FAMOUS MOVIE DETECTIVES II

MICHAEL R. PITTS

THE SCARECROW PRESS, INC.
METUCHEN, N.J., & LONDON
1991

Also by Michael R. Pitts

Kate Smith: A Bio-Bibliography
Western Movies
The Great Western Pictures
The Great Western Pictures II
Hollywood and American
    History
Horror Film Stars
The Great Gangster Pictures
The Great Gangster Pictures II
The Bible on Film
Hollywood on Hollywood
Hollywood on Record: The Film
    Stars' Discography

The Great Science Fiction
    Pictures
Radio Soundtracks: A Reference
    Guide
Radio Soundtracks: A Reference
    Guide, *second edition*
Film Directors: A Guide to Their
    American Films
The Great Spy Pictures
The Great Spy Pictures II
Famous Movie Detectives

British Library Cataloguing-in-Publication data available

Library of Congress Cataloging-in-Publication Data

Pitts, Michael R.
    Famous movie detectives II / Michael R. Pitts.
        p.   cm.
    Includes bibliographical references and index.
    ISBN 0-8108-2345-4
    1. Detective and mystery films—History and criticism. I. Title. II. Title:
Famous movie detectives two. III. Title: Famous movie detectives 2.
PN1995.9.D4P53   1991
791.43'655—dc20   90-9083

For my parents,

ROY AND GERTRUDE PITTS

CONTENTS

PREFACE

OVER A DECADE AGO my book *Famous Movie Detectives* (Scarecrow, 1979) was published, and this follow-up volume continues to look at the careers of noted celluloid sleuths. (In this supplement, "B/V" refers to that base volume.) Detective films have been popular cinema fare for more than a half-century, and the genre shows no signs of letting up—as noted by the number of recent films covered in the text, along with their counterparts going back to the silent days. Like the first book, this one looks at not only the careers of the detectives on film but also their radio, television, stage, and literary careers as well. More coverage is given to the first fourteen detectives, including detailed filmographies, while those in the "Other Movie Detectives" category (sleuths with two or more films to their credit) get less coverage. This section also includes a trio (Frank Cannon, Joe Dancer, Kojak) of television detectives who have been the subjects of movies made for TV.

When I wrote the first volume, I deleted planned chapters on Sherlock Holmes and Philip Marlowe because those characters were subjects of books published at the same time by Scarecrow Press. In the last decade there have been more films and other media activities by these detectives, so I have included them in this volume with up-to-date coverage.

In regard to the filmographies, the following abbreviations are used: **P:** Producer. **EP:** Executive Producer. **AP:** Associate Producer. **D:** Director. **SC:** Script. **ST:** Story. **PH:** Photography. **ED:** Editor. **AD:** Art Director. **MUS:** Music Director. **TD:** Technical Director. **ASST DIR:** Assistant Director. **PROD MGR:** Production Manager. **SP EFF:** Special Effects.

I would like to thank several people and organizations for their help in preparing this volume, especially my wife, Carolyn, for typing the Sherlock Holmes chapter, and Sam Rubin, former editor of *Classic Images*, for granting permission to use the Holmes chapter, in a revised version, as it originally appeared in his publication under one of my pen names. Thanks also go to Dr. Ray White, Pierre Guinle, Barbara Hoover, Richard Bojarski, James Robert Parish, Film Favorites, Nicole Schmitt of France's Service des Archives du Film, the British Film Institute (Sue Wilson, Paramjit Dhanda), Ken Hanke, James L. Limbacher, Vincent Terrace, and Centro Sperimentate Di Cinematografica Cine Nazionale (Mario Musumeci).

As with the previous volume, I hope this book will provide the reader and researcher with a well-balanced history of the movie detectives included here. Movies are to be enjoyed and so is reading about them. I hope this book will provide its readers pleasure as well as a good perspective on the fictional detectives it covers. Any additions, corrections, or comments regarding this book will be appreciated by the author, sent in care of the publisher.

MICHAEL R. PITTS

Chapter 1

ARSENE LUPIN

FRENCH NEWSPAPER REPORTER Maurice Leblanc created the character of suave criminal Arsène Lupin as a fiction story assignment, and he wrote several books and short stories about the French "Prince of Thieves." Lupin used many disguises and aliases and always managed to outwit the police detectives on his trail. Like Raffles (q.v.) and the Lone Wolf (see B/V), Arsène Lupin eventually came over to the side of the law and became a master detective, although he retained his good humor and penchant for the ladies. Leblanc's first Arsène Lupin novel was *Arsène Lupin, Gentleman Burglar* in 1907, and he continued to write about the character through 1925's *Memoirs of Arsène Lupin.*

In some of his early Arsène Lupin stories, Maurice Leblanc used the character of Herlock Sholmes, a word-play on "Sherlock Holmes," in order to avoid copyright problems with the Arthur Conan Doyle character. When the German company Vitascope filmed some of these stories, they were called ARSENE LUPIN VS. SHERLOCK HOLMES, since copyright laws regarding film adaptations were lax at that time. Issued in 1910, this series contained five one- and two-reel films with Paul Otto as Arsène Lupin and Viggo Larsen, who also directed, as Holmes. Each of the films had Lupin committing some criminal act with Holmes on his trail, until the final episode, ARSENE LUPINS ENDE (The Finish of Arsène Lupin), when Holmes finally gets Lupin behind bars for good. The first feature-length film about Arsène Lupin came in 1916 from Great Britain with Gerald Ames playing the title role in ARSENE LUPIN, made by London Films. The film was based on the play by Maurice Leblanc and François de Crosset, and the plot had police Inspector Guerchard (Kenelm Foss) on the trail of the suave Arsène Lupin. Kenelm Foss also adapted the play for the film, and in 1921 Gerald Ames had the title role in another British feature, MR. JUSTICE RAFFLES (q.v.).

Vitagraph produced its own version of the Leblanc–de Crosset play the next year, and its ARSENE LUPIN starred Earle Williams as the gentleman thief. The script for this feature pretty much followed that of the British version, with Arsène Lupin romancing beautiful Sonia (Ethel Gray Terry) while trying to sidestep being put in jail by Detective Guerchard (Brinsley Shaw). The result, however, was none too good, according to *Variety*, which claimed that the film "is an insult to the intelligence of a ten-year-old schoolboy. The most impossible situations are dished up in all seriousness, and you are asked to believe they actually occurred . . . Vitagraph's screen adaptation is a joke."

In 1919 Paramount filmed Maurice Leblanc's 1914 novel *The Teeth of the Tiger* under that title with David Powell in the title role. Here Arsène Lupin is named in a man's will, and as each of the other heirs is killed off, Lupin ends up being one of the two murder suspects. To clear his name, the Frenchman does his own detecting and uncovers the identity of the killer. The next year, Robertson-Cole issued 813, from the 1910 novel by Leblanc. The title referred to a clock containing the number "813," which was a clue in a murder case in which Arsène Lupin (Wedgewood Newell) is the main suspect. To clear himself, Lupin volunteers to lead the murder investigation, with most of the action taking place in an old, spooky house. Wallace Beery co-starred, playing dual roles. In 1921 Paul Fejos directed the Hungarian feature, ARSEN LUPIN UTOLSO KAL-ANDJA. Fejos later directed the Hollywood features LONESOME ('28), BROADWAY ('29), and THE LAST PERFORMANCE ('29).

The first sound version of ARSENE LUPIN was made by Metro-Goldwyn-Mayer in 1932. It teamed brothers John and Lionel Barrymore as Lupin and his adversary, Guerchard. Masquerading as the Duke of Charmerace, Arsène

Lupin works out an elaborate plan to steal the Mona Lisa from Paris's Louvre. Detective Guerchard knows Lupin is up to no good, and to get him he has pretty Sonia (Karen Morley) paroled from prison in order to catch Lupin in a romantic trap. The ploy works as Sonia and Lupin fall in love, but when the gentleman thief is at last captured by the policeman, he is allowed to escape. "A neat angle of the film version is the fact that the audience never sees Lupin in the act of larceny itself, a trick of indirection that works out well. His campaign is always foreshadowed vaguely or revealed after it has been accomplished," noted *Variety*. John Barrymore was especially good as the romantically inclined Lupin, and his work was matched by brother Lionel as the gruff but admiring detective. Karen Morley was also effective as the young woman torn between love and not wanting to return to prison.

While the character of Arsène Lupin was French, it was not until 1937 that a film about the gentleman crook was made in that country. ARSENE LUPIN, DETECTIVE, based on Maurice Leblanc's *L'Agence Barnett*, told of Detective Barnett (Jules Berry), who is on the trail of a murderer. One of the suspects tells a journalist that Barnett is really Arsène Lupin, but the real gentleman thief comes to his defense, the murderer is captured, and the thief runs away with the killer's mistress. The French magazine *L'Oeuvre* noted of this comedy-mystery, "The film is amusing."

After having played the part of Michael Lanyard in Columbia's LONE WOLF RETURNS (see B/V) in 1935, Melvyn Douglas was assigned to the title role in M-G-M's ARSENE LUPIN RETURNS three years later, after William Powell rejected the part. This tame but slickly made outing had gentleman burglar Arsène Lupin, along with fiancée Lorraine DeGrissac (Virginia Bruce) and helpers Joe Doyle (Nat Pendleton) and Alf (E. E. Clive), joining forces with American detective Steve Emerson (Warren William) to find the culprit who stole Lorraine's jewels from her father's (John Halliday) estate.

In 1944 Universal made the programmer ENTER ARSENE LUPIN, which introduced Charles Korvin to the

Lionel Barrymore *(left)* and John Barrymore in ARSENE LUPIN (M-G-M, 1932)

screen in the title role. Produced and directed by Ford Beebe, the feature had Lupin robbing beautiful Stacie (Ella Raines) while they are passengers on the Paris-Constantinople express, then falling in love with her. He returns her jewels and follows her to her English country estate where he learns that her cousins (Gale Sondergaard and Miles Mander) are planning to kill the young woman for her money. Lupin decides to help the girl but is also allied with fence Ganimard (J. Carrol Naish) and eventually is captured by the law, but not until after saving Stacie from her greedy relatives. Discussing the film in their career study of Ford Beebe in *Screen Facts* (no. 13, 1966), Elaine M. Geltzer and George Geltzer noted that the feature was "a slick and glossy production. . . . The sets were handsome, and made to look even more so by one of Hollywood's top cameramen, Hal Mohr. . . . Audiences at previews loved it. Reviews were uniformly enthusiastic. Universal had a real sleeper on their hands. Curiously, like so many 'sleepers' which seemed so superior to competitive products at the time, it does not wear too well today. It remains a handsome production without that extra sparkle to make it unique."

The next year Pereda Films in Mexico made ARSENIO LUPIN based on the Maurice Leblanc stories. Ramon Pereda produced and directed the feature and also played the lead role of Lupin. The feature contained the usual plot ploys of the slick thief outwitting the law, and in one sequence he is at odds with detective Herlock Sholmes.

Arsène Lupin returned to his homeland in 1956, where a trio of films were made based on Leblanc's works in the

Ella Raines and Charles Korvin in ENTER ARSENE LUPIN (Universal, 1944)

next half-dozen years. First Robert Lamoureux portrayed Arsène Lupin in THE ADVENTURES OF ARSENE LUPIN, directed by Jacques Becker. Set in Germany in 1912, the story has Lupin devising an elaborate scheme to rob the kaiser's treasure chest—and succeeding. Three years later Robert Lamoureux reprised the part in SIGNE ARSENE LUPIN (Signed Arsène Lupin), directed by Yves Robert. Set in the post–World War I period, the plot has Arsène Lupin getting out of the army and onto the trail of a missing medieval treasure. He romances beautiful Aurelia (Alida Valli), whom he discovers is on the same quest. *Variety* commented, "Pic is refreshingly told but leisurely paced."

ARSENE LUPIN CONTRE ARSENE LUPIN (Arsène Lupin against Arsène Lupin), was issued in 1962. The story opens with the burial of the real Arsène Lupin. He left behind two sons, François (Jean-Pierre Cassel) and Gérard (Jean-Claude Brialy), and the two young men begin a series of daring robberies which baffle the police. When a princess (Françoise Dorleac) has her jewels stolen, the two brothers join forces to regain them for her. The comedy-mystery was set in the 1920s. "Director Edouard Molinaro uses many varied and speeded up shots plus a lot of period dancing and music. But the right balance of time and pace eludes him. He sacrifices the satire for flashy camera work," wrote *Variety*. The French publication *Juvenal* said the tone of the film was "light."

In 1970-1971 the "Arsène Lupin" television series was shown in France and Sweden. Georges Descrieres portrayed Arsène Lupin. Episode titles include "L'Arrestation d'Arsène Lupin," "La Vengeance d'Arsène Lupin," and "Arsène Lupin contre Sherlock Holmes." The last segment thus placed the character of Arsène Lupin against the master detective he had fought in his initial screen outing some six decades before.

Filmography

1. ARSENE LUPIN VS. SHERLOCK HOLMES. Vitascope [Germany], 1910. One- and two-reel series.
   D: Viggo Larsen. From the stories by Maurice Leblanc.

Cast: Viggo Larsen (Sherlock Holmes), Paul Otto (Arsène Lupin).
Series Titles: DER ALTE SEKRETAR (The Old Secretaire), DER BLAUE DIAMANT (The Blue Diamond), DIE FLASHEN REMBRANDTS (The Fake Rembrandts), DIE FLUCHT (Arsène Lupin's Escape), ARSENE LUPINS ENDE (The Finish of Arsène Lupin).

2. ARSENE LUPIN. London Films, 1916. 6,400 feet.
   D: George L. Tucker. **SC:** Kenelm Foss, from the play by Maurice Leblanc & François de Crosset.
   Cast: Gerald Ames (Arsène Lupin), Manora Thew (Sonia), Kenelm Foss (Inspector Guerchard), Douglas Munro (Gournay-Martin), Marga la Rubia, Philip Hewland.

3. ARSENE LUPIN. Vitagraph, 1917. 5,000 feet.
   D: Paul Scardon.
   Cast: Earle Williams (Arsène Lupin), Brinsley Shaw (Detective Guerchard), Mr. Leone (Gournay-Martin), Ethel Gray Terry (Sonia), Billie Billings (Germaine), Julia Swayne Gordon (Victoria), Bernard Siegel (Charolais), Gordon Gray (Anastase), Logan Paul (Firmid), Hugh Wynn (Alfred).

4. THE TEETH OF THE TIGER. Paramount, 1919.
   From the novel by Maurice Leblanc.
   Cast: David Powell (Arsène Lupin), Myrtle Steadman, Marguerite Courtot, Charles Gerrard, Temple Saxe.

5. 813. Robertson-Cole, 1920. Five reels.
   D: Scott Sydney. **SC:** W. Scott Darling, from the novel by Maurice Leblanc.
   Cast: Wedgewood Newell (Arsène Lupin), Wallace Beery (Major Parbury/Ribiera), Laura La Plante, Kathryn Adams, Joseph P. Lockney, Frederick Vroom.

6. ARSEN LUPIN UTOLSO KALANDJA. [Hungary], 1921.
   P: Paul Fejos.

7. ARSENE LUPIN. Metro-Goldwyn-Mayer, 1932. 64 minutes.
   D: Jack Conway. **SC:** Carey Wilson, Rayard Veiller & Lenore Coffee, from the play by Maurice Leblanc & François de Crosset. **PH:** Oliver T. Marsh. **ED:** Hugh Wynn.
   Cast: John Barrymore (Arsène Lupin), Lionel Barrymore (Inspector Guerchard), Karen Morley (Sonia), John Miljan (Prefect of Police), Tully Marshall (Gournay-Martin), Henry Armetta, George Davis (Sheriff's Men), John Davidson (Butler), James Mack (Laurent), Mary Jane Irving (Marie).

8. ARSENE LUPIN, DETECTIVE. Parisienne de Films [France], 1937. 98 minutes.

D: Henri Diamant-Berger. **SC:** Henri Diamant-Berger & Jean Nohain, from the novel *L'Agence Barnett* by Maurice Leblanc. **PH:** Maurice Desaffiaux & André Dantan. **MUS:** Jean Lenoir. **Design:** Hugues Laurent & Raymond Druart. **Sound:** Igor B. Kalinowski.

Cast: Jules Berry (Detective Barnett/Arsène Lupin), Suzy Prim (Olga Vauban), Rosine Derean (Germaine Laurent), Mady Berry (Victorie), Suzanne Dehelly (Olga's Friend), Marcelle Monthil (Cook), Denise Kerny (Burglar), Yvonne Rozille (Suzanne), Gabriel Signoret (Inspector Bechoux), Aimé Simon-Girard (Journalist), Thomy Bourdelle (Cassire), Aimos (Barnett's Friend), Abel Jacquin (Bremond), Serjius (Joseph), Robert Ozanne (Maitre d'), René Navarre (Inspector), Balder (Bobby), Georges Bever (Fake Clergyman), Gilles & Julien (Vanier & Del Preco), René Hieronimus (Night Guard), Gaston Mauger, Albert Broquin, Christiane Ribes, Luce Fabiole, Arlette Stavisky.

9. ARSENE LUPIN RETURNS. Metro-Goldwyn-Mayer, 1938. 81 minutes.

   P: John W. Considine, Jr. **D:** George Fitzmaurice. **SC:** James Kevin McGuinness, Howard Emmett Rogers & George Harmon Coxe. **PH:** George Fosley. **ED:** Gene Lewis. **MUS:** Franz Waxman. **AD:** Cedric Gibbons.

   Cast: Melvyn Douglas (Arsène Lupin/René Ferrand), Virginia Bruce (Lorraine DeGrissac), Warren William (Steve Emerson), John Halliday (Count DeGrissac), Nat Pendleton (Joe Doyle), Monty Woolley (George Bouchet), George Zucco (Martell), E. E. Clive (Alf), Rollo Lloyd (Duval), Vladimir Sokoloff (Ivan Pavloff), Tully Marshall (Monelli), Leonard Pen, Harry Tyler, Chester Clute (Reporters), Jonathan Hale (D.C.I. Chief), Lillian Rich (Telephone Operator), Harvey Clark (Assistant Manager), Jack Norton (Hotel Manager), Robert Emmett Keane (Watkins), Pierre Watkin (Mr. Carter), Joseph King (Inspector Hennessey), Dell Henderson (Plainclothes Policeman), George Davis (Dock Guard), Frank Dawson (Franz), Stanley Fields (Groom), Mitchell Lewis, William Norton Bailey, Chris Frank (Detectives), Robert Middlemass (Sergeant), Perry Ivins (Fingerprint Man), Egon Brecher (Vasseur), Ian Wolfe (A. LeMarchand), Ruth Hart (Telephone Girl), Otto Fries (Truck Driver), Priscilla Lawson (Switchboard Operator), Jacques Vanair, Robert O'Connor (Gendarmes), Sid D'Albrook (Detective Alois), William H. Royle (Burly Detective), George Douglas, Jean Perry (Policemen), Frank Leigh (English Eddie).

10. ENTER ARSENE LUPIN. Universal, 1944. 72 minutes.

    P-D: Ford Beebe. **SC:** Bertram Millhauser. **PH:** Hal Mohr. **ED:** Saul A. Goodkind.

    Cast: Charles Korvin (Arsène Lupin), Ella Raines (Stacie), J. Carrol Naish (Ganimard), George Dolenz (Dubosc), Gale Sondergaard (Bessie Seagrave), Miles Mander (Charles Seagrave), Leland

Hodgson (Constable Ryder), Tena Pilkington (Pollett), Lillian Bronson (Wheeler), Holmes Herbert (Jobson), Charles LaTorre (Inspector Cogswell), Gerald Hamer (Doc Marling), Ed Cooper (Cartwright), Art Foster (Superintendent), Clyde Kenny (Beckwith), Alphonse Martell (Conductor).

11. ARSENIO LUPIN (Arsène Lupin). Pereda Films, S.A. [Mexico], 1945.

P-D: Ramon Pereda. **SC:** Antonio Helu, from the stories by Maurice Leblanc. **PH:** Jesus Hernandez. **AD:** Ramon Rodriguez Granada. **ED:** Alfredo Rosas Piego. **MUS:** Rosalio Ramirez. **SOUND:** José B. Carles.

Cast: Ramon Pereda (Arsène Lupin), Adriana Lamar, José Baviera, Victor Argota.

12. LES ADVENTURES D'ARSENE LUPIN (The Adventures of Arsène Lupin). Chavane/SNEG/Gaumont, 1956. 103 minutes.

P: Robert Sussfield. **D:** Jacques Becker. **SC:** Albert Simonin & Jacques Becker. **PH:** Edmond Sechan. **AD:** Rino Mondellini.

Cast: Robert Lamoureux (Arsène Lupin), O. E. Hasse, Lisolette Pulver, Henri Rolland.

13. SIGNE ARSENE LUPIN (Signed Arsène Lupin). Chavane/SNEG/Lambor-Costellacione/Gaumont, 1960. 100 minutes.

D: Yves Robert. **SC:** J. P. Rappeneau. **PH:** Maurice Barry. **ED:** G. Natot.

Cast: Robert Lamoureux (Arsène Lupin), Alida Valli (Aurelia), Yves Robert (Labellu), Roger Dumas (Isidore), Michel Etcheverry (Collector), Gisele Grandpré (Friend), Jacques Dufiho (Albert).

14. ARSENE LUPIN CONTRE ARSENE LUPIN (Arsène Lupin against Arsène Lupin). Gaumont/Cinephonic/DAMA/Chavane, 1962. 110 minutes.

D: Edouard Molinaro. **SC:** Georges Neveux, Edouard Molinaro & François Chavane. **PH:** Pierre Pelit. **ED:** Robert Isnardon.

Cast: Jean-Claude Brialy (François), Jean-Pierre Cassel (Gérard), Françoise Dorleac (Nathalie), Geneviève Grad (Catherine), Daniel Cauchy (Charly), Jean Le Poulain (Prefect), Anne Vernon.

Chapter 2

HERCULE POIROT

AGATHA CHRISTIE'S ECCENTRIC Belgian detective, Hercule Poirot, has proven to be one of the most popular of fictional sleuths, having been featured in scores of books written between 1920 and 1975. He has also been adapted to other mediums, including the stage, films, radio, and television. While several performers have excelled as Poirot, none has totally captured his persona—although Harold Huber on radio, and Albert Finney in MURDER ON THE ORIENT EXPRESS ('74) have come the closest. Along with Miss Jane Marple (q.v.), Poirot has continued to be the most enduring of the myriad of characters created by the prolific Christie.

Hercule Poirot first appeared on the literary scene in 1920 in *The Mysterious Affair at Styles,* and his fourth appearance came in 1926's *Murder of Roger Ackroyd,* which Michael Morton adapted for the stage in 1928 as *Alibi.* Charles Laughton was impressive as Poirot in the mystery play, and in 1931 Twickenham Films purchased the screen rights and filmed ALIBI on a $50,000 budget, casting Austin Trevor as the Belgian detective. Poirot is called to the country estate of his pal Roger Ackroyd (Franklin Dyall) to investigate his supposed suicide, but he uncovers a bogus crime. Trevor, who was a dapper actor totally unlike the literary figure, proved popular in the role and repeated it in two more features, BLACK COFFEE ('31) and LORD EDGWARE DIES ('34). In 1932 the play was brought to Broadway as *Fatal Alibi,* with Charles Laughton again as Poirot, but it failed to find an audience and ran for only two dozen performances.

In 1930 Agatha Christie wrote an original Hercule Poirot stage play, *Black Coffee*, which was produced on the London stage in 1931 with Francis L. Sullivan as the sleuth. Again Twickenham purchased the rights to the work and filmed it with Austin Trevor as Poirot. The plot had Poirot and friend Captain Hastings (Richard Cooper) called to Sir Claude Amory's (C. V. France) country estate to help protect the formula he has developed for a new weapon, but Amory is killed. Working with local Inspector Japp (Melville Cooper), Poirot realizes Amory was poisoned by drinking black coffee and that his formula has been stolen. *Black Coffee* was novelized by Christie in 1934.

Austin Trevor's third and final work as Poirot came in LORD EDGWARE DIES, a 1934 Real Art release which got minor issuance in the U.S. by RKO Radio. In addition to Austin Trevor, the film brought back Richard Cooper as Captain Hastings. Based on the 1933 novel *Thirteen at Dinner*, the production had Poirot looking into the murder of elderly Lord Edgware (C. V. France) whose young wife (Jane Carr) said she wanted him dead so she could marry a nobleman (Esmé Percy). Again Poirot and Hastings work with Inspector Japp (John Turnbull) in bringing the case to a satisfactory conclusion. The property was remade as THIRTEEN AT DINNER in 1985 as a TV movie.

Austin Trevor (1897-1978) is said to have been cast as Hercule Poirot because he could speak French. Throughout his long career he was often cast as a Frenchman although he was Irish. He made his stage debut in 1915 and came to films in 1930. Among his many movies were DEATH AT BROADCASTING HOUSE ('34), THE SILENT PASSENGER ('35), REMBRANDT ('36), DARK JOURNEY ('37), KNIGHT WITHOUT ARMOUR ('37), GOODBYE, MR. CHIPS ('39), NIGHT TRAIN TO MUNICH ('40), ANNA KARENINA ('48), THE RED SHOES ('48), HORRORS OF THE WAX MUSEUM ('59), and NEVER BACK LOSERS ('62). His final film was THE ALPHABET MURDERS ('66), the first Hercule Poirot film to be made since his own LORD EDGWARE DIES more than three decades before. In it he was cast in a supporting role.

In 1940 Francis L. Sullivan again portrayed Poirot on the

London stage in *Peril at End House*, which Arnold Ridley adapted from Christie's 1932 novel. Harold Huber portrayed the Belgian sleuth in the 1945 Mutual radio series "Hercule Poirot," and he was ideally cast in the role. A veteran movie character actor who looked somewhat like Agatha Christie's conception of the detective, Huber was an expert at dialects and had portrayed a variety of ethnic detectives in several of the Charlie Chan films.

In the early 1960s Metro-Goldwyn-Mayer purchased the rights to Agatha Christie's 1935 novel *The A.B.C. Murders* as a vehicle for Zero Mostel, to be called AMANDA AND THE ABC MURDERS. Christie, however, did not like the script; when the project was finally made, it starred Tony Randall as a comic Poirot and was called THE ALPHABET MURDERS. This 1966 release had Poirot in London, followed by British intelligence agent Hastings (Robert Morley), and becoming embroiled in a series of killings in which letters of the alphabet are clues. Although Inspector Japp (Maurice Denham) believes the real killer has been dispatched, Poirot persists in the case and uncovers the culprit. *Variety* said the vehicle got the "travesty treatment with mildly diverting results."

The most satisfying of all the screen adaptations to date of an Agatha Christie work, and one which is said to be the author's favorite, is the 1974 EMI production of MURDER ON THE ORIENT EXPRESS, based on the 1934 novel *Murder on the Calais Coach*. Not only was this a posh production with an all-star cast, but the film was highlighted by Albert Finney's performance as Hercule Poirot; he played the part as it was written in the Christie novels and he looked the role—even to Poirot's exaggerated waxed mustache. Finney was nominated for an Academy Award for his work as Poirot, as was Ingrid Bergman for best supporting actress, along with other nominations for the script, photography, costumes, and music. Richard Rodney Bennett won the British Film Academy award for his musical score for the feature; John Gielgud and Ingrid Bergman were winners for their supporting performances. The movie made over $19 million at the box office. Its plot had Poirot traveling on the Orient Express to Constanti-

From left: Martin Balsam, Albert Finney, and George Coulouris in MURDER ON THE ORIENT EXPRESS (EMI/Paramount, 1974)

nople in the 1920s with a diverse group of passengers, all of whom are suspects with motives for the stabbing death of grasping American industrialist Ratchett (Richard Widmark). With the Calais coach detached from the rest of the train in wintertime Yugoslavia, Poirot sets out to solve the killing.

In 1976 the character of Hercule Poirot, along with several other noted fictional sleuths, was satirized in the overly praised mystery-farce MURDER BY DEATH. Here Poirot was called Milo Perrier and was hammed up by James Coco as the Belgian investigator out to win $1 million tax-free and the title of the world's greatest detective by beating his rivals in solving a murder.

The huge success of MURDER ON THE ORIENT EXPRESS caused that film's producers, Richard Goodwin and John Brabourne, to do a follow-up feature, DEATH ON THE NILE, taken from the 1937 novel of the same title. The film was made on location in Egypt; its settings, even more posh than those of the first film, are its highlight, along with another all-star cast. Perhaps its biggest weakness was the casting of Peter Ustinov as Poirot, who molded the character to fit his own persona rather than the Christie novel. The leisurely paced feature made almost $9 million. On vacation in Egypt, Poirot is on a cruise along the Nile River when an attempt is made on the life of wealthy Linnet Ridgeway (Lois Chiles). Later her new husband, Simon Doyle (Simon MacCorkindale), is wounded by his former fiancée, Jacqueline de Bellefort (Mia Farrow), who lost him to Linnett, her former best friend. When Linnet is murdered on the boat, Poirot attempts to solve the case with the other passengers as suspects.

Although Peter Ustinov hardly satisfied Christie purists as Poirot, he apparently caught the fancy of the viewing public—in 1982 he was back in the role in EVIL UNDER THE SUN, taken from the 1941 novel. Again Poirot is on holiday, this time at a lush resort on the island of Tyrrhenian, where nasty stage star Arlena Marshall (Diana Rigg) is dispatched. The island is filled with suspects, including her husband (Dennis Quilley), stepdaughter (Emily Hone), the resort owner (Maggie Smith), and a bitchy magazine writer (Roddy McDowall). While the film was satisfying to the eye, the production was slow moving and uninteresting; it proved to be the last Poirot theatrical feature for six years, although the property was transferred to television in the interim.

Between 1982 and 1985, CBS-TV presented four telefilms based on Agatha Christie works, two of them with Helen Hayes as Miss Jane Marple (q.v.). On October 19, 1985, the fifth Christie TV film, THIRTEEN AT DINNER, a remake of LORD EDGWARE DIES, was telecast with Peter Ustinov portraying Poirot for the third time. Appearing on David Frost's (himself) TV program, Poirot meets actress Jane Wilkinson (Faye Dunaway) who confides that she will kill her husband, Lord Edgware (John Barron), to obtain her freedom. Later at the Edgware estate, the lord says that he will give her a divorce, but he is soon murdered. While Scotland Yard Inspector Japp (David Suchet) believes the

Advertisement for 13 AT DINNER (CBS-TV, 1985)

wife is guilty, Poirot pursues the case to a satisfactory conclusion. The TV movie was well made, and on January 8, 1986, Ustinov was back as Poirot in DEAD MAN'S FOLLY, taken from the 1956 novel. Here Poirot and mystery writer Ariadne Oliver (Jean Stapleton) are involved in a murder hunt game at a remote British estate with Poirot accompanied by friend Captain Hastings (Jonathan Cecil). During the entertainment, an actual murder takes place, and the guests are the suspects. Filmed at West Wycombe Park in Buckinghamshire, the feature "emerges as one of the best of the TV-movies based on Christie's works" (Judith Crist, *TV Guide*). Peter Ustinov was again Hercule Poirot in a third telefilm, MURDER IN THREE ACTS, telecast by CBS-TV on September 30, 1986, and based on Agatha Christie's 1934 novel. This one had Poirot and Captain Hastings (Jonathan Cecil) on holiday in Acapulco where several murders occur. The Belgian detective finds a link among the killings involving poison to dispatch the victims. Like its two TV predecessors, this Poirot adventure was well produced and a satisfying mystery.

Peter Ustinov portrayed Hercule Poirot for the sixth time, and for the third time on the big screen, when the character returned to theaters in APPOINTMENT WITH DEATH, an Israeli-made production taken from the 1938 novel of the same title. Poirot is again on holiday in Egypt and among his fellow travelers are greedy Mrs. Emily Boulton (Piper Laurie) who is traveling with her unhappy family, and British Parliament member Lady Westholme (Lauren Bacall). When Emily is found murdered on an archaeological dig, Poirot must fathom the case. He is aided by Palestine's British army chief (John Gielgud). The *Hollywood Reporter* said this handsomely made feature was "a deadly bore." The movie proved to be the least successful of all the Hercule Poirot big-screen features, and its distribution was limited.

Having portrayed Hercule Poirot six times on film and TV, Peter Ustinov is certainly the performer most associated with the role, although (as noted earlier) his interpretation of the part is hardly how Poirot appeared in the

Christie books. Born in 1921, Peter Ustinov made his stage debut at age seventeen and his first film in 1940. In the ensuing years, he has won fame as an actor, writer, director, and narrator. He won an Academy Award as best supporting actor in SPARTACUS ('60). Among his other films are ODETTE ('50), HOTEL SAHARA ('51), QUO VADIS ('51), WE'RE NO ANGELS ('55), THE SUNDOWN-ERS ('60), BLACKBEARD'S GHOST ('67), VIVA MAX ('70), LOGAN'S RUN ('76), THE MOUSE AND HIS CHILD ('78), and his disappointing performance as the Chinese detective in CHARLIE CHAN AND THE CURSE OF THE DRAGON QUEEN ('81).

Certainly Hercule Poirot has been one of the most continuously popular of all fictional detectives with his literary adventures reprinted in many languages. Although Agatha Christie finally killed off the fussy, self-centered little Belgian investigator in her last novel about him, *Curtain*, in 1975, Poirot continues to delight generation after generation of mystery lovers. Cinematically Poirot has not been so successful as he has been on the printed page, but in the past two decades Poirot has come to the fore as one of the most filmed of fictional sleuths, thanks to Albert Finney's definitive performance in MUR-DER ON THE ORIENT EXPRESS and Peter Ustinov's half-dozen less-than-reverent portrayals in films and television. In the spring of 1988, CBS-TV announced plans to produce more movies based on the works of Agatha Christie—no doubt some of these will be about Hercule Poirot.

Filmography

1. ALIBI. Twickenham, 1931. 75 minutes.
   P: Julius Hagen. **D:** Leslie Hiscott. **SC:** H. Fowler Mear, from the play by Michael Morton and the novel *The Murder of Roger Ackroyd* by Agatha Christie.
   Cast: Austin Trevor (Hercule Poirot), Franklin Dyall (Sir Roger Ackroyd), Elizabeth Allan (Ursula Browne), J. H. Roberts (Dr. Sheppard), John Deverell (Lord Halliford), Ronald Ward (Ralph Ackroyd), Mary Jerrold (Mrs. Ackroyd), Mercia Swinburne (Caryll

Sheppard), Harvey Braban (Inspector Davis), Clare Greet, Diana Beaumont, Earle Grey.

2. BLACK COFFEE. Twickenham, 1931. 78 minutes.
   P: Julius Hagen. **D:** Leslie Hiscott. **SC:** Brock Williams & H. Fowler Mear, from the play by Agatha Christie.
   Cast: Austin Trevor (Hercule Poirot), Adrianne Allen (Lucia Amory), Richard Cooper (Captain Hastings), Elizabeth Allan (Barbara Amory), C. V. France (Sir Claude Amory), Philip Strange (Richard Amory), Dino Galvani (Dr. Carelli), Michael Shepley (Raynor), Melville Cooper (Inspector Japp), Marie Wright (Miss Amory), Leila Page, Harold Meade, S. A. Cookson.

3. LORD EDGWARE DIES. Real Art, 1934. 81 minutes.
   P: Julius Hagen. **D:** Henry Edwards. **SC:** H. Fowler Mear, from the novel *Thirteen at Dinner* by Agatha Christie. **PH:** Sydney Blythe.
   Cast: Austin Trevor (Hercule Poirot), Jane Carr (Lady Edgware), Richard Cooper (Captain Hastings), John Turnbull (Inspector Japp), Michael Shepley (Captain Ronald Marsh), Leslie Perrins (Bryan Martin), C. V. France (Lord Edgware), Esmé Percy (Duke of Merton).

4. THE ALPHABET MURDERS. Metro-Goldwyn-Mayer, 1966. 90 minutes.
   P: Lawrence P. Bachmann. **D:** Frank Tashlin. **SC:** David Pursall & Jack Seddon, from the novel *The A.B.C. Murders* by Agatha Christie. **PH:** Desmond Dickinson. **ED:** John Victor Smith. **MUS:** Ron Goodman. **ASST DIR:** David Tomblin.
   Cast: Tony Randall (Hercule Poirot), Anita Ekberg (Amanda Beatrice Cross), Robert Morley (Hastings), Maurice Denham (Inspector Japp), Guy Rolfe (Duncan Doncaster), Sheila Allen (Lady Diane), James Villiers (Franklin), Julian Glover (Don Fortune), Grazina Frame (Betty Barnard), Clive Morton ("X"), Cyril Luckham (Sir Carmichael Clarke), Richard Wattis (Wolfe), David Lodge (Sergeant), Patrick Newell (Cracknell), Austin Trevor (Judson), Alison Seebohm (Miss Sparks), Margaret Rutherford (Miss Jane Marple), Stringer Davis (Mr. Stringer).

5. MURDER ON THE ORIENT EXPRESS. EMI/Paramount, 1974. 128 minutes. Color.
   P: John Brabourne & Richard Goodwin. **D:** Sidney Lumet. **SC:** Paul Dehn, from the novel by Agatha Christie. **PH:** Geoffrey Unsworth. **ED:** Anne V. Coates. **MUS:** Richard Rodney Bennett. **AD:** Jack Stephens. **DESIGN:** Tony Walton.
   Cast: Albert Finney (Hercule Poirot), Lauren Bacall (Mrs. Hubbard), Martin Balsam (Bianchi), Ingrid Bergman (Greta Ohlsson), Jacqueline Bisset (Countess Andrenyi), Jean-Pierre Cassel (Pierre Paul Michel), Sean Connery (Colonel Arbuthnot), John Gielgud

(Beddoes), Wendy Hiller (Princess Dragomiroff), Anthony Perkins (Hector McQueen), Vanessa Redgrave (Mary Debenham), Rachel Roberts (Hildegarde Schmidt), Richard Widmark (Ratchett), Michael York (Count Andrenyi), Colin Blakely (Hardman), George Coulouris (Dr. Constantine), Denis Quilley (Foscarelli), Vernon Dobtcheff (Concierge), Jeremy Lloyd (A.D.C.), John Moffatt (Chief Attendant).

6. DEATH ON THE NILE. EMI/Paramount, 1978. 140 minutes. Color.
   P: John Brabourne & Richard Goodwin. **AP:** Norton Knatchbull. **D:** John Guillermin. **SC:** Anthony Shaffer, from the novel by Agatha Christie. **PH:** Jack Cardiff. **ED:** Malcolm Cooke. **MUS:** Nino Rota. **AD:** Brian & Terry Ackland. **DESIGN:** Peter Murton. **COSTUMES:** Anthony Powell.
   Cast: Peter Ustinov (Hercule Poirot), Harry Andrews (Barnstaple), Jane Birkin (Louise Bourger), Lois Chiles (Linet Ridgeway), Bette Davis (Mrs. Van Schuyler), Mia Farrow (Jacqueline de Bellefort), Jon Finch (Ferguson), Olivia Hussey (Rosalie Otterbourne), I. S. Johar (Karnak Manager), George Kennedy (Andrew Pennington), Angela Lansbury (Mrs. Salome Otterbourne), Simon MacCorkindale (Simon Doyle), David Niven (Colonel Rice), Maggie Smith (Miss Bowers), Jack Warden (Dr. Bessner), Sam Wanamaker (Rockford).

7. EVIL UNDER THE SUN. Universal, 1982. 117 minutes. Color.
   P: John Brabourne & Richard Goodwin. **AP:** Michael-John Knatchbull. **D:** Guy Hamilton. **SC:** Anthony Shaffer, from the novel by Agatha Christie. **PH:** Christopher Challis. **ED:** Richard Marden. **MUS:** Cole Porter. **DESIGN:** Elliot Scott. **COSTUMES:** Anthony Powell. **ASST DIR:** Derek Cracknell.
   Cast: Peter Ustinov (Hercule Poirot), Colin Blakely (Sir Horace Blatt), Jane Birkin (Christine Redfern), Nicholas Clay (Patrick Redfern), Maggie Smith (Daphne Castle), Roddy McDowall (Rex Brewster), Sylvia Miles (Myra Gardner), James Mason (Odell Gardner), Denis Quilley (Kenneth Marshall), Diana Rigg (Arlena Marshall), Emily Hone (Linda Marshall), Cyril Conway (Surgeon), Barbara Hicks (Flewitt's Secretary), Richard Vernon (Flewitt), Robert Dorning (Concierge), Dimitri Andreas (Gino).

8. THIRTEEN AT DINNER. CBS-TV, 1985. 100 minutes. Color.
   P: Neil Hartley. **D:** Lou Antonio. **SC:** Rod Browning, from the novel by Agatha Christie. **PH:** Curtis Clark. **ED:** David A. Simmons. **MUS:** John Addison. **DESIGN:** Andrews Sanders.
   Cast: Peter Ustinov (Hercule Poirot), Faye Dunaway (Lady Edgware), Lee Horsley (Martin), Bill Nighy (Marsh), Amanda Pays (Geraldine), Jonathan Cecil (Captain Hastings), David Suchet (Inspector Japp), John Barron (Lord Edgware), David Frost (Himself), Diane Keen (Jenny Driver), John Stride (Director), Benedict

Taylor (Donald Ross), Allan Cuthbertson (Sir Montague Corner), Glyn Baker (Butler), Peter Clapham (Wildburn), Geoffrey Rose (Duke of Merton), Lou Antonio (Producer).

9. DEAD MAN'S FOLLY. CBS-TV, 1986. 100 minutes. Color.
    P: Neil Hartley. **D:** Clive Donner. **SC:** Rod Browning, from the novel by Agatha Christie. **PH:** Curtis Clark. **ED:** Donald R. Rode. **MUS:** John Addison. **DESIGN:** Brian Ackland-Snow.
    Cast: Peter Ustinov (Hercule Poirot), Jean Stapleton (Ariadne Oliver), Constance Cummings (Mrs. Folliot), Susan Wooldridge (Miss Brewis), Tim Pigott-Smith (Sir George Stubbs), Nicolette Sheridan (Lady Hattie Stubbs), Jonathan Cecil (Captain Hastings), Kenneth Cranham (Inspector Bland), Ralph Arliss (Michael Weyman), Christopher Guard (Alec Legge), Caroline Langrishe (Sally Legge), Jimmy Gardner (Merdell), Jeff Yahger (Eddie South), James Gaddas (Foreign Man), Pippa Hinchley (Marlene Tucker), Marjorie Yates (Mrs. Tucker).

10. MURDER IN THREE ACTS. CBS-TV, 1986. 100 minutes. Color.
    P: Paul Waigner. **D:** Gary Nelson. **SC:** Scott Swanton, from the novel by Agatha Christie. **PH:** Neal Roach. **ED:** Donald R. Rode. **AD:** Fernando Ramirez. **MUS:** Alf Clausen.
    Cast: Peter Ustinov (Hercule Poirot), Tony Curtis (Charles Cartwright), Emma Samms (Egg Eastman), Jonathan Cecil (Captain Hastings), Dana Elcar (Dr. Strange), Frances Lee McCain (Miss Milray), Concetta Tomei (Janet Crisp), Diana Muldaur (Angela Stafford), Marian Mercer (Daisy Eastman), Fernando Allende (Ricardo Montoya), Lisa Eichorn (Cynthia Dayton), Pedro Armendariz [Jr.] (Colonel Mateo), Nicholas Pryor (Freddie Dayton), Jacqueline Evans (Mrs. Babbington), Angeles Gonzalez (Housekeeper), Claudia Guzman (Rosa), Alma Levy (Nurse).

11. APPOINTMENT WITH DEATH. Cannon Group, 1988. 108 minutes. Color.
    P-D: Michael Winner. **EP:** Menaham Golan & Yoram Globus. **SC:** Anthony Shaffer, Peter Buckman & Michael Winner, from the novel by Agatha Christie. **PH:** David Gurfinkel. **ED:** Arnold Crust [Michael Winner]. **MUS:** Pino Donaggio. **DESIGN:** John Blezard. **COSTUMES:** John Bloomfield.
    Cast: Peter Ustinov (Hercule Poirot), Lauren Bacall (Lady Westholme), Carrie Fisher (Nadine Boynton), John Gielgud (Colonel Carbury), Piper Laurie (Emily Boynton), Hayley Mills (Miss Quinton), Jenny Seagrove (Sarah King), David Soul (Jefferson Cope), John Terlesky (Raymond Boynton), Valerie Richards (Carol Boynton), Nicholas Guest (Lennon Boynton), Amber Bezer.

Chapter 3

INSPECTOR CLOUSEAU

THE BRAINCHILD OF writer-producer-director Blake Edwards, Inspector Jacques Clouseau has become one of the most popular cinema detectives despite the fact that he is the antithesis of the accepted image of the screen sleuth. Clouseau is an incompetent bumbler who murders languages as he stumbles through a variety of cases, always doing the wrong thing yet by fate always solving the matter at the end as well as winning the girl. Clouseau's inane actions, his disastrous detection methods which drive his superior, Dreyfus, mad, and the perennial attacks on his person by his manservant Cato are common denominators which link the various features made about Clouseau. Also linking the adventures is the use of the cartoon character of the Pink Panther, an ingratiating feline, who is used to introduce the film's opening credits. Monetarily, the Clouseau films have been among the most successful of all detective features, the nine movies having grossed well over $80 million at the box office.

Blake Edwards produced, directed, and co-wrote (with Maurice Richlin) the initial series feature, THE PINK PANTHER, which was issued in March 1964. The story has bumbling but optimistic French police Inspector Jacques Clouseau (Peter Sellers) on the trail of the notorious jewel thief Sir Charles Litton (David Niven), known as the Phantom, for fifteen years. Clouseau does not realize that his wife, Simone (Capucine), is really Litton's mistress and accomplice. Sir Charles is after a priceless gem called the Pink Panther which belongs to Princess Dala (Claudia Cardinale). Also after the jewel is Sir Charles's nephew,

Advertisement for INSPECTOR CLOUSEAU (United Artists, 1968)

George Litton (Robert Wagner), also a jewel thief, although this is not known by his uncle. When the princess gives a party, the Pink Panther is stolen. After many adventures it is Clouseau who is arrested for stealing the jewel, while Sir George and Simone escape to South America, although they plan to send a letter clearing the detective, who is now an object of public adulation. THE PINK PANTHER was shot in Italy and the Swiss Alps; it grossed nearly $6 million in the U.S. *Variety* called the feature "high-gloss nonsense with standout comic highlights and brilliant playing by Peter Sellers." On the other hand, Georges Millau wrote in *Films in Review* (May 1964), "Screwball comedy has to be a lot wackier to succeed with me, and have fresher material."

The success of THE PINK PANTHER led Blake Edwards to churn out a quick sequel, A SHOT IN THE DARK, released in the early summer of 1964. Edwards co-wrote the screenplay with William Peter Blatty, and it was based on Harry Kunritz's play (which had had a 388 performance run on Broadway in 1961–1962) and on Marcel Archard's 1960 play *L'idiot*. Here Inspector Clouseau (Peter Sellers) comes to the aid of beautiful French parlormaid Maria Gambrelli (Elke Sommer) when she is accused of killing her lover. Clouseau believes she is innocent, but his superior, Chief Inspector Dreyfus (Herbert Lom), thinks otherwise and has the girl arrested. Pressure is brought on Dreyfus to put Clouseau back on the case, and Maria is released only to be found near the dead body of her employer's (Benjamin Ballon, played by George Sanders), gardener. Again Maria is arrested and again Clouseau has her released. When she goes to a nudist camp he follows, only to find her suspected of murdering Ballon's chambermaid. When another of Ballon's servants is eliminated, Maria is again arrested, and Clouseau is taken off the case. Again pressure is put on Dreyfus, and Clouseau is reassigned to the affair, and he again releases Maria. They go to a nightclub where four people die in unsuccessful attempts on Clouseau's life. Finally he and Maria take six suspects to Ballon's home, but they all escape in the detective's car, which has been wired with a bomb, and they are killed in the explosion. Having perpetrated all the murders to get rid of Clouseau, Dreyfus goes mad and is committed to an asylum. Filmed in Paris, A SHOT IN THE DARK has all the plot elements associated with the Pink Panther features, and it grossed $6.7 million at the box office. "The laughs are fairly constant, but unfortunately, Edwards now and then remembers that play he adapted and things tend to bog down," wrote the *Saturday Review of Literature*. *Films in Review* (August-September 1964) was still not impressed, as Louise Corbin opined, "I didn't think much of Peter Sellers as Inspector Clouseau in THE PINK PANTHER and I think even less of him as Clouseau in A SHOT IN THE DARK."

The role of Inspector Clouseau solidified Peter Sellers' popularity as a screen comic star. Born in 1925, he worked in radio, stage, and television and made his first film in 1951. Among his many features were THE LADYKILLERS ('55), THE SMALLEST SHOW ON EARTH ('57), TOM THUMB ('58), THE MOUSE THAT ROARED ('59), I'M ALL RIGHT, JACK ('59), TWO-WAY STRETCH ('60), WALTZ OF THE TOREADORS ('62), LOLITA ('62), THE WRONG ARM OF THE LAW ('63), DR. STRANGELOVE ('64), THE WORLD OF HENRY ORIENT ('64), WHAT'S NEW PUSSYCAT? ('65), THE WRONG BOX ('66), AFTER THE FOX ('66), CASINO ROYALE ('67), I LOVE YOU, ALICE B. TOKLAS ('68), UNDERCOVER HERO ('74), MURDER BY DEATH ('76), THE PRISONER OF ZENDA ('79), and THE FIENDISH PLOT OF DR. FU MANCHU ('80), his last completed film before his death from heart failure in 1980. Just as associated with the Pink Panther films as Sellers is Herbert Lom as Inspector Dreyfus. Born in 1917, the Czech actor came to the stage in 1936 and then moved to Great Britain in 1939 and made his stage debut there the next year. A very versatile performer, Lom has appeared in many films, including TOMORROW WE LIVE ('41), THE DARK TOWER ('43), THE SEVENTH VEIL ('45), NIGHT BOAT TO DUBLIN ('46), THE BLACK ROSE ('50), MR. DENNING DRIVES NORTH ('51), THE RINGER ('53), PARIS EXPRESS ('53), THE LADYKILLERS ('55), WAR AND PEACE ('56), FIRE DOWN BELOW ('57),

THE ROOTS OF HEAVEN ('58), THE BIG FISHERMAN ('59), SPARTACUS ('60), EL CID ('61), MYSTERIOUS ISLAND ('61), THE PHANTOM OF THE OPERA ('62), THE TREASURE OF SILER LAKE ('65), GAMBIT ('66), COUNT DRACULA ('70), TEN LITTLE INDIANS ('75), THE LADY VANISHES ('80), and THE MAN WITH BOGART'S FACE ('80). He starred in the British television series "The Human Jungle" in the early 1960s. Another asset in the Pink Panther series is the work of Burt Kwouk as Clouseau's predatory servant, Cato, who is continually using martial arts against his boss at the most inopportune times.

In 1968 the British-made INSPECTOR CLOUSEAU was released by United Artists. It is the only Pink Panther feature to date not made by Blake Edwards. Bud Yorkin directed this unpopular effort, and Alan Arkin proved inadequate compared to Peter Sellers in the part of Clouseau. Scotland Yard calls in Clouseau to locate money taken from England's great train robbery, as it is believed that a government operative is involved with the gang who stole the loot. He goes to a prison to meet one of the gang members and gets on the trail of the prison superintendent's (Frank Finlay) pretty maid Lisa (Delia Boccardo) while trying to avoid the man's sexually voracious wife (Beryl Reid). At a fair, Clouseau is drugged, and a plaster mask is made of his face. Later Clouseau masks are used by bandits who pull off a series of bank robberies in Switzerland. The money is hidden in candy wrappers placed on a barge in the Rhine River. The gang takes Clouseau and Lisa, who is really an Interpol agent on the case, prisoners, but using a laser-beam lighter the French detective sinks the barge and the gang is captured.

While no new Pink Panther films appeared for several years after the disappointing INSPECTOR CLOUSEAU, the cartoon character of the always silent and perennially nonplussed Pink Panther was featured in the animated thirty-minute NBC-TV series "The Pink Panther Show" in the fall of 1969. Lennie Schultz and the Ritts Puppets served as hosts for the series, while the cartoon voices were performed by Marvin Miller, Paul Frees, John Byner,

Rich Little, Athena Forde, and Dave Barry. Henry Mancini's theme music, which highlighted all the Pink Panther features, was used; the Warner Bros.–produced program was also telecast in England on BBC-TV. The series has remained popular through the years in syndication, and the Pink Panther cartoon character has also been used in television commercials.

With his screen popularity waning in the mid-1970s, Peter Sellers reteamed with Blake Edwards for his third Pink Panther comedy, THE RETURN OF THE PINK PANTHER, which United Artists issued in the spring of 1975. In many ways the film was a rehash of THE PINK PANTHER, but it was a "very funny film . . . in many ways a time capsule film, full of brilliant sight gags and comedic innocence" (*Variety*). When the famous Pink Panther jewel is again stolen, Chief Inspector Dreyfus (Herbert Lom) is again forced to reinstate Inspector Clouseau (Peter Sellers), who gets on the trail of supposedly retired thief Sir Charles Litton (Christopher Plummer), who is also out to find the culprit. The quest takes Clouseau and Litton to a resort hotel in Switzerland where the French detective tries to seduce Litton's wife (Catherine Schell). Grossing over $25 million, THE RETURN OF THE PINK PANTHER spawned two equally successful series features starring Peter Sellers.

Next came THE PINK PANTHER STRIKES AGAIN, released late in 1976. On the day he is about to be released from his sanitarium confinement, Inspector Dreyfus (Herbert Lom) is paid a courtesy call by Clouseau (Peter Sellers), who now has his old job, and as a result Dreyfus has a relapse and escapes. Now totally mad and seeking to eliminate his nemesis Clouseau from his life, Dreyfus takes possession of an old castle and kidnaps a mastermind (Richard Vernon), who has invented a doomsday machine. Dreyfus promises not to use the machine to destroy the world if Clouseau is liquidated. A beautiful Russian spy (Lesley-Anne Down) is also after the machine, and Clouseau must try to keep it out of her hands, save the professor, and capture Dreyfus. "For some reason, quite a bit of this basic action is rather lamely executed. One

Peter Sellers in THE PINK PANTHER STRIKES AGAIN (United Artists, 1976)

suspects that the film makers were so busy devising good stuff for Peter Sellers to do in his fourth impersonation of the serenely incompetent Clouseau that they neglected the long periods when he is not on screen," wrote *Time*. The reviewer added, however, "Better an indifferent PAN-THER than none at all." Grossing $20 million, THE PINK PANTHER STRIKES AGAIN took some comic jabs at horror films: Clouseau masquerades as Quasimodo, the Hunchback of Notre Dame; Herbert Lom madly plays the organ as he did when he starred in 1962's PHANTOM OF THE OPERA; and a brief animated scene shows King Kong atop the Empire State Building. Overall, though, this outing was Peter Sellers' weakest Pink Panther effort to date.

In the summer of 1978 Peter Sellers was Clouseau again in REVENGE OF THE PINK PANTHER, a United Artists release. An international drug operation pinpoints Inspector Clouseau (Peter Sellers) for elimination, and dope pusher Douvier (Robert Webber) is to carry out the mission. Clouseau, however, is robbed and a thief is killed in his stead. The inspector then masquerades as a priest and oversees his own funeral. The case takes him to Hong Kong where he tracks Douvier, aided by Simone (Dyan Cannon), Douvier's wife, as she, too, is marked for murder. *Newsweek* termed the feature "a slapstick farce with raucous sight gags, wild chases and crass jokes that must be inspired by *Playboy* cartoons." Again the film was very successful, making some $25 million at the box office. The film's weakest point was that it gave Herbert Lom very little to do as Dreyfus.

New Pink Panther features were planned by Blake Edwards, but Peter Sellers died in 1980. Footage of Sellers (some of it outtakes from the Pink Panther films) was used for TRAIL OF THE PINK PANTHER, which M-G-M/ United Artists issued late in 1982. Edwards fashioned a story which used this footage along with new material into a film dedicated to Sellers. Unfortunately the plot line was very jumbled. The first part of the film had Clouseau (Peter Sellers) in various predicaments brought about by his innate bumbling and his effect on the raving Dreyfus (Herbert Lom). When Clouseau is reported missing in a plane crash, French TV newswoman Marie Jouvet (Joanna Lumley) conducts a series of interviews with people who knew him, and they recount various episodes in his checkered career. Among those she talks to are Sir Charles Litton (David Niven) and his wife (Capucine), servant Cato (Burt Kwouk), gangster Bruno (Robert Loggia), and Clouseau's father (Richard Mulligan). *Variety* termed this mishmash "a thin, peculiar picture unsupported by the number of laughs one is accustomed to in this series."

Filmed simultaneously with TRAIL OF THE PINK PANTHER was an entirely new feature, CURSE OF THE PINK PANTHER, the last outing to date in the grouping by Blake Edwards, who again produced, directed, and co-scripted the film. The plot has loony Dreyfus (Herbert Lom) using a computer to locate incompetent Gotham cop Clinton Sleigh (Ted Wass) in order to find not only the

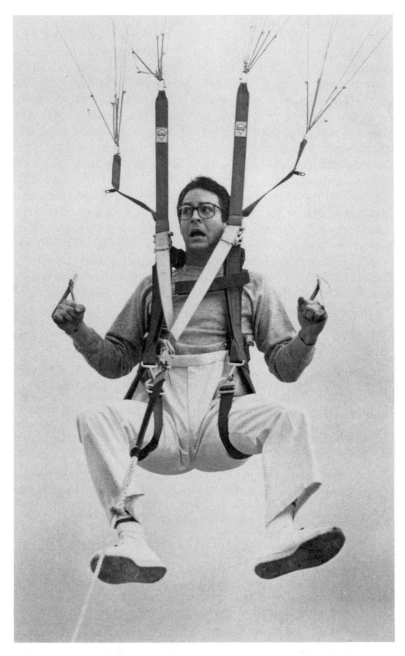

Ted Wass in CURSE OF THE PINK PANTHER (M-G-M/United Artists, 1983)

missing Clouseau but also the Pink Panther gem, which again has been stolen. Clinton takes on the case and talks with people from Clouseau's past, such as Sir Charles Litton (David Niven), his wife (Capucine) and his nephew, George (Robert Wagner). Finally, Clouseau (Roger Moore), who has had plastic surgery, shows up, and the affair is solved. Little more than a rehash of earlier Pink Panther efforts, the film suffered from the loss of Peter Sellers as Clouseau, although Roger Moore's surprise cameo in the part is amusing. By the time the last two Pink Panther films were made David Niven was in such poor health that his voice had to be dubbed by Rich Little. Issued in the summer of 1983, CURSE OF THE PINK PANTHER met with tepid critical reception and definitely showed that without the genius of Peter Sellers the series could not stay afloat.

Filmography

1. THE PINK PANTHER. United Artists, 1964. 113 minutes. Color.
   P: Martin Jurow. **AP:** Dick Crockett. **D:** Blake Edwards. **SC:** Maurice Richlin & Blake Edwards. **PH:** Philip Lathrop. **ED:** Ralph E. Winters. **MUS:** Henry Mancini. **AD:** Fernando Carrere. Title song sung by Fran Jeffries.
   Cast: David Niven (Sir Charles Litton), Peter Sellers (Inspector Jacques Clouseau), Capucine (Simone Clouseau), Robert Wagner (George Litton), Claudia Cardinale (Princess Dala), Fran Jeffries (The Greek Cousin), Brenda De Banzie (Angela Dunning), James Lanphier (Saloud), Colin Gordon (Tucker), John Le Mesurier (Defense Attorney), Guy Thomajan (Artoff), Michael Trubshawe (Novelist), Riccardo Billi (Greek Shipowner), Meri Welles (Starlet), Martin Miller (Photographer).

2. A SHOT IN THE DARK. United Artists, 1964. 101 minutes. Color.
   P-D: Blake Edwards. **AP:** Cecil F. Ford. **SC:** Blake Edwards & William Peter Blatty. **PH:** Christopher Challis. **ED:** Bert Bates. **MUS:** Henry Mancini. **ASST DIR:** Derek Cracknell. **PROD MGR:** Denis Johnson.
   Cast: Peter Sellers (Inspector Jacques Clouseau), Elke Sommer (Maria Gambrelli), George Sanders (Benjamin Ballon), Herbert Lom (Chief Inspector Charles Dreyfus), Tracy Reed (Dominique Ballon), Graham Stark (Hercule Lajoy), André Maranne (François), Douglas

Wilmer (Henri Lafarge), Maurice Kaufmann (Pierre), Ann Lynn (Dudu), David Lodge (Georges), Moira Redmond (Simone), Reginald Beckwith (Camp Sunshine Receptionist), Turk Thrust [Bryan Forbes] (Charlie), John Herrington (Doctor), Jack Melford (Psychoanalyst).

3. INSPECTOR CLOUSEAU. United Artists, 1968. 98 minutes. Color.
    P: Lewis J. Rachmil. **D:** Bud Yorkin. **SC:** Tom Waldman & Frank Waldman. **PH:** Arthur Ibbetson. **ED:** John Victor Smith. **MUS:** Ken Thorne. **AD:** Norman Dorme. **SP EFF:** Malcolm King.
    Cast: Alan Arkin (Inspector Jacques Clouseau), Delia Boccardo (Lisa Morrel), Frank Finlay (Superintendent Weaver), Beryl Reid (Mrs. Weaver), Patrick Cargill (Sir Charles Braithwaite), Barry Foster (Addison Steele), Clive Francis (Clyde Hargreaves), John Bindon (Bull Parker), Michael Ripper (Frey), Tutte Lemkow (Frenchy LeBec), Anthony Ainsley (Bomber LeBec), Wallas Eaton (Hoeffler), David Bauer (Geffrion), Richard Pearson (Shockley), George Pravda (Wulf), Eric Pohlmann (Bergesch), Geoffrey Bayldon (Gutch), Arthur Lovegrove (Innkeeper), Kathya Wyeth (Meg), Tracey Crisp (Julie), Marjie Lawrence (Peggy), Craig Booth (David), Julie Croft (Nicole), Robert Russell (Stockton), Susan Engel (Policewoman), Will Stampe (Fishmonger), Barbara Dana (Nun).

4. THE RETURN OF THE PINK PANTHER. United Artists, 1975. 115 minutes. Color.
    P-D: Blake Edwards. **SC:** Frank Waldman & Blake Edwards. **PH:** Geoffrey Unsworth. **ED:** Tom Priestley. **MUS:** Henry Mancini. **ASST DIR:** Guy Sauteret & Derek Kavanagh.
    Cast: Peter Sellers (Inspector Jacques Clouseau), Christopher Plummer (Sir Charles Litton), Catherine Schell (Claudine Litton), Herbert Lom (Chief Inspector Charles Dreyfus), Peter Arne (Colonel Sharki), Grégoire Aslan (Police Chief), Peter Jeffrey (General Wadafi), Eric Pohlmann (The Fat Man), Burt Kwouk (Cato), André Maranne (François), Victor Spinetti (Concierge) Mike Grady (Bellboy).

5. THE PINK PANTHER STRIKES AGAIN. United Artists, 1976. 103 minutes. Color.
    P-D: Blake Edwards. **SC:** Blake Edwards & Frank Waldman. **PH:** Harry Waxman. **ED:** Alan Jones. **MUS:** Henry Mancini. Title song sung by Tom Jones.
    Cast: Peter Sellers (Inspector Jacques Clouseau), Herbert Lom (Charles Dreyfus), Lesley-Anne Down (Olga), Colin Blakely (Alec Drummond), Leonard Rossiter (Quinlin), Burt Kwouk (Cato), André Maranne (François), Marne Maitland (Deputy Commissioner), Richard Vernon (Dr. Fassbender), Michael Robbins (Jarvis), Briony McRoberts (Margo Fassbender), Dick Crockett (President), Byron Kane (Secretary of State).

6. REVENGE OF THE PINK PANTHER. United Artists, 1978. 98 minutes. Color.

   P-D: Blake Edwards. **EP:** Tony Adams. **SC:** Ron Clark, Blake Edwards & Frank Waldman. **PH:** Ernie Day. **ED:** Alan Jones. **AD:** John Siddall. **MUS:** Henry Mancini.

   Cast: Peter Sellers (Inspector Jacques Clouseau), Herbert Lom (Charles Dreyfus), Dyan Cannon (Simone Legree), Robert Webber (Douvier), Burt Kwouk (Cato), Paul Stewart (Scallini), Robert Loggia (Bruno Marchione), Graham Stark (Auguste), Sue Lloyd (Russo), Tony Beckley (Guy Algo), Valerie Leon (Tanya).

7. TRAIL OF THE PINK PANTHER. Metro-Goldwyn-Mayer/United Artists, 1982. 97 minutes. Color.

   P: Blake Edwards & Tony Adams. **EP:** Jonathan D. Krane. **D:** Blake Edwards. **SC:** Frank Waldman, Tom Waldman, Blake Edwards & Geoffrey Edwards. **PH:** Dick Bush. **ED:** Alan Jones. **MUS:** Henry Mancini. **AD:** Alan Tomkins & John Siddall. **ASST DIR:** Ray Corbett & Michel Cheyko.

   Cast: Peter Sellers (Inspector Jacques Clouseau), David Niven (Sir Charles Litton), Herbert Lom (Charles Dreyfus), Capucine (Lady Simone Litton), Richard Mulligan (Mr. Clouseau), Joanna Lumley (Marie Jouvet), Robert Loggia (Bruno Marchione), Harvey Korman (Professor Balls), Burt Kwouk (Cato), Graham Stark (Hercule), Peter Arne (Colonel Bufoni), André Maranne (François), Ronald Fraser (Dr. Longet), Leonard Rossiter (Quinlin).

8. CURSE OF THE PINK PANTHER. Metro-Goldwyn-Mayer/United Artists, 1983. 109 minutes. Color.

   P: Blake Edwards & Tony Adams. **EP:** Jonathan D. Krane. **D:** Blake Edwards. **SC:** Blake Edwards & Geoffrey Edwards. **PH:** Dick Bush. **ED:** Ralph E. Winters, Bob Hathaway & Alan Jones. **MUS:** Henry Mancini. **AD:** Alan Tomkins & John Siddall. **ASST DIR:** Ray Corbett.

   Cast: Ted Wass (Clifton Sleigh), David Niven (Sir Charles Litton), Robert Wagner (George Litton), Herbert Lom (Charles Dreyfus), Capucine (Lady Simone Litton), Joanna Lumley (Chandra), Robert Loggia (Bruno Marchione), Harvey Korman (Professor Balls), Burt Kwouk (Cato), Leslie Ash (Juleta Shane), Graham Stark (Hercule), André Maranne (François), Peter Arne (Colonel Bufoni), Roger Moore (Inspector Jacques Clouseau), Patricia Davis, William Hootkins.

Chapter 4

INSPECTOR MAIGRET

INSPECTOR JULES MAIGRET has been one of the most popular and enduring of fictional police detectives. Georges Simenon created Maigret in 1929, and he continued to produce Maigret works through the late 1970s, a total of nearly fifty novels. In addition, Simenon wrote under a number of other names, making him one of the most prolific writers of this century. In addition to the sixteen films made about Inspector Maigret, more than two dozen movies have been produced from other Simenon fiction works, including PARIS EXPRESS ('52), FORBIDDEN FRUIT ('52), A LIFE IN THE BALANCE ('55), THE BOTTOM OF THE BOTTLE ('56), THE BROTHERS RICO ('57), and LE PRESIDENT ('61).

The character of Jules Maigret is an interesting one in that the books on his cases have revealed the various changes in his life over the years, much like Rex Stout's Nero Wolfe (see B/V) or Erle Stanley Gardner's Perry Mason (q.v.). A quiet, methodical investigator, Maigret is forever smoking a pipe, and in his work no clue is so small that it will be overlooked. His wife, Louise, is loyal to him but has long since realized that Maigret's work is the most important aspect of his life. In *The Private Lives of Private Eyes, Spies, Crime Fighters and Other Good Guys* (1977), Otto Penzler called Inspector Maigret ''one of the towering figures of mystery fiction.''

Jean Renoir directed the initial Inspector Maigret film, LA NUIT DU CARREFOUR (Night at the Crossroads), starring his brother Pierre Renoir as Maigret. The story had the Paris police inspector out to solve the murder of a diamond merchant, finally tracing it to a gang using a remote garage as its headquarters. Apparently the producers ran out of money before the film was finished, but the completed footage was edited into a feature and released successfully. However, *Variety* complained that the "film attempts to be exceedingly arty, resulting in confusion, many sequences being apparently shot for mere atmosphere."

LA NUIT DU CARREFOUR was released in 1932, as was the second Maigret outing, LE CHIEN JAUNE (The Yellow Dog). This feature was directed by Jean Tarride and starred his father Abel Tarride, as Maigret. Based on the Simenon novel of the same title, the film had Inspector Maigret at the seaport town of Concarneau trying to solve a crime involving a corrupt physician who had returned to France after working as a bootlegger in the United States. The plot of the film was somewhat reminiscent of the Sherlock Holmes (q.v.) work, *The Valley of Fear*, by Arthur Conan Doyle.

The third Inspector Maigret feature to be made in France was LA TETE D'UN HOMME (A Man's Head), issued in 1933, which Julien Duvivier directed and scripted, with Harry Bauer cast as Maigret. The plot had the inspector on the trail of a crook from Czechoslovakia who has murdered two women in Paris. The film was remade in 1949 as THE MAN ON THE EIFFEL TOWER (q.v.).

In 1933 Georges Simenon ceased writing Maigret novels for five years, and it was not until the Nazi occupation of France during World War II that more Maigret films were made. Apparently the first of these was called MAIGRET, but the 1941 production was never finished. From 1943 to 1945, however, Albert Préjean portrayed Maigret in a trio of French-made feature films, beginning with 1943's PICPUS, from the novella *Signé Picpus*. The story has Maigret on the trail of a murderer who is really the writer of a letter exposing the crime to the police. Next came CECILE EST MORTE in 1944, directed by Maurice Tourneur. Here a young woman (Santa Relli) has fallen in love with Maigret (Albert Préjean). She tells him her aunt is in danger, and soon both women are murdered, and

Maigret must solve the case. The final German-supervised Maigret feature was LES CAVES DU MAJESTIC (Majestic Hotel Cellars), issued in 1945, and taken from Simenon's 1941 novel of the same title. Here Inspector Maigret (Albert Préjean) investigates the murder of a woman guest in a fashionable Paris hotel, with a chef (Jacques Baumer) accused of the crime. *Variety* noted, "Direction is good, with an especially good scene when Préjean stages a dinner party, inviting both suspects to decide who is guilty and should be adjudged the father of the dead woman's child."

The first English-language Maigret feature came in 1949 with RKO'S THE MAN ON THE EIFFEL TOWER, which producer Irving Allen filmed in Paris. Actor Burgess Meredith, who also played a co-staring role, directed the

Charles Laughton *(left)* and Chaz Chase in THE MAN ON THE EIFFEL TOWER (RKO Radio, 1949)

feature, although some sources claim Charles Laughton, who played Maigret, was an unofficial co-director. The film was a remake of the 1933 feature, LA TETE D'UN HOMME (q.v.). The story has a young man, Bill Kirby (Robert Hutton), hire a psychopath, Radek (Franchot Tone), to murder his old aunt so he could leave his wife (Patricia Roc) to marry beautiful Edna (Jean Wallace). After the crime is committed, the chief suspect is the nearly blind scissors-grinder, Huertin (Burgess Meredith), but Inspector Maigret (Charles Laughton), who is in charge of the case, eventually captures the real killer after an extended chase through Paris. While most critics lauded Stanley Cortez's color photography which highlighted the city of Paris, most were not happy with the film's plot or Charles Laughton's overly mannered performance as Maigret.

For the French inspector's next film appearance in BRELAN D'AS (Full House) in 1952, Maigret had to share screen time with two other detectives, Belgian sleuth Wens (Raymond Rouleau) and American private eye Lemmy Caution (see B/V) (Van Dreelan) in a three-part story. The Maigret segment was "Le Témoignage d'un Enfant de Choeur" (The Choir Boy's Testimony), and in it Inspector Maigret (Michel Simon) interrogates a choir boy (Christian Fourcade) about a murder he witnessed. *Variety* commented, "Simon brings depth to the Maigret character in the short running time."

Next Inspector Maigret came to French television in 1953 in a series starring Maurice Manson in the title role. In 1955 Pathé took three segments from the series and tied them together into a feature film called MAIGRET DIRIGE L'ENQUETE (Maigret in Charge of the Inquest) which was released to French theaters. The three episodes making up the film were "Maigret Cherche un Cadavre," "Maigret et la Vieille Fille," and "Maigret Cherche un Motif."

Jean Gabin, the most popular actor in the history of French cinema, took over the role of Inspector Maigret in MAIGRET TEND UN PIEGE (Maigret Sets a Trap) in 1957. He proved so popular in the part that he played it twice more in 1959's MAIGRET ET L'AFFAIRE ST.-FIACRE and MAIGRET VOIT ROUGE in 1963. Born in 1907, Gabin had

Jean Gabin and Annie Girardot in MAIGRET TEND UN PIEGE (Maigret Sets a Trap) (Intermondia/Jolly Film, 1957)

stage experience before coming to films in 1931. During the 1930s he was a matinee idol in France in such features as COEUR DE LILAS ('32), GOLGOTHA ('35), PEPE LE MOKO ('37), LA GRANDE ILLUSION ('37), and LA BETE HUMAINE ('38). During World War II he starred in two Hollywood productions, MOONTIDE ('42) and THE IM-POSTER (THE STRANGE CONFESSION) ('44). After the war he returned to France and made films like MARTIN ROUMAGNAC ('45) with Marlene Dietrich, but his popularity had slipped and he did not regain it until he made TOUCHEZ PAS AU GRISBI in 1953. Thereafter, until his death in 1976, Gabin remained France's most popular male film star, appearing in such features as L'AIR DE PARIS

('54), CRIME ET CHATIMENT ('56), LE CAS DU
DOCTEUR LAURET ('57), LES MISERABLES ('58), EN
CAS DE MALHEUR ('58), LE PRESIDENT ('61), MON-
SIEUR ('64), DU RIFIFI A PANAME ('66), LE SOLEIL DES
VOYOUS ('67), FIN DE JOURNEE ('69), LE CLAN DES
SICILIENS ('69, released in the U.S. in an English-
language version called THE SICILIAN CLAN), LE
TUEUR ('71), and L'AFFAIRE DOMINICI ('72).

MAIGRET TEND UN PIEGE had Inspector Jules Maigret
(Jean Gabin) on the trail of a psychopath who had killed
four women in Paris. Arresting a bogus suspect, Maigret
sets policewomen up as decoys in order to catch the real
killer, who manages to escape. Maigret begins to suspect
architect Marcel Maurin (Jean Desailly) of the crimes,
despite the fact that the man is well-to-do and has a loyal
wife (Annie Girardot). As he is about to pin the crimes on
Maurin, another murder takes place, but eventually Maigret is able to solve the case. In *Cinema: The Magic Vehicle: A
Guide to Its Achievement* (1979), Adam Garbicz and Jacek
Klinowski wrote, "Relief is the only positive feeling in
MAIGRET SETS A TRAP; the rest is gloomy and dusky—
and this is well rendered by the photography and the
music. The picture has a good pace and realistic character
description." The film was released in 1958 in Great Britain
as MAIGRET SETS A TRAP, and in the United States the
same year by Lopert as INSPECTOR MAIGRET.

Jean Gabin's second Maigret outing was MAIGRET ET
L'AFFAIRE ST.-FIACRE, issued in 1959 and directed by
Jean Delannoy, who had directed Gabin's initial Maigret
feature. Here Maigret is contacted by an old friend, a
countess, who has received a threatening letter. When she
is found dead, the inspector believes she has been
murdered and goes to the small town of St.-Fiacre to find
her killer. *Variety* noted "Gabin's quizzical figure of the
plodding but shrewd detective who unknots the tangled
skeins of provincial avarice and intrigue rather than arrive
at a solution by slick police work." MAIGRET VOIT
ROUGE, issued in 1963, was Jean Gabin's final Maigret
film. This time out, American gangsters in Paris murder a
young woman witness who could have sent their leader

back to the States and into prison. Maigret sets out to bring in the killers and finds himself aided by the FBI. The film was based on Georges Simenon's 1952 novel *Maigret, Lognon et les Gangsters.*

Prior to Jean Gabin's portraying Maigret, Jean Morel had done the part on the Paris stage in 1955 in *Liberty Bar,* and that vehicle was done for French television in 1960 with Louis Arbessier as Maigret. That year also saw the beginning of the British television series "Maigret," starring Rupert Davies as the pipe-smoking sleuth. The BBC series ran from 1960 to 1970, and in 1965 Davies also did the role of the French detective on stage in *Maigret and the Lady* at London's Strand Theatre. In 1966 Rupert Davies was signed to play Maigret in the West German production MAIGRET SPIELT FALSCH, but after it went into production Davies was not happy with the script and withdrew from the project, being replaced by German actor Heinz Ruhmann.

When the film was released in 1966 it was called MAIGRET UND SEIN GROSSTER FALL (Maigret and His Biggest Case), and it was an Austrian–West German–French–Italian co-production directed by Alfred Weidenmann. Based on Georges Simenon's 1931 novel *La Danseuse du Gai Moulin,* it told of a murder committed at an art gallery and a precious Van Gogh painting being stolen. The main suspect is British art collector Holoway (Gunther Ugeheuer), but he is murdered in Switzerland. Assigned to the case, Inspector Maigret (Heinz Ruhmann) goes to Lausanne and there eventually finds the culprits responsible for the two killings. The film was released to U.S. TV by International Television Corporation (ITC) as ENTER INSPECTOR MAIGRET.

The year 1966 also saw another Maigret feature, MAIGRET À PIGALLE (Maigret at the Pigalle), a French-Italian co-production, starring Gino Cervi as Maigret. Based on the 1951 book *Maigret au Picratt's,* the film told of a stripper killed at the Pigalle nightclub, with Inspector Maigret investigating the matter. When a countess and a club doorman are also killed at the Pigalle, Maigret sets up a witness to the crimes as a target, stops the arrest of a suspect, and finally captures the real murderer.

The international popularity of Inspector Maigret was shown by the fact that in the mid-1960s he was portrayed on West German television by Kees Bruce, on the Japanese small screen by Kinya Aikowa, and on Dutch television by Jan Teulings. In October 1967 Jean Richard starred in the title role of the French "Maigret" series, and several of the episodes were television remakes of earlier feature films, such as "Cécile Est Morte," "La Tête d'un Homme," "Le Chien Jaune," "Signé Picpus," and "La Nuit du Carrefour." Running through 1969, the French TV series produced nearly three dozen episodes. In 1976 Michel Bouquet portrayed Maigret in the French television program "Les Anneaux de Bicetre," directed by Louis Grospierre, and in 1977 Jean Richard reprised the Maigret role in still another television production in France, a small-screen remake of "Maigret, Lognon et les Gangsters."

In 1988 Inspector Maigret finally came to American television in the made-for-TV movie MAIGRET, starring Richard Harris in the title role. When a former colleague, now a detective, is found murdered, Inspector Maigret and his partner Lucas (Andrew McCullough) are assigned to the case. The trail leads Maigret to wealthy American recluse Kevin Partmann (Patrick O'Neal) who is about to take back his huge business holdings from his sons, Daniel (Ian Ogilvy) and Tony (Eric Deacon). Maigret and his wife Louise (Barbara Shelley) go on a cruise with Partmann and his family, and an attempt is made on the detective's life. Victoria Partmann (Victoria Tennant), Daniel's wife and Kevin's ex-lover, is murdered. Getting all the suspects together, Maigret solves the case by naming two killers caught in a web of deceit and greed. Although well made with European locales, MAIGRET was a slow-moving telefilm, and Richard Harris portrayed Maigret in a bizarre, lethargic, absentminded manner, topping the characterization with a slight Irish accent!

Filmography

1. LA NUIT DU CARREFOUR (Night at the Crossroads). Comptoir Cinematographique Français, 1932. 90 minutes.

D: Jean Renoir. **ASST DIR:** Jacques Becker.
Cast: Pierre Renoir (Inspector Jules Maigret), Winna Winfried, Georges Koudria, Michel Duran, Jean Gehret, Max Dalban, Luci Vallat, Jean Mitry.

2. LE CHIEN JAUNE (The Yellow Dog). Ord Halk, 1932. 95 minutes.
   D: Jean Tarride. From the novel by Georges Simenon.
   Cast: Abel Tarride (Inspector Jules Maigret), Rolla Norman (Gangster), Robert Le Vigan (Crook), Rosine Derean (Servant), Jacques Henley, Fred Marche, Paul Azias, Jane Lory, Sylvette Fillacier, Germaine Essler.

3. LA TETE D'UN HOMME (A Man's Head). [France], 1933.
   D-SC: Julien Duvivier. **PH:** Armand Thirard. **SETS:** George Wakheuitck.
   Cast: Harry Bauer (Inspector Jules Maigret), Valery Inkijinoff, Gina Manes, Marie-Louise Damiens, Line Noro, Alexandre Rignault, Gaston Jacquet.

4. PICPUS. [France], 1943.
   D: Richard Pottier. From the novel *Signé Picpus* by Georges Simenon.
   Cast: Albert Préjean (Inspector Jules Maigret), Juliette Faber, Jean Tissier, Noël Roquevert, Guillaume de Sax, Antoine Balpetre.

5. CECILE EST MORTE (Cécile Is Dead). [France], 1944.
   D: Maurice Tourneur.
   Cast: Albert Préjean (Inspector Maigret), Santa Relli (Cécile), André Reybaz, Germaine Kerjean, Jean Brochard.

6. LES CAVES DU MAJESTIC (Majestic Hotel Cellars). Domaines, 1945. 95 minutes.
   D: Richard Pottier. **SC:** Charles Spaak, from the novel by Georges Simenon.
   Cast: Albert Préjean (Inspector Jules Maigret), Suzy Prim (Victim), Jacques Haumer (Chef), Denise Grey (Secretary), Jean Marchat (Victim's Husband), Gabriello (Detective), Florelle (Hotel Guest), Charpin (Judge).

7. THE MAN ON THE EIFFEL TOWER. RKO Radio, 1949. 94 minutes. Color.
   P: Irving Allen. **D:** Burgess Meredith (& uncredited Charles Laughton). **SC:** Harry Brown, from the novel *A Battle of Nerves* by Georges Simenon. **PH:** Stanley Cortez. **ED:** Louis H. Sackin. **MUS:** Michel Michelet.
   Cast: Charles Laughton (Inspector Jules Maigret), Franchot Tone (Radek), Burgess Meredith (Huertin), Robert Hutton (Bill Kirby), Jean Wallace (Edna Kirby), Patricia Roc (Helen Kirby), Belita

(Gisella), George Thorpe (Comelieu), William Phipps (Jamvier), William Cothrell (Moers), Chaz Chase (Waiter), Wilfred Hyde-White (Professor Grollet).

8. BRELAN D'AS. Pathé-Consortium, 1952. 118 minutes.
   D: Henri Verneuil. **SC:** Jacques Campanez, from stories by Peter Cheney, Georges Simenon & S. A. Steeman. **PH:** André German. **ED:** Georges Rongier.
   Cast: Michel Simon (Inspector Jules Maigret), Raymond Rouleau (Detective Wens), Van Dreelan (Lemmy Caution), Arlette Merry (Florence), Natalie Nattier (Micheline), Christian Fourcade (Christian), Claire Olivier.

9. MAIGRET DIRIGE L'ENQUETE (Maigret in Charge of the Inquest). Pathé-Consortium-Cinema, 1955. 90 minutes.
   P: Marcel Provençal. **D:** Stany Cordier. **PH:** Raymond Clunie. **MUS:** Joseph Kosma. **DESIGN:** Robert Dumesnil.
   Cast: Maurice Manson (Inspector Jules Maigret), Peter Walker (Janvier), Michel André (Janvier's Associate), Svetlana Pitoeff (Cécile Pardon), Ben Omanoff (Lucas), Joseph Weiner (Dandurand), Jacques Laurent (Verne), Georges Tabet (Restaurant Patron), Lucien Desagneaux (Sad Freddy), Anne-Marie Duverney (Secretary), Bruce Kay (Glass Clerk), Gladis Gould (Lanky Liz), Marcel Bothier (M. Tremblet), Laurence Badie (Francine), Martha Labarr (Mme. Maigret), Duncan Elliot (Mauvre), Jo Warfield (Jussiaume), Sue Graham (Louise), Colin Drake (Teddy), Marcel Journet (The Commissioner), Louise Vincent (Marie), Louise Nowa (Mme. Vye Boynet), Frank MacDonald.

10. MAIGRET TEND UN PIEGE (Maigret Sets a Trap). Intermondia/Jolly Film, 1957. 119 minutes.
    D: Jean Delannoy. **SC:** Michel Audiard, from the novel by Georges Simenon. **PH:** Louis Page. **ED:** Henri Taverna. **MUS:** Paul Misraki. **AD:** René Renoux.
    Cast: Jean Gabin (Inspector Jules Maigret), Annie Girardot (Yvonne Maurin), Jean Desailly (Marcel Maurin), Olivier Hussenot (Lagrume), Lucienne Bogaert (Mme. Maurin), Jeanne Boitel (Mme. Maigret), Alfred Adam (Barberot), Paulette Dubost (Mme. Barberot), Gerard Sety (Jojo), Lino Ventura (Inspector Torrence), Jean Tissier (Older Reporter), Guy Decomble (Suspect).
    British Title: MAIGRET SETS A TRAP.
    U. S. Title: INSPECTOR MAIGRET ('58).

11. MAIGRET ET L'AFFAIRE ST.-FIACRE (Maigret and the St.-Fiacre Case). Cinedis/Intermondia, 1959. 100 minutes.
    D: Jean Delannoy. **SC:** R. M. Arlaud, Michel Audiard & Jean Delannoy, from the novel by Georges Simenon. **PH:** Louis Page. **ED:** Henri Taverna.

Cast: Jean Gabin (Inspector Jules Maigret), Valentine Tessier (The Countess), Michel Auclair (The Count), Michel Vitold (Priest), Robert Hirsch (Lucien), Gabrielle Fontan, Paul Frankeur.

12. MAIGRET VOIT ROUGE (Maigret Sees Red). Comacico/Films Copernic/Titanus, 1963. 90 minutes.

   D: Gilles Grangier. **SC:** Jacques Robert & Gilles Grangier, from the novel by Georges Simenon. **PH:** Louis Page. **ED:** Sophie Dubus.

   Cast: Jean Gabin (Inspector Jules Maigret), Françoise Fabian (Lilli), Guy Decomble (Lognon), Vittorio Sanipoli (Pozzo), Brad Harris (Charlie), Ricky Cooper (Cicero), Paul Carpenter.

13. MAIGRET UND SEIN GROSSTER FALL (Maigret and His Biggest Case). Intercontinental/Terra Film/Carmina Films, 1966. 90 minutes. Color.

   D: Alfred Weidenmann. **SC:** Herbert Reinecker, from the novel *Maigret et l'Espion* by Georges Simenon. **PH:** Heinz Holscher. **ED:** Gretl Girinec & Uli Kirsch. **MUS:** Ervin Halletz. **DESIGN:** Herta Harider. **ASST DIR:** Wieland Liebske.

   Cast: Heinz Ruhmann (Inspector Jules Maigret), Françoise Prevost (Simone), Gunther Stoll (Alain Robin), Eddi Arent (Labat), Gunther Strack (Commissioner Delvigne), Gerd Vespermann (Inspector Caselle), Alexander Kerst (Delfosse), Christo Negas (Adriano), Ulli Lommel (René), Rudolf Barry (Inspector Lucas), Gunther Ugeheuer (Holoway), Peter Gross (Inspector Lapointe), Edwin Noel (Jean), Giacomo Furia (Genaro), Francesca Rosano (Franchita), Claudio Camaso, Pier Paolo Caffoni, Peter Gerhard, Silvana Sansoni, Hans Habietinek, Walter Varndal, Ralf Boddenhuser, Toni Wagner.

   Italian Title: IL CASO DIFFICILE DEL COMMISSARIO MAIGRET (Maigret's Difficult Case).

   French Title: MAIGRET FAIT MOUCHE.

   U. S. TV Title: ENTER INSPECTOR MAIGRET.

14. MAIGRET A PIGALLE (Maigret at the Pigalle). Riganti-Cervi/Les Films Number One, 1966. Color.

   P: Franco Riganti & Antonio Cervi. **D:** Mario Landi. **SC:** Sergio Amedei & Mario Landi, from the novel *Maigret au Picratt's* by Georges Simenon. **PH:** Giuseppe Ruzzolini. **MUS:** Armando Trovajoli.

   Cast: Gino Cervi (Inspector Jules Maigret), Lila Kedrova, Raymond Pellegrin, Alfred Adam, Daniel Ollier, Jose Greci, Enzo Cerusico.

   French Title: LE COMMISSAIRE MAIGRET A PIGALLE.

15. MAIGRET. HTN/Columbia, 1988. 100 minutes. Color.

   P-SC: Arthur Weingarten. **EP:** Robert Connor. **AP:** Steve Groves.

D: Paul Lynch. **PH:** Bob Edwards. **ED:** Lyndon Matthews. **MUS:** Alan Lisk. **DESIGN:** Caroline Smith.

Cast: Richard Harris (Chief Inspector Jules Maigret), Patrick O'Neal (Kevin Partmann), Victoria Tennant (Victoria "Vicky" Partmann), Ian Ogilvy (Daniel Partmann), Barbara Shelley (Louise Maigret), Dominique Barnes (Tara Partmann), Caroline Munro (Carolyn Page), Richard Durden (Julian Brady), Andrew McCullough (Lucas), Eric Deacon (Tony Partmann), Annette Andre (Judith Hollenbeck), Don Henderson (Captain), Mark Audley (Ekers).

Chapter 5

MIKE HAMMER

MIKE HAMMER IS ONE of the most widely read yet vilified of post–World War II fictional detectives. As created by Mickey Spillane, Hammer is a tough, no-nonsense private eye who hates corruption and Communism in equal doses. To him the end justifies the means, and in his novels he is as brutal, perhaps more brutal, than his foes. Many writers have claimed Hammer was a product of the McCarthy era of the early 1950s and that he is basically a self-centered anarchist. A loner, Hammer has few friends and is only close to his secretary-lover Velda, although women are greatly attracted to him. Unlike most fictional detectives, Hammer spends little time analyzing a case or looking for clues. He simply gets on a killer's trail and stays on it until the culprit is found, and often dispatched by Hammer's vengeance.

Beginning in 1947 with *I, the Jury*, Mickey Spillane has turned out more than a baker's dozen books about Mike Hammer through the 1980s. Born Frank Morrison in Brooklyn in 1918, the author was an Air Force instructor during World War II and later became a crime reporter before becoming a fiction writer. Spillane has portrayed the character Mike Hammer on film and recordings, and as himself has appeared in the film RING OF FEAR ('54). Spillane may be the most readily recognizable mystery writer of the day, thanks to his appearances on TV talk shows and commercials. Spillane has also written several non-Hammer books, including *The Delta Factor* ('67), which was filmed under that title in 1970 and featured Spillane's wife Sherri Spillane, who also appeared on the cover of his book, *The Erection Set* (1972).

In 1953 producer-director Victor Saville formed Park Lane Productions for the purpose of making films based on Mickey Spillane's novels. In the next five years he produced four features: three Mike Hammer adventures and one non-Hammer outing—1954's THE LONG WAIT, the second of the quartet of productions. The initial Park Lane film was I, THE JURY; based on the first Hammer novel, it was issued in 1953 in 3-D. The story had private eye Mike Hammer (Biff Elliott) out to get revenge on the killer of a wartime pal who had lost an arm saving Hammer's life in combat. Police Captain Chambers (Preston Foster) tries to get Hammer to work within the framework of the law in tracking down the murderer, but the gumshoe has his own ideas of right and wrong. He eventually meets and is attracted to beautiful psychiatrist Charlotte Manning (Peggie Castle), who turns out to be the killer. When she offers him her body, Hammer kills Charlotte in retribution. A film noir offering of the early 1950s, I, THE JURY was a brutal feature, the 3-D effects were weak, and Biff Elliott was somewhat stiff as Hammer. Peggy Castle, however, was quite alluring as the scheming murderess.

After making THE LONG WAIT in 1954, Victor Saville joined director Robert Aldrich's Associates and Aldrich Company to make KISS ME, DEADLY, based on Mickey Spillane's 1952 novel. Of all the Mike Hammer films, this is probably the best known and analyzed, although its plot is fuzzy and convoluted. Its best aspect is the casting of Ralph Meeker as Mike Hammer, for he looked the role and handled the assignment with tough intensity. The story opens with Mike Hammer picking up blond hitchhiker Christina (Cloris Leachman), and the two being attacked by thugs who beat up the private eye and murder the woman. Recovering, Hammer delves into the case, and a gangster (Paul Stewart) and his promiscuous sister (Marian Carr) try to buy him off the matter. He persists, and when a friend (Nick Dennis) is murdered after finding two bombs in Hammer's new car (given to him by the gangster), he provides protection for Lily (Gaby Rodgers),

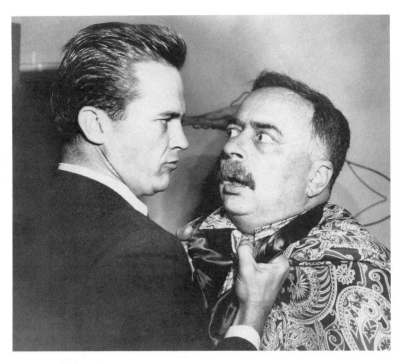

Ralph Meeker *(left)* and Silvio Minciotti in KISS ME, DEADLY (United Artists, 1955)

Christina's roommate. Hammer is captured by the hood-lum and his gang, and at their hideout he sees Dr. Soberin (Albert Dekker) whom he remembers had tortured Christina. Mike escapes only to find his secretary Velda (Maxine Cooper) has been abducted. Hammer is then able to locate a locker containing a box sought after by the hoodlums, and police Captain Pat Chambers (Wesley Addy) tells him that it holds atomic material which foreign spies want to obtain. He takes the box to a beach home belonging to Soberin, and there he finds the captive Velda. Lily is also there, and she kills Soberin and wounds Mike, who manages to save Velda. The two escape just as Lily dies in an atomic blast after opening the box Mike has brought with him. KISS ME, DEADLY got tepid reviews but grossed nearly $1 million at the box office and eventually developed a cult following in Europe.

In the mid-1950s Ted de Corsia portrayed Mike Hammer in the radio series "That Hammer Guy," also called "Mike Hammer." In 1954 Mickey Spillane wrote and portrayed Mike Hammer on the extended-play, 45 RPM record "Mickey Spillane's Mike Hammer" for V-Records (V-2501). The original story told how Hammer met Velda, who was portrayed by Betty Ackerman. The background music on the disk was written by Stan Purdy, who performed it with his orchestra. Also issued was a companion EP, "Mickey Spillane's Mike Hammer, Volume II" (V-2502) with Purdy and his orchestra performing four Purdy compositions, "Velda," "Oh, Mike!" "The Woman," and "The Mike Hammer Theme."

Victor Saville's last Mike Hammer production was MY GUN IS QUICK, issued by United Artists in the summer of 1957 and based on the 1950 novel of the same title, the second Hammer book. This time out Mike Hammer (Robert Bray) is drawn into the hunt for treasure that Holloway (Donald Randolph) took from the Nazis during World War II. Hammer and secretary Velda (Pamela Duncan) find out that two gangs are after the gems, and several young women are killed as a result. An intended victim, Nancy (Whitney Blake), comes to Hammer for help and joins him and his police captain friend (Booth Colman) in trying to locate the jewels. Eventually the private eye is able to get the two opposing sides on a fishing boat, and a showdown ensues. Hammer eliminates one of the gangs only to find out that Nancy is the head of the other group. Mike then captures her and turns her over to his cop friend. *Variety* complained about the film's "senseless brutality, murky plotting and unsubtle sex," and wrote that star Robert Bray "has enough masculine appeal and acting ability to do better in a more sensible role."

Darren McGavin was well cast in the title role of the half-hour TV series "Mike Hammer, Detective" (CBS-TV, 1958-1959), produced by MCA-TV. McGavin also served as the narrator for the series, which was set in New York City and told of the private eye's various adventures. In

England the program was telecast as "Mickey Spillane's Mike Hammer."

In 1962 Mickey Spillane penned the Mike Hammer adventure *The Girl Hunters*, and the next year it was filmed under that title in England although set in Gotham, and Spillane himself made a most satisfying Hammer. The plot had Mike Hammer as a gutter lush after the disappearance of his beloved Velda. An old friend, Police Captain Pat Chambers (Scott Peters), asks Mike to see a dying sailor (Murray Kash), who says he will talk only to the gumshoe. A sobered Hammer talks with the man, who was shot with the same weapon used to kill a senator. The sleuth does not divulge to Chambers that the man told him he had been the target of Communist agents led by a mysterious figure called the Dragon. Federal operative Art Rickerby (Lloyd Nolan) informs Mike that the sailor, too, was a spy, but for the United States, and Hammer pledges to work on the case. He goes to columnist pal Hy Gardner (himself) for

Mickey Spillane *(left)* and Lloyd Nolan in THE GIRL HUNTERS (Columbia, 1963)

help, and the newsman puts him in touch with the murdered senator's beautiful young widow, Laura Knapp (Shirley Eaton). Hammer comes to believe that Velda is a prisoner of the spy ring he is after, and he also thinks that Laura is involved with the enemy agents. He finds the Dragon headquartered at a chicken farm and in a showdown eliminates him by driving nails through the man's hands and into the floor. Laura shows up, and when Hammer accuses her of aiding the Reds in killing her husband, she pulls a shotgun and attempts to kill Hammer—but he has set the weapon to backfire, and Laura is killed. *Variety* termed THE GIRL HUNTERS a "tough private eye melodrama with effective treatment."

While the character of Mike Hammer remained popular in literature, he did not return to films until 1981 when MICKEY SPILLANE'S MARGIN FOR MURDER was shown on CBS-TV on October 15. Kevin Dobson was cast as Hammer, tracking down the murderer of his best friend, with help of secretary-girlfriend Velda (Cindy Pickett) and policeman Pat Chambers (Charles Hallahan). For the first time, a Hammer telefilm was not based on a Mickey Spillane novel but was instead an original story by Alex Lucas, the film's producer. It also served as a pilot for a TV series which did not sell at the time.

I, THE JURY was remade in 1982 and upon its London opening was given an X-rating for sex and violence. Issued in the U.S. by 20th Century–Fox, it obtained an R-rating but failed to generate much business and was soon being shown on cable television. Basically staying close to the concept of the 1953 original, the remake "has all the updated violence, nudity, wit and style that was missing from the puritanical original" (*Variety*). Set in Manhattan, the film has private investigator Mike Hammer (Armand Assante) trying to find out who killed his Vietnam War pal, with the trail leading him to sex clinic operator Charlotte Bennett (Barbara Carrera) and former government agent Romero (Barry Snider), who now leads his own private army from a computerized headquarters. The film was extremely violent, filled with vulgarities and nudity. Unlike the Mickey Spillane works of the late 1940s and

1950s, when Hammer was a rabid Communist hater, here the villains are not Reds but the Central Intelligence Agency. *The Film Yearbook 1983* (1982) said that the Larry Cohen (who was originally set to direct) script "is punctuated with numerous grisly deaths, a surfeit of random sadism and the full complement of miscellaneous unpleasantness, which it details with ostentatious relish," but added that the film "is not without its redeeming factors, however: pace, occasional wit and self-parody on overtime."

On April 9, 1983, CBS-TV made a second attempt at a Mike Hammer telefilm pilot with MICKEY SPILLANE'S MIKE HAMMER: MURDER ME, MURDER YOU, this time with Stacy Keach as Hammer. The movie involved Hammer finding out that he has a grown daughter (Lisa Blount) when his ex-girlfriend (Michelle Phillips) asks him for protection because she has to testify before a grand jury investigating an all-female courier service which she co-owns. She tells him about their daughter before being murdered, and Mike tries to find the killer, enlisting the aid of his daughter as well as Velda (Tanya Roberts) and policeman Pat Chambers (Don Stroud). In *TV Guide* Judith Crist wrote that Stacy Keach was "probably the classiest incarnation to date of Mike Hammer." Gayne Rescher's photography on the film won an Emmy Award and the telefilm itself was given the Mystery Writers of America's Edgar Award.

As a result of the success of the second Mike Hammer pilot, "Mickey Spillane's Mike Hammer" became a weekly one-hour series on CBS-TV early in 1984, with Stacy Keach playing the title role, Lindsay Bloom portraying Velda, and Don Stroud as Captain Pat Chambers. The series was inaugurated by a third Mike Hammer TV movie, MICKEY SPILLANE'S MIKE HAMMER: MORE THAN MURDER, on January 26, 1984. During a poker game, Pat Chambers is shot and then accused of being a drug pusher; his friend Mike Hammer tries to prove his innocence. As a result he has an affair with Eve Warwick (Robyn Douglass), who is actually an undercover agent. When the young woman is murdered, Hammer is eventually able to find the crooks

Advertisement for MIKE HAMMER: MURDER ME, MURDER YOU
(CBS-TV, 1983)

responsible and also clear Chambers. Of this series opener, *Variety* noted "future Hammer's will have to take advantage of Keach's strong presence without resorting to the clichés of the '50s in dialog and plot devices." The new Mike Hammer TV show was a ratings success, but it came to an end in 1985 when star Stacy Keach was arrested in Great Britain on drug charges and given a short prison sentence. After his release, CBS-TV announced it would resume the program under the title "The New Mike Hammer."

On April 18, 1986, the network telecast THE RETURN OF MICKEY SPILLANE'S MIKE HAMMER, a telefilm which ushered in the new Hammer series. Here Mike Hammer (Stacy Keach) accidentally thwarts the kidnapping of a movie star's (Lauren Hutton) little girl and is hired by her studio to be the child's bodyguard. Going with her to Hollywood, Hammer is unable to prevent a second kidnapping. In trying to find the child he gets mixed up with a ransom and gangsters, the latter led by bitter Vietnam veterans who run a child kidnapping racket. *TV Movies and Video Guide* (1988) thought it "Average." The second attempt at a Mike Hammer TV series with Stacy Keach also proved unsuccessful, and the show lasted for only a few months.

In the spring of 1988, CBS-TV announced its continuing faith in telefilms about detectives and said that it would continue to produce Mike Hammer movies on a regular basis.

MIKE HAMMER: MURDER TAKES ALL was telecast on CBS-TV on May 21, 1989, with Stacy Keach reprising the role of the tough detective hero. Directed by John Nicolella and written by Mark Edward Edens, the telefilm had Hammer in Las Vegas investigating a homicide. Lynda Carter, Michelle Phillips, and Lyle Alzado co-starred.

Filmography

1. I, THE JURY. United Artists, 1953. 87 minutes.
   P: Victor Saville. **D:** Harry Essex. **SC:** Harry Essex, from the novel by Mickey Spillane. **PH:** John Alton.

Cast: Biff Elliott (Mike Hammer), Preston Foster (Captain Pat Chambers), Peggie Castle (Charlotte Manning), Margaret Sheridan (Velda), Alan Reed (George Kalecki), Frances Osborne (Myrna), Robert Cunningham (Hal Kines), Elisha Cook, Jr. (Bobo), Paul Dubov (Marty), Mary Anderson (Eileen Vickers), Tani Seitz (Mary Bellamy), Dran Seitz (Esther Bellamy), Robert Swanger (Jack Williams), John Qualen (Dr. Vickers).

2. KISS ME, DEADLY. United Artists, 1955. 105 minutes.

P-D: Robert Aldrich. **EP:** Victor Saville. **SC:** A. I. Bezzerides, from the novel by Mickey Spillane. **PH:** Ernest Laszlo. **ED:** Michael Luciano. **MUS:** Frank DeVol. Title song sung by Nat "King" Cole & Kitty White. **ASST DIR:** Robert Justman.

Cast: Ralph Meeker (Mike Hammer), Gaby Rodgers (Lily Carver), Maxine Cooper (Velda), Albert Dekker (Dr. Soberin), Cloris Leachman (Christina), Wesley Addy (Captain Pat Chambers), Nick Dennis (Nick), Paul Stewart (Carl Evello), Juano Hernandez (Eddie Yaeger), Marian Carr (Friday Evello), Jack Lambert (Sugar Smallhouse), Jack Elam (Charlie Max), Jerry Zinneman (Sammy), Leigh Snowden (Girl at Pool), Percy Helton (Dr. Kennedy), Madi Comfort (Singer), Fortunio Bonanova (Carmen Trivaco), James McCallian (Super), Silvio Minciotti (Older Mover), Robert Cornthwaite, James Seay (FBI Agents), Mort Marshall (Ray Diker), Jesslyn Fax (Mrs. Super), Strother Martin (Harvey Wallace), Paul Richards (Gangster with Knife), Ben Morris, Sam Balter, Joe Hernandez (Radio Announcers), Marjorie Bennett (Hotel Manager), Kitty White (Kit), Art Loggins (Bartender), Robert Sherman (Gas Station Attendant), Keith McConnell (Athletic Club Clerk), Eddie Real (Sideman).

3. MY GUN IS QUICK. United Artists, 1957. 91 minutes.

P: Victor Saville. **D:** George A. White & Phil Victor. **SC:** Richard Powell & Richard Collins, from the novel by Mickey Spillane. **PH:** Harry Neuman. **ED:** Frank Sullivan. **AD:** Boris Leven. **MUS:** Marlin Skiles.

Cast: Robert Bray (Mike Hammer), Whitney Blake (Nancy), Pat Donahue (Dione), Donald Randolph (Holloway), Pamela Duncan (Velda), Booth Colman (Captain Pat Chambers), Jan Chaney (Red), Gina Core (Maria), Richard Garland (Lou), Charles Bosz (Gangster), Peter Mamakos (La Roche), Claire Carleton (Proprietress), Phil Arnold (Shorty), John Dennis (Al), Terence De Marney (Jean), Jackie Paul (Stripper), Leon Askin (Teller), Jack Holland (Hotel Clerk).

4. THE GIRL HUNTERS. Columbia, 1963. 103 minutes.

P: Robert Fellows. **AP:** Charles Reynolds. **D:** Roy Rowland. **SC:** Mickey Spillane, Roy Rowland & Robert Fellows, from the novel by Mickey Spillane. **PH:** Ken Talbot. **ED:** Sidney Stone. **MUS:** Phil Green. **AD:** Tony Inglis. **ASST DIR:** George Polland.

Cast: Mickey Spillane (Mike Hammer), Shirley Eaton (Laura Knapp), Lloyd Nolan (Art Rickerby), Hy Gardner (Himself), Scott Peters (Captain Pat Chambers), Guy Kingsley Poynter (Dr. Larry Snyder), James Dyrenforth (Bayliss Henry), Charles Farrell (Joe Grissi), Kim Tracy (Nurse), Benny Lee (Nat Drutman), Murray Kash (Richie Cole), Bill Nagy (Georgie), Olive Endersby (Duck Duck), Richard Montez (Skinny Guy), Larry Cross (Red Markham), Tony Arpino (Cab Driver), Hal Galilli (Bouncer), Nelly Hanham (Landlady), Bob Gallico (Dr. Leo Daniels), Michael Brennan, Howard Greene, Grant Holden (Policemen), Francis Napies (Detective), Larry Taylor (The Dragon).

5. MICKEY SPILLANE'S MARGIN FOR MURDER. CBS-TV, 1981. 100 minutes. Color.

P-ST: Alex Lucas. EP: Jay Bernstein, Larry Thompson & Robert Hamner. D: Daniel Haller. SC: Calvin Clements, Jr. PH: Michael D. Marguiles. ED: John M. Woodcock. MUS: Nelson Riddle. AD: Kenneth S. Davis.

Cast: Kevin Dobson (Mike Hammer), Charles Hallahan (Captain Pat Chambers), Cindy Pickett (Velda), Donna Dixon (Daisy), Asher Brauner (Jerry Adams), Floyd Levine (Geraldo Machetti), Aarika Wells (Lindsey Brooks), John Considine (Lou Krone), Renata Vanni (Mama De Fellita), Charles Picerni (Glover), Nicholas Hormann (John O'Hare), David Downing, John Alderman, A. Gerald Singer, Ralph Strait, Glenn Wilder.

6. I, THE JURY. 20th Century–Fox, 1982. 109 minutes. Color.

P: Robert Solo. D: Richard T. Heffron. SC: Larry Cohen, from the novel by Mickey Spillane. PH: Andrew Laszlo. ED: Garth Craven. MUS: Bill Conti. ASST DIR: Jerry Shapiro & Henry Brochtein.

Cast: Armand Assante (Mike Hammer), Barbara Carrera (Charlotte Bennett), Laurence Landon (Velda), Geoffrey Lewis (Joe Butler), Paul Sorvino (Captain Pat Chambers), Judson Scott (Kendricks), Barry Snider (Romero), Julia Barr (Norma Childs), Jessica James (Hilda Kendricks), Alan King (Charles Kalecki), Lee Anne Harris, Lynette Harris (Twins).

7. MICKEY SPILLANE'S MIKE HAMMER: MURDER ME, MURDER YOU. CBS-TV, 1983. 100 minutes. Color.

P: Lew Gallo. EP: Jay Bernstein & Larry Thompson. AP: Lana Wood. D: Gary Nelson. SC: William Stratton. PH: Gayne Rescher. ED: Donald R. Rode. MUS: Earle Hagen. AD: Frederic P. Hope & Ross Bellah.

Cast: Stacy Keach (Mike Hammer), Tanya Roberts (Velda), Michelle Phillips (Chris Jameson), Don Stroud (Captain Pat Chambers), Lisa Blount (Michelle Jameson), Delta Burke (Paula Corey), Tom Atkins (Jack Vance), Jonathan Banks (Janos Saracen), Kent Williams (Lawrence Barrington), Bert Rosario (Duardo), Randi

Brooks (Arla), Lee Meredith (Marty), Ric Mancini (Cal Pope), Eddie Egan (Hennessey), Madison Arnold (Conlin), Ava Lazar (Janice Wells), James Arone (Bumpo), Michele Avonne (Betty Geraldo), Julie Hayek (Second French Courier), Quinn Kessler (Karen Marshall), William Vincent Kulak (Paramedic), Carol Pritiken (Second Receptionist), Timothy Stack (Natty), Michael A. Andrews (Isadora Shepperton).

8. MICKEY SPILLANE'S MIKE HAMMER: MORE THAN MURDER. CBS-TV, 1984. 100 minutes. Color.

P: Lew Gallo. **EP:** Jay Bernstein. **D:** Gary Nelson. **SC:** William Stratton & Stephen Downing. **MUS:** Earle Hagen.

Cast: Stacy Keach (Mike Hammer), Lindsay Bloom (Velda), Don Stroud (Captain Pat Chambers), Kent Williams (Barrington), Tim McIntire (Malcolm Dobbs), Lynn-Holly Johnson (Sandy), Robyn Douglass (Eve Warwick), Sam Groom, Richard Romanus, Denny Miller, Danny Goldman, Gail Rae Carlson, Kevin King, Ingrid Anderson, John Hancock, Stephanie Blackmore, David Haskell, Martin West, Lee Meredith, Norman Matlock, Mike Glassman, Jay Bernstein.

9. THE RETURN OF MICKEY SPILLANE'S MIKE HAMMER. CBS-TV, 1986. 100 minutes. Color.

P: Gary Frederickson. **EP:** Jay Bernstein. **D:** Ray Danton. **SC:** Larry Brody, Janis Hendler & James M. Miller. **PH:** Hector Figueroa & Warren Rothenberg. **MUS:** Earle Hagen.

Cast: Stacy Keach (Mike Hammer), Lauren Hutton (Joanna Lake), Lindsay Bloom (Velda), Don Stroud (Captain Pat Chambers), Vince Edwards (Inspector Walker), Mickey Rooney (Jack Bergen), Kent Williams (Barrington), Mike Preston (Dak), Stephen Macht (Nick), John Karlen (Chapel), Leo Penn (Leo Hawkins), Frank McRae (Herschel Dean), Bruce Boxleitner, Dabney Coleman, JoAnn Pflug, Dionne Warwick, Danny Goodman, Tom Everett, Emily Chance, Lee Benton, David Chow, Peter Iacangelo, Kieu Chinh, Hunter Von Leer, Dawn Mangrum, Don Lewis, Andre (Rosey) Brown, Andre Feijoo, Jeannie Martin Austin.

Chapter 6

MISS JANE MARPLE

ALONG WITH HERCULE POIROT (q.v.), Miss Jane Marple is the most enduring of the fictional characters created by Agatha Christie, and of the two she was the author's favorite. An elderly English spinster who lived in the small village of St. Mary Mead, Miss Marple became entwined in a whole series of literary homicides, beginning with *Murder at the Vicarage* in 1930 and carrying through more than a dozen novels, ending with *The Sleeping Murder* in 1976, the year Christie died. Despite her long-running popularity, Miss Marple did not appear on film until the early 1960s, more than three decades after her literary inception.

Prior to coming to films, Miss Marple was dramatized on stage when *Murder at the Vicarage* was adapted as a play of the same title by Moie Charles and Barbara Toy. Barbara Mullen portrayed Miss Marple in 1949 when the play opened at London's Playhouse Theatre. Miss Marple came to American television when NBC-TV presented "A Murder Is Announced," from the 1950 novel, as an episode of "The Goodyear Theatre," telecast December 30, 1956. Popular British star Gracie Fields played Miss Marple, and co-stars were Roger Moore (later the Saint on television and James Bond in films) and Jessica Tandy. A television series based on the Christie works was planned in 1960 when Metro-Goldwyn-Mayer purchased the rights for most of the author's books and short stories for $3 million, but the studio decided to make a feature film about Miss Jane Marple instead.

MEET MISS MARPLE, taken from the 1957 novel *4:50*

from Paddington (called *What Mrs. McGullicuddy Saw!* in the U.S.), starred Margaret Rutherford, while her husband, Stringer Davis, was cast in a role especially written for him, that of local librarian and confidant Mr. Stringer. Although she hardly looked like the frail little lady of the Agatha Christie novels, Margaret Rutherford proved to be very popular in the part and is the actress most associated with Miss Marple. Born in 1892, Margaret Rutherford made her stage debut in 1925 and her first film, DUSTY ERMINE, in 1936. In later years she became one of the most beloved character actresses in British films; she was knighted in the 1960s. Among her films were THE YELLOW CANARY ('43), BLITHE SPIRIT ('45), PASSPORT TO PIMLICO ('49), THE MAGIC BOX ('51), THE IMPORTANCE OF BEING EARNEST ('52), INNOCENTS IN PARIS ('53), AUNT CLARA ('54), THE SMALLEST SHOW ON EARTH ('57), I'M ALL RIGHT, JACK ('59), MOUSE ON THE MOON ('63), THE VIPs ('63, for which she received an Academy Award as best supporting actress), CHIMES AT MID-NIGHT ('66), and A COUNTESS FROM HONG KONG ('66). She died in 1972.

MEET MISS MARPLE became MURDER SHE SAID and was issued in 1961 to good reviews and audience response, the public especially taken with Margaret Rutherford as the eccentric Miss Marple. On a train, Miss Marple witnesses a murder committed on a passing train. When police Inspector Craddock (Charles Tingwell) does not believe her story, she takes a position as a maid on the estate near where she saw the incident. Eventually she finds the body of the murdered woman, who had been married to the estate's owner (James Robertson-Justice), and he and his family are suspects, as is the local physician, Dr. Quimper (Arthur Kennedy). Five more murders take place before Miss Marple pinpoints the killer.

For the second Miss Marple feature, MURDER AT THE GALLOP, M-G-M adapted a Hercule Poirot novel, 1953's *After the Funeral,* with the elderly spinster taking over for the Belgian investigator. While collecting funds for an organization for reformed criminals, Miss Marple and Mr. Stringer (Stringer Davis) witness the supposedly accidental death of wealthy Enderby (Finlay Currie), and Miss Marple becomes suspicious. She attends the reading of the dead man's will and finds that four relatives are named in it. After one of them, a sister (Katya Douglas), is killed, her friend (Flora Robson) says that Miss Marple committed the crime, but Inspector Craddock (Charles Tingwell) clears her. Moving to a riding academy called the Gallop run by Enderby's nephew, Hector (Robert Morley), Miss Marple finds that the crimes center on the possession of a French masterpiece belonging to the estate, a painting thought to be valueless. Setting herself up as the next victim, Miss Marple is able to trap the murderer and even receives a marriage proposal from Hector, which she declines.

For the third Miss Marple feature, an original screenplay was devised not based on any Agatha Christie work. MURDER AHOY ('64) had Miss Marple as a member of an organization aiding delinquent juveniles. When another trustee (Henry Longhurst) suddenly dies, Miss Marple suspects foul play and finds he was murdered. The case leads her and Mr. Stringer (Stringer Davis) to a docked ship used as a home for the wayward boys. There she learns that the youths are being trained to carry out petty crimes under the instruction of supposed teacher Mr. Compton (Francis Matthews). He and a matron (Norma Foster) are murdered before Miss Marple corners the killer and Inspector Craddock (Charles Tingwell) arrives to arrest the culprit. At the climax, Miss Marple engages in a fencing match with the murderer before Craddock's arrival. Released in the U.S. in 1964, MURDER AHOY was not shown in its homeland of England until the next year, and then it was missing nearly twenty minutes of footage.

MURDER AHOY was actually the last of four Miss Marple films made by M-G-M, but it was issued prior to MURDER MOST FOUL, which was released in 1965. Again a Hercule Poirot novel, *Mrs. McGinty's Dead* (1952), was used for the plot, with Miss Marple taking over for Poirot. Here Miss Marple is on a jury hearing a case about a man accused of killing his landlady. A mistrial is declared when Miss Marple is the only juror voting for acquittal; as a result, she plans to prove herself correct and find the

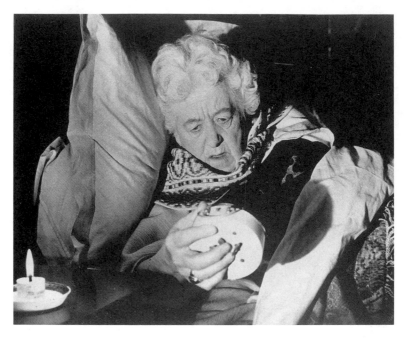

Margaret Rutherford in MURDER MOST FOUL (M-G-M, 1965)

killer. She and Mr. Stringer (Stringer Davis) go to the victim's home and find that she was once an actress who worked in a theatrical touring company managed by Driffold Cosgood (Rod Moody). Taking on the guise of an actress, Miss Marple gets a job with the company with Cosgood hoping to get money from her to keep his repertory outfit afloat financially. Miss Marple tells Inspector Craddock (Charles Tingwell) that she believes the murderer is part of the company, but he refuses to believe her until two cast members are killed and Miss Marple is able to connect the trio of murders and point out the killer.

Following her very successful quartet of Miss Marple features for M-G-M, Margaret Rutherford reprised the part in a guest appearance in the Hercule Poirot (q.v.) 1966 feature, THE ALPHABET MURDERS, with Stringer Davis also appearing with her as Mr. Stringer.

In 1976 the character of Miss Marple was satirized in the

comedy-mystery MURDER BY DEATH. Elsa Lanchester played Miss Jessica Marbles, and Estelle Winwood was her elderly nanny, in a tale of world-famous detectives vying to solve a murder and win $1 million tax-free and the title of the world's greatest detective. The previous year *Murder at the Vicarage* was revived on the London stage with Barbara Mullen as Miss Marple, and in 1976 Avril Angers took over the part.

Following the box office successes of MURDER ON THE ORIENT EXPRESS ('74) and DEATH ON THE NILE ('78), both Hercule Poirot features, the producers of the two films, John Brabourne and Richard Goodwin, turned to the Miss Marple character for the 1981 release, THE MIRROR CRACK'D, based on the 1962 book *The Mirror Crack'd from Side to Side*. An American movie company is filming in Kent near the home of Miss Jane Marple (Angela Lansbury). On the set, a busboy dies after drinking a poisoned drink meant for a member of the film's cast, and Miss Marple is called in to investigate along with Inspector Craddock (Edward Fox). On the set Miss Marple finds feuding between the film's two stars, Marina Gregg (Elizabeth Taylor) and Lola Brewster (Kim Novak), both hoping for a comeback in the production about Mary, Queen of Scots. Hampered by a sprained ankle, Miss Marple is eventually able to ferret out the murderer. Like the two previous Hercule Poirot features, THE MIRROR CRACK'D is a lushly made, leisurely film which provided Elizabeth Taylor and Kim Novak their best film roles in several years. Angela Lansbury, however, was the highlight of the feature as Miss Marple, and her portrayal of the character is the closest to its literary source to be performed to date. Four years later Lansbury would star in the CBS-TV program "Murder, She Wrote," a highly rated show in which she plays mystery writer and amateur sleuth, Jessica Fletcher, a somewhat Americanized Miss Marple. An interesting aspect of THE MIRROR CRACK'D was that it opened by showing a film within a film called *Murder at Midnight*, a mystery which Miss Marple walked out on because she readily spotted the murderer.

In 1980 producer Stan Margulies and Warner Bros.

Television announced that five Agatha Christie telefilms would be made for CBS-TV, although none of them was to be a Miss Marple adventure. The initial film was MURDER IS EASY ('82), from the 1939 novel, and it featured Helen Hayes. In reviewing the film in *TV Guide*, Judith Crist commented that Hayes "makes us realize she'd be the ultimate Marple." Helen Hayes did, in fact, portray Miss Marple in the second TV feature film outing, A CARIB-BEAN MYSTERY, taken from the 1964 novel, telecast October 22, 1983. The plot has Miss Marple at a Caribbean resort resting from a bout with pneumonia; there she meets Major Palgrave (Maurice Evans), who is murdered. As Miss Marple investigates, two more homicides occur, and the suspects include the various other guests, the house doctor (Brock Peters), and the debt-ridden resort owners.

A CARIBBEAN MYSTERY proved to be a satisfying TV movie with Helen Hayes an energetic Miss Marple. She was cast in the part for a second time in MURDER WITH MIRRORS, telecast February 20, 1985. Based on the 1952 novel, called *They Do It with Mirrors* in England, the telefilm found Miss Marple coming to the estate of her longtime friend Carrie Louise Serrocold (Bette Davis), whose step-son (John Woodvine) is murdered. The estate is used by Carrie Louise's second husband, Lewis (John Mills), to house delinquent boys, and he confides to Miss Marple that he believes his wife is being poisoned. Local Inspector Curry (Leo McKern) investigates the case, and many of the family members are suspects. It is Miss Marple who is able to name the killer, who was after her friend's money. Filmed at thirteenth-century Brocket Hall in Hertfordshire, MURDER WITH MIRRORS was a handsome production, and Helen Hayes again was outstanding as Miss Marple. The main drawback to the TV movie was co-star Bette Davis, who was recovering from cancer surgery and several strokes; in her fragile condition her performance was painful to behold.

Following the two Miss Marple TV movies with Helen Hayes, CBS-TV produced a trio of Hercule Poirot films with Peter Ustinov. In 1986 the PBS-TV series "Mystery!"

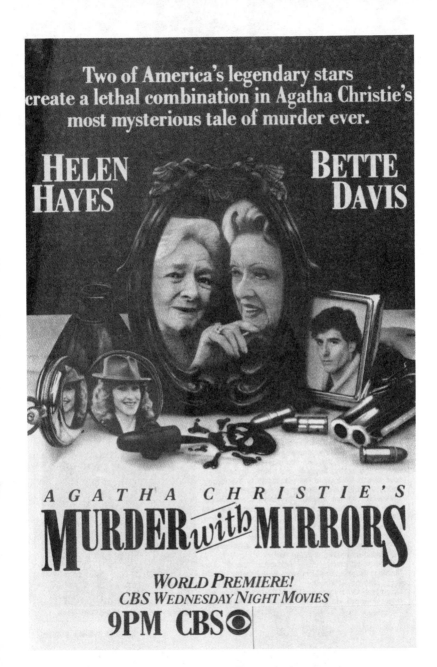

Advertisement for MURDER WITH MIRRORS (CBS-TV/Warner Bros., 1985)

telecast "Agatha Christie's Miss Marple," a British program starring Joan Hickson as Miss Marple. Joan Hickson had a supporting role in the initial Miss Marple film, MURDER SHE SAID. Continuing through 1988, this PBS miniseries presented such Agatha Christie works as "At Bertram's Hotel," "The Body in the Library," "The Moving Finger," "A Murder Is Announced," "Nemesis," "A Pocketful of Rye," and "The Sleeping Murder." In the spring of 1988, CBS-TV announced it would produce more telefilms based on Agatha Christie's works, no doubt some with Miss Marple.

Filmography

1. MURDER SHE SAID. Metro-Goldwyn-Mayer, 1961. 87 minutes.
   P: George H. Brown. **D:** George Pollock. **SC:** David Pursall, Jack Seddon & David Osborn, from the novel *4:50 from Paddington* by Agatha Christie. **PH:** Geoffrey Faithfull. **ED:** Ernest Walter. **MUS:** Ron Goodwin. **AD:** Harry White. **ASST DIR:** Douglas Hicks. **PROD MGR:** Jan Darnley-Smith. **MAKEUP:** Eddie Knight.
   Cast: Margaret Rutherford (Miss Jane Marple), Arthur Kennedy (Dr. Quimper), Muriel Pavlow (Emma Ackenthorpe), James Robertson-Justice (Ackenthorpe), Thorley Walters (Cedric Ackenthorpe), Charles Tingwell (Inspector Craddock), Conrad Phillips (Harold), Ronald Howard (Brian Eastley), Joan Hickson (Mrs. Kidder), Stringer Davis (Mr. Stringer), Ronnie Raymond (Alexander Eastley), Gerald Cross (Albert), Michael Golden (Hillman), Barbara Leake (Mrs. Stainton), Gordon Harris (Bacon), Peter Butterworth (Ticket Man), Richard Biers (Mrs. Binster), Lucy Griffith (Lucy).

2. MURDER AT THE GALLOP. Metro-Goldwyn-Mayer, 1963. 81 minutes.
   P: George H. Brown. **EP:** Lawrence P. Bachmann. **D:** George Pollock. **SC:** James P. Cavanagh, David Pursall & Jack Seddon, from the novel *After the Funeral* by Agatha Christie. **PH:** Arthur Ibbetson. **ED:** Bert Rule. **MUS:** Ron Goodwin. **AD:** Frank White. **ASST DIR:** Jonathan Barry. **PROD MGR:** Sydney Streeter. **MAKEUP:** Eddie Knight.
   Cast: Margaret Rutherford (Miss Jane Marple), Robert Morley (Hector Enderby), Flora Robson (Miss Gilchrist), Charles Tingwell (Inspector Craddock), Stringer Davis (Mr. Stringer), Duncan Lamont (Hillman), James Villiers (Michael Shane), Robert Urquhart (George Crossfield), Katya Douglas (Roasmund Shane), Gordon

Harris (Sergeant Bacon), Noel Howlett (Mr. Trundell), Finlay Currie (Enderby), Kevin Stoney (Dr. Markwell).

3. MURDER AHOY. Metro-Goldwyn-Mayer, 1964. 93 minutes.
   P: Lawrence P. Bachmann. **AP:** Ben Arbeid. **D:** George Pollock. **SC:** David Pursall & Jack Seddon. **PH:** Desmond Dickinson. **ED:** Ernest Walter. **MUS:** Ron Goodwin. **AD:** Bill Andrews. **ASST DIR:** David Tomblin. **PROD MGR:** Sydney Streeter.

   Cast: Margaret Rutherford (Miss Jane Marple), Lionel Jeffries (Captain de Courey Rhumstone), Charles Tingwell (Inspector Craddock), William Mervyn (Commander Breeze-Connington), Joan Benham (Matron Alice Fanbraid), Stringer Davis (Mr. Stringer), Nicholas Parsons (Dr. Crump), Miles Malleson (Bishop Faulkner), Henry Oscar (Lord Rudkin), Derek Nimmo (Sub-Lieutenant Humbert), Gerald Cross (L. W. Brewer Dimchurch), Norma Foster (Assistant Matron Shirley Boston), Terence Edmond (Sergeant Bacon), Francis Matthews (Lieutenant Compton), Lucy Griffith (Millie), Bernard Adams (Dusty Miller), Tony Quinn (Kelly), Edna Petrie (Miss Pringle), Roy Holder (Petty Officer Lamb), Henry Longhurst (Cecil Folly-Hardwicke).

4. MURDER MOST FOUL. Metro-Goldwyn-Mayer, 1965. 90 minutes.
   P: Ben Arbeid. **EP:** Lawrence P. Bachmann. **D:** George Pollock. **SC:** David Pursall & Jack Seddon, from the novel *Mrs. McGinty's Dead* by Agatha Christie. **PH:** Desmond Dickinson. **ED:** Ernest Walter. **MUS:** Ron Goodwin. **AD:** Frank White. **ASST DIR:** David Tomblin. **PROD MGR:** Sydney Streeter.

   Cast: Margaret Rutherford (Miss Jane Marple), Ron Moody (Driffold Cosgood), Charles Tingwell (Inspector Craddock), Andrew Cruickshank (Justice Crosby), Megs Jenkins (Mrs. Thomas), Dennis Price (Harris Tumbrill), Terry Scott (Police Constable Wells), Ralph Michael (Ralph Summers), James Bolam (Bill Hanson), Stringer Davis (Mr. Stringer), Francesca Annis (Sheila Howard), Alison Seebohm (Eva McGonigall), Pauline Jameson (Maureen Summers), Maurice Good (George Rowton), Annette Kerr, Windsor Davies, Neil Stacey, Stella Tanner.

5. THE ALPHABET MURDERS. Metro-Goldwyn-Mayer, 1966. 90 minutes.
   P: Lawrence P. Bachmann. **D:** Frank Tashlin. **SC:** David Pursall & Jack Seddon, from the novel *The A.B.C. Murders* by Agatha Christie. **PH:** Desmond Dickinson. **ED:** John Victor Smith. **MUS:** Ron Goodwin. **ASST DIR:** David Tomblin.

   Cast: Tony Randall (Hercule Poirot), Anita Ekberg (Amanda Beatrice Cross), Robert Morley (Hastings), Maurice Denham (Inspector Japp), Guy Rolfe (Duncan Doncaster), Sheila Allen (Lady Diane), James Villiers (Franklin), Julian Glover (Don Fortune), Grazina Frame (Betty Barnard), Clive Morton ("X"), Cyril Luckham

(Sir Carmichael Clarke), Richard Wattis (Wolfe), Patrick Newell (Cracknell), David Lodge (Sergeant), Austin Trevor (Judson), Alison Seebohm (Miss Sparks), Margaret Rutherford (Miss Jane Marple), Stringer Davis (Mr. Stringer).

6. THE MIRROR CRACK'D. Columbia/EMI/GW Films, 1981. 105 minutes. Color.

P: John Brabourne & Richard Goodwin. **D:** Guy Hamilton. **SC:** Jonathan Hales & Barry Sandler, from the novel by Agatha Christie. **PH:** Christopher Challis. **ED:** Richard Marden. **MUS:** John Cameron.

Cast: Angela Lansbury (Miss Jane Marple), Elizabeth Taylor (Marina Gregg), Kim Novak (Lola Brewster), Rock Hudson (Jason Rudd), Tony Curtis (Marty N. Fein), Geraldine Chaplin (Ella Zielinsky), Edward Fox (Inspector Craddock), Wendy Morgan (Cherry), Margaret Courtenay (Mrs. Bantry), Charles Gray (Bates), Maureen Bennett (Heather Babcock), Carolyn Pickles (Miss Giles), Charles Lloyd Pack (Vicar), Richard Pearson (Dr. Haydock), Peter Woodthorpe (Scoutmaster), Anthony Steel (Sir Derek Ridgeley), Dinah Sheridan (Lady Amanda), Oriane Grieve (Kate Ridgeley), Kenneth Fortescue (Charles Foxwell), Hildegard Neil (Lady Foxcroft), Allan Cuthbertson (Peter Montrose), Nigel Stock (Inspector Gates).

7. A CARIBBEAN MYSTERY. CBS-TV/Warner Bros., 1983. 100 minutes. Color.

P: Stan Margulies. **D:** Robert Michael Lewis. **SC:** Steven Humphrey & Sue Grafton, from the novel by Agatha Christie. **PH:** Ted Voigtlander. **ED:** Les Green. **MUS:** Lee Holdridge. **AD:** Robert MacKichan.

Cast: Helen Hayes (Miss Jane Marple), Maurice Evans (Major Geoffrey Palgrave), Barnard Hughes (Mr. Rafiel), Season Hubley (Molly Kendall), Jameson Parker (Tim Kendall), Swoosie Kurtz (Ruth Walter), Cassie Yates (Lucky Dyson), Zakes Mokae (Captain Daventry), Beth Howland (Evelyn Hillingdon), Lynne Moody (Victoria Johnson), George Innes (Edward Hillingdon), Brock Peters (Dr. Graham), Mike Preston (Arthur Jackson), Bernard McDonald (Minister), Santos Morales (Miguel), Sam Scarber (Police Sergeant), Cecil Smith (Guest).

8. MURDER WITH MIRRORS. CBS-TV/Warner Bros., 1985. 100 minutes. Color.

P: Stan Margulies. **AP:** Maria Padilla. **D:** Dick Lowry. **SC:** George Eckstein, from the novel by Agatha Christie. **PH:** Brian West. **ED:** Richard Bracken. **AD:** Leigh Malone. **MUS:** Richard Rodney Bennett.

Cast: Helen Hayes (Miss Jane Marple), Bette Davis (Carrie Louise Serrocold), John Mills (Lewis Serrocold), Leo McKern (Inspector

Curry), John Woodvine (Christian Serrocold), Liane Langland (Gina), John Laughlin (Wally), Dorothy Tutin (Mildred), Anton Rodgers (Dr. Hargrove), Frances de la Tour (Miss Bellever), Tim Roth (Edgar), Christopher Fairbank (Sergeant Lake), James Coombes (Steve Restarick), Amanda Maynard (Miss Valentine).

Chapter 7

NURSE SARAH KEATE

IN THE MID-1930s WARNER BROS. purchased the screen rights to Mignon G. Eberhart's literary works about nurse-detective Sarah Keate. No doubt the studio intended to use Nurse Keate as a screen rival to RKO's successful Hildegarde Withers series (see B/V), although Eberhart's Nurse Keate predated Stuart Palmer's Miss Withers by two years since the first Nurse Keate novel appeared in 1929 while *The Penguin Pool Murder*, the initial Hildegarde Withers book did not come out until 1931. At any rate, Warners turned out a quintet of movies based on the Eberhart works, and 20th Century–Fox also issued a programmer based on one of the author's Miss Keate short stories. None of the films was particularly satisfying, due in part to the fact they were sloppily brought to the screen. The character created by Mignon G. Eberhart was a middle-aged woman who was often aided in her cases by young policeman Lance O'Leary. On film Miss Keate was rarely middle-aged, O'Leary appeared in only half the feature films, and rarely was the nurse's surname the same from picture to picture—as she was sometimes called Sally Keating, Miss Keats, or Sara (not Sarah) Keate.

Aline MacMahon and Guy Kibbee were a popular Warner Bros. screen team in the 1930s, so when the studio filmed WHILE THE PATIENT SLEPT, from Eberhart's 1930 novel, MacMahon was cast as wisecracking Nurse Sarah Keate, while Kibbee was the bald, middle-aged police detective Lance O'Leary. Nurse Keate is working for a wealthy man (Walter Walker), whose relatives flock to his mansion when he goes into a coma. When a murder

From left: Aline MacMahon, Patricia Ellis, and Brandon Hurst in WHILE THE PATIENT SLEPT (Warner Bros./First National, 1935)

takes place, Miss Keate and policeman O'Leary set out to solve it. Although the *New York Times* complained that the film was "quite unsatisfactory," *Variety* noted that it would be popular with mystery fans and added, "Adapted from 'Nurse Keate,' big-selling novel, so that may help too." The reviewer also said, "Miss MacMahon and Kibbee play for maximum laughs, and Allen Jenkins muggs his stooge role up to the neckline." Released in March 1935, the film apparently was planned as a series for the two stars, but they were not a part of any further studio efforts in the Nurse Keate outings.

Nearly a year after the release of WHILE THE PATIENT SLEPT, Warner Bros. released THE MURDER OF DR. HARRIGAN, based on Eberhart's 1931 book *From This Dark Stairway*. Here Nurse Keate was dubbed Nurse Sally Keating, and comely Kay Linaker was cast in the part, in deference to the book's middle-aged Miss Keate, while

Lance O'Leary was dropped from the script. The plot has Nurse Keating working at a big-city hospital and in love with Dr. Lambert (Ricardo Cortez). A doctor who is about to operate on hospital chief Dr. Harrigan (John Eldredge) dies, and it is believed that Harrigan was murdered. The police are called in, and after an attempt is made to kill Sally, she and Lambert unmask the murderer, who was shielded by another nurse, Lillian Ash (Mary Astor). *Variety* commented, "It's along formula lines. . . . As usual, also, everyone looks suspicious except the cops." While Lance O'Leary was missing, it should be noted that he did have a counterpart in the feature, as Joseph Crehan played police Lieutenant Lamb who investigated the complicated case, although Lamb was middle-aged and not a young man like O'Leary.

Warners continued to call Miss Keate Sally Keating in their third series film, MURDER BY AN ARISTOCRAT, issued in the summer of 1936 and taken from the 1932 novel of the same title. When a blackmailer who has been preying on a family is murdered, Nurse Sally Keating (Marguerite Churchill) and her lover, Dr. Allen Carick (Lyle Talbot), get embroiled in the affair. It is Sally who is able to deduce the culprit. The film was produced as a part of Warner Bros./First National's Clue Club film series, and *Variety* called it "routine mediocrity" and subtitled the feature, "Murder by Bryan Foy." Mr. Foy was the film's producer.

After three tepid efforts in the Nurse Keate series, Warners temporarily halted the films. Then 20th Century–Fox made an attempt with THE GREAT HOSPITAL MYSTERY, a 1937 release taken from "Dead Yesterday," a short story by Mignon G. Eberhart about Nurse Keate. Again the character had name problems and was called Miss Keats. While Jane Darwell was nicely cast in the role she had little to do other than shout orders to her nursing staff and look stern. Miss Keats is the head of nursing at a big-city hospital where one of the patients is a young man who was ambushed by gangsters after he witnessed two gangland murders. The hoodlums plan to finish off the witness and are not aware that he has died and that the police have placed one of their own in his place hoping to capture the hit man. Romance was supplied by a staff doctor (Thomas Beck) and a young nurse (Sally Blane), while most of the film's enjoyment came from the comic antics of Joan Davis as another floor nurse.

Early in 1938 Warner Bros. revived the Nurse Keate films with THE PATIENT IN ROOM 18, based on Eberhart's first Miss Keate book published in 1929. Here the character returned to her book name, although her first name was now spelled Sara, not Sarah. In the film, Ann Sheridan was billed third as Nurse Sara Keate while Patric Knowles was top billed as Lance O'Leary and Eric Stanley was billed second as his comic servant, Bentley. O'Leary is a patient in a hospital recovering from a nervous breakdown after coming under the spell of detective stories. Nurse Keate is assigned to minister to him and keep him away from pulp fiction. When a murder takes place at the hospital, policeman Foley (Cliff Clark) investigates, but Lance and Miss Keate do their own detective work and find that the man was murdered with stolen radium. Eventually Lance and Sara solve the case. "A modest little mystery-comedy" is what the *New York Times* called the effort, while *Variety* said the picture "appears to be another unit to fill quota of mystery pics on the [studio] schedule."

The final Nurse Keate film was MYSTERY HOUSE, taken from the 1930 novel *Mystery of Hunting's End*. Ann Sheridan, now billed second, was back as Nurse Sarah (now spelled as originally) Keate, while Dick Purcell took top billing as Lance O'Leary. When a bank president calls his board of directors to his remote mountain lodge to expose who is stealing bank funds, the man is murdered, and his daughter (Anne Nagel) asks Lance O'Leary to investigate. He is aided by his girlfriend, Nurse Sarah Keate. "Situations aren't clearly cut, nor are motives established with much clarity. Dialog is often hackneyed and run-of-mine. Humor gets about a complete overlooking," according to *Variety*.

While the half-dozen features based on the character of Nurse Sarah Keate were mediocre affairs, the books about the nurse-detective were quite popular, and the prolific

Ben Welden, Ann Sheridan, Elspeth Dudgeon, Anne Nagel, Hugh O'Connell, Dick Purcell, and Anthony Averill in MYSTERY HOUSE (Warner Bros./First National, 1938)

Eberhart continued to headline the character in such novels as *Wolf in Man's Clothing* (1942) and *Man Missing* (1954), although Nurse Keate was never adapted to other entertainment mediums.

Nurse Sarah Keate was just one of several female fictional sleuths (others included Hildegarde Withers, Nancy Drew, Torchy Blane) who populated 1930s films. Despite being successful in literature, Miss Keate failed to catch on cinematically, although the problem appears to have been with Hollywood in tampering with Eberhart's novels and not in the innate appeal of Nurse Keate, whose literary career lasted for a quarter of a century.

Filmography

1. WHILE THE PATIENT SLEPT. Warner Bros./First National, 1935. 66 minutes.

D: Ray Enright. SC: Robert Lee & Gene Solow, from the novel by Mignon G. Eberhart. PH: Arthur Edeson. ED: Owen Marks. AD: Esdras Hartley.

Cast: Aline MacMahon (Nurse Sarah Keate), Guy Kibbee (Lance O'Leary), Lyle Talbot (Deke Lonegan), Patricia Ellis (March Federic), Allen Jenkins (Jackson), Robert Barrat (Adolphe Federic), Hobart Cavanaugh (Eustace Federic), Dorothy Tree (Mittel Brown), Henry O'Neill (Elihu Dimeick), Russell Hicks (Dr. Jay), Helen Flint (Isobel Federic), Brandon Hurst (Groudal), Eddie Shubert (Muldoon), Walter Walker (Richard Federic).

2. THE MURDER OF DR. HARRIGAN. Warner Bros./First National, 1936. 67 minutes.

P: Bryan Foy. D: Frank McDonald. SC: Peter Milne & Sy Bartlett, from the novel *From This Dark Stairway* by Mignon G. Eberhart. PH: Arthur Todd. ED: William Clemens. AD: Robert M. Haas. MUS: Leo F. Forbstein.

Cast: Kay Linaker (Nurse Sally Keating), Ricardo Cortez (Dr. George Lambert), Mary Astor (Lillian Ash), John Eldredge (Dr. Harrigan), Joseph Crehan (Lieutenant Lamb), Frank Reicher (Dr. Coate), Anita Kerry (Agnes), Philip Reed (Simon), Robert Strange (Peter Melady), Mary Treen (Margaret Brody), Gordon [Bill] Elliott (Ladd), Don Barclay (Jackson), Johnny Arthur (Wentworth), Joan Blair (Ina).

3. MURDER BY AN ARISTOCRAT. Warner Bros./First National, 1936. 59 minutes.

P: Bryan Foy. D: Frank McDonald. SC: Luci Ward & Roy Chanslor, from the novel by Mignon G. Eberhart. PH: Arthur Todd. ED: Louis Hesse.

Cast: Lyle Talbot (Dr. Allen Carick), Marguerite Churchill (Nurse Sally Keating), Claire Dodd (Janice Thatcher), Virginia Brissac (Adela Thatcher), William Davidson (Bayard Thatcher), John Eldredge (John Tweed), Gordon [Bill] Elliott (Dave Thatcher), Joseph Crehan (Hilary Thatcher), Florence Fair (Evelyn Thatcher), Stuart Holmes (Higby), Lottie Williams (Emeline), Mary Treen (Florrie), Milton Kibbee (Cab Driver), Henry Otho (Sheriff).

4. THE GREAT HOSPITAL MYSTERY. 20th Century–Fox, 1937. 59 minutes.

AP: John Stone. D: James Tinling. SC: William Conselman, Rose Meredith & Jerry Cady, from the story "Dead Yesterday" by Mignon G. Eberhart. PH: Harry Jackson. ED: Nick DeMaggio. MUS: Samuel Kaylin.

Cast: Sally Blane (Ann Smith), Thomas Beck (Dr. David McKerry), Jane Darwell (Nurse Keats), Sig Rumann (Dr. Triggert), Joan Davis (Nurse Flossie Duff), William Demarest (Beatty), George Walcott (Allen Tracy), Wade Boteler (Madoon), Howard Phillips

(Tom Kirby), Ruth Peterson (Desk Nurse), Carl Faulkner, Frank C. Fanning (Policemen), Margaret Brayton (Chart Room Nurse), Lona Andrews (Miss White), Tom Mahoney (Bank Guard).

5. THE PATIENT IN ROOM 18. Warner Bros./First National, 1938. 58 minutes.

P: Bryan Foy. D: Bobby Connolly. SC: Eugene Solow & Robertson White, from the novel by Mignon G. Eberhart. PH: James Van Trees. ED: Lou Hesse.

Cast: Patric Knowles (Lance O'Leary), Eric Stanley (Bentley), Ann Sheridan (Nurse Sara Keate), Rosella Towne (Maida), Jean Benedict (Carol), Charles Trowbridge (Doctor), Cliff Clark (Foley), John Ridgely, Harland Tucker, Edward Raquello, Vicki Lester, Edward McWade, Ralph Sanford, Frank Orth.

6. MYSTERY HOUSE. Warner Bros./First National, 1938. 56 minutes.

P: Bryan Foy. D: Noel Smith. SC: Sherman Lowe & Robertson White, from the novel *Mystery of Hunting's End* by Mignon G. Eberhart. PH: L. W. O'Connell. ED: Frank Magee.

Cast: Dick Purcell (Lance O'Leary), Ann Sheridan (Nurse Sarah Keate), Anne Nagel (Gwen Kingery), William Hopper (Lal Killian), Anthony Averill (Julian Barre), Dennie Moore (Annette), Hugh O'Connell (Newell Morse), Ben Welden (Gerald Frawley), Sheila Bromley (Terice Von Elm), Elspeth Dudgeon (Aunt Lucy Kingery), Anderson Lawlor (Joe Paggi), Trevor Bardette (Bruker).

Chapter 8

PERRY MASON

PERRY MASON'S CREATOR, Erle Stanley Gardner, was one of the most prolific writers of the twentieth century. A native of Massachusetts, Gardner had a variety of jobs before becoming a lawyer and moonlighting as a fiction writer. He sold his first story in 1923 and a decade later began writing the Perry Mason novels. In the next four decades he turned out over seventy Mason books with sales of over 200 million copies. In addition he used various pseudonyms, and besides Mason he wrote books about other detectives, including Terry Clane, Doug Selby (the D.A.), Sheriff Bill Eldon, Lester Leith, Grampa Wiggins, and Sidney Zoom.

In 1934 Warner Bros. purchased the screen rights to seven Perry Mason works and began a series of feature films about the character, although Erle Stanley Gardner never liked the resulting films and eventually refused to allow any more of his properties to be filmed. While the films highlighted the romantic feeling that existed in the books between Mason and his secretary, Della Street, the cinema adaptations often roamed too far from Gardner's conceptions to make them enjoyable. Mason was sometimes pictured as a heavy drinker, à la the Thin Man (see B/V), and he was usually portrayed as a debonair sleuth, like Philo Vance (see B/V), in deference to the down-to-earth lawyer created by Gardner.

The first Warner Bros. Perry Mason feature was THE CASE OF THE HOWLING DOG, taken from the fourth Mason novel, published in 1934, the year of the film's release. Warren William was cast as Perry Mason, a part he

From left: Allen Jenkins, Grant Mitchell, Addison Richards, Warren William, Dorothy Tree, and James Burtis in THE CASE OF THE HOWLING DOG (Warner Bros., 1934)

would play a total of four times. William is associated with detective films, having also portrayed such screen sleuths as Philo Vance (see B/V), the Lone Wolf (see B/V), and Ted Shayne (Sam Spade) (see B/V). His portrayal of Perry Mason was highly satisfying, and his fine acting ability and charm added much to the delineation of the lawyer-sleuth. THE CASE OF THE HOWLING DOG involved Mason in defending a young woman (Mary Astor) accused of murdering her husband. With the aid of secretary Della Street (Helen Trenholme) and police Sergeant Holcomb (Allen Jenkins), Mason is able to solve the case and pinpoint the real killer. One of the main clues which helps Mason solve the affair is a mad watchdog. The *New York Times* felt the feature was "a well-knit story, swiftly paced, dramatically punctuated and, above all, honest with its audience."

THE CASE OF THE CURIOUS BRIDE, the next Mason novel published in 1934, was also the next Warners film in the Mason series, and it was shown theatrically in 1935. A friend (Margaret Lindsay) of Perry Mason's (Warren William) comes to him about the return of her first husband (Errol Flynn), whom she thought was deceased. The man has threatened her new husband (Donald Woods) and is soon murdered. The woman is accused of the killing, and Mason comes to her defense, aided by Della Street (Claire Dodd) and man Friday Spudsy (Allen Jenkins). Rounding up all the suspects at a cocktail party, Mason is able to re-create the homicide and name the murderer. This "good whodunit entertainment" (*Variety*) interestingly cast future Perry Mason, Donald Woods, as one of the suspects, while future star Errol Flynn had a brief role as the murder victim.

The third Perry Mason outing, THE CASE OF THE LUCKY LEGS, was also issued in 1935. It was based on the third Mason novel, published two years before. The *New York Times* lauded the feature: "A gay, swift and impertinent excursion into the sombre matter of murder . . . at once the best of the Erle Stanley Gardner collection and deserves being rated close to the top of this season's list of mystery films." There were detractors, however, who felt that Perry Mason drank too much in the feature and was near inebriation much of the time. Here Perry Mason (Warren William) is representing a man (Porter Hall) who wants him to investigate the killing of a promoter who staged crooked beauty contests and who had absconded with prize money. Allen Jenkins again played associate Spudsy, while Mason carried on a rather bland relationship this time with Della Street (Genevieve Tobin).

The first Perry Mason novel, *The Case of the Velvet Claws* (1933), was filmed as the fourth Perry Mason movie. Released in 1936, THE CASE OF THE VELVET CLAWS found Mason in "a murky mélange of malefice and murder" (*New York Times*). It was Warren William's last film in the series, as he soon left Warners to free-lance. The picture opens with Perry Mason (Warren William) and Della Street (Claire Dodd) getting married—the groom promising his new bride he will give up sleuthing. No sooner is this said than Eva Belton (Wini Shaw) asks Perry to help her because she is being blackmailed and accused of killing her wealthy father for his money. Mason finds that the case has eight other suspects, and he is able to pinpoint the murderer before resuming his honeymoon.

Late in 1936, Warners released THE CASE OF THE BLACK CAT, based on the 1935 novel *The Case of the Caretaker's Cat*. Ricardo Cortez, a silent-film romantic idol who had made a successful transition to talkies and had played Sam Spade in the original MALTESE FALCON (see B/V) in 1931, was cast as Perry Mason. A young woman (Jane Bryan) is accused of murdering her grandfather because the rich old man took her out of his will for marrying a man (Craig Reynolds) he detested. Prosecutor Hamilton Burger (Guy Usher) feels the woman is guilty, but Mason is able to prove her innocence and name the guilty party. Here Mason and Della Street (June Travis) are not married, and the film also featured Mason's own private investigator, Paul Drake (Garry Owen). The *New York Times* felt the film was "a frugal, though somewhat complex, mystery."

In the summer of 1937 Warner Bros. issued THE CASE

Donald Woods in THE CASE OF THE STUTTERING BISHOP (Warner Bros./First National, 1937)

OF THE STUTTERING BISHOP, from Erle Stanley Gardner's 1936 novel of the same title. Donald Woods, who was a suspect in THE CASE OF THE CURIOUS BRIDE two years before, was now cast as Perry Mason, but he appeared too young for the role. The plot has Bishop Mallory (Edward McWade) asking Mason to look into the murder of a man whose daughter-in-law (Anne Nagel) is accused of the crime. Crooks bring in another girl (Linda Perry) to claim the estate, but Mason solves the matter and reveals the murderer. Della Street (Ann Dvorak) again aided Mason in the case, as did an older Paul Drake (Joseph Crehan), while Hamilton Burger (Charles Wilson) led the prosecution. *Variety* opined, "While suspense is cleverly sustained, the romantic side of this film is painfully neglected and it is light on humor, so that this Erle Stanley Gardner mystery story is slow going." The reviewer also complained, "In the customary whodunit fashion, solution of the case is made via an extra added fact never before in the plot . . . Just one of those things, apparently to render a happy ending, but it's too artificial."

Warner Bros. also owned the rights to Erle Stanley Gardner's book *The Case of the Dangerous Dowager* (1937) and planned to film this Perry Mason story, but the author was fed up with the Mason series. After negotiating with him, the studio took the lawyer-detective out of the scenario and filmed it as GRANNY GET YOUR GUN, a 1940 programmer starring May Robson.

Perry Mason came to radio in 1943 on CBS (it ran until 1955), and the fifteen-minute program "Perry Mason" ran weekdays with Bartlett Robinson playing the title role. Later the part was taken over by Santos Ortega, Donald Briggs, and John Larkin.

If purists felt Perry Mason was not properly done on the big screen, few could argue with the way the character was presented in the long-running television series "Perry Mason" (CBS-TV, 1957-1966) starring Raymond Burr as Mason, Barbara Hale as Della Street, William Talman as Hamilton Burger, Ray Collins as Lieutenant Tragg, and William Hopper as Paul Drake. Erle Stanley Gardner was a consultant on the scripts for the series, and in its final episode he portrayed the courtroom judge. With good scripts and production values, plus all-star casts, the Mason episodes are topnotch TV entertainment, still popular in syndication since it left CBS in 1966.

Born in British Columbia in 1917, Raymond Burr came to films in the late 1940s, usually as a thug or psychotic, in such features as SAN QUENTIN ('47), RAW DEAL ('48), PITFALL ('48), RUTHLESS ('48), BLACK MAGIC ('49), THE RED LIGHT ('50), A PLACE IN THE SUN ('51), BRIDE OF THE GORILLA ('51), MARA MARU ('52), GORILLA AT LARGE ('54), REAR WINDOW ('54), PASSION ('54), GODZILLA ('56), CRIME OF PASSION ('57), DESIRE IN THE DUST ('60), PJ ('68), THE KILLER PRIEST (NBC-TV, 1971), THE RETURN ('80), and GODZILLA 1985 ('85). Burr also starred in such TV series as "Ironside" (NBC-TV, 1967-1975) and "Kingston: Confidential" (NBC-TV, 1977). The role of Perry Mason netted Raymond Burr several Emmy Awards and changed his image to that of a romantic leading man. He is considered to be the epitome of the role, and in 1972 when Nicaragua instituted a series of postage stamps commemorating fictional detectives, Raymond Burr was used as the model for the portrait of Perry Mason.

After 270 one-hour episodes, "Perry Mason" left the CBS-TV network in the fall of 1966. Seven years later, in September 1973, "The New Adventures of Perry Mason" was shown on CBS-TV with Monte Markham in the title role. This new one-hour series also featured Sharon Acker as Della Street, Dane Clark as Lieutenant Tragg, Albert Stratton as Paul Drake, Harry Guardino as Hamilton Burger, and Brett Somers as another Mason secretary, Gertrude Lade. This series lasted only five months before leaving the airwaves early in 1974.

After nearly two decades away from the Perry Mason role, Raymond Burr, much heavier and now sporting a beard, returned to the part in the NBC-TV movie, PERRY MASON RETURNS, telecast December 1, 1985. Dean Hargrove's script had Mason a judge who leaves the bench to defend Della Street (Barbara Hale) when she is accused

Monte Markham in "The New Adventures of Perry Mason" (CBS-TV, 1973)

of murder. Mason finds himself opposed by a female district attorney (Cassie Yates) and he enlists the aid of Paul Drake, Jr. (William Katt), the son of his former investigator, in proving Della's innocence. "It's all pleasantly old hat," Judith Crist wrote in *TV Guide*. Mason's return to network television was a huge ratings success, resulting in a whole series of Perry Mason TV movies. It should be noted that William Katt, who portrayed Paul Drake, Jr., is the son of Barbara Hale and actor Bill Williams.

The second Perry Mason TV film, PERRY MASON: THE CASE OF THE NOTORIOUS NUN, telecast May 25, 1986, was just as good as its predecessor. The complicated plot had Perry Mason coming to the defense of a young nun (Michele Greene), at the behest of his old friend Archbishop Corro (William Prince). The nun is accused of

Advertisement for PERRY MASON RETURNS (NBC-TV, 1985)

murdering a priest (Timothy Bottoms) who had allegedly spurned her romantic overtures while investigating corruption involving church funds. Embroiled in the case are a corrupt hospital chief (Jon Cypher), his administrative chief and lover (Barbara Parkins), and a scheming lawyer (Arthur Hill). Mason, with the help of Paul Drake, Jr. (William Katt), proves that a hit man was used to kill the priest as he uncovers the misuse of parish monies and names the person behind the nefarious activities. The film greatly benefited from an ingratiating performance by Michele Greene as the accused nun.

Next came PERRY MASON: THE CASE OF THE SHOOTING STAR, which NBC-TV presented on November 9, 1986. A none-too-popular actor (Joe Penny) murders a bad-mouthing TV talk show host (Alan Thicke) during the man's program. Perry Mason agrees to defend him, although District Attorney Michael Reston (David Ogden Stiers), a character first introduced in the preceding Mason film, seems to have an airtight case against the thespian. *TV Movies and Video Guide* (1988) noted, "Thicke is puckishly cast as the TV talker . . . Average." The fourth Mason TV film was PERRY MASON: THE CASE OF THE LOST LOVE, shown February 23, 1987. Its tale of blackmail and murder had Perry Mason coming to the defense of an ex-love (Jean Simmons) who is running for a Senate seat and who is being blackmailed by a man (Jonathan Banks) who has information that she was once institutionalized. When the blackmailer is found murdered, the woman's husband (Gene Barry) is accused of the crime. Mason defends him and proves his innocence. In the *Hollywood Reporter*, Miles Beller opined that the feature "is a solid chunk of entertainment, as durable and dependable as the TV attorney, a TV courtroom figure who continues to cast a long shadow."

On May 24, 1987, NBC-TV showed PERRY MASON: THE CASE OF THE SINISTER SPIRIT. The eerie plot had a mystery writer (Matthew Falson) inviting a number of guests to a remote hotel for a party celebrating his new book. When they arrive, the writer taunts his guests, and he ends up being pushed from a bell tower. The main suspect is his publisher (Robert Stack), who is accused of the crime and defended by Perry Mason. "Red herrings abound and you might beat Mason to the solution this time, but the old gang . . . is appealing," Judith Crist wrote in *TV Guide.*

PERRY MASON: THE CASE OF THE MURDERED MADAM, the sixth Mason telefilm, was broadcast on NBC-TV on October 4, 1987. Murder, blackmail, and prostitution made up the plot line of this film. A jealous husband (Vincent Baggetta) is accused of murdering his former wife (Ann Jillian), a former madam. Perry Mason defends the man. Helped by a former associate (Daphne Ashbrook) of the murdered woman, he finds that she had taped a luncheon where a quartet of supposedly honest businessmen had planned to commit bank fraud. *Daily Variety* complained that the TV movie was "not up to norm for the Mason mysteries, long on talk, short on action." A few weeks later, on November 15, 1987, NBC-TV presented PERRY MASON: THE CASE OF THE SCANDALOUS SCOUNDREL. Here Perry Mason is defending a young reporter (Susan Wilder) accused of murdering her nasty tabloid publisher (Robert Guillaume). Among the other suspects are a banker and a woman rejected by the victim. In *TV Guide* Judith Crist referred to Mason as the "old reliable" and commented, "This one doesn't play quite fair with mystery-solvers, but in this series it's the old familiars who count."

On February 28, 1988, the eighth Perry Mason movie, PERRY MASON: THE CASE OF THE AVENGING ACE, was telecast. "The beautiful victim always got what she wanted . . . except once," read the advertisement for this film, which had Perry Mason defending an Air Force officer (Larry Wilcox) accused of murdering his two-timing wife, with Mason believing that his client has been framed. *TV Guide* complained it was "run-of-the-mill." The ninth Perry Mason movie, and the fourth to be shown during the 1987–1988 TV season, was PERRY MASON: THE CASE OF THE LADY IN THE LAKE, broadcast May 15, 1988. A tennis star (David Hasselhoff) is accused of murdering his wife (Doran Clark) by drowning her, and he is defended by

Perry Mason. The attorney discovers a variety of suspects, including the victim's guardian (John Ireland), Mason's longtime friend; her ex-boyfriend (John Beck), who managed her mining company; her estate manager (Audra Lindley); and the accused's gambler brother (George Deloy) and ex-girlfriend (Liane Langland). With the aid of private eye Paul Drake, Jr. (William Katt), Mason is able to break the baffling case and prove his client's innocence as well as point out the culprit behind an elaborate blackmail and murder scheme. While the telefilm had nothing to do with Raymond Chandler's Philip Marlowe (q.v.) novel *The Lady in the Lake* (1943), it was a well-made and satisfying mystery movie.

A trio of "Perry Mason" TV movies were telecast by NBC-TV in 1989, all starring Raymond Burr as Mason and Barbara Hale as Della Street. PERRY MASON: THE CASE OF THE LETHAL LESSON, broadcast February 12, 1989, had Mason defending the son (William R. Moses) of an old friend (Brian Keith) after the young law student is accused of killing a nasty classmate. This well-done TV film was directed by Christian Nyby II. Even better was PERRY MASON: THE CASE OF THE MUSICAL MURDER, shown April 9, 1989. This time, Mason tries to find out who bumped off a mean-tempered stage director; among the suspects is a once-famous actress, played by Debbie Reynolds. Regarding this outing, *Daily Variety* said "Erle Stanley Gardner's 'Perry Mason' creation holds up surprisingly well after all these years." On November 19, 1989, PERRY MASON: THE CASE OF THE ALL-STAR ASSASSIN appeared. Here Perry Mason comes to the aid of a hockey player (Jason Beghe) who is accused of killing his former boss (Pernell Roberts), a man who destroyed his career. *TV Guide* termed it "an agreeable little puzzler."

All of the Mason movies have won high ratings, and NBC-TV plans to continue broadcasting made-for-TV movies about the popular character. The secret of the film's success seems to be that not only do they contain a nostalgic appeal but they all have been elaborately produced, well written, and well acted. The plots have stayed within the bounds of the mystery genre without resorting to sensationalism to draw viewers. Basically, the Mason movies are fairly cerebral family entertainment, a formula whose appeal now dates back more than three decades.

Filmography

1. THE CASE OF THE HOWLING DOG. Warner Bros., 1934. 75 minutes.

    D: Alan Crosland. **SC:** Ben Markson, from the novel by Erle Stanley Gardner. **PH:** William Rees. **AD:** John Hughes.

    Cast: Warren William (Perry Mason), Mary Astor (Bessie Foley), Helen Trenholme (Della Street), Allen Jenkins (Sergeant Holcomb), Grant Mitchell (Claude Drumm), Dorothy Tree (Lucy Benton), Helen Lowell (Elizabeth Walker), Gordon Westcott (Arthur Cartwright), Harry Tyler (Sam Martin), Arthur Aylesworth (Bill Pemberton), Russell Hicks (Clinton Foley), Frank Reicher (Dr. Cooper), Addison Richards (Judge Markham), James Burtis (George Dobbs), Eddie Shubert (Ed Wheeler), Harry Seymour (David Clark).

2. THE CASE OF THE CURIOUS BRIDE. Warner Bros., 1935. 80 minutes.

    AP: Harry Joe Brown. **D:** Michael Curtiz. **SC:** Tom Reed & Brown Holmes, from the novel by Erle Stanley Gardner. **PH:** David Abel. **ED:** Terry O. Morse. **AD:** Carl Jules Weyl & Anton Grot. **SP EFF:** Fred Jackman & Fred Jackman, Jr. **SOUND:** Dolph Thomas. **ASST DIR:** Jack Sullivan.

    Cast: Warren William (Perry Mason), Margaret Lindsay (Rhoda Montaine), Donald Woods (Carl Montaine), Claire Dodd (Della Street), Allen Jenkins (Spudsy), Philip Reed (Dr. Claude Millbeck), Barton MacLane (Joe Lucas), Winifred [Wini] Shaw (Doris Pender), Warren Hymer (Oscar Pender), Olin Howland (Coroner Wilbur Strong), Charles Richman (G. Philip Montaine), Thomas Jackson (Toots Howard), Errol Flynn (Gregory Moxley), Robert Gleckler (Detective Byrd), James Donlan (Detective Fritz), Mayo Methot (Florabelle Morgan), George Humbert (Luigi), Henry Kolker (District Attorney Stacey), Paul Hurst (Fibo Morgan).

3. **THE CASE OF THE LUCKY LEGS.** Warner Bros./First National, 1935. 77 minutes.

    P: Henry Blanke. **D:** Archie Mayo. **SC:** Brown Holmes & Ben Markson, from the novel by Erle Stanley Gardner. **PH:** Tony Gaudio. **ED:** James Gibbon. **AD:** Hugh Reticker. **MUS:** Leo F. Forbstein. **ASST DIR:** Lee Katz.

    Cast: Warren William (Perry Mason), Genevieve Tobin (Della Street), Patricia Ellis (Margie Clune), Lyle Talbot (Dr. Doray), Allen Jenkins (Spudsy), Barton MacLane (Bissonette), Peggy Shannon

(Thelma Bell), Porter Hall (Bradbury), Anita Kerry (Eva Jamont), Craig Reynolds (Frank Patton), Henry O'Neill (Manchester), Charles Wilson (Ricker), Joseph Crehan (Johnson), Olin Howland (Doctor), Mary Treen (Mrs. Spudsy), Joseph Downing (Sanborne).

4. THE CASE OF THE VELVET CLAWS. Warner Bros./First National, 1936. 63 minutes.
   P: Bryan Foy. D: William Clemens. SC: Tom Reed, from the novel by Erle Stanley Gardner. PH: Sid Hickox. ED: Jack Saper. AD: Esdras Hartley.
   Cast: Warren William (Perry Mason), Claire Dodd (Della Street), Winifred [Wini] Shaw (Eva Belton), Gordon [Bill] Elliott (Carl Griffin), Joseph King (George C. Better), Addison Richards (Frank Locke), Eddie Acuff (Spudsy Drake), Olin Howland (Wilbur Strong), Kenneth Harlan (Peter Milnor), Dick Purcell (Crandall), Clara Blandick (Judge Mary F. O'Daugherty), Ruth Robinson (Mrs. Velta), Paula Stone (Norma Velta), Robert Middlemass (Sergeant Hoffman), Stuart Holmes (Digley), Carol Hughes (Esther Linton).

5. THE CASE OF THE BLACK CAT. Warner Bros./First National, 1936. 66 minutes.
   P: Bryan Foy. D: William McGann. SC: F. Hugh Herbert, from the novel *The Case of the Caretaker's Cat* by Erle Stanley Gardner. PH: Allen G. Siegler. ED: Frank Magee.
   Cast: Ricardo Cortez (Perry Mason), June Travis (Della Street), Jane Bryan (Wilma Laxter), Craig Reynolds (Frank Dafley), Carlyle Moore, Jr. (Douglas Keene), Gordon [Bill] Elliott (Sam Laxter), Nedda Harrington (Louise De Vol), Garry Owen (Paul Drake), Harry Davenport (Peter Laxter), George Rosener (Ashton), Clarence Wilson (Shuster), Guy Usher (Hamilton Burger), Gordon Hart, Lottie Williams, Harry Hayden, Milton Kibee, John Sheehan.

6. THE CASE OF THE STUTTERING BISHOP. Warner Bros./First National, 1937. 70 minutes.
   P: Bryan Foy. D: William Clemens. SC: Don Ryan & Kenneth Gamet, from the novel by Erle Stanley Gardner. PH: Rex Wimpey. ED: Jack Saper.
   Cast: Donald Woods (Perry Mason), Ann Dvorak (Della Street), Anne Nagel (Janice Alma Brownley), Linda Perry (Janice Seaton), Craig Reynolds (Gordon Bixter), Gordon Oliver (Philip Brownley), Joseph Crehan (Paul Drake), Helen MacKellar (Stella Kenwood), Edward McWade (Bishop Mallory), Tom Kennedy (Jim Magooney), Mira McKinney (Ida Gilbert), Frank Faylen (Charles Downs), Douglas Wood (Ronald C. Brownley), Veda Ann Borg (Gladys), George Lloyd (Peter Sacks), Selmer Jackson (Victor Stockton), Gordon Hart (Judge Knox), Charles Wilson (Hamilton Burger), Eddie Chandler (Detective), Jack Richardson (Taxi Driver).

7. PERRY MASON RETURNS. NBC-TV, 1985. 100 minutes. Color.
   P: Barry Steinberg. **EP:** Fred Silverman & Dean Hargrove. **AP:** Jeff
   Peters. **D:** Ron Satlof. **SC:** Dean Hargrove. **PH:** Albert J. Dunk. **ED:**
   Robert L. Kimble & Edwin F. England. **MUS:** Dick DeBenedictis &
   Fred Steiner. **AD:** David Jaquest.
   Cast: Raymond Burr (Perry Mason), Barbara Hale (Della Street),
   William Katt (Paul Drake, Jr.), Patrick O'Neal (Arthur Gordon),
   Richard Anderson (Ken Braddock), Cassie Yates (Barbara Scott),
   James Kidnie (Bobby Lynch), Holland Taylor (Paula Gordon),
   David McIlwraith (David Gordon), Roberta Weiss (Laura Gordon),
   Kerrie Keane (Kathryn Gordon), Al Freeman, Jr. (Lieutenant
   Cooper), Paul Hubbard (Sergeant Stratton), Lindsay Merrithew
   (Chris), Kathy Lasky (Lianne), Charles Macaulay (Judge Norman
   Whitewood), Mag Huffman (Salesgirl), Carolyn Hetherington
   (Mrs. Jeffries), Cec Linder (District Attorney Jack Welles), John
   MacKenzie (Gas Station Attendant), David Bolt (Dr. Henderson),
   Doug Lennox (Vinnie), Frank Adamson (Mr. Williams), Lee Miller
   (Security Guard), Nerene Virgin (Minicam Reporter), Ken Pogue
   (Frank Lynch), Doris Petrie (Mrs. Lynch), Lillian Lewis (Customer),
   Perek Keurworst (Court Clerk).

8. PERRY MASON: THE CASE OF THE NOTORIOUS NUN. NBC-
   TV, 1986. 100 minutes. Color.
   P: Barry Steinberg. **EP:** Fred Silverman & Dean Hargrove. **AP:** Jeff
   Peters. **D:** Ron Satlof. **SC:** Joel Steiger. **PH:** Hector Figueroa. **ED:**
   Robert L. Kimble & George Chanian. **DESIGN:** Richard Wilcox.
   MUS: Dick DeBenedictis & Fred Steiner.
   Cast: Raymond Burr (Perry Mason), Barbara Hale (Della Street),
   William Katt (Paul Drake, Jr.), Michele Greene (Sister Margaret),
   Timothy Bottoms (Father Thomas O'Neill), William Prince (Arch-
   bishop Stefan Corro), Barbara Parkins (Ellen Cartwright), David
   Ogden Stiers (District Attorney Michael Reston), Tom Bosley
   (Father DeLeon), Arthur Hill (Thomas Shea), Jon Cypher (Dr. Peter
   Lattimore), James McEachin (Detective Brock), Gerald S. O'Lough-
   lin (Monsignor Kyser), Edward Winter (Jonathan Eastman), Hagan
   Beggs (Richard Logan), Donna Cox, Alex Diakun, Dennis Kell, Jane
   Mortifee, David Petersen, Marie Stillin.

9. PERRY MASON: THE CASE OF THE SHOOTING STAR. NBC-TV,
   1986. 100 minutes. Color.
   P: Barry Steinberg. **EP:** Dean Hargrove & Fred Silverman. **AP:** Jeff
   Peters. **D:** Ron Satlof. **SC:** Anne C. Collins. **ST:** Dean Hargrove &
   Joel Steiger. **PH:** Hector Figueroa. **ED:** David Solomon. **MUS:** Dick
   DeBenedictis & Fred Steiner.
   Cast: Raymond Burr (Perry Mason), Barbara Hale (Della Street),
   William Katt (Paul Drake, Jr.), Jennifer O'Neill (Alison Carr), Joe
   Penny (Robert McCay), Ron Glass (Eric Brenner), Alan Thicke
   (Steve Carr), Ivan Dixon (Judge), David Ogden Stiers (District

Attorney Michael Reston), Wendy Crewson (Michelle Benti), Ross Betty (Peter Towne), Mary Kane (Kate Huntley), Lisa Howard (Sharon Loring), J. Kenneth Campbell, Lee Wilkof, Bryan Genesse, John Evans, Cec Linder, Ken James, Michael Donaghue, Mag Huffman.

10. PERRY MASON: THE CASE OF THE LOST LOVE. NBC-TV, 1987. 100 minutes. Color.

P: Barry Steinberg. **EP:** Fred Silverman & Dean Hargrove. **AP:** Jeff Peters. **D:** Ron Satlof. **SC:** Anne C. Collins. **PH:** Arch Bryant. **ED:** David Solomon. **AD:** Paul Staheli. **MUS:** Dick DeBenedictis & Fred Steiner.

Cast: Raymond Burr (Perry Mason), Barbara Hale (Della Street), William Katt (Paul Drake, Jr.), Jean Simmons (Laura Robertson), Gene Barry (Glen Robertson), David Ogden Stiers (District Attorney Michael Reston), Robert Mandan (Dr. Michaels), Robert Walden (Robert Lane), Stephen Elliott (Elliott Moore), Robert F. Lyons (Pete Dickson), Stephanie Dunham (Jennifer Parker), Gordon Jump, Jonathan Banks, Leslie Wing, Lucien Berrier, Julian Gamble, Virginia Gregory, Victor Morris, Dee Dee Olinyk, Norvell Rose, Pam Ward.

11. PERRY MASON: THE CASE OF THE SINISTER SPIRIT. NBC-TV, 1987. 100 minutes. Color.

P: Barry Steinberg. **EP:** Fred Silverman & Dean Hargrove. **AP:** Jeff Peters. **D:** Richard Lang. **SC:** Anne C. Collins. **PH:** Arch Bryant. **ED:** David Solomon. **AD:** Paul Staheli. **MUS:** Dick DeBenedictis & Fred Steiner.

Cast: Raymond Burr (Perry Mason), Barbara Hale (Della Street), William Katt (Paul Drake, Jr.), Robert Stack (Jordan White), Leigh Taylor-Young (Maura McGuire), Dwight Schultz (Andrew Lloyd), David Ogden Stiers (District Attorney Michael Reston), Kim Delaney (Susan Warrenfield), Dennis Lipscomb (Michael Light), Jack Bannon (Donald Sayer), Matthew Falson, Burt Douglas.

12. PERRY MASON: THE CASE OF THE MURDERED MADAM. NBC-TV, 1987. 100 minutes. Color.

P: Peter Katz. **EP:** Fred Silverman & Dean Hargrove. **D:** Ron Satlof. **SC:** Patricia Green. **PH:** Arch Bryant. **ED:** David Solomon. **AD:** Paul Staheli. **MUS:** Dick DeBenedictis & Fred Steiner.

Cast: Raymond Burr (Perry Mason), Barbara Hale (Della Street), William Katt (Paul Drake, Jr.), Ann Jillian (Suzanne Dominico), Bill Macy (Richard Wilson), Anthony [Tony] Geary (Steve Reynolds), John Rhys-Davies (Edward Tremayne), Vincent Baggetta (Tony Dominico), Daphne Ashbrook (Miranda), James Noble (Leonard Weeks), David Ogden Stiers (District Attorney Michael Reston), Jason Bernard, Kim Ulrich, Jamie Horton, Richard Portnow, Mike Moroff, Wendeline Harstone, John Nance, Michael Osborn.

13. PERRY MASON: THE CASE OF THE SCANDALOUS SCOUN-
DREL. NBC-TV, 1987. 100 minutes. Color.
EP: Philip Saltzman, Fred Silverman & Dean Hargrove. **D:**
Christian Nyby II. **SC:** Anthony Spinner. **PH:** Arch Bryant. **ED:**
David Solomon. **MUS:** Dick DeBenedictis & Fred Steiner.
Cast: Raymond Burr (Perry Mason), Barbara Hale (Della Street),
William Katt (Paul Drake, Jr.), Morgan Brittany (Marianne Clay-
man), Robert Guilliaume (Harlen Wade), Yaphet Kotto (General
Sorensen), Susan Wilder (Michele), Rene Enriquez (Oscar Ortega),
George Grizzard (Dr. Clayman), Wings Hauser (James Rivers),
David Ogden Stiers (District Attorney Michael Reston).

14. PERRY MASON: THE CASE OF THE AVENGING ACE. NBC-TV,
1988. 100 minutes. Color.
P: Peter Katz. **EP:** Fred Silverman & Dean Hargrove. **D:** Christian
Nyby II. **SC:** Lee David Zlotoff. **PH:** Arch Bryant. **ED:** David
Solomon. **MUS:** Dick DeBenedictis & Fred Steiner. **AD:** Paul
Staheli.
Cast: Raymond Burr (Perry Mason), Barbara Hale (Della Street),
William Katt (Paul Drake, Jr.), Patty Duke (Althea Sloan), Don
Galloway (General Hobart), Erin Gray (Captain O'Malley), Charles
Siebert (James Sloan), David Ogden Stiers (District Attorney
Michael Reston), Larry Wilcox (Lieutenant Colonel Kevin Parks),
Gary Hershberger (Lieutenant Wilkins), Regina Krueger (Mrs.
Parks), James McEachin (Police Detective), James Sutorius, Arthur
Taxier, Richard Sanders, James McIntire, Joel Colodner, Pam Ward,
Tony Higgins, Dotty Coloroso, Michael X. Martin, Caitlin O'Con-
nell, Sue Hoffman, Tupper Cullum, Wendeline Harstone, Burt
Goodman.

15. PERRY MASON: THE CASE OF THE LADY IN THE LAKE.
NBC-TV, 1988. 100 minutes. Color.
P: Peter Katz. **EP:** Fred Silverman & Dean Hargrove. **D:** Ron
Satlof. **SC:** Shel Williams. **PH:** Arch Bryant. **ED-AP:** David Solo-
mon. **MUS:** Dick DeBenedictis & Fred Steiner. **AD:** Paul Staheli.
Cast: Raymond Burr (Perry Mason), Barbara Hale (Della Street),
William Katt (Paul Drake, Jr.), David Hasselhoff (Billy Travis),
Doran Clark (Sara Wingate Travis), David Ogden Stiers (District
Attorney Michael Reston), Audra Lindley (Mrs. Chaney), Liane
Langland (Lisa Blake), John Beck (Doug Vickers), Darrell Larson
(Skip Wingate), George Deloy (Frank Travis), John Ireland (Uncle
Walter), Terence Evans, Ric Jury, Nadya Starr, Wendy MacDonald,
Jim Beaver, Michael Flynn, Carl Morrow, David Watson, Michael
Preston.

Chapter 9

PHILIP MARLOWE

RAYMOND CHANDLER was past fifty when his first Philip Marlowe novel, *The Big Sleep*, was published in 1939. The Depression had put an end to his job with the oil industry, and in 1933 he began writing stories about hard-boiled detectives for *Black Mask* magazine, slowly developing the character of Philip Marlowe. Although his Los Angeles–based sleuth had other names, in later years some of these stories were reprinted with the detective now called Philip Marlowe. In all, Chandler wrote seven books about Philip Marlowe, and all have been filmed except the last, *Playback* (1958), which was originally conceived as a screenplay. Chandler also wrote or collaborated on the scripts for DOUBLE INDEMNITY ('44), AND NOW TOMORROW ('44), THE UNSEEN ('45), THE BLUE DAHLIA ('46), and STRANGERS ON A TRAIN ('51). A private person, Chandler often conceived convoluted plots, and his feel for Los Angeles and its environs in the 1930s and 1940s highlights his works, as does his ability to entwine his knightlike hero Philip Marlowe with numerous interesting and offbeat characters and situations.

Unlike Dashiell Hammett's Sam Spade (see B/V), his chief rival in hard-boiled-detective popularity, Philip Marlowe is not a shady character but an ethical man who likes the independence of his job (he had once briefly been a cop) and the feeling that he is righting some of the world's wrongs. Fairly well educated, with a liking for literature and good music, Marlowe is not so much bright as honest in many of his cases, and while he eventually gets them solved, the investigations often require involved explanations on the part of his creator to tie all the loose ends together. Still, the Marlowe books and stories contain action, menace, some romance, and a look at the seamy underside of the West Coast of Chandler's day. They have been popular reading for several decades.

Ironically, the first two films to be made from Raymond Chandler's Philip Marlowe novels did not contain the character of Marlowe, yet both were surprisingly good adaptations of the original works. The first of these was THE FALCON TAKES OVER, issued in the spring of 1942, which was based on Chandler's second "Marlowe" book, *Farewell, My Lovely* (1940). The plot was used for the third entry in RKO Radio's Falcon series, the penultimate feature with George Sanders as Gay Falcon, a character created by Michael Arlen. Here Gay Falcon took over the Philip Marlowe role in a story which had the Falcon and his ex-safecracker associate Goldy Locke (Allen Jenkins) becoming involved with hulking former wrestler Moose Malloy (Ward Bond), who has just gotten out of prison and is looking for his former girlfriend. He hires the Falcon to find the woman, but the path leads through many murders while he tries to romance and yet protect newspaper reporter Ann Riordan (Lynn Bari), who is also on Moose's trail for a big story. Gamblers and a phony fortune-telling racket also become part of the case before the girlfriend (Helen Gilbert) is finally located and the Falcon aids police Captain Mike O'Hara (James Gleason) and Sergeant Bates (Edward Gargan) in winding up the case. While the script took some liberties with Chandler's work, it stayed close enough to the original to give the film a classy look. Helen Gilbert was especially good as the murderous girlfriend, as were Ann Revere as Jesse Florian, Hans Conreid as Lindsay Marriot, and Turhan Bey as fake medium Jules Amthor.

The second Philip Marlowe film adaptation not to contain the title character was TIME TO KILL, which 20th Century–Fox released late in 1942. It was based on Raymond Chandler's novel *The High Window*, published the same year, and was the seventh and final entry in the studio's Michael Shayne series starring Lloyd Nolan as the

Brett Halliday–created gumshoe. A rare coin, the Brasher Doubloon, is missing from Mrs. Murdock's (Ethel Griffies) collection, and the elderly eccentric hires private eye Michael Shayne (Lloyd Nolan) to find it. Shayne tries to woo the woman's pretty young secretary, Merle (Heather Angel), as does his client's son, Leslie (James Seay). Shayne is led to believe that gangster Morney (Morris Ankrum) may be involved in the theft of the coin. After a murder is committed and linked to the doubloon, the police, led by Lieutenant Breeze (Richard Lane), get involved in the case. A tip from Merle, however, leads Shayne to photographer Louis Venter (Ralph Byrd), and he learns that the man has been blackmailing Mrs. Murdock and the supposed theft of the coin was just a dodge to keep him away from the real truth. He finds out that Venter, who is also murdered, had taken a photograph showing Mrs. Murdock killing her two-timing husband, a crime she had claimed Merle had committed. Before Breeze can arrest Mrs. Murdock, however, she chokes to death while eating. Again, this non-Marlowe movie was a pretty fair adaptation of Chandler's work. In fact, in *The Detective in Hollywood* (1978), Jon Tuska claimed it "is in every way superior to the later remake, THE BRASHER DOUBLOON."

Officially, the first Philip Marlowe movie was 1945's MURDER, MY SWEET, which RKO Radio assigned to director Edward Dmytryk. In 1941 RKO had paid $2,000 for the screen rights to the second Philip Marlowe novel, *Farewell, My Lovely*, which had been filmed the next year as THE FALCON TAKES OVER. Thus MURDER, MY SWEET (its working title was the same as the novel) was really a remake of the Falcon picture. With the offbeat casting of fading film crooner Dick Powell as the shamus Marlowe "the film represents the breakthrough in popularity for the hard-boiled private-eye film. This is what audiences were waiting for: the toughness of Sam Spade minus his less endearing qualities, the seediness of the Continental Op without the bad looks. Powell could snarl with the best of them, but he was handsomer than Bogart and, after all, he wasn't too far from Chandler's Marlowe"

*From left:*Dick Powell, Miles Mander, and Anne Shirley in MURDER, MY SWEET (RKO Radio, 1945)

(Don Miller, "Private Eyes," *Focus on Film* [Autumn, 1975]).

Several murders are tied to a case involving Hollywood private detective Philip Marlowe (Dick Powell) and he relates the story, under police grilling, to Randall (Don Douglas) and Nulty (Paul Phillips). He tells them he accidentally met huge Moose Malloy (Mike Mazurki), who hired him to find his lost love, Velma, who has disappeared while Moose was in prison. Since the girl once worked as a singer in a bar called Florian's, Marlowe goes to see the widow of the owner, but Jessie Florian (Esther Howard) claims that Velma is dead. Marlowe is hired for another case, to buy back stolen jade for Lindsay Marriott (Douglas Walton), but the man is murdered. He finds that Marriott was mixed up with phony spiritualist Jules Amthor (Otto Kruger) and that the jade belonged to wealthy collector Grayle (Miles Mander), who has a young wife (Claire Trevor), and a grown-up daughter, Ann (Anne Shirley). A visit to Amthor ends with Marlowe beaten and drugged, but he learns that the spiritualist was blackmailing Mrs. Grayle because he had proof that she had been unfaithful to her husband. Marlowe tells Mrs. Grayle he will help her stop Amthor, but the latter is murdered by Malloy, whom Marlowe takes to a beach house where he discovers that Mrs. Grayle is really Velma. Grayle and Ann arrive, and the collector kills his wife and Moose. After Ann confirms Marlowe's story, they leave the police station together.

Although there was some tampering with the Chandler novel (Grayle in the novel was a judge, Ann was a newspaperwoman and not his daughter, gangster Laird Burnette was totally eliminated), MURDER, MY SWEET beautifully captured the aura of the Los Angeles of the Chandler work. Dick Powell was superb as the gumshoe, as was wrestler-actor Mike Mazurki as the hulking Moose Malloy. The film breathed new life into Dick Powell's waning film career, and he repeated the part of Marlowe in "Murder, My Sweet" on two radio adaptations of the film: on "Lux Radio Theatre" (CBS, June 11, 1945) with Claire Trevor repeating her role as the femme fatale, and on "Hollywood Star Time" (CBS, June 6, 1946) with Mary Astor as Mrs. Grayle. In England the RKO film was issued under its original title, FAREWELL, MY LOVELY.

Following the box office success of MURDER, MY SWEET, Warner Bros. purchased the screen rights to the first Philip Marlowe novel and filmed THE BIG SLEEP late in 1944. The book's plot proved so complicated that filming began without a finished script, and even after lensing was completed the film appeared so mixed up that new shooting took place along with extensive reediting. Hollywood insiders expected the finished product to be a bust, but when Warners finally issued the film late in the summer of 1946 it proved to be a satisfying feature, which like MURDER, MY SWEET, retained Raymond Chandler's flavorful depiction of the Los Angeles he loved so well. Also Humphrey Bogart, as expected, was well cast as Philip Marlowe and Lauren Bacall was acceptable as the leading lady, although her work was overshadowed by Martha Vickers as the sex-crazy, thumb-sucking younger sister. Cowboy star Bob Steele was outstanding as the hired killer, Canino. *Daily Variety* termed the feature "a first-rate melodrama."

Aged General Sternwood (Charles Waldron) hires detective Philip Marlowe (Humphrey Bogart) to buy some incriminating pictures taken of his youngest daughter Carmen (Martha Vickers) by Arthur Geiger (Theodore Von Eltz). Carmen's lover, the family chauffeur, murders Geiger but is himself found dead, while the photos fall into the hands of Joe Brody (Louis Jean Heydt) via his girlfriend, Agnes (Sonia Darrin), who works in Geiger's rare book store. Brody attempts to peddle the pictures to Carmen's older sister Vivian (Lauren Bacall), who believes her father hired Marlowe to find his missing friend, Shawn Regan. When Brody is killed by Carol Lundgren (Tom Rafferty), Geiger's lover, he is captured by Marlowe, who turns him over to his police pal, Detective Bernie Olds (Regis Toomey). Since the nude photos of Carmen have been recovered, Vivian asks Marlowe to get off the case, but he thinks she is connected with gambler Eddie Mars (John Ridgely), who was Geiger's landlord. It is also rumored that Mars's wife (Peggy Knudsen) is Regan's lover and that the two have left the city together. Following an unsuccessful attempt to rob Vivian outside Mars's casino, the detective is approached by Agnes's new boyfriend, Harry Jones (Elisha Cook, Jr.), who says he can take the gumshoe to Mars's wife. Returning to his office, Marlowe sees Jones murdered by the gambler's hired gunman, Canino (Bob Steele). From Agnes, Marlowe learns that Mrs. Mars is at a garage owned by Art Huck (Trevor Bardette), but when he goes there he is captured by Canino. Vivian arrives and sets him free, and when Canino returns Marlowe kills him. Taking Vivian to Geiger's home, Marlowe has a showdown with Eddie Mars and ties up the case, proving that Mars was blackmailing Vivian because he knew it was Carmen who had murdered Regan when he refused to sleep with her.

When he tries to escape, Mars is ambushed by his own men as Marlowe telephones the police.

Three months after the release of THE BIG SLEEP, Metro-Goldwyn-Mayer issued THE LADY IN THE LAKE, based on Raymond Chandler's fourth Philip Marlowe novel, published in 1943. Chandler had been signed by the studio to adapt his novel to the screen, but his final script proved too long and Steve Fisher rewrote it. Robert Montgomery was to direct the picture as well as portray Philip Marlowe. In reality, the *camera* plays Marlowe, as Montgomery is seen only occasionally in the film, mainly as a mirror reflection. Montgomery used the subjective-camera technique to portray Marlowe: the audience, via the camera, saw what Marlowe saw as the action took place. The technique proved quite successful in the feature, although the involved plot line made the movie hard to follow at times. Still, the picture proved to be very successful, grossing over $4 million at the box office, four times its original cost.

Philip Marlowe (Robert Montgomery) writes a magazine story and takes it to Kingsby Publications, where it is rejected by editor Adrienne Fromsett (Audrey Totter). She hires him to find Chrystal, the missing wife of her employer, Derace Kingsby (Leon Ames), who wants to divorce the woman. Trying to find Chrystal, he goes to see her rumored lover, Chris Lavery (Richard Simmons), but the two have a fight and Marlowe ends up in the Bay City drunk tank before being released by Captain Kane (Tom Tully) and Lieutenant DeGarmot (Lloyd Nolan). On a tip from Adrienne, Marlowe goes to the Little Fawn Lake resort in the mountains to find Chrystal, but instead he learns that the owner's wife has been drowned and he is being held for the crime. Adrienne tells the private eye that Chrystal may have killed Muriel Chess, the supposedly drowned woman, whom Marlowe discovers was really Mildred Haviland (Jayne Meadows), on the run from the law. Marlowe returns to see Lavery and finds his landlady present. After she leaves, the sleuth discovers that Lavery has been murdered. Since he thinks Adrienne committed the murder, Marlowe calls Kingsby who tells him to stay on the case although he, too, thinks his editor may have committed the crime. Marlowe then calls in Kane and DeGarmot and accuses the latter of having traced Mildred to Little Fawn Lake. He is beaten for his troubles. The two cops let him go, however, when he says he has proof that DeGarmot knew both Lavery and Mildred. From Adrienne, Marlowe learns that DeGarmot once investigated a case involving the mysterious death of a doctor's wife and that Mildred had worked for the physician. Following an unfruitful visit with the dead woman's parents (Morris Ankrum and Kathleen Lockhart), Marlowe is waylayed by DeGarmot, who beats him up again and reports him drunk. The fast-thinking Marlowe knocks out a real drunk and leaves him in his place on the highway. Going to Adrienne's apartment, Marlowe is told by the young woman to get off the case because she loves him and fears for his safety. As they are talking, Kingsby arrives and tells Marlowe that Chrystal needs money and that he should take it to her. When he does, after leaving a trail of rice for Adrienne to follow, he realizes that Chrystal is the landlady who murdered Lavery. In reality, the woman is really Mildred Haviland, since the real Chrystal was the woman who drowned in Little Fawn Lake. DeGarmot, who had been blackmailing the woman, shows up and shoots her, but before he can do the same to Marlowe, Adrienne arrives with Kane and his men, and the crooked cop is arrested. Marlowe and Adrienne then decide to stay together.

Within three months of the release of THE LADY IN THE LAKE, another Philip Marlowe feature was issued, THE BRASHER DOUBLOON, which 20th Century–Fox had made earlier as the Michael Shayne feature, TIME TO KILL. Both features were taken from the 1942 book *The High Window*. Well directed by John Brahm, THE BRASHER DOUBLOON is often vilified by critics, but in reality it is a moody, film noir presentation of the novel, somewhat hurt by a limited budget, the bland rendering of the leading-lady role, and a hokey finale. While George Montgomery gave a workmanlike performance as Mar-

Nancy Guild and George Montgomery in THE BRASHER DOUBLOON
(20th Century–Fox, 1947)

lowe, character actress Florence Bates stole the film's
acting honors as the self-centered Mrs. Murdock. Adding
to the film's entertainment value is its somber atmosphere
of hovering evil, exemplified by the gangsters portrayed by
Marvin Miller and Alfred Linder.

Wealthy socialite Mrs. Elizabeth Murdock (Florence
Bates) retains private eye Philip Marlowe (George
Montgomery) to recover a priceless Dutch coin, the
Brasher Doubloon, missing from her collection. The
woman's pretty secretary, Merle Davis (Nancy Guild),
persuades Marlowe to take the case, despite the fact he
detests Mrs. Murdock and her momma's-boy son, Leslie
(Conrad Janis), who is attracted to Merle. After refusing
the offer of gunman Eddie Prue (Alfred Linder) to meet

with his boss, nightclub proprietor Blair (Marvin Miller), Marlowe goes to see coin dealer Morningstar (Houseley Stevenson) who says someone tried to sell him the doubloon. Overhearing the coin dealer call a man about his visit, Marlowe goes to see the person and finds him murdered. He also finds a claim check, and redeeming it he obtains the doubloon. When he goes back to see Morningstar, he discovers that the coin dealer has also been killed. Police officers Breeze (Roy Roberts) and Spangler (Bob Adler) suspect Marlowe is involved in the killings but lack the proof to arrest him. Leslie then tells Marlowe he has been fired from the case and that he himself took the doubloon to pay a gambling debt. He also tells Marlowe that Merle is mentally unstable and has been since she saw his father, for whom she worked, fall to his death from an office building window some years before. Later, photographer Rudolph Vannier (Fritz Kortner) tries to steal the coin from Marlowe, and Merle threatens to kill him unless he turns the doubloon over to her. Merle feels she is to blame for Mr. Murdock's fall since she pushed him aside because he was trying to seduce her, and he fell to his death. She also tells the sleuth that Vannier has a movie of the fall and has been using it to blackmail Mrs. Murdock. Blair, Prue, and their henchmen then abduct Marlowe and take him to Blair's club to try to find the whereabouts of the coin. Leslie arrives, and he and Prue fight, and Marlowe escapes. Getting a call from Merle, Marlowe meets her at Vannier's house. They find him murdered, but Marlowe also finds the blackmail film. He calls Breeze and Spangler, and he has them come to his office along with Mrs. Murdock and Leslie. There Marlowe shows the movie footage which reveals that it was Mrs. Murdock who pushed her husband to his death, and Marlowe also proves she murdered Vannier. The socialite is arrested, and Marlowe and Merle begin a romance.

The year 1947 also saw the debut of the "Philip Marlowe" radio series on NBC. Academy Award–winner Van Heflin portrayed the title role, and the series was sponsored by Pepsodent toothpaste. Two years later, the program switched to CBS and was titled "The Adventures of Philip Marlowe," with Gerald Mohr, who had played the Lone Wolf (q.v.) in three films at Columbia in 1946–1947, cast as Marlowe.

Philip Marlowe came to television on October 7, 1954, in the debut episode of the CBS-TV series "Climax!" Dick Powell returned to the role of Marlowe in this adaptation of "The Long Goodbye," based on Raymond Chandler's penultimate Marlowe novel, published in 1953. Co-starred were Teresa Wright, Cesar Romero, Tom Drake, and Horace MacMahon. The program was telecast live and was most memorable for the scene in which an actor, portraying a murdered character, got up and walked off screen in full view of the TV camera! Chandler's detective became a TV series five years later when "Philip Marlowe," a half-hour, filmed program, debuted on ABC-TV with Philip Carey in the title role. The Tuesday night series lasted for six months before leaving the air in March 1960.

During the 1960s there was a revival in interest in the Philip Marlowe works, and by the early 1970s all of Chandler's novels and most of his short stories had been reprinted and had found an avid reading public. In 1969 Metro-Goldwyn-Mayer released MARLOWE, based on the sixth Philip Marlowe book, *The Little Sister* (1949). It told of the Hollywood private eye (James Garner) being commissioned by attractive Orfamay Quest (Sharon Farrell) to find her missing brother, Orrin (Roger Newman). The trail leads to a Bay City hotel where Marlowe finds the manager, Clausen (Warren Finnerty), murdered, while Dr. Lagardie (Paul Stevens) says he does not know either Orrin Quest or Clausen. Going to the Alvardo Hotel to meet Grant Hicks (Jackie Coogan), who has told the sleuth he has information on the case, Marlowe is blackjacked. When he awakens, he finds Hicks murdered and takes a photo claim check from his effects. Policemen Christy French (Carroll O'Connor) and Sergeant Beifus (Kenneth Tobey) are called into the latest homicide by Marlowe, who uses the claim check to locate incriminating photographs of television star Mavis Wald (Gayle Hunnicutt) with hoodlum Sonny Steelgrave (H. M. Wynant). When he goes to interview Mavis, Marlowe meets her friend Dolores

Gonzales (Rita Moreno), and is beaten by Steelgrave's hoods. At his office Marlowe is offered money by Winslow Wong (Bruce Lee) to drop the case, and when he refuses the man destroys his furniture. That night the detective takes his lady friend, Julie (Corinne Camacho), to Sonny's nightclub. While they are there, Wong tries to kill Marlowe, but misses with a lunging kick and falls out a window and is killed. The case then leads to Mavis's agent (William Daniels), who pays Marlowe to protect his client's interests. Later he finds Orrin with Dr. Lagardie and learns that the medical man once worked for Steelgrave. Marlowe is doped and Orrin is found dead, but the police do not arrest the detective since they think Orrin committed the two murders. Marlowe burns the photos of Mavis, and then learns that Steelgrave has been bumped off. When he finds Orfamay going through his personal belongings, Marlowe learns that Mavis is really her younger sister, and that she and Orrin had been blackmailing their sibling about the photographs. Mavis arrives on the scene, and she and Orfamay have a fight. Marlowe stops them, saying that the pictures have been destroyed. He then goes to see Dolores who tells him that she killed Sonny to save Mavis from marrying the gangster. Dr. Lagardie, who was once married to Dolores, arrives and kills her and then shoots himself. Marlowe drops the case in order to protect Mavis and her career. F. Maurice Speed in *Film Review 1970-71* (1970) called MARLOWE a "fast, furious [and commendable] detection thriller." Still the feature did mediocre box office business; it was later reissued as THE LITTLE SISTER.

Raymond Chandler's most personal Philip Marlowe novel was his sixth book about the detective, *The Long Goodbye* (1953), which had the sleuth mellowing with age and having an extended romance. The plot was also very involved and probably the least interesting of the Marlowe books, although it received the Mystery Writers of America Award as 1954's best mystery novel. As noted, Dick Powell played Marlowe in a TV adaptation in 1954, and nearly two decades later the story was brought to the big screen in the worst Philip Marlowe movie to date. The story was updated, and the casting of Elliott Gould as a modern Marlowe was disastrous, as was the foggy direction by Robert Altman. The production cost $1.7 million, and despite two releases never recouped its costs.

When his pal Terry Lennox (Jim Boulton) has a fight with his wife, Sylvia, the man asks private eye Philip Marlowe (Elliott Gould) to take him to Tijuana. Returning to Hollywood, Marlowe learns that the woman has been murdered, but he remains mum and is arrested, then released when a confession to the crime written by Terry is found before he commits suicide. Later Marlowe gets a letter and $5,000 from his supposedly dead friend. Meanwhile Marlowe is hired by wealthy Eileen Wade (Nina Van Pallandt) to find her husband Roger (Sterling Hayden), whom he locates at a clinic run by Dr. Verringer (Henry Gibson). Gangster Marty Augustine (Mark Rydell) hires Marlowe to locate money that Terry took with him to Mexico, and he learns from Roger that Marty owes him a large sum of money. Later Marlowe finds out that Roger actually owes the hoodlum $10,000, has committed suicide, and once had an affair with Sylvia. Eventually Marlowe learns that Terry is alive and that he killed his wife because she found out from Roger that Terry was having an affair with Eileen. In revenge Sylvia planned to tell the law about the money Terry was carrying for Augustine. Eileen arrives to run away with Terry, but Marlowe kills him. It is hard to imagine a worse Philip Marlowe movie.

For years it had been suggested that Robert Mitchum would be perfect for the part of Philip Marlowe. Producers Elliott Kastner and Jerry Bick, after the fiasco of their THE LONG GOODBYE, played it safe and cast Mitchum as Marlowe in their 1975 remake of FAREWELL, MY LOVELY, which had been filmed earlier as THE FALCON TAKES OVER and MURDER, MY SWEET. Although Mitchum was in his late fifties when he made the film, he was still the screen's finest Philip Marlowe. His performance, along with the movie's ability to capture the aura of the 1940s, made FAREWELL, MY LOVELY a success which grossed over $5 million at the box office.

Charlotte Rampling and Robert Mitchum in FAREWELL, MY LOVELY
(Avco/Embassy, 1975)

The plot of the third version of the Chandler novel was changed somewhat from the book and the two prior filmings, but overall it retained the flavor and basic outline of the novel. The main character changes were the elimination of the Ann Riordan part and the changing of psychic Jules Amthor into politically corrupt lesbian madam Frances Amthor, well played by Kate Murtagh. Otherwise the film remained close to its source in its involved and sordid tale of Philip Marlowe (Robert Mitchum) corralled by oafish Moose Malloy (Jack O'Halloran) into finding his lost lady love Velma, on a trail leading into a maze of murder, blackmail, and police corruption. Charlotte Rampling was adequately alluring as the femme fatale, while Sylvia Miles was nominated for an Academy Award for her performance as lush Jessie Florian. Unlike MURDER, MY SWEET, this version retained the major character of gangster Laird Brunette (Anthony Zerbe) who knew the true identity of Mrs. Grayle (Charlotte Rampling), a former hooker and Moose's ex-love, who was now married to an aged jurist. Brunette had been blackmailing her to keep her past a secret. The film retained the romantic interest between Marlowe and the sexy Mrs. Grayle, and displayed the cinema's more relaxed showings of violence (especially the early sequence where Moose single-handedly mops up the denizens of a black bar, leaving behind several corpses) and nudity. Perhaps the film's only real weakness was the inclusion of second-rate musician Tommy Ray (Walter McGinn), who was murdered because he also knew Mrs. Grayle's secret, and Marlowe's giving the reward money at the finale to his wife and son. This was not part of Chandler's novel.

The success of FAREWELL, MY LOVELY resulted in the teaming of producer Elliot Kastner with writer-director Michael Winner to produce a remake of THE BIG SLEEP, with Robert Mitchum again cast as Philip Marlowe. Here Chandler's novel is followed more closely than in FAREWELL, MY LOVELY, but with two exceptions: the locale was changed to London and the time period was updated to the present. As a result the critics lambasted the feature, and it failed to do more than moderate box office business.

Still, the 1978 release is a worthy screen rendering of Chandler's work. Again Robert Mitchum's performance as Philip Marlowe is its highlight. Maybe the film was too close to the original, because in order to tie all the plot elements together at the finale, flashbacks within flashbacks had to be utilized to make sense of it all.

As was the case with FAREWELL, MY LOVELY, the permissiveness of the modern big screen allowed the more unsavory aspects of THE BIG SLEEP to be shown, where they were only hinted at in the 1946 version. The character of thumb-sucking nymphomaniac Camilla (she was named Carmen in the book) Sternwood (Candy Clark) was shown in the nude on more than one occasion, and older sister Charlotte (changed from Vivian in the novel) Sternwood (Sarah Miles) wears a see-through blouse and no bra near the end of the film. The movie correctly named Shawn Regan as Charlotte's husband; his murder by Camilla, who tried to seduce him, is shown in one of the flashbacks explaining the overall events of the picture. THE BIG SLEEP is a handsome feature which makes good utilization of its London locales. The film had a star-studded cast, with especially good work by Joan Collins as the scheming Agnes, James Stewart as the dying General Sternwood (the title *The Big Sleep* refers to death), and Colin Blakely as loser Harry Jones. Less satisfying was Oliver Reed's work as the gangster Eddie Mars and Richard Boone's scenery-chewing hit man Canino. Unfortunately the critical blasting and the meager profits of the film ended any hope of a continuing series of Philip Marlowe features with Robert Mitchum.

The most recent attempt to recreate the Philip Marlowe character came in the Home Box Office miniseries "Philip Marlowe—Private Eye," telecast in five episodes from April 16 to May 14, 1983. Powers Boothe portrayed Marlowe, while other regulars were Kathryn Leigh Scott as Annie Riordan, shown here as Marlowe's lady love, and William Kearns as Los Angeles homicide cop, Lieutenant Violets Magee. The series, which opened with "Smart Aleck Kill" from Raymond Chandler's 1934 *Black Mask* story, was produced by David Wickes and directed by

Peter Hunt. Like THE BIG SLEEP, "Philip Marlowe—
Private Eye" was made in London and of the taped
segments *Variety* reported that "the old L.A. atmosphere
was conveyed well enough," since the shows were set in
the 1930s.

Filmography

1. THE FALCON TAKES OVER. RKO Radio, 1942. 63 minutes.
    P: Howard Benedict. **D:** Irving Reis. **SC:** Lynn Root & Frank
    Fenton, from the novel *Farewell, My Lovely* by Raymond Chandler.
    PH: George Robinson. **ED:** Harry Marker. **AD:** Albert S.
    D'Agostino & F. M. Gray. **MUS:** C. Bakaleinikoff.
    Cast: George Sanders (Gay Lawrence), Lynn Bari (Ann Riordan),
    James Gleason (Mike O'Hara), Allen Jenkins (Jonathan G. "Goldy"
    Locke), Helen Gilbert (Diana Kenyon), Ward Bond (Moose Malloy),
    Edward Gargan (Sergeant Bates), Anne Revere (Jessie Florian),
    George Cleveland (Jerry), Harry Shanon (Grimes), Hans Conreid
    (Lindsay Marriot), Mickey Simpson (Bartender), Turhan Bey (Jules
    Amthor), Selmer Jackson (Laird Brunette).

2. TIME TO KILL. 20th Century–Fox, 1942. 61 minutes.
    P: Sol M. Wurtzel. **D:** Howard I. Leeds. **SC:** Clarence Upson
    Young, from the novel *The High Window* by Raymond Chandler.
    PH: Charles Clarke. **ED:** Alfred Day. **AD:** Richard Day & Chester
    Gore. **MUS:** Emil Newman.
    Cast: Lloyd Nolan (Michael Shayne), Heather Angel (Merle),
    Ralph Byrd (Louis Venter), Richard Lane (Lieutenant Breeze),
    Sheila Bromley (Lois Morney), Morris Ankrum (Alex Morney),
    Ethel Griffies (Mrs. Murdock), James Seay (Leslie Murdock), Ted
    Hecht (Phillips), William Pawley (Hench), Syd Saylor (Postman),
    Lester Sharpe (Washburn), Charles Williams (Dental Assistant),
    LeRoy Mason (Headwaiter), Phyllis Kennedy (Ena), Paul Guifoyle
    (Manager), Helen Flint (Marge), Bruce Wong (Houseboy).

3. MURDER, MY SWEET. RKO Radio, 1945. 95 minutes.
    P: Adrian Scott. **D:** Edward Dmytryk. **SC:** John Paxton, from the
    novel *Farewell, My Lovely* by Raymond Chandler. **PH:** Harry J. Wild.
    ED: Jospeh Noriega. **AD:** Albert S. D'Agostino & Carroll Clark.
    MUS: Roy Webb. **ASST DIR:** William Dorfman.
    Cast: Dick Powell (Philip Marlowe), Claire Trevor (Mrs. Grayle),
    Anne Shirley (Anne Grayle), Otto Kruger (Jules Amthor), Mike
    Mazurki (Moose Malloy), Miles Mander (Grayle), Douglas Walton
    (Lindsay Marriott), Don Douglas (Lieutenant Randall), Esther
    Howard (Jessie Florian), Ralf Harolde (Dr. Sonderborg), Paul
    Phillips (Detective Nulty), Ernie Adams (Bartender), Dewey Robin-

son (Boss), Ralph Dunn, George Anderson (Detectives), Jack Carr (Short Man). **British Title:** FAREWELL, MY LOVELY.

4. THE BIG SLEEP. Warner Bros., 1946. 114 minutes.

P-D: Howard Hawks. **SC:** William Faulkner, Leigh Brackett & Jules Furthman, from the novel by Raymond Chandler. **PH:** Sid Hickox. **ED:** Christian Nyby. **AD:** Carl Jules Weyl. **MUS:** Max Steiner. **ASST DIR:** Robert Vreeland.

Cast: Humphrey Bogart (Phillip Marlowe), Lauren Bacall (Vivian Sternwood), Martha Vickers (Carmen Sternwood), John Ridgely (Eddie Mars), Regis Toomey (Detective Bernie Olds), Bob Steele (Canino), Charles Waldron (General Sternwood), Elisha Cook, Jr. (Harry Jones), Sonia Darrin (Agnes Lowzier), Louis Jean Heydt (Joe Brody), Theodore Von Eltz (Arthur Gwynne Geiger), Peggy Knudsen (Mona Mars), Charles D. Brown (Norris the Butler), Dorothy Malone (Girl in Bookshop), Joy Barlowe (Girl in Taxi), Tom Rafferty (Carol Lundgren), Tom Fadden (Sidney), Ben Welden (Pete), Trevor Bardette (Art Huck), James Flavin (Captain Cronjager), Joseph Crehan (Medical Examiner), Emmett Vogan (Deputy), Forbes Murray (Furtive Man), Pete Kooy (Motorcycle Officer), Carole Douglas (Librarian), Jack Chefe (Croupier), Paul Weber, Jack Perry, Wally Walker (Mars's Henchmen), Lorraine Miller (Hatcheck Girl), Shelby Payne (Cigarette Girl), Tanis Chandler, Deannie Best (Waitresses).

Cut from Film: Thomas Jackson (District Attorney Wilde), Dan Wallace (Owen Taylor).

5. THE LADY IN THE LAKE. Metro-Goldwyn-Mayer, 1946. 105 minutes.

P: George Haight. **D:** Robert Montgomery. **SC:** Steve Fisher [& uncredited Raymond Chandler], from the novel by Raymond Chandler. **PH:** Paul C. Vogel. **ED:** Gene Ruggiero. **AD:** Cedric Gibbons & Preston Ames. **MUS:** David Snell. **ASST DIR:** Dolph Zimmer.

Cast: Robert Montgomery (Philip Marlowe), Lloyd Nolan (Lieutenant DeGarmot), Audrey Totter (Adrienne Fromsett), Tom Tully (Captain Kane), Leon Ames (Derace Kingsby), Jayne Meadows (Mildred Haviland), Morris Ankrum (Eugene Grayson), Kathleen Lockhart (Mrs. Grayson), Richard Simmons (Chris Lavery), Lila Leeds (Receptionist), Ellen Ross (Elevator Girl), William Roberts (Artist), Cy Kendall (Jaibi), Ralph Dunn (Sergeant), Wheaton Chambers (Property Clerk), Frank Orth (Greer), William McKeever Riley (Bunny), Robert Williams (Detective), Fred E. Sherman (Reporter), Jack Davis, Tom Murray, John Gallaudet, George Magrill, Bud Fine, John Webb Dillon (Policemen), Robert Spencer (Double for Marlowe), Bill Newell (Drunk), Eddie Acuff (Coroner),

Charles Bradstreet, Bert Moorehouse, Fred Santley, Sherry Hall, James Nolan, Nina Ross, George Travell, William O'Leary, Florence Stephens, Sandra Morgan, Laura Treadwell, Kay Wiley, Frank Dae, David Cavendish, Ann Lawrence, Roger Cole (Party Guests).

6. THE BRASHER DOUBLOON. 20th Century–Fox, 1947. 72 minutes. **P:** Robert Brassier. **D:** John Brahm. **SC:** Dorothy Hannah & Leonard Praskins, from the novel *The High Window* by Raymond Chandler. **PH:** Lloyd Ahern. **ED:** Harry Reynolds. **AD:** James Basevi & Richard Irvine. **MUS:** David Buttolph.

   Cast: George Montgomery (Philip Marlowe), Nancy Guild (Merle Davis), Conrad Janis (Leslie Murdock), Florence Bates (Mrs. Elizabeth Murdock), Roy Roberts (Lieutenant Breeze), Fritz Kortner (Rudolph Vannier), Marvin Miller (Blair), Houseley Stevenson (Morningstar), Bob Adler (Sergeant Spangler), Jack Conrad (George Anson), Alfred Linder (Eddie Prue), Jack Overman (Manager), Jack Stoney (Mike), Ray Spiker (Figaro), Paul Maxey (Coroner), Joe Palma (Attendant), Al Eben (Baggage Room Attendant).

7. MARLOWE. Metro-Goldwyn-Mayer, 1969. 95 minutes. Color. **P:** Gabriel Katzka & Sidney Beckerman. **D:** Paul Bogart. **SC:** Stirling Silliphant, from the novel *The Little Sister* by Raymond Chandler. **PH:** William H. Daniels. **ED:** Gene Ruggiero. **AD:** George W. Davis & Addison Hehr. **MUS:** Peter Matz. **ASST DIR:** Bud Grace. Title song sung by Orpheus.

   Cast: James Garner (Philip Marlowe), Gayle Hunnicutt (Mavis Wald), Carroll O'Connor (Lieutenant Christy French), Rita Moreno (Dolores Gonzales), Sharon Farrell (Orfamay Quest), William Daniels (Mr. Crowell), H. M. Wynant (Sonny Steelgrave), Jackie Coogan (Grant Hicks), Kenneth Tobey (Sergeant Fred Beifus), Bruce Lee (Winslow Wong), Christopher Cary (Chuck), George Tyne (Oliver Hady), Corinne Camacho (Julie), Paul Stevens (Dr. Vincent Lagardie), Roger Newman (Orrin Quest), Read Morgan (Gumpshaw), Warren Finnerty (Haven Clausen).

   Reissued as THE LITTLE SISTER.

8. THE LONG GOODBYE. United Artists, 1973. 112 minutes. Color. **P:** Jerry Bick. **EP:** Elliott Kastner. **D:** Robert Altman. **SC:** Leigh Brackett, from the novel by Raymond Chandler. **PH:** Vilmostz Sigmond. **ED:** Lou Lombardo. **MUS:** John Williams.

   Cast: Elliott Gould (Philip Marlowe), Nina Van Pallandt (Eileen Wade), Sterling Hayden (Roger Wade), Mark Rydell (Marty Augustine), Henry Gibson (Dr. Verringer), David Arkin (Harry), Jim Boulton (Terry Lennox), Warren Berlinger (Morgan), Jo An Brody (Jo Ann Eggenweiler), Pepe Callahan (Pepe), Jack Knight, Vince Palmieri, Arnold Strong (Hoodlums), Rutanya Alda, Tammy Shaw (Marlowe's Neighbors), Jack Riley (Piano Player), Ken Sansom

(Colony Guard), Danny Goldman (Bartender), Sybil Scottford (Real Estate Lady), Steve Colt (Detective Farmer), Jerry Jones (Detective Green), Tracy Harris (Detective), Rodney Moss (Clerk).

9. FAREWELL MY LOVELY. Avco/Embassy, 1975. 97 minutes. Color.
   P: Jerry Bruckheimer & George Pappas. **EP:** Jerry Bick & Elliott Kastner. **D:** Dick Richards. **SC:** David Zelag Goodman, from the novel by Raymond Chandler. **PH:** John Alonzo. **ED:** Joel Cox & Walter Thompson. **AD:** Angelo Graham. **MUS:** David Shire.

   Cast: Robert Mitchum (Peter Marlowe), Charlotte Rampling (Mrs. Grayle), John Ireland (Lieutenant Nulty), Sylvia Miles (Jessie Florian), Jack O'Halloran (Moose Malloy), Anthony Zerbe (Laird Brunette), Harry Dean Stanton (Billy Rolfe), Jim Thompson (Judge Grayle), John O'Leary (Lindsay Marriott), Kate Murtagh (Frances Amthor), Walter McGinn (Tommy Ray), Jimmy Archer (Georgie), Joe Spinell (Nick), Sylvester Stallone (Jonnie), Burton Gilliam (Cowboy).

10. THE BIG SLEEP. United Artists, 1978. 99 minutes. Color.
    P: Elliott Kastner & Michael Winner. **D:** Michael Winner. **SC:** Michael Winner, from the novel by Raymond Chandler. **PH:** Robert Paynter. **ED:** Freddie Wilson. **MUS:** Jerry Fielding.

    Cast: Robert Mitchum (Philip Marlowe), Sarah Miles (Charlotte Sternwood), Candy Clark (Camilla Sternwood), Richard Boone (Lash Canino), James Stewart (General Sternwood), Oliver Reed (Eddie Mars), Joan Collins (Agnes Lozelle), John Mills (Inspector Carson), Colin Blakely (Harry Jones), Edward Fox (Joe Brody), Harry Andrews (Butter Norris), Richard Todd (Barker), Diana Quick (Mona Grant), James Donald (Inspector Gregory), John Justin (Arthur Gwynne Geiger), Simon Turner (Karl Lundgren), Martin Potter (Owen Taylor), David Savile (Regan), Dudley Sutton (Lanny), Don Henderson (Lou), Nik Forster (Croupier), Joe Ritchie (Taxi Driver), Patrick Durkin (Reg), Derek Deadman (Man in Bookstore).

Chapter 10

RAFFLES

THE BROTHER-IN-LAW OF Sherlock Holmes's (q.v.) creator Sir Arthur Conan Doyle, Ernest William Hornung wrote a number of books and short stories about gentleman thief, or cracksman, A. J. Raffles, who spent most of his literary career baffling detectives with his robbery exploits. In his later years, however, Raffles turned to detection and aided the law like his French counterpart Arsène Lupin (q.v.) and later American thief-turned-sleuth Michael Lanyard, the Lone Wolf (see B/V). Like Sherlock Holmes's Dr. Watson, Raffles had a chronicler, his friend and helper, Bunny Manders. Most of the films about Raffles deal with his ability to outwit the law although he was usually reformed by the love of a fair damsel.

E. W. Hornung's initial Raffles novel, *The Amateur Cracksman*, was published in 1899, and two years later *Raffles: The Further Adventures of the Amateur Cracksman* appeared. In 1903 the play *Raffles: The Amateur Cracksman* by Eugene Wiley Presbrey appeared on Broadway. In 1905 Hornung's novel about Raffles, *Thief in the Night*, was published; in 1909 *Mr. Justice Raffles* appeared. Following Hornung's death in 1921, Barry Perowne wrote more Raffles adventures, such as *The Return of Raffles* (1933), *Raffles in Pursuit* (1934), *Raffles vs. Sexton Blake* (1937), and *Raffles and the Key Man* (1940).

Raffles' first screen outing came in 1905 when Vitagraph made the one-reeler THE ADVENTURES OF RAFFLES, THE AMATEUR CRACKSMAN starring J. Barney Sherry as Raffles. The film was the first to be made by the company's Flatbush Studios. Between 1908 and 1911 the

Danish Nordisk Company made a baker's dozen Sherlock Holmes films, and a trio of them featured the Baker Street sleuth at odds with Raffles. Viggo Larsen starred in the series as Holmes and also wrote and directed the series entries. Raffles, who was portrayed by Forrest Holger-Madsen, was featured in the first three films in the Nordisk series, SHERLOCK HOLMES IN DEATHLY DANGER (also known as SHERLOCK HOLMES RISKS HIS LIFE), RAFFLES ESCAPES FROM PRISON, and THE SECRET DOCUMENT, all issued in 1908. SHERLOCK HOLMES IN DEATHLY DANGER found Holmes at odds with both Raffles and Professor Moriarty (Otto Dethlefsen), who had teamed up to get rid of their common nemesis. By the film's end both the villains were behind bars, but in the follow-up, RAFFLES ESCAPES FROM PRISON, the cracksman is free again with Holmes on his trail, a plot device used in the final effort, THE SECRET DOCUMENT. While the Holmes series then carried on without Raffles, the character was the subject of the 1910 Danish production, RAFFLES, as well as a 1911 Italian serial also called RAFFLES.

By the teens, the Raffles character was well known enough to be satirized on film—in 1914 Mack Sennett's Keystone Films made the two-reel comedy BAFFLES, GENTLEMAN BURGLAR, directed by Harry Lehrmann and starring Ford Sterling in the title role. In Britain Raffles' name was used in a series of comedies in the "Pimple" series about a silly character played by Fred Evans. Joe Evans appeared as Raffles in the series in: WHAT HAPPENED TO PIMPLE, THE GENTLEMAN BURGLAR; PIMPLE AND THE STOLEN PLANS; THE ADVENTURES OF PIMPLE, THE SPIRITUALIST (all 1914); MRS. RAFFLES NEE PIMPLE; JUST PIMPLE; PIMPLE COPPED (all 1915); PIMPLE'S A WOMAN IN THE CASE; PIMPLE'S MONKEY BUSINESS (both 1916); and SAVING RAFFLES (1917).

In 1917 John Barrymore starred in RAFFLES, THE AMATEUR CRACKSMAN for the newly formed L. Lawrence Weber Photodrama Corporation. The story had Raffles at a country estate where he is suspected of stealing the Melrose diamonds, and Detective Bedford (Frederick Perry) swears to apprehend him for the crime. To save himself, as well as to win the love of beautiful Gwendolyn (Evelyn Brent), Raffles takes the gems from the real thief (Mike Donlin) and returns them. *Variety* stated, "By virtue of its artistry, intensely sustained suspense and irrefutable logic, [the film] must grip audiences for many seasons." In 1920 the Hornung character was the subject of a second Italian production, RAFFLES, LADRA GENTILUOMO. The next year, Gerald Ames, who had earlier had the title role in London Films' ARSENE LUPIN (1916) (q.v.), starred as Raffles in MR. JUSTICE RAFFLES, taken from E. W. Hornung's 1909 novel. The plot had Raffles helping a young woman blackmailed by a moneylender.

In 1925 Universal made RAFFLES, THE AMATEUR CRACKSMAN, which former film idol King Baggot directed from E. W. Hornung's 1901 novel and Eugene Wiley Presbrey's 1903 play. *Photoplay* termed the film a "good crook story," but said it was "marred by some slow direction." On a cruise Raffles (House Peters) warns Gwendolyn Amersteth (Miss Du Pont) that her diamond necklace will be stolen. It is, but it is returned to her before the ship docks. The woman then invites Raffles to her country estate, and there detective Captain Bedford (Frederick Esmelton) plans to use a paroled crook to help him trap Raffles. Gwendolyn warns the cracksman, and the two run away and get married.

For Raffles' sound debut, producer Samuel Goldwyn began work on RAFFLES in 1930 for United Artists release, with Harry D'Arrast directing. The producer and director were soon disagreeing, and George Fitzmaurice took over and finished directing the production in which Ronald Colman played the title role. The previous year Colman had portrayed BULLDOG DRUMMOND (see B/V) for Samuel Goldwyn. RAFFLES had the cracksman falling in love with heiress Gwen (Kay Francis) and promising her he would give up being a thief, but when his friend Bunny (Bramwell Fletcher) needs money, Raffles plans to steal Lady Melrose's (Alison Skipworth) diamond necklace. Detective MacKenzie (David Torrence) of Scotland Yard

Kay Francis, Ronald Colman *(center)* and Bramwell Fletcher in RAFFLES
(United Artists, 1930)

gets wind of Raffles' plan, but the cracksman steals the
necklace and is cornered by MacKenzie. With Gwen's aid,
Raffles is able to escape through a secret passage in a clock,
and they head to Paris to get married.

THE RETURN OF RAFFLES was produced in England
by director Mansfield Markham in 1932, and it was based
on the E. W. Hornung stories. The plot had Raffles
(George Barraud) at a house party given by Lady Truwode
(Sydney Fairbrother) and being framed for stealing a
necklace. With the aid of pal Bunny (Claud Allister),
Raffles is able to clear himself as well as win the love of
beautiful Elga (Camilla Horn).

Nearly a decade after his 1930 version of RAFFLES,
Samuel Goldwyn remade the film in 1939 with David
Niven in the title role. The story had cracksman Raffles
foiling Scotland Yard Detective MacKenzie (Dudley
Digges) in a series of robberies with the lawman vowing to

From left: Douglas Walton, David Niven, and Olivia de Havilland in RAFFLES (United Artists, 1939)

bring in the debonair crook. Loving beautiful Gwen (Olivia de Havilland), Raffles plans to give up his profession, but when friend Bunny (Douglas Walton) needs money to pay his gambling debts, Raffles plans to steal Lady Melrose's (Dame May Whitty) necklace. He does so, but MacKenzie has crook Crawshaw (Peter Godfrey) accused of the crime in order to capture Raffles. Lord Melrose (Lionel Pape) offers a reward for the return of the necklace. Raffles accepts the reward money, which he gives to Bunny. At the finale, Raffles agrees to pay his debt to society before returning to Gwen. RAFFLES was a successful remake, but a sequel to it was shelved when star David Niven left Hollywood to return to England to join that country's entry into World War II.

The gentleman thief was featured on CBS radio's "Raffles, the Amateur Cracksman" in 1934. In 1945 Horace Braham portrayed the sleuth in the radio series "Raffles."

In 1958 a Mexican version of the Hornung character appeared in RAFFLES, also called EL RAFFLES MEXICANO, with Rafael Bertrand in the title role. It was filmed at Churubusco Studios in Mexico City.

Filmography

1. THE ADVENTURES OF RAFFLES, THE AMATEUR CRACKSMAN. Vitagraph, 1905. One reel.
   Cast: J. Barney Sherry (Raffles).

2. SHERLOCK HOLMES IN DEATHLY DANGER. Nordisk, 1908. One reel.
   D-SC: Viggo Larsen.
   Cast: Viggo Larsen (Sherlock Holmes), Forrest Holger-Madsen (Raffles), Otto Dethlefsen (Professor Moriarty), Elith Pio (Billy), Paul Gregaard, Gustav Lund, Aage Brandt, August Blom.
   Also called SHERLOCK HOLMES RISKS HIS LIFE.

3. RAFFLES ESCAPES FROM PRISON. Nordisk, 1908. One reel.
   D-SC: Viggo Larsen.
   Cast: Viggo Larsen (Sherlock Holmes), Forrest Holger-Madsen (Raffles), Elith Pio (Billy), Paul Gregaard, Gustav Lund, Aage Brandt, August Blom.

4. THE SECRET DOCUMENT. Nordisk, 1908. One reel.
   D-SC: Viggo Larsen.
   Cast: Viggo Larsen (Sherlock Holmes), Forrest Holger-Madsen (Raffles), Elith Pio (Billy), Paul Gregaard, Gustav Lund, Aage Brandt, August Blom.

5. RAFFLES. Nordisk, 1910.

6. RAFFLES. Italian, 1911. Serial.

7. WHAT HAPPENED TO PIMPLE, THE GENTLEMAN BURGLAR. Folly Films, 1914. 745 feet.
   D-SC: Fred Evans & Joe Evans.
   Cast: Fred Evans (Pimple), Joe Evans (Raffles).

8. PIMPLE AND THE STOLEN PLANS. Folly Films, 1914. 975 feet.
   D-SC: Fred Evans & Joe Evans.
   Cast: Fred Evans (Pimple), Joe Evans (Raffles).

9. THE ADVENTURES OF PIMPLE, THE SPIRITUALIST. Folly Films, 1914. 810 feet.

D-SC: Fred Evans & Joe Evans.
Cast: Fred Evans (Pimple), Joe Evans (Raffles).

10. MRS. RAFFLES NEE PIMPLE. Folly Films, 1915. 892 feet.
D-SC: Fred Evans & Joe Evans.
Cast: Fred Evans (Pimple), Joe Evans (Raffles).

11. JUDGE PIMPLE. Folly Films, 1915. 756 feet.
D-SC: Fred Evans & Joe Evans.
Cast: Fred Evans (Pimple), Joe Evans (Raffles).

12. PIMPLE COPPED. Folly Films, 1915. 745 feet.
D-SC: Fred Evans & Joe Evans.
Cast: Fred Evans (Pimple), Joe Evans (Raffles).

13. PIMPLE'S A WOMAN IN THE CASE. Piccadilly, 1916. 980 feet.
D-SC: Fred Evans & Joe Evans.
Cast: Fred Evans (Pimple), Joe Evans (Raffles).

14. PIMPLE'S MONKEY BUSINESS. Piccadilly, 1916. 1,800 feet.
D-SC: Fred Evans & Joe Evans.
Cast: Fred Evans (Pimple), Joe Evans (Raffles).

15. SAVING RAFFLES. Piccadilly, 1916. 940 feet.
D-SC: Fred Evans & Joe Evans.
Cast: Fred Evans (Pimple), Joe Evans (Raffles).

16. RAFFLES, THE AMATEUR CRACKSMAN. L. Lawrence Weber Photodrama Corporation, 1917.
P: L. Lawrence Weber. **D:** George Irving. **SC:** Anthony B. Kelly, from the play by Eugene Wiley Presbrey.
Cast: John Barrymore (Raffles), Evelyn Brent (Gwendolyn Vidal), Frederick Perry (Detective Bedford), Frank Morgan (Bunny), Mike Donlin (Thief), H. Cooper Cliffe, Christine Mayo, Mathilda Brundage, Nita Allen.

17. RAFFLES, LADRA GENTILUOMO. Italian, 1920.

18. MR. JUSTICE RAFFLES. Hepworth, 1921. Six reels.
D: Gerald Ames & Gaston Quiribet. **SC:** Blanche McIntosh, from the novel by E. W. Hornung.
Cast: Gerald Ames (Raffles), Eileen Dennes (Camilla Belsize), James Carew (Dan Levy), Hugh Clifton (Teddy Garland), Lionel Watts (Bunny), Gwynne Herbert (Lady Laura Belsize), Henry Vibart (Mr. Garland), Peggy Patterson (Dolly Fairfield), Pino Conti (Foreigner), Townsend Whitling (Tough).

19. RAFFLES, THE AMATEUR CRACKSMAN. Universal/Jewel, 1925. Six reels.
    D: King Baggot. **SC:** Harvey Thew, from the novel by E. W. Hornung and the play by Eugene Wiley Presbrey. **PH:** Charles Stumar.
    Cast: House Peters (Raffles), Miss Du Pont (Gwendolyn Amersteth), Frederick Esmelton (Detective Bedford), Hedda Hopper (Mrs. Clarice Vidal), Walter Long (Crawshaw), Winter Hall (Lord Amersteth), Kate Lester (Lady Amersteth), Freeman Wood (Bunny Manners), Roland Bottomley (Lord Crowley), Lillian Langdon (Mrs. Tilliston), Robert Bolder (Mr. Tilliston).

20. RAFFLES. United Artists, 1930. Eight reels.
    P: Samuel Goldwyn. **D:** Harry D'Arrast & George Fitzmaurice. **SC:** Sidney Howard, from the novel by E. W. Hornung and the play by Eugene Wiley Presbrey. **PH:** George Barnes & Gregg Toland. **ED:** Stuart Heisler. **AD:** William Cameron Menzies & Park French. **RECORDER:** Oscar Lagerstrom. **ASST DIR:** H. Bruce Humberstone. **TD:** Gerald Grove & John Howell.
    Cast: Ronald Colman (Raffles), Kay Francis (Gwendolyn), Bramwell Fletcher (Bunny), Frances Dade (Ethel), David Torrence (Detective MacKenzie), Alison Skipworth (Lady Melrose), Frederick Kerr (Lord Melrose), John Rogers (Crawshaw), Wilson Benge (Barraclough).

21. THE RETURN OF RAFFLES. Markham, 1932. 71 minutes.
    P-D: Mansfield Markham. **SC:** W. J. Balef.
    Cast: George Barraud (Raffles), Camilla Horn (Elga), Claud Allister (Bunny), A. Bromley Davenport (Sir John Truwode), Sydney Fairbrother (Lady Truwode), H. Saxon-Snell (Von Spechen).

22. RAFFLES. United Artists, 1939. 71 minutes.
    P: Samuel Goldwyn. **D:** Sam Wood. **SC:** John Van Druten & Sidney Howard, from the novel by E. W. Hornung and the play by Eugene Wiley Presbrey. **PH:** Gregg Toland. **ED:** Sherman Todd. **MUS:** Victor Young. **SETS:** Julie Heron. **COSTUMES:** Travis Banton.
    Cast: David Niven (Raffles), Olivia de Havilland (Gwendolyn), Dame May Whitty (Lady Melrose), Dudley Digges (Detective MacKenzie), Douglas Walton (Bunny), Lionel Pape (Lord Melrose), E. E. Clive (Barraclough), Peter Godfrey (Crawshaw), Margaret Seddon (Maude Holden), Gilbert Emery (Bingham), Hilda Plowright (Wilson), Vesey O'Davoren (Butler), George Cathrey (Footman), Keith Hitchcock (Merton), Forrester Harvey (Umpire), Jimmy Finlayson (Cabby), George Atkinson (Attendant), Gibson Gowland, George Kirby, Herbert Clifton (Villagers), Wilfred Lucas,

Larry Dodds, John Power, Colin Kenny, Charles Coleman (Bobbies).

23. RAFFLES. Almaneda Films, S. de R. L., 1958.
    D-SC: Alejandro Galindo. **PH:** Raul Martinez Solares. **ED:** Fernando Martinez. **MUS:** Gustavo Cesar Carrion. **AD:** Gunther Gerszo. **SOUND:** Ernesto Caballero.
    Cast: Rafael Bertrand (Raffles), Martha Mijares, Arturo Martinez, José Baviera, Pedro D'Aguillon, León Barroso, Prudencia Griffel, Alfonso Carti, Mario Chavez, Miguel Arenas, Quentin Bulnes.
    Also called EL RAFFLES MEXICANO.

Chapter 11

SEXTON BLAKE

FIRST APPEARING IN *The Halfpenny Marvel* boy's weekly magazine in 1893, the character of Sexton Blake, as created by Hal Meredith, soon developed into a popular literary figure, a crime fighter who was both athletic and cerebral. By the time the stories about Blake were appearing in the *Union Jack* weekly tabloid later in the decade, he had taken up residence at London's Baker Street and carried on scientific detection in the best Sherlock Holmes tradition. He acquired a Cockney paperboy assistant, Tinker, as well as a landlady, Mrs. Bardell. Amalgamated Press began publishing *The Sexton Blake Library* in 1915, and the series continued until 1959, while Blake remained the major attraction of the *Union Jack* until 1933 when it became *Detective Weekly* and continued with the Sexton Blake stories. Fleetway Publications produced *Detective Weekly*, and in 1938 they came out with *The Sexton Blake Annual*. From 1959 to 1963 Mayflower-Dell Publications put out *The Sexton Blake Library*.

In addition to his literary exposure, Sexton Blake proved to be a popular stage attraction in Great Britain. In 1907 C. Douglas Carlile's play *Sexton Blake* appeared in London, and the next year Horace Hunter toured in the title role of *Sexton Blake, Detective*, a variation of Carlile's play. In 1909 the actor-playwright adapted it to the screen and also directed SEXTON BLAKE, in which Carlile portrayed Blake, who tries to save the daughter of a squire from matrimony with a killer. The same year Carlile was Blake again in THE COUNCIL OF THREE; here he takes on the guise of a go-between for a gang in order to save a young woman they have kidnapped. In 1910 C. Douglas Carlile portrayed Sexton Blake in two more films, LADY CANDALE'S DIAMONDS, in which the detective is on the trail of jewel thieves, and THE JEWEL THIEVES RUN TO EARTH BY SEXTON BLAKE, where Blake saves a jewelry store clerk from being killed by a gun operated by a clock. Carlile played the sleuth for the fifth time in the 1912 film SEXTON BLAKE VS. BARON KETTLER, a Humanity Story Films release about the detective on the trail of stolen plans.

In 1914 a trio of Sexton Blake films appeared—all written and directed by Charles Raymond with Phillip Kay as Blake and Lewis Carlton as Tinker. THE MYSTERY OF THE DIAMOND BELT had Blake on the trail of a robber who poses as a lord in order to rob a businessman; BRITAIN'S SECRET TREATY found Blake posing as a foreign war minister in order to capture a notorious German spy; and THE KAISER'S SPY had Blake tracking down the leader of a German spy ring, a scientist operating in a remote forest tower. In 1915 James Duncan played the sleuth in J. Russell Bogue's play *Sexton Blake on the East Coast*, and Charles Raymond directed another trio of Blake movies, this time starring Harry Lorraine as the detective and Bert Rex as Tinker. The first of the film trio was THE STOLEN HEIRLOOMS, which had Blake trying to save a former gambler from a theft charge and nearly being done in by the real crook. THE COUNTERFEITERS had Blake and Tinker on the trail of a forgery gang and being captured in an old windmill, but escaping to round up the criminals. THE THORNTON JEWEL MYSTERY found Blake trying to aid a man framed on a robbery charge by a young woman. In 1919 Harry Lorraine produced and directed THE FURTHER EXPLOITS OF SEXTON BLAKE: THE MYSTERY OF S. S. *OLYMPIC*, but Douglas Payne, who had been the villain in THE MYSTERY OF THE DIAMOND BELT, portrayed Blake with the sleuth out to capture a gang that has murdered a scientist for his formula and kidnapped his daughter. Douglas Payne portrayed Sexton Blake for the second time in the 1922 British feature film, THE DORRINGTON DIAMONDS, with the detective again on the trail of a gang of jewel thieves.

By the midteens the character of Sexton Blake was popular enough in British films to be satirized. In 1915 Folly Films issued SEXTON PIMPLE, with Fred Evans as a comic sleuth who saves the King of Cork from foreign agents. Prior to this, in 1913, a detective called Bexton Slake set out to save a kidnapped infant in THE WOULD-BE DETECTIVE, and in 1919 a comedy called I WILL, I WILL, I WILL combined the characters of Sherlock Holmes and Sexton Blake into one Sherlock Blake, played by Wally Bosco, who helps a young man win the love of a society girl.

Toward the end of the silent-film era, Sexton Blake was featured in a series of a half-dozen two-reelers made by British Filmcraft. The umbrella title for the series was SEXTON BLAKE, and Langhorne Burton played the title role, while Mickey Brantford was Tinker, and Mrs. Fred Emney played Mrs. Bardell. The plots of these short subjects had Blake and Tinker involved in the solving of various crimes, and the titles were THE CLUE OF THE SECOND GOBLET, BLAKE THE LAWBREAKER, SEXTON BLAKE—GAMBLER, SILKEN THREADS, THE GREAT OFFICE MYSTERY, and THE MYSTERY OF THE SILENT DEATH.

In the 1930s George Curzon portrayed Sexton Blake in a trio of features, probably the best known of all the movies based on the Sexton Blake character, each based on a novel about the detective. George Curzon (1896–1976) was a naval officer who began acting on stage in 1924 and in films in 1930. Among his screen works were AFTER THE BALL ('32), MURDER AT COVENT GARDEN ('34), THE SCOTLAND YARD MYSTERY ('34), THE MAN WHO KNEW TOO MUCH ('34), LORNA DOONE ('35), YOUNG AND INNOCENT ('37), THE MIND OF MR. REEDER ('39), UNCLE SILAS ('47), THE CRUEL SEA ('53), and WOMAN OF STRAW ('64). Curzon's Sexton Blake was a handsome, solid, and intellectual hero involved in almost serial-like adventures.

The initial George Curzon film in the series was SEX-

TON BLAKE AND THE BEARDED DOCTOR, issued in 1935 and made by British Fox. Produced and directed by George A. Cooper, the film was adapted to the screen by Rex Hardinge from his book *The Blazing Launch Murder*. The plot had Sexton Blake on the trail of a bearded doctor (Henry Oscar) who murders men for their insurance and here tries to blackmail a young woman (Gillian Maude) and an insurance agent (Phil Ray) before Blake stops him. British Fox then produced a second 1935 release, SEXTON BLAKE AND THE MADEMOISELLE, which Alex Bryce directed and photographed from producer Michael Barringer's script, based on G. H. Teed's novel. Here Blake is hired by a financier to retrieve stolen bonds, but the detective finds that the man is really a crook and that the young woman (Lorraine Grey) took the bonds to get revenge on the financier for cheating her father. In both features, Tony Sympson played Tinker.

In 1936 Arthur Wontner portrayed Sexton Blake in Donald Stuart's play *Sexton Blake* at London's Prince Edward Theatre. Detective film fans best remember Wontner for having played Sherlock Holmes (q.v.) in five British films in the 1930s.

George Curzon returned to the role of Sexton Blake for the third and final time in the best known of all the films based on the character, SEXTON BLAKE AND THE HOODED TERROR, based on Pierre Quiroule's novel *Mystery of Caversham Square*. The reason the film is so well known is that British bogeyman Tod Slaughter co-starred as a master criminal known as the Snake. An international crime ring called the Hooded Terror plagues London, and Sexton Blake is called in to stop it and its leader, the Snake. Eventually he discovers that wealthy Michael Larron (Tod Slaughter) is really the Snake, but Blake is forced to let him escape as he rescues beautiful Julie (Greta Gynt) from the master criminal's clutches. Evidently the film was to have a sequel which never materialized, although the feature itself was reissued in 1942.

In SEXTON BLAKE AND THE HOODED TERROR David Farrar played a character called Granite Charlie, and in 1944 Farrar took over the role of Blake in two features for

H. B. Hallam *(left)* and George Curzon in SEXTON BLAKE AND THE HOODED TERROR (M-G-M, 1938)

Anglo-American, MEET SEXTON BLAKE and THE ECHO MURDERS. Born in 1908 and a newspaperman before coming to films in 1937, David Farrar appeared in British features like A ROYAL DIVORCE ('38), DANNY BOY ('41), PENN OF PENNSYLVANIA ('41), THE DARK TOWER ('43), and BLACK NARCISSUS ('47), before work in Hollywood in films like THE SEA CHASE ('55), ESCAPE TO BURMA ('55), and PEARL OF THE SOUTH PACIFIC ('55), plus a couple of Spanish-made epics, SOLOMON AND SHEBA ('59), and JOHN PAUL JONES ('59). MEET SEXTON BLAKE had the detective and Tinker (John Varley) on the trail of photographs and a ring taken from a man killed in an air raid. The pictures hold the key to a formula for a new type of metal for the construction of aircraft, and the two track down the thief. THE ECHO MURDERS was a spy thriller in which Blake is asked to come to Cornwall by a man who is found murdered. The detective eventually links the killing to a German plot to set up an invasion base on the Cornwall coast, and he thwarts the spies' efforts.

Sexton Blake, in a much modernized version, returned to the screen in 1958 in still another spy melodrama, MURDER AT SITE THREE, based on H. Howard Baker's novel. On the east coast of England, a Royal Air Force security officer is murdered at an intercontinental ballistic missile base. Sexton Blake (Geoffrey Toone) and pal Tinker (Richard Burrell) are called in to investigate, and they uncover a plot by foreign spies to take over the site. The film was in the programmer class and marked Sexton Blake's final film appearance to date.

In 1967 and 1968 Laurence Payne portrayed Sexton Blake in the British Associated Rediffusion television series "Sexton Blake."

Filmography

1. SEXTON BLAKE. Melodrama Production Syndicate (Gaumont), 1909. Two reels.
   D: C. Douglas Carlile, from his play *Sexton Blake, Detective* and the story "Five Years Later" by W. Murray Graydon.
   Cast: C. Douglas Carlile (Sexton Blake), Russell Barry (Roger Blackburn).

2. THE COUNCIL OF THREE. London Cinematograph Company, 1909. Two reels.
   D: S. Wormald.
   Cast: C. Douglas Carlile (Sexton Blake).

3. LADY CANDALE'S DIAMONDS. London Cinematograph Company, 1910. Two reels.
   D-SC: S. Wormald.
   Cast: C. Douglas Carlile (Sexton Blake).

4. THE JEWEL THIEVES RUN TO EARTH BY SEXTON BLAKE. Gaumont, 1910. 810 feet.
   D-SC: S. Wormald.
   Cast: C. Douglas Carlile (Sexton Blake).

5. SEXTON BLAKE VS. BARON KETTLER. Humanity Story Films, 1912. 645 feet.

D: Hugh Moss.
Cast: C. Douglas Carlile (Sexton Blake).

6. THE MYSTERY OF THE DIAMOND BELT. I. B. Davidson, 1914. 39 minutes.
   D-SC: Charles Raymond.
   Cast: Phillip Kay (Sexton Blake), Lewis Carlton (Tinker), Douglas Payne (George Marsden Plummer), Eve Balfour (Kitty the Moth), Percy Moran (Flash Harry), Austin Camp (Jack Braham), Lily Maxwell (Nora Plummer), Harry Graham (Maurice Braham).

7. BRITAIN'S SECRET TREATY. I. B. Davidson, 1914. Three reels.
   D-SC: Charles Raymond. **ST:** Andrew Murray.
   Cast: Phillip Kay (Sexton Blake), Lewis Carlton (Tinker), Thomas Canning (The Count).

8. THE KAISER'S SPY. I. B. Davidson, 1914. Three reels.
   D-SC: Charles Raymond.
   Cast: Phillip Kay (Sexton Blake), Lewis Carlton (Tinker).

9. THE STOLEN HEIRLOOMS. I. B. Davidson/Walthurdaw, 1915. Three reels.
   D-SC: Charles Raymond.
   Cast: Harry Lorraine (Sexton Blake), Bert Rex (Tinker).

10. THE COUNTERFEITERS. I. B. Davidson, 1915. Three reels.
    D-SC: Charles Raymond. **ST:** John W. Bobin.
    Cast: Harry Lorraine (Sexton Blake), Bert Rex (Tinker), Jack Jarman, N. Watts-Phillips.

11. THE THORNTON JEWEL MYSTERY. I. B. Davidson, 1915. Three reels.
    D-SC: Charles Raymond.
    Cast: Harry Lorraine (Sexton Blake), Bert Rex (Tinker), Miss Vere (Flash Kate).

12. THE FURTHER EXPLOITS OF SEXTON BLAKE: THE MYSTERY OF THE S. S. *OLYMPIC*. Atlantic Films (Gaumont), 1919. Four reels.
    P-D: Harry Lorraine.
    Cast: Douglas Payne (Sexton Blake), Marjorie Villis (Gwendolyn Howard), Jeff Barlow (Mr. Reece), Frank Dane (Hamilton), Neil Warrington (Tinker), William Brandon.

13. THE DORRINGTON DIAMONDS. Screen Plays, 1922.
    P: Percy Nash. **D-SC:** Jack Denton.
    Cast: Douglas Payne (Sexton Blake), George Bellamy (Tinker), Mildred Evelyn, Jeff Barlow, Cecil Burke.

14. SEXTON BLAKE. British Filmcraft (Paramount), 1928. Two reels
each.
P: George J. Banfield.
Series Titles:
- THE CLUE OF THE SECOND GOBLET.
  D: George A. Cooper. **SC:** G. H. Teed.
  Cast: Langhorne Burton (Sexton Blake), Mickey Brantford
  (Tinker), Fred Raynham (George Marsden-Plummer), Gabrielle
  Morton (Helen), Leslie Perrins (Fairbairn).
- BLAKE THE LAWBREAKER.
  D: George A. Cooper.
  Cast: Langhorne Burton (Sexton Blake), Mickey Brantford
  (Tinker), Fred Raynham, Thelma Murray, Leslie Perrins, Philip
  Desborough.
- SEXTON BLAKE—GAMBLER.
  D: George J. Banfield.
  Cast: Langhorne Burton (Sexton Blake), Mickey Brantford
  (Tinker), Marjorie Hume (Joan Fairfield), Frank Atherley (Lord
  Fairfield), Adeline Hayden Coffin (Lady Fairfield), Oscar Rosan-
  der (Ralph Garvin).
- SILKEN THREADS.
  D: Leslie Eveleigh.
  Cast: Langhorne Burton (Sexton Blake), Mickey Brantford
  (Tinker), Leslie Perrins (Stormcroft), Marjorie Hume (Nadia
  Petrowski), Frank Atherley (Man), Mrs. Fred Emney (Mrs.
  Bardell).
- THE GREAT OFFICE MYSTERY.
  SC: Lewis Jackson.
  Cast: Langhorne Burton (Sexton Blake), Mickey Brantford
  (Tinker), Fred Raynham (Gordon Wincliffe), Gabrielle Morton
  (Sadie), Ronald Curtis (Kestrel).
- THE MYSTERY OF THE SILENT DEATH.
  D: Leslie Eveleigh.
  Cast: Langhorne Burton (Sexton Blake), Mickey Brantford
  (Tinker), Roy Travers (Reece), Thelma Murray (Peggy), Ray
  Raymond (Ross), Mrs. Fred Emney (Mrs. Bardell).

15. SEXTON BLAKE AND THE BEARDED DOCTOR. British Fox
(M-G-M), 1935. 64 minutes.
P-D: George A. Cooper. **SC:** Rex Hardinge, from his novel *The
Blazing Launch Murder*.

Cast: George Curzon (Sexton Blake), Henry Oscar (Dr. Gibbs), Gillian Maude (Janet), Tony Sympson (Tinker), Phil Ray (Jim Cameron), John Turnbull (Inspector Donnell), Edward Dignon (Hawkins), James Knight (Red), Donald Wolfit (Percy), Johnnie Schofield, Ben Williams.

16. SEXTON BLAKE AND THE MADEMOISELLE. Fox British (M-G-M), 1935. 63 minutes.

   P-SC: Michael Barringer, from the novel by G. H. Teed. **D-PH:** Alex Bryce.

   Cast: George Curzon (Sexton Blake), Lorraine Gray (Roxanne), Edgar Norfolk (Inspector Thomas), Tony Sympson (Tinker), Raymond Lovell (Captain), Ian Fleming (Henry Norman), Vincent Holman (Carruthers), Wilson Coleman (Pierre), Ben Williams, Henry Peterson, William Collins.

17. SEXTON BLAKE AND THE HOODED TERROR. M-G-M, 1938. 70 minutes.

   P-D: George King. **SC:** A. R. Rawlinson, from the novel *Mystery of Caversham Square* by Pierre Quiroule. **PH:** Hone Glendinning. **ED:** John Seabourne. **MUS:** Jack Beaver. **AD:** Philip Rawcombe.

   Cast: George Curzon (Sexton Blake), Tod Slaughter (Michael Larron), Greta Gynt (Julie), Tony Sympson (Tinker), Charles Oliver (Max Fleming), Marie Wright (Mrs. Bardell), David Farrar (Granite Charlie), Norman Pierce (Inspector Bramley), H. B. Hallam (Bertrand), Pedro (Himself), Max Faber, Carl Melene, Alex Huber, Philip Holles, Len Sharpe.

18. MEET SEXTON BLAKE. Anglo-American, 1944. 80 minutes.

   P: Louis H. Jackson. **D-SC:** John Harlow, from the novel *The Case of the Stolen Dispatches* by Anthony Parsons. **PH:** Geoffrey Faithfull.

   Cast: David Farrar (Sexton Blake), John Varley (Tinker), Magda Kun (Yvonne), Gordon McLeod (Inspector Venner), Manning Whiley (Raoul Sudd), Kathleen Harrison (Mrs. Bardell), Dennis Arundell (Johann Sudd), Cyril Smith (Belford), Ferdi Mayne (Slant-Eyes), Betty Huntley-Wright (Nobby), Jean Simmons (Eva Watkins), Roddy Hughes, Charles Farrell, Tony Arpino, Charles Rolfe, Philip Godfrey, Billy Howard, John Powe, Mark Jones, Jack Vyvan, Henry Wolston, David Keir, Elsie Wagstaffe, Brookes Turner, Alfred Harris, Margo Johns, Olive Walter.

19. THE ECHO MURDERS. Anglo-American, 1945. 75 minutes.

   P: Louis H. Jackson. **D-SC:** John Harlow, from the novel *Terror of Tregarwyth* by John Sylvester. **PH:** James Wilson.

   Cast: David Farrar (Sexton Blake), Pamela Stirling (Stella Duncan), Dennis Price (Dick Warren), Julien Mitchell (James Duncan), Dennis Arundell (Rainsford), Cyril Smith (Morgan), Ferdi Mayne (Dacier), Kynaston Reeves (Beales), Patric Curwen (Dr. Grey),

Johnnie Schofield, Paul Groft, Desmond Roberts, Danny Green, Tony Arpino, Vincent Holman, Howard Douglas, Billy Howard, Anders Timberg, Victor Weske, Gerald Pring, Noel Dainton, Charles Hersee, Olive Walter.

20. MURDER AT SITE THREE. Exclusive, 1958. 67 minutes.
    P: Charles Leeds. **D:** Francis Searle. **SC:** Paddy Manning O'Brine, from the novel *Crime Is My Business* by W. Howard Baker. **PH:** Bert Mason.
    Cast: Geoffrey Toone (Sexton Blake), Barbara Shelley (Susan), Jill Melford (Paula Dane), John Warwick (Commander Chambers), Richard Burrell (Tinker), Reed de Rouen (McGill), Harry Towb (Kenney), Gordon Sterne, Theodore Wilhelm.

Chapter 12

THE SHADOW

WALTER S. GIBSON, using the pseudonym of Maxwell Grant, wrote 282 novels about the mysterious crime fighter–detective the Shadow for *The Shadow Magazine*, from 1931 to 1949. In addition he provided the continuities for *The Shadow Comics*, which began in 1940. Since the Shadow was known as Lamont Cranston after the character's first adventures, it was in that guise that he came to radio in 1936 on "The Shadow" starring Orson Welles. The half-hour series ran for two decades on radio with Robert Hardy Andrews and Bill Johnstone also playing the title role, although Bret Morrison is the actor most associated with the part, since he played it from 1944 to 1956. By the late 1930s Lamont Cranston had a lady love, Margo Lane, and on radio she was played by a number of actresses, including Agnes Moorehead and Lesley Woods. On radio the Shadow used invisibility to thwart his foes, while in print he wore a black cape and slouch hat and often remained in the shadows but was not invisible. This latter aspect of the character was the one adopted to films for most of the Shadow's rather diverse screen career.

Maxwell Grant's magazine novel *The Ghost of the Manor* was adapted to the screen for the Shadow's first film adventure, THE SHADOW STRIKES, issued by Grand National in the summer of 1937. The adventure had Lamont Cranston (Rod La Rocque) stopping a bank heist, with the police believing he is behind the caper. Cranston pretends to be a lawyer in order to get the goods on the real robber, and two murders occur before he is able to wrap up the case. While *Boxoffice* magazine called the film the

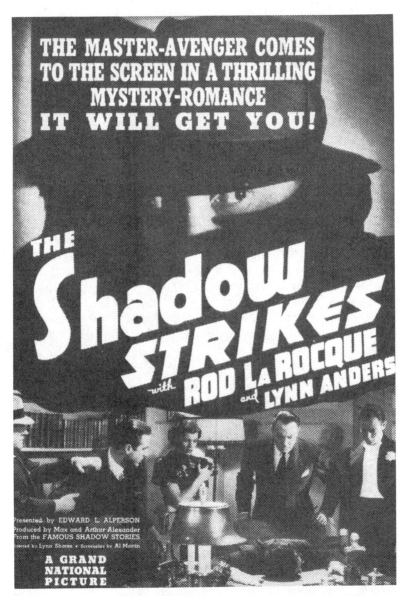

Advertisement for THE SHADOW STRIKES (Grand National, 1937)

"chilliest," *Variety* said it was "marred by stupid dialog, feeble acting, misdirection and dangling continuity." Undaunted, Grand National starred Rod La Rocque in a second Shadow outing, INTERNATIONAL CRIME, issued in the spring of 1938 and based on Maxwell Grant's *Fox Hound*. This movie had Lamont Cranston as a newspaper reporter romancing another newshound, Phoebe Lane (Astrid Allwyn), who tries to aid him in solving the murder of a rich businessman. Eventually Cranston uncovers the fact that a foreign spy (William Von Bricken) was behind the killing, as he is working with gangsters in trying to stop a large bond issue. The film was one of the first to hint that Germany was an enemy of the U.S. in the pre–World War II era, and it was certainly a big improvement over THE SHADOW STRIKES, but by the time it was released Grand National was in financial troubles and no further celluloid Shadow adventures came from the company before it folded in 1939.

In 1937 Columbia released a B-picture called THE SHADOW, but it was a crime melodrama and not based on the Maxwell Grant creation. In 1940, however, Columbia did release the fifteen-chapter serial, THE SHADOW, which was based on the radio and magazine stories by Maxwell Grant. Victor Jory took on the title role. Lamont Cranston is asked by a group of government and civic leaders to stop the Black Tiger and his minions, who have been sabotaging strategic government installations, railroads, and aircraft to obtain materials needed to produce his weapons. During the course of the action, Cranston appears not only as the Shadow but also as Chinese merchant Lin Chang in his efforts to infiltrate the Black Tiger's headquarters. The serial was an action filled one, and the villain not only used a death ray but also spoke to his minions via the electrified head of the statue of a cat.

Kane Richmond (1906-1973) is the actor most associated with the Shadow on film, having starred as the character in a trio of popular movies issued by Monogram in 1946. Richmond came to films in 1930; during the 1930s and 1940s he was a leading man in B-pictures and serials. Among his many films were DEVIL TIGER ('34), LET'S FALL IN LOVE ('34), THE LOST CITY ('35, serial), BORN

TO FIGHT ('36), CHARLIE CHAN IN PANAMA ('40), KNUTE ROCKNE—ALL AMERICAN ('40), MURDER OVER NEW YORK ('40), PLAYGIRL ('41), GREAT GUNS ('41), HARD GUY ('41), STAGE STRUCK ('46), and BRICK BRADFORD ('47, serial).

THE SHADOW RETURNS, issued early in 1946, was the first of the Monogram films, and its plot had Lamont Cranston (Kane Richmond) and Margo Lane (Barbara Reed) looking into the matter of the theft of precious gems allegedly stolen from a grave. The Shadow discovers that the jewels contain the secret for the formula to a plastic material which would revolutionize the business world. Despite the fact *Variety* termed the film a "trite whodunit," it was followed in the spring by BEHIND THE MASK, also called THE SHADOW BEHIND THE MASK. Here a blackmailing newspaper gossip columnist (Robert Shayne) is murdered, and Lamont Cranston (Kane Richmond) is blamed for the crime. Taking on his alter ego, the Shadow, Cranston tries to solve the case and clear his name with the aid of girlfriend Margo Lane (Barbara Reed). They discover that the killing was connected with a bookmaking racket and that one of the murdered man's associates is behind the illegal activities. *Variety* noted, "Meller factors are excellent, but comedy, introduced frequently, is too contrived and obvious."

Late in the summer of 1946 Monogram issued its final Shadow feature, THE MISSING LADY, also known as THE SHADOW AND THE MISSING LADY. The plot has Lamont Cranston (Kane Richmond) on the trail of a precious jade statuette and the killer of the art dealer who owned it. When another art dealer (Douglas Wood) is also killed, Lamont is blamed for the crime, and he and Margo Lane (Barbara Reed) try to prove his innocence. When another murder takes place, Cranston gets into further trouble but plays a hunch that the trio of killings is hooked up with the missing jade. He is able finally to solve the case and turn two killers over to the law. While the film's poster announced, "It's Mystery at Its Best . . . Greatest of Year's Detective Thrillers," THE MISSING LADY proved to be the end of the trail for Monogram's Shadow series.

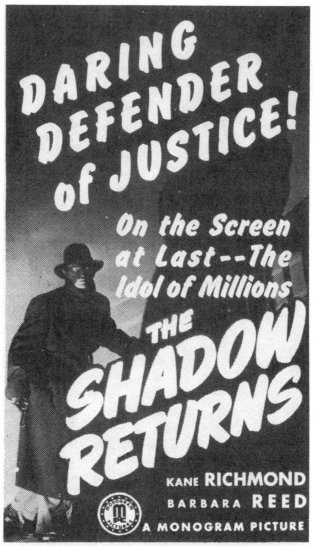

Advertisement for THE SHADOW RETURNS (Monogram, 1946)

During the course of this brief series, Barbara Reed portrayed Margo Lane in all three films, and Pierre Watkin enacted the role of Police Commissioner Weston, Lamont Cranston's uncle. In the last two films, George Chandler played Cranston's butler, Shrevvie.

Although *The Shadow Magazine* ceased publication in 1949, Republic Pictures attempted to produce a television series based on the Maxwell Grant character in the mid-1950s. Starring Richard Derr as Cranston, several episodes of "The Shadow" TV series were produced, but the project failed to sell and Republic ceased production in 1958. Late that year, however, the studio pasted together several of the filmed segments from the series and issued the feature film, INVISIBLE AVENGER. The plot has Lamont Cranston (Richard Derr) and Jogendra (Mark Daniels) coming to New Orleans to investigate the murder of jazz musician Tony Alcalde (Steve Dano) and getting involved with an exiled Central American revolutionary. They eventually put a stop to the group that is trying to keep the rightful ruler (Dan Mullin) of Santa Cruz from returning to power. Noted cinematographer James Wong Howe directed some of the footage used in the film. In 1962 MPA Films released the feature film BOURBON STREET SHADOWS, which added footage to INVISIBLE AVENGER although retaining its basic plot line.

By the mid-1960s a resurgence of interest in the Shadow took place and several of *The Shadow Magazine* novels were reissued. In 1974 Pyramid Publications began a series of new Shadow novels, which resulted in nearly two dozen books. In the 1980s several old and new Shadow novels remained in print, and plans were afoot for a new Shadow feature film.

While the Shadow has had a long and successful sleuthing career, the adventures of Lamont Cranston have had their best success on the printed page and on radio. While the movies made about the character have not been without interest, they have failed to capture the flavor of mystery and adventure which made the character so popular.

Filmography

1. THE SHADOW STRIKES. Grand National, 1937. 61 minutes.
   P: Max & Arthur Alexander. **D:** Lynn Shores. **SC:** Al Martin. **ST:** George Herman Coxe, from the novel *The Ghost of the Manor* by Maxwell Grant.
   Cast: Rod La Rocque (Lamont Cranston), Lynn Anders (Marcia Delthern), Walter McGrail (Winstead Comstock), James Blakely (Jasper Delthern), Kenneth Harlan (Captain Breen), Norman Ainsley (Kendricks), John Carnavale (Warren Berrenger).

2. INTERNATIONAL CRIME. Grand National, 1938. 64 minutes.
   P: Max & Arthur Alexander. **D:** Charles Lamont. **SC:** Jack Natteford, from the novel *Fox Hound* by Maxwell Grant. **PH:** Marcel Piccard. **ED:** Charles Henkell.
   Cast: Rod La Rocque (Lamont Cranston), Astrid Allwyn (Phoebe Lane), Thomas Jackson (Commissioner Weston), Oscar O'Shea (Heath), William Von Bricken (Flotow), William Pawley (Honest John), Walter Bonn (Stefan), William Moore (Burke), Lew Hearn (Moe Shrevnitz).

3. THE SHADOW. Columbia, 1940. 15 chapters.
   P: Larry Darmour. **D:** James V. Horne. **SC:** Joseph Poland, Ned Dandy & Joseph O'Donnell. **PH:** James S. Brown, Jr. **ED:** Dwight Caldwell. **MUS:** Lee Zahler.
   Cast: Victor Jory (Lamont Cranston), Veda Ann Borg (Margo Lane), Roger Moore (Vincent), Robert Fiske (Turner), J. Paul Jones (Marshall), Jack Ingram (Flint), Charles Hamilton (Roberts), Ed Peil, Sr. (Inspector Cardona), Frank LaRue (Commissioner Weston), Charles King (Russell), Gordon Hart (Hill), Lloyd Ingraham, Kit Guard, George De Normand, Lew Sergant, Charles Sullivan Constantine Romanoff, Joe Caits.
   Chapter Titles: The Doomed City, The Shadow Attacks, The Shadow's Peril, In the Tiger's Lair, Danger Above, The Shadow's Trap, Where Horror Waits, The Shadow Rides the Rails, The Devil in White, The Underground Trap, Chinatown at Dark, Murder by Remote Control, Wheels of Death, The Sealed Room, The Shadow's Net Closes.

4. THE SHADOW RETURNS. Monogram, 1946. 61 minutes.
   P: Joe Kaufman. **D:** Phil Rosen. **SC:** George Callahan. **PH:** William A. Sickner. **ED:** Ace Herman. **AD:** Dave Milton.
   Cast: Kane Richmond (Lamont Cranston), Barbara Reed (Margo Lane), Joseph Crehan (Inspector Cardona), Pierre Watkin (Commissioner Weston), Tom Dugan, Robert Emmett Keane, Frank Reicher, Lester Dorr, Rebel Randall, Emmett Vogan, Sherry Hall, Cyril Delevanti.

5. BEHIND THE MASK. Monogram, 1946. 67 minutes.
    P: Joe Kaufman. **AP:** Lou Brock. **ED:** Phil Karlson. **SC:** George
    Callahan. **ST:** Arthur Hoerl. **PH:** William A. Sickner. **ED:** Ace
    Herman. **AD:** Dave Milton.
    Cast: Kane Richmond (Lamont Cranston), Barbara Reed (Margo
    Lane), George Chandler (Shrevvie), Joseph Crehan (Inspector
    Cardona), Pierre Watkin (Commissioner Weston), Dorothea Kent
    (Jennie), Joyce Compton (Lulu), Marjorie Hoshelle (Mae Bishop),
    June Clyde (Edith Merrill), Robert Shayne (Brad Thomas), Lou
    Crosby (Marty Greene), Edward Gargan (Dixon), Bill Christy (Copy
    Boy), James Cardwell (Jeff Mann), Nancy Brickman (Susan), Dewey
    Robinson (Head Waiter), Marie Harmon (Girl), Ruth Cherrington
    (Dowager), James Nataro (Reporter).
    Also called THE SHADOW BEHIND THE MASK.

6. THE MISSING LADY. Monogram, 1946. 60 minutes.
    P: Joe Kaufman. **AP:** George Callahan. **D:** Phil Karlson. **SC:** George
    Callahan. **PH:** William A. Sickner. **ED:** Ace Herman. **AD:** Dave
    Milton. **ASST DIR:** Doo Joos & Kenny Kossler. **SETS:** Ray Bolts.
    Cast: Kane Richmond (Lamont Cranston), Barbara Reed (Margo
    Lane), George Chandler (Shrevvie), James Flavin (Inspector Car-
    dona), Pierre Watkin (Commissioner Weston), Dorothea Kent
    (Jennie), Jack Overman (Ox Welsh), George J. Lewis (Jon Field),
    James Cardwell (Terry Blake), Bert Roach (Waldo), Douglas Wood
    (Alfred Kester), Gary Owen (Johnson), Ray Teal (Slater), Jo Carroll
    Dennison (Gilda Marsh), Ralph Dunn (Clark), Dewey Robinson
    (Bartender), Frances Robinson (Ann Walsh), Anthony Warde
    (Lefty), Claire Carleton (Rose Dawson), Almira Sessions (Effie),
    Nora Cecil (Millie).
    Also called THE SHADOW AND THE MISSING LADY.

7. INVISIBLE AVENGER. Republic, 1958. 60 minutes.
    P: Eric Sayers & Emanuel Demby. **D:** James Wong Howe & John
    Sledge. **SC:** George Bellak & Betty Jeffries. **PH:** Willis Winford &
    Joseph Wheeler. **ED:** John Hemel. **MUS:** Edward Dutreil. **SETS:**
    Sam Leve & Bernard Weist.
    Cast: Richard Derr (Lamont Cranston), Helen Westcott (Tara),
    Mark Daniels (Jogendra), Dan Mullin (Pablo & Victor Ramirez),
    Jeanne Neher (Felicia Ramirez), Steve Dano (Tony Alcalde), Lee
    Edwards (Colonel), Jack Doner (Billy), Leo Bruno (Rocco), Sam
    Page (Charlie).

8. BOURBON STREET SHADOWS. MPA Films, 1962. 70 minutes.
    P-D: Ben Parker. **SC, PH, ED, MUS, SETS, Cast:** see INVISIBLE
    AVENGER, above.

Chapter 13

SHERLOCK HOLMES

THE CHARACTER OF SHERLOCK HOLMES, created by Arthur
Conan Doyle in 1887 in his first novel, *A Study in Scarlet*,
has proved to be the most popular of all fictional detectives. Doyle was a London physician who decided to write
a detective novel after studying the methods of Dr. Joseph
Bell of Edinburgh University, who was well known for his
powers of deductive reasoning. To his character, Doyle
gave not only the powers of deductive reasoning but also
a series of characteristics which endeared him to millions
of mystery fans for generations.

The combination of Doyle's five novels and fifty-six
short stories revolving around the adventures of the sleuth
provided a lengthy biography of the character. The
fictional Holmes was born circa 1858, the grandson of the
sister of the French military painter Vernet. He was the
younger brother of Mycroft Holmes. He attended London
University and for a time attended anatomical classes at St.
Bartholomew's Hospital, eventually developing a new test
for bloodstains, which replaced the guaiacum test.

Holmes began his private detective practice in 1877 and
continued for some quarter of a century, though from 1891
to 1893 he toured parts of Tibet and the Near East under
assumed names, after having been thought killed by his
notorious archenemy, Dr. Moriarty. Returning to London
in 1893, Holmes destroyed the remnants of Moriarty's
power structure and continued practicing until 1903 when
he retired to Sussex Downs and his hobby of beekeeping.
During World War I he was recalled to active service by the
king and broke up several espionage rings, residing for a

time in the United States and Ireland. For this work he received the Congressional Medal of Honor, a diamond sword from the king of Belgium, and the Versailles Plaque.

Holmes was the author of several monographs on various aspects of deductive reasoning and a couple of short accounts of his cases. He was most proud of his work, "Practical Handbook of Bee Culture with Some Observations on Segregation of the Queen." Practically all of Holmes's casework was compiled by his friend and colleague, Dr. John H. Watson, who was associated with him in most of his cases.

Arthur Conan Doyle was still creating new cases for his famous detective when, in 1900, Holmes came to the screen in American Mutoscope and Biograph's short film, SHERLOCK HOLMES BAFFLED. This early flicker was actually a comedy using stop-action photography and had Holmes failing to apprehend a burglar! Five years later, Vitagraph made THE ADVENTURES OF SHERLOCK HOLMES, which was also released under the alternate title of HELD FOR RANSOM.

A third Holmes film appeared in 1908, produced by an Italian company, Ambrosio, called RIVAL SHERLOCK HOLMES. Of this 584-foot film, the *Moving Picture World* said, "A pictorial detective story of merit, with many lightning changes of disguise by the detective in his pursuit of lawbreakers. Exciting scenes and physical encounters are numerous. A sensational subject of superb dramatic effect, without objectionable features."

Later in the same year, Crescent Films released SHERLOCK HOLMES AND THE GREAT MURDER MYSTERY, based on Doyle and Edgar Allan Poe's "Murders in the Rue Morgue," which had the detective going into a trance to pin a murder on an escaped gorilla.

In December 1908 another foreign-made Holmes product hit the American shores in a production called SHERLOCK HOLMES IN DEATHLY DANGER. Made by the Nordisk Film Company of Copenhagen, this was the first Holmes film to list players, a practice which was then coming into vogue. Thus the first screen-credited Holmes was Viggo Larsen, who also directed the film, which was not based on any Doyle work, though the character of Moriarty was in the plot. Larsen and Alwin Neuss, among others, played the detective in other one-reel films for Nordisk until 1911. Other titles included SHERLOCK HOLMES IN THE GAS CHAMBER in 1908 and THE MURDER AT BAKER STREET in 1911. All the films were shown in the U.S. by the Great Northern Film Company.

With the demise of the Nordisk series, a German company, Vitascope, produced a group of films based on the works of Maurice Leblanc with Sherlock in a game of wits with the French jewel thief Arsène Lupin. Five titles were filmed in the series which had the umbrella title of ARSENE LUPIN VS. SHERLOCK HOLMES. In the 1945 Mexican film ARSENIO LUPIN (q.v.), the jewel thief is at odds with detective Herlock Shlomes.

In 1912 a co-production outfit, the Franco-British Film Company, made eight two-reelers which were supervised by Doyle himself. A French actor named Georges Treville played Holmes in the films. THE SPECKLED BAND was released in U.S. by Union Features.

The same year Thanhouser starred Harry Benham in SHERLOCK HOLMES SOLVES THE SIGN OF THE FOUR, in which Holmes uncovered the efforts of a British army officer's son to secure the half of his father's fortune which had been bequeathed to the daughter of a family friend. Benham was a matinee idol of the silent screen and played a number of classical characters on film, including Robert Louis Stevenson's DR. JEKYLL AND MR. HYDE ('12).

In 1914 Vitascope issued the first German version of DER HUND VON BASKERVILLE with Alwin Neuss back as Holmes. Rudolph Meinert directed and Richard Oswald (who would helm the 1929 German version of the same novel) adapted the Doyle work to the screen. The film was so successful that it resulted in a series of sequels: DAS EINSAME HAUS (The Isolated House), WIE ENTSTAND DER HUND VON BASKERVILLE (How the Hound of the Baskervilles Returned), DAS UNHEIMLICHE ZIMMER (The Uncanny Room), DAS DUNKEL SCHLOSS (The

Dark Castle), DR. MacDONALD'S SANITARIUM (all '15), and THE HOUSE WITHOUT ANY WINDOWS ('16).

British producer G. B. Samuelson turned out A STUDY IN SCARLET in 1914 starring James Braginton as Holmes; the same year Universal issued its shorter version of the same book with Francis Ford, who also directed, as the sleuth. In this two-reeler, Ford's younger brother, Jack, played Dr. Watson. Jack Ford later became famous as director John Ford. In 1916 G. B. Samuelson did another Holmes film, THE VALLEY OF FEAR, with H. A. Saintsbury as the Baker Street detective.

The most famous of all stage Sherlock Holmes, William Gillette, also brought his version of the sleuth to the screen in 1916. Essanay released SHERLOCK HOLMES, based on Gillette's 1899 play, which he had written with Doyle's consent. The stage work had incorporated a young helper for Holmes, named Little Billy, and a love interest, Alice Faulkner. Gillette was sixty-three when he made the film, and he would continue to tour in his play about Holmes until his death in 1937. He also became the first radio Holmes, doing the part on NBC on October 20, 1930, in "The Adventure of the Speckled Band."

William Gillette's stage version of SHERLOCK HOLMES was remade in 1922 by Goldwyn Pictures, with John Barrymore as the sleuth. Though his greatest stage and film triumphs still lay ahead of him, Barrymore was very popular at this time, and his casting as Sherlock was a good one. Filmed in the U.S., some location shots were made in London, adding authenticity to the whole affair, directed by Albert Parker. Barrymore played the part to the hilt, using several disguises. Gustav von Seyffertitz, one of film's greatest villains, was a very evil and spiderlike Moriarty; Carol Dempster was Alice Faulkner, whom Holmes married at the film's end; Roland Young was Dr. Watson. Barrymore later described Young as apparently "modest, self-effacing," but then complained, "When I saw the completed film, I was flabbergasted, stunned and almost became an atheist on the spot. That quiet, agreeable bastard had stolen, not one, but every damned scene!"

John Barrymore *(left)* and Gustav von Seyfferitz in SHERLOCK HOLMES (Goldwyn, 1922)

Also in the cast were Louis Wolheim, Hedda Hopper, William Powell, and Reginald Denny. Released in the U.S. in May 1922, it played in Britain as MORIARTY.

The year before the Barrymore SHERLOCK HOLMES was made, another of Doyle's novels, THE HOUND OF THE BASKERVILLES, was filmed in England. This version of the book starred Eille Norwood as Holmes; Maurice Elvey directed it in five reels. Films Booking Office released this rather mediocre film in the U.S. in 1922. In 1921, Norwood and Elvey began a collaboration on fifteen two-reel shorts with Norwood as Holmes. It was called THE ADVENTURES OF SHERLOCK HOLMES. With screenplays by Elvey, William J. Elliott, and Arthur Conan

Doyle himself, the series contained such titles as A SCANDAL IN BOHEMIA, YELLOW FACE, THE COPPER BEECHES, THE BERYL CORONET, THE DYING DETECTIVE, THE RED-HEADED LEAGUE, and THE MAN WITH THE TWISTED LIP.

This group and its successor, another group of fifteen two-reelers with Norwood, called THE FURTHER ADVENTURES OF SHERLOCK HOLMES, were released in Britain in 1922 by the Alexander Film Corporation and in the U.S. by Educational Films. In these groups of films, Dr. Watson was portrayed by Hubert Willis, who carried on with Norwood in the third and last series of fifteen, released in 1923 in Britain by the Stoll Film Corporation and called THE LAST ADVENTURES OF SHERLOCK HOLMES.

In 1923 Elvey and Norwood did a second feature from Doyle, THE SIGN OF FOUR. Thus Eille Norwood portrayed Sherlock Holmes more times on screen than has any other actor, in two features and forty-five shorts. Born in Yorkshire in 1861, Norwood began working on the stage in 1884 and made his film debut in 1911. Practically all of his film appearances were as Holmes, though he did star in Edgar Wallace's CRIMSON CIRCLE in 1922. Norwood died in 1948.

The Germans did another version of DER HUND VON BASKERVILLE in 1929 with Richard Oswald directing matinee idol Carlyle Blackwell portraying Holmes. Though he was the last silent-film Holmes, Blackwell's career was on the quick descent after having been a star for some twenty years, since the early days of films. His broad acting style was not suitable to the talking era, though he still worked in supporting roles in B-films and bits in A-films, almost up until his death in 1955. Oswald's version of DER HUND VON BASKERVILLE was a good one, but it got little showing in the English-speaking world, though Grande/Bregtagne released it in Britain.

The best known of the early talking Holmeses was Clive Brook. Born Clifford Brook in London in 1891, he was a journalist and soldier before turning to the stage in 1919 and films three years later. At first a villain, he soon became a hero in films made on both sides of the Atlantic, most notably in UNDERWORLD ('27) and FOUR FEATHERS ('28). In 1929 Paramount cast him as Sherlock Holmes in the modern-day RETURN OF SHERLOCK HOLMES, which was based on Doyle's "Dying Detective" and "His Last Bow," with Basil Dean directing from his and Garrett Fort's screen adaption. The film had Holmes attending the wedding of Watson's daughter (Betty Lawford) to Roger Longmore (Phillips Holmes), which ends in tragedy when the groom's father is murdered. Delving into the case, Holmes finds that the murdered man was poisoned by one of Professor Moriarty's (Harry T. Morey) people, because the man had once worked with Moriarty on a transatlantic steamship and knew his identity. Using several disguises, Holmes clears the man's name and has Moriarty convicted of murder. Critic Mordaunt Hall said, "Clive Brook gives a nice easy performance." Dr. Watson was played by British actor H. Reeves-Smith.

In 1930 Sir Arthur Conan Doyle died; the year before he had made a fifteen-minute short for Fox Movietone in which he told how he created Sherlock Holmes. By this time, his opinion of his most famous character must have mellowed, for he claimed he enjoyed hearing from Holmes fans, though many years before he had tried to kill off his sleuth in the story "The Final Problem." An angry public, however, demanded Holmes's return, and although Doyle tried his hand at other forms of literature, including political writing, history, science fiction (the most famous of which was *The Lost World*), and even spiritism, his lasting contribution to the world of literature and film was Sherlock Holmes.

In the same year as Doyle's death, Clive Brook made his second appearance as Sherlock, in Paramount's all-star PARAMOUNT ON PARADE. In one sequence, which was a satire on detective films, William Powell was Philo Vance, Eugene Pallette was Sergeant Ernest Heath, both from the Philo Vance films, and Warner Oland was Sax Rohmer's Chinese villain, Dr. Fu Manchu. This very comical sketch had Jack Oakie as a murder victim, with

Holmes and Vance tracking down the killer, Fu Manchu, who did in both of the famous sleuths.

In 1930 the British began making a series of Holmes films, which though competently made were inferior to the U.S. releases of the period, due mainly to poor technical facilities. The first of these was THE SLEEPING CARDINAL, made by Twickenham, which introduced Arthur Wontner as Holmes and Ian Fleming as Watson. Wontner was a silent-film star in Britain whose descending career was given a much-needed boost with his Holmes films of the 1930s. The actor made his stage debut in 1897 and began in films in 1916, most notably starring in the JOSE COLLINS series in the 1920s. He worked in films into the 1950s and died in 1960 at the age of eighty-five. Australian born Ian Fleming, no relation to the James Bond creator, received his greatest acclaim as Dr. Watson in his films with Wontner, though he was continuously active in British films in a myriad of roles until his death in 1969 at the age of eighty-one.

THE SLEEPING CARDINAL was based on two Doyle stories, "The Final Problem" and "The Empty House," and was directed by Leslie S. Hiscott, who collaborated on the screenplay with Cyril Twyford. The complicated plot had Holmes again pitted against Professor Moriarty (Norman McKinnel), in a case involving gambling, an international counterfeiting ring, bank robberies, the British Foreign Office, and murder. The cast also contained two other Doyle characters: Minnie Rayner as Mrs. Hudson, the owner of the house at 221B Baker Street where Holmes had rooms, and Philip Hewland as Inspector Lestrade of Scotland Yard, Holmes's perennial nemesis on the side of the law. The film was shown in the U.S. in 1932 by First Division as SHERLOCK HOLMES' FATAL HOUR.

In 1931 the company Gaumont British made a seven-reel version of THE HOUND OF THE BASKERVILLES, with script and direction by V. Garteth Gundrey and dialogue by Edgar Wallace. The film, which had Robert Rendel as Holmes and Frederick Lloyd as Watson, was mediocre with poor production values. First Division showed it in the U.S. in 1932.

THE SPECKLED BAND was made by the British and Dominions Studios in 1931, with Raymond Massey making a believable Holmes. W. P. Lispcomb's screenplay had Holmes facing the evil Dr. Rylott (Lyn Harding), who planned to murder both of his stepdaughters for their inheritances. He killed the first of the girls, but the latter was saved by Holmes. Critics of the period, including Mordaunt Hall, thought Massey better than Clive Brook, and Herbert Wilcon said, "Mr. Massey's performance is pleasing, intelligent, and restrained." This seven-reeler was directed by Jack Raymond, with Athole Steward as Dr. Watson; it got U.S. release by First Division late in 1931.

Arthur Wontner made his second appearance as Holmes in Twickenham's MISSING REMBRANDT, which First Division released here in 1932. Ian Fleming, Minnie Raynor, and Philip Hewland repeated their roles. Directed by Leslie Hiscott, and based on Doyle's "Adventure of Charles Augustus Milverton," the film had Holmes against the evil Baron von Guntermann (Francis L. Sullivan), who stole a Rembrandt painting. In the course of the action, Holmes disguised himself as an old woman and a clergyman. One scene contained a police raid on a Limehouse opium den. Holmes eventually captured von Guntermann as well as his secretary (Dino Galvani), the latter wanted on a blackmail charge.

Associated Talking Pictures next starred Wontner and Fleming as Holmes and Watson in THE SIGN OF FOUR, which Graham Cutts and Rowland V. Lee directed. The plot had evil Jonathan Small (Gilbert Davis), a man with a wooden leg, coming from the mysterious East to terrorize the family of Major Sholto and acquire certain valuable jewels. Though the film closely stayed with Doyle's novel, the poor production values and photography were liabilities, as were the almost incomprehensible English accents, though most critics thought Wontner excellent as Holmes. World Wide released the film in the U.S.

Clive Brook portrayed Holmes for the third and last time in 1932 in Fox's SHERLOCK HOLMES. Directed by

William K. Howard and written by Bertram Millhauser, who later did five of the Universal films with Basil Rathbone, the plot had Holmes again against Moriarty (Ernest Torrance), who was using Chicago gangsters in an attempt to have London pub owners pay him protection money. Holmes disguised himself at times as an old aunt and a workman, and after apprehending Moriarty and putting an end to his evil scheme, he married Alice Faulkner (Miriam Jordan), and took up chicken farming. The film was based partially on William Gillette's play; Reginald Owen was Dr. Watson, and Howard Leeds played Little Billy. Mordaunt Hall thought, "Mr. Brook . . . is [a] quite engaging Holmes," though a number of reviews noted that Sherlock no longer used the needle, a practice he rarely engaged in on film.

Reginald Owen became the only screen actor to portray both Holmes and Watson when he played the former in A STUDY IN SCARLET, a film produced by World Wide in 1932, but sold to Fox, who released it in 1933. Owen was also given credit for continuity and dialogue. Robert Florey's screenplay had nothing to do with the Doyle novel. Here Holmes battled a criminal organization called the Scarlet Ring which in its Grange-like activities stole money and committed several murders. Edwin L. Marin directed, with Warburton Gamble as Dr. Watson, Alan Mowbray as Lestrade, and Tempe Pigott as Mrs. Hudson. Mordaunt Hall said, "Mr. Owen gives quite an effective performance as Holmes."

Two years passed before any new Holmes features were made, but in 1935 Gaumont-British and director Leslie S. Hiscott reunited Arthur Wontner and Ian Fleming in THE TRIUMPH OF SHERLOCK HOLMES. Holmes is about to retire when a man is murdered in an old castle. The man's wife tells Holmes the story in flashbacks. The man had been a member of a secret society called the Scourers, a terrorist group, and had given information to the police. Lestrade (Charles Mortimer) believed that one of the members had done the man in, but Holmes proved that Moriarty (Lyn Harding) was behind the murder. The film was based somewhat on "The Valley of Fear" by Doyle.

The (London) Times said, ''As a thriller . . . it has quite a lot to recommend it.'' Set in modern times, the film was shown in the U.S. by Olympia Macri Excelsior.

In 1937 Twickenham produced THE SILVER BLAZE from Doyle's short story, with Thomas Bentley directing. Arthur Wontner and Ian Fleming made their last screen appearances as the famous duo in this story, with Professor Moriarty (Lyn Harding) behind the disappearance of a racehorse in order to prevent it from running in a race. Again in a modern-day setting, the film was shown under a number of titles including SHERLOCK HOLMES' SILVER BLAZE and SHERLOCK HOLMES AND THE SILVER BLAZE. Astor released the film in the U.S. in 1941 under the title of MURDER AT THE BASKERVILLES, and it now plays on U.S. TV under the alternate title of ADVENTURE AT THE BASKERVILLES.

Lobby card for MURDER AT THE BASKERVILLES (Astor, 1941), U.S. release title for THE SILVER BLAZE (Twickenham, 1937)

The Germans returned to making Holmes films in 1937 with still another version of DER HUND VON BASKER-VILLES, which Karl Lamac directed, with Bruno Guttner as Holmes and photography by Willy Winterstein. The same year, Erich Engles directed Herman Speelmans as Holmes in DIE GRAUE DAME, which was based on the Muller-Puzika play *The Deed of the Unknown.*

In 1937 the Germans also produced a psuedo-Holmes film called DER MANN DER SHERLOCK HOLMES WAR, which had Hans Albers and Heinz Ruhmann as two down-and-out private detectives who masquerade as Holmes and Watson and who are brought to trial for their murders. In the trial sequence, an actor, playing Doyle, testifies on the defendant's behalf, causing them to be acquitted. Karl Hartl directed this UFA production, which had limited English-language release as TWO JOLLY ADVENTURERS, though the Doyle estate sued to have its U.S. exhibition halted.

In March of 1939, 20th Century-Fox released the most definitive, and perhaps the best, of all Sherlock Holmes films, THE HOUND OF THE BASKERVILLES, with the most popular actor to portray the detective on screen, Basil Rathbone. Born in South Africa in 1892, Rathbone made his stage debut in England in 1910 and came to the U.S. in 1912 in Shakespeare's TAMING OF THE SHREW. After serving in World War I, he returned to the stage and made his film debut for director Maurice Elvey in THE FRUIT-FUL VINE in 1921. Thereafter, he worked in British stage and films; in 1924 he made his U.S. film debut in PITY THE CHORUS GIRL? and began working on Broadway. With his good looks and fine voice, Rathbone had no trouble making it in talking films, and during the 1930s he established himself (as William K. Everson called him in *The Bad Guys)* as "probably the best all around villain the movies ever had." In DAVID COPPERFIELD ('35) he was the vicious Mr. Murdstone; in A TALE OF TWO CITIES ('35), the effete and cruel marquis de St. Evrémonde; in ANNA KARENINA ('35), he was the cold Karenin; and Tybalt in ROMEO AND JULIET ('36). He twice dueled with Errol Flynn, first time as the pirate Levasseur in

Clockwise, from top: Nigel Bruce, Basil Rathbone, and Nigel De Brulier in THE HOUND OF THE BASKERVILLES (20th Century–Fox, 1939)

CAPTAIN BLOOD ('35) and then as Sir Guy of Gisbourne in THE ADVENTURES OF ROBIN HOOD ('38). When he took on the role of Sherlock Holmes in 1939, Rathbone became typecast as the detective—so much so that in later years he was to develop a dislike for Doyle's character.

Director Sidney Lanfield and scripter Ernest Pascal closely followed the Doyle novel in filming THE HOUND OF THE BASKERVILLES, which opened with the credits superimposed over a shot of the misty, ancient Stonehenge, and then cut to a man running from something not seen in the night, something which emitted terrible inhuman cries. The actual plot centered around the murder of the Baron Baskerville and a similar attempt on the life of his son (Richard Greene, who oddly enough was billed before Rathbone and Nigel Bruce). The film was filled with red herrings (Lionel Atwill, John Carradine, Ralph Forbes, Beryl Mercer, Morton Lowery, Eily Malyon, among others); the climax with Holmes in the fog-shrouded cemetery, both hunting and hunted by the hound of the title, made this one of the best mystery films of all time. A good budget was allotted to the picture, but its main success rested with the perfect casting of the two principals, Basil Rathbone as Holmes and Nigel Bruce as Dr. Watson.

As Basil Rathbone was to become typecast as Holmes, so too did Nigel Bruce become his comrade, Dr. Watson. Bruce presented the picture of the lovable, loyal, and bumbling Watson, not really like the erudite physician whom Doyle used to relate Holmes's casework. Born in 1895, Bruce became a stage actor in 1920, working mostly in comedy. He made his screen debut in 1930. Later he came to Hollywood, where he became a staple of the British colony in the film capital. Among his better pre-Holmes films were TREASURE ISLAND ('34), BECKY SHARP ('35), and THE TRAIL OF THE LONESOME PINE ('36). With THE HOUND OF THE BASKERVILLES, however, he became firmly associated with Dr. Watson, and he played the role with Rathbone's Holmes until 1946. During those years, he also played the part on radio opposite Rathbone, and he continued to do so after the latter left the series. Bruce also made numerous appearances outside the Sherlock Holmes series, including THE CHOCOLATE SOLDIER ('41), LASSIE COME HOME ('43), THE CORN IS GREEN ('45), HONG KONG ('51), and LIMELIGHT ('53). In 1953 the actor was scheduled to portray Dr. Watson opposite Basil Rathbone in the latter's revival of the William Gillette play, but a heart attack forced him out of the show. Early in 1954, he did appear on TV on CBS's "Four Star Playhouse," but he died the same year.

So successful was THE HOUND OF THE BASKER-VILLES, that five months later in August 1939, 20th Century–Fox released the THE ADVENTURES OF SHER-LOCK HOLMES, still another adaption of William Gillette's play, with screenplay by Edwin Blum and William

Drake. Again with Rathbone and Bruce, the film eliminated the Alice Faulkner character, but Little Billy (Terry
Kilburn) was present, as was Mary Gordon as Mrs.
Hudson, a role she originated in THE HOUND and one
she would continue through the later Universal series.

Mary Gordon, a short Scottish actress of considerable
depth, was perfectly cast as the fussy but lovable owner of
221-B Baker Street, and was most famous for her cameos in
these films, despite having made hundreds of other films
in Hollywood during her career. She also portrayed Mrs.
Hudson in the radio series with Rathbone and Bruce. She
died in 1963 at the age of eighty-one.

THE ADVENTURES OF SHERLOCK HOLMES was as
disappointing as THE HOUND OF THE BASKERVILLES
had been satisfying. Although it boasted the same fine
production values as the earlier film, the picture never
seemed to jell in its plot, though several sequences were
good in themselves. Rathbone, in disguise as a cockney
entertainer at a garden party, was well done, and George
Zucco made an excellent Moriarty. In one scene, his cohort
Bassick (Arthur Hohl) inquires of the professor, "Holmes
again?" to which Moriarty replies, "Always Holmes—until
the end." The end comes in the Tower of London, from
which the professor was trying to lift the Crown Jewels,
when in a fight to the finish, Holmes knocks Moriarty off a
ledge to his death. This film did not arouse the interest or
acclaim the earlier film did, and the series was not
continued.

Rathbone and Bruce, however, continued to portray the
characters of Holmes and Watson on radio on NBC's
"Adventures of Sherlock Holmes," and did 273 broadcasts
in seven years, from 1939 to 1946. In one of these live
broadcasts, Rathbone made the boo-boo of his career. He
was supposed to say, "Watson, the board of directors is
nothing but a hoard of bores," though the spoken line was
not delivered in that manner.

Three years after the release of the second Fox film,
Universal issued SHERLOCK HOLMES AND THE VOICE
OF TERROR, which starred Basil Rathbone and Nigel
Bruce as Holmes and Watson in a modern-day setting.

Directed by John Rawlins, with screenplay by Lynn Riggs and Robert D. Andrews, the film was supposed to be based on Doyle's "His Last Bow," though the plot centered around the blitzkreig attack by the Germans on England. Holmes was called in by Sir Evan Barham (Reginald Denny, who had appeared in the 1922 SHER-LOCK HOLMES) of the Home Office, to find out the identity of the "voice of terror" who correctly prognosticated the exact time and place of the Nazi attacks. Also in the cast were Henry Daniell, as a red herring; Evelyn Ankers, as a Limehouse whore who aided Holmes in uncovering the identity of the "voice of terror"; and Thomas Gomez, as a British traitor collaborating with the Nazis. Mary Gordon was back as Mrs. Hudson; and Hillary Brooke, later the leading lady in a couple of the Universal-Holmes films, had a cameo as a cabbie. The end found the Nazi invasion of England thwarted and the "voice of terror" captured. Holmes delivered a soliloquy on patriotism and optimism which would become a standard feature for the series.

At Christmastime of 1942, Universal released the second in the series, SHERLOCK HOLMES AND THE SECRET WEAPON, which was directed by Roy William Neill, who was to continue in that capacity for the rest of the series. Born Roland de Gostrie in Ireland in 1890, Neill came to Hollywood in 1917 and began directing low-budget films with mysteries becoming his forte, as shown by LADY RAFFLES ('28), BLACK MOON ('34), THE BLACK ROOM ('35, with Boris Karloff), EYES OF THE UNDERWORLD ('41), and later BLACK ANGEL ('46, the year of his death).

The film also introduced British actor Dennis Hoey as Inspector Lestrade, a role he would play off and on throughout the series. Hoey, whose real name was Samuel Hyams, was born in England in 1893. After working as a singer, he made his stage debut in 1918 and went to Hollywood in 1931 where he worked steadily in films, his major success being in the Holmes series. In 1943 he played a Lestrade-like role for director Neill in FRANKEN-STEIN MEETS THE WOLFMAN. He died in 1960.

SHERLOCK HOLMES AND THE SECRET WEAPON

took a bit of its plot from Doyle's "Adventure of the Dancing Men," but was mainly an original screenplay by Edward T. Lowe, W. Scott Darling, and Edmund Hartmann. The plot had Professor Moriarty (played with great skill by Lionel Atwill) trying to locate the "secret weapon" of the title, a new bombsight developed by an inventor (William Post, Jr.) whom Holmes is assigned to protect. This time the evil professor meets his doom, after trying unsuccessfully to drain Holmes of all his blood, by falling through a trapdoor he himself had conceived, and drowning in the Thames.

In March 1943 Universal released SHERLOCK HOLMES IN WASHINGTON, which had the sleuth and Dr. Watson in that city on the track of a microfilm copy (concealed in a matchbook) of a highly secret government document. The

From left: George Zucco, Henry Daniell, Basil Rathbone, and Bradley Page in SHERLOCK HOLMES IN WASHINGTON (Universal, 1943)

film was from an original story by Bertram Millhauser, with a screenplay by Millhauser and Lynn Riggs. German agent Richard Stanley (George Zucco) is trying to get hold of the document as the matchbook passes from person to person. Henry Daniell had a secondary role as one of Stanley's henchman, and Thurston Hall gave a bravura performance as a United States senator whom Stanley tried to kill. The film was definitely not up to the standard of the previous entries in the series.

Bertram Millhauser also did the screenplay for SHERLOCK HOLMES FACES DEATH, which was based on Doyle's "Musgrave Ritual." In this, one of the best in the series, Holmes is called to spooky Musgrave Manor, the ancestral home of the accursed Musgraves, which for the war effort has been turned into a convalescent home for battle-fatigued soldiers, ministered over by Dr. Watson. With the murders of the last two male Musgraves, the focus of attention falls on an American soldier (Milburn Stone, Doc of TV's "Gunsmoke"), who is in love with the last of the Musgraves (Hillary Brooke). During a howling thunderstorm, Brooke reads the Musgrave Ritual, which ends when a lightning bolt breaks through a window and strikes a suit of armor.

The climax of the film occurs in a subterranean crypt, the set for which had first been used in DRACULA ('31). Halliwell Hobbes, in one of his many appearances in Holmes films, gave a sterling performance as the butler; Norma Varden was a cockney barmaid; and Peter Lawford had a bit part as a sailor in a pub sequence.

In 1943 Rathbone and Bruce made gag appearances as Holmes and Watson in the looney Olsen and Johnson comedy, CRAZY HOUSE. In one brief sequence, the camera cuts to Holmes, with Watson coming to bring him some vital news. Before the good doctor can divulge his message, Holmes announced, "I know Watson, Olsen and Johnson are coming." "But how did you know?" inquired the astonished doctor. "I am Sherlock Holmes. I know everything," said the sleuth.

Three Sherlock Holmes films appeared in 1944, the first of which was the poorest in quality. Based on Doyle's

"Final Problem" and a bit of *The Sign of the Four*, Bertram Millhauser's screenplay had Holmes at odds with a female villain, Adrea Spedding (Gale Sondergaard), the leader of a notorious murder ring, in THE SPIDER WOMAN, also known as SHERLOCK HOLMES AND THE SPIDER WOMAN. Though Spedding proved an admirable foe for the detective, her two attempts to do him in failed—as did this short film in keeping up with the quality of the series.

THE SCARLET CLAW, which Universal released in June 1944, was many pegs above its predecessor, with a screenplay by Edmund L. Hartmann and director Neill based on an original story by Paul Gangelin and Brenda Weisberg. The setting for the film was an isolated Canadian village in which a supernatural-like figure stalked the night murdering inhabitants with the weapon of the title. The viewer was hard-pressed to identify the villain, who turned out to be played in three different disguises by Gerald Hamer. One particularly poignant scene was the aftermath of the murder of the innkeeper's little daughter (Kay Harding). The film boasted a good cast including Paul Cavanagh, who appeared in three films in the series, as did Ian Wolfe, here as Drake the butler, and included a brief shot of one-time film idol William Desmond.

Director Neill introduced in PEARL OF DEATH one of the movies' most horrifying villains in the person of the Creeper, played by Rondo Hatton. Hatton, a victim of a disease of the pituitary gland called acromegaly, had been doing bits in films since 1930, but was "introduced" in this movie. So successful was his character that Universal starred him in two other "Creeper" films, HOUSE OF HORRORS ('46) and THE BRUTE MAN ('46), which the studio sold to PRC for release. Before his death in 1946, he also appeared with Gale Sondergaard in THE SPIDER WOMAN STRIKES BACK, a sequel to THE SPIDER WOMAN, though Holmes and Watson were not in the film.

Bertram Millhauser's screenplay for PEARL OF DEATH, which partially borrowed from Doyle's "Adventure of the Six Napoleons," had evil Naomi Drake (Evelyn Ankers) smuggling into England the notorious Borgia pearl, which

Advertisement for THE SCARLET CLAW (Universal, 1944)

had on it the blood of dozens of evildoers who had tried to possess it. A cohort of jewel thief Giles Conover (Miles Mander), Drake loses the pearl to Holmes, who gives it to the British Museum, from which it is then stolen by one of Conover's agents. He hides it in a wet plaster bust of Napoleon before he is apprehended. Conover sends out his agent, the Creeper, a madman who kills by snapping the spine of his victim, to locate the pearl among the six persons who have each bought a statue. The Creeper is shown in low lighting or in shadow and does not appear in full view until the startling climax when he is shot to death by Holmes after killing Conover, who planned to double-cross Drake, with whom the Creeper is in love.

The next entry in the series, THE HOUSE OF FEAR, was released in March 1945, the first of three Holmes films that year. Based on the Doyle story "The Five Orange Pips," with screenplay by Roy Chanslor, the film takes place in a haunted Scottish mansion in which are assembled the members of a group called the Good Comrades, all members of a club who are beneficiaries in the deaths of the other members. Holmes is called in when the members begin dropping off one by one, after receiving an envelope containing orange pips with the number of the remaining members. The so-called murderer is revealed in an exciting climax.

Bertram Millhauser's last screenplay in the series was WOMAN IN GREEN, which contained shades of Doyle's "Adventure of the Empty House," and centered on the murders of several young women, all of whom have their right forefinger amputated by the killer. Hillary Brooke was featured as Lydia, a hypnotist and murderer, in association with Dr. Moriarty (Henry Daniell, who lent a certain evil charm to the part). The killings, ministered to by Moriarty, prove to be part of a plan to blackmail a wealthy nobleman (Paul Cavanagh), who commits suicide. At the climax of the film, Lydia puts Holmes under her spell and tries to force him to walk off the ledge of a high building, but is thwarted by the appearance of Watson and the police. The not-really-hypnotized detective takes off

SHERLOCK HOLMES **159**

after Moriarty, who falls to his death when the drain pipe he grabs hold of breaks away from the building.

The last 1945 entry was a fast-paced one called PURSUIT TO ALGIERS, in which the action of Leonard Lee's original screenplay occurs on board an ocean liner on which Holmes and Watson are escorting an heir to an Eastern throne who is endangered by assassins. Dr. Watson pulls his usual bumbling antics, and the film is loaded with villains (Martin Kosleck, John Abbott, Frederick Worlock, Morton Lowry, and gigantic wrestler Wee Willie Davis). Although the film is well done, it lacks the flair of the better entries in the series.

In 1946 two Holmes films were issued by Universal which proved to be the last of the series. TERROR BY NIGHT, with an original screenplay by Frank Gruber, was one of the best of them all, a surprise for a film coming so late in the series. A number of murders take place on a train traveling from London to Edinburgh at night. Holmes and Watson are on board protecting the priceless diamond, the Star of India. The villain of the piece turns out to be a friend of Dr. Watson, Major Duncan-Bleek (Alan Mowbray), who is actually an imposter and a jewel thief after the diamond. The murder-on-a-train motif has often been used in films but rarely to better advantage than in this mystery.

The series ended in May 1946 when Universal released DRESSED TO KILL. Frank Gruber and Leonard Lee's screenplay had Holmes at odds with another female archcriminal, Hilda Courtney (Patricia Morison), who with her cohort Hamid (Harry Cording) are out to find the hiding place of engraving plates stolen from the Bank of England. The riddle to the hiding place is hidden in the tune of three music boxes produced in a Dartmoor prison by the plates' thief. The unusual climax of the film takes place in the library of the home of Samuel Johnson, where the plates have been secreted in a bookcase.

The Sherlock Holmes series could have continued at Universal, but Basil Rathbone refused to renew his contract. The actor also terminated his radio broadcasts as the famous sleuth, although Nigel Bruce remained for a time in the role of Watson. Among those who succeeded Rathbone as Holmes were Richard Gordon, Louis Hector, Tom Conway (famous in films as the Falcon and on radio as the Saint), Ben Wright, and John Stanley. Others to portray Dr. Watson were Leigh Lovel, Eric Snowden, Alfred Shipley, and Ian Martin. Besides playing Holmes, Louis Hector was also often cast as Dr. Moriarty on the series.

Rathbone continued to appear in films after leaving the series, and in 1950 he made his dramatic television debut on NBC's "Tele-Theatre" playing Sherlock Holmes. In 1953 he appeared in a limited run of the William Gillette play which his wife, Ouida Rathbone, adapted. Jack Raine played Dr. Watson (replacing the ailing Nigel Bruce) and Thomas Gomez was Moriarty. In the late 1950s, Rathbone made a series of long-playing record albums for the Caedmon label, and on them he read several Sherlock Holmes stories. On "The Stories of Sherlock Holmes" (LP-171) he read "The Adventure of the Speckled Band" and "The Final Problem," and on volume 2 of the record (LP-1208) he read "The Red Headed League." Volume 3 (LP-1120) contained "A Scandal in Bohemia," and volume 4 (LP-1240) had Rathbone reading "Silver Blaze."

In the 1950s Basil Rathbone centered his professional activities on stage and television, although he did make occasional film appearances, such as the villain in WE'RE NO ANGELS ('55) and as the snobbish political leader in John Ford's LAST HURRAH ('58). In the 1960s he toured the college campus circuit reading from the classics. One critic referred to him as "the Heifetz of the spoken word." His last years, however, were spent in cheap horror films—although TALES OF TERROR ('62) and A COMEDY OF TERRORS ('64) were a cut above the ordinary—and the movies' greatest villain and sleuth ended his career in HILLBILLYS IN A HAUNTED HOUSE ('67) and AUTO-SIA DE UN FANTASMA ('68), one of the most inane films ever made, before his sudden death from heart failure in the summer of 1967.

For a number of years, no new Holmes material

appeared on celluloid, though in 1954 British television carried a series of thirty-nine half-hour episodes of a series, "The New Adventures of Sherlock Holmes," which starred Ronald Howard as Holmes and Howard Marion-Crawford as Dr. Watson. This Paris-made series was syndicated on U.S. television at the same time. Howard, the son of actor Leslie Howard, made a pleasing Holmes; Crawford, who died in 1969, was a stage and radio actor who made a good Dr. Watson.

In 1959 Hammer Films of England produced THE HOUND OF THE BASKERVILLES, which starred Peter Cushing as the sleuth and André Morell as Watson. This film compared favorably with the Basil Rathbone version. Terence Fisher directed from Peter Bryan's script, which closely followed the Doyle novel. It was made on a low budget, as had been Hammer's previous box office

Eille Norwood (1), John Barrymore (2), Clive Brook (3), Raymond Massey (4), Arthur Wontner (5), Basil Rathbone (6) as Sherlock Holmes; Peter Cushing in THE HOUND OF THE BASKERVILLES (Hammer Films/United Artists, 1959)

smashes, THE CURSE OF FRANKENSTEIN ('56) and HORROR OF DRACULA ('57), which Fisher directed with Cushing and Christopher Lee, who played the younger Baskerville in the Holmes film. The film turned out well though it did not make so much money as the studio had hoped, and a projected Holmes series was not continued. Cushing, who had a well-rounded career before becoming almost exclusively a horror star since 1957, was well cast as Holmes and did quite well in the part. Most critics considered André Morell an ideal Watson.

Four years after the Hammer film, a German company, CCC/Omnia, produced VALLEY OF FEAR, which took only Doyle's title and nothing else. Curt Siodmak's screenplay was a conglomerate of a series of events centered around Holmes's and Moriarty's attempts to get hold of a stolen necklace once worn by Cleopatra. Made in Germany, partially directed by Terence Fisher (with Frank Witherstein), the film made little sense and was so poorly put together that it did not get British release until 1968 under the title SHERLOCK HOLMES AND THE DEADLY NECKLACE. This dubbed version could get no U.S. playdates and was sold directly to television. The film was so poor that at its finale Moriarty (Hans Sohnker) was allowed to escape right in front of Holmes and Watson, which would seem to intimate that a series of films was to follow. This, mercifully, did not occur. Christopher Lee, who was Sir Henry Baskerville in the previous Hammer film, was Sherlock Holmes, and he claimed to be quite proud of his performance, though not of the film itself. Thorley Walters, also a British actor, made a very commendable Dr. Watson.

The British tried again with Holmes in 1965 with FOG. Produced by Herman Cohen and directed by James Hill, Donald and Derek Ford's screenplay had the sleuth at odds with Jack the Ripper in his attempt to solve the infamous Ripper murders which gripped London in terror at the turn of the century. Released in the U.S. early in 1966 by Columbia as A STUDY IN TERROR, Sy Oshinsky in the *Motion Picture Herald* said, "John Neville is superb as Sherlock Holmes; he may very well be the best interpreter

SHERLOCK HOLMES   **163**

of the . . . character . . . [this] fine production [is] . . . an intelligent and exciting vehicle for the return of Sherlock Holmes." Despite the quality of the film, it did very little business at the box office, and a series with Neville was not forthcoming. Donald Houston was Dr. Watson, and Frank Finlay played Lestrade.

In 1965 the British also made a second attempt at a Sherlock Holmes TV series with Douglas Wilmer as Holmes and Nigel Stock as Watson. Peter Cushing, the star of Hammer's HOUND OF THE BASKERVILLES, later replaced Wilmer. To date none of the episodes, all filmed in color, has played U.S. television.

Two Italian TV movies—THE HOUND OF THE BASKERVILLES and THE VALLEY OF FEAR, with Nando Gazzolo as Holmes—were produced in 1968 by Italy's official network, RAI—Radiotelevisione Italiane.

Veteran writer, producer, and director Billy Wilder attempted to make a definitive Sherlock Holmes film in 1970 with THE PRIVATE LIFE OF SHERLOCK HOLMES. The screenplay by Wilder and I.A.L. Diamond attempted to follow closely Doyle's stories in making a conglomerate picture of the detective, but it ended up as merely a series of dull episodes. The result was another SHERLOCK HOLMES AND THE DEADLY NECKLACE with good production values.

The screenplay was inconsistent with the Doyle works and even tried to make the detective a pervert. For one of the few times in his screen history, Holmes was actually shown indulging in the needle. In one ridiculous scene, Holmes spurned the affections of a forty-nine-year-old ballerina (Genevieve Page), who wished to have a child by him, and hinted that he had more of an interest in Dr. Watson. Under normal circumstances, Robert Stephens as Holmes and Colin Blakely as Watson might have made something of their parts, but both seemed to be lost in the maze of nonsense that Wilder and Diamond concocted in this film. Irene Handl played Mrs. Hudson, and Christopher Lee, the only actor to play both Sherlock Holmes and his brother on screen, portrayed Mycroft Holmes in a fine manner. However, the gaunt actor was hardly the corpulent character Doyle devised. Wilder spent over $10 million and three years in making the film, which proved to be a financial disaster as well as a critical one.

Another pseudo-Holmes film appeared in 1971, called THEY MIGHT BE GIANTS. Here George C. Scott played a retired judge named Justin Playfair who was under the delusion that he was the real Sherlock Holmes. With inverness, magnifying glass, and a female psychiatrist named Dr. Watson (Joanne Woodward), he went around modern-day New York City looking for an imaginary Moriarty. This Anthony Harvey–directed film proved to be unpopular both as a commercial and as a critical venture, although it was a pleasant comedy.

In the mid-1960s, Fritz Weaver played Holmes in the successful Broadway musical *Baker Street* which produced the best-selling song, "Married Man." Plans to film the musical never jelled, however.

Still another version of THE HOUND OF THE BASKER-VILLES, was made by Universal and shown over ABC-TV in 1972. Adapted by Robert E. Thompson, the telefilm served as a pilot for a series which did not sell. The seventy-three-minute color melodrama was shot on a low budget and was surprisingly dull despite an excellent performance by Stewart Granger as a white-haired Holmes. Bernard Fox as Watson, however, seemed to be doing a takeoff on Nigel Bruce, and the overall effect of the film was vapid.

In 1974 Keith McConnell portrayed Sherlock Holmes in the British-made MURDER IN NORTHUMBERLAND, for West End Productions, with Anthony Seerl as Watson. The plot had the duo traveling to York to investigate a murder involving a high-ranking British family. Sadly, the film has seen no U.S. release. Keith McConnell is widely associated with the role of Holmes due to his having portrayed the detective in another medium. In 1973 McConnell and Laurie Main portrayed Holmes and Watson on a Schlitz Malt Liquor TV commercial, followed by another the following year. In 1976 McConnell and Richard Peel were Holmes and Watson in Columbia's MURDER BY DEATH, but their parts were cut from most release prints, some say due to jealousy by big-name stars who played takeoffs on other famous fictional detectives trying to solve a mystery. It seems that Holmes and Watson arrive on the scene, solve the mystery, and depart, making the other characters look silly. On December 26, 1980, on CBS-TV's "Children's Mystery Theatre," Keith McConnell and Laurie Main again were Holmes and Watson in "The Treasure of Alpheus T. Winterborn," about a young boy (Keith Mitchell) trying to solve the mystery of a town's eccentric benefactor.

Douglas Wilmer and Thorley Walters returned to the roles of Sherlock Holmes and Dr. Watson in THE ADVENTURES OF SHERLOCK HOLMES' SMARTER BROTHER (20th Century–Fox, 1975), a spoof of the Doyle works, with Gene Wilder (who also wrote and directed the feature) as Sigi Holmes, the younger brother of the detective who outwits his more famous sibling in a case involving the theft of a secret document vital to British security. A pleasant affair, the film boasted good supporting work from Marty Feldman as Scotland Yard Sergeant Orville Sacker and Dom DeLuise as an opera singer. The same year also saw a pornographic Holmes film entitled THE AMERICAN ADVENTURES OF SURELICK HOLMES.

In the 1970s a number of novels appeared by various authors which were further adventures of Sherlock Holmes as related by Dr. Watson. The best known of these was Nicholas Meyer's *The Seven Percent Solution*, which Universal filmed under that title and issued in 1976. Nicol Williamson was interesting as Holmes, while Robert Duvall was quite good as Watson in this tale of the doctor taking his friend to Vienna to see Sigmund Freud (Alan Arkin) in order to get to the bottom of the detective's dependence on drugs. The film was a good one, and Universal planned to follow it with Nicholas Meyer's *The West End Horror*, another Holmes-Watson adventure, but to date it has not been filmed.

Another spoof of Doyle's famous detective came in 1978 with the British-made HOUND OF THE BASKERVILLES, directed by Paul Morrissey and starring Peter Cook (who co-wrote the script) as Holmes and Dudley Moore as the

Larry Hagman in THE RETURN OF THE WORLD'S GREATEST DETECTIVE (NBC-TV, 1976)

detective's mother. A more awful film would be hard to imagine; this so-called takeoff was a dreary affair from start to finish with almost no laughs and plenty of boredom. This is probably the worst Sherlock Holmes film ever produced.

The previous year a far better Sherlock Holmes adventure was made for television in SHERLOCK HOLMES IN NEW YORK, telecast October 18, 1976, by NBC-TV. Roger Moore (most noted as the Saint on TV and James Bond in the movies) played Holmes, and Patrick MacNee was Watson. The story had the detective coming to New York City to stop Professor Moriarty (John Huston), who planned to hoard the world's gold supply, as well as to kidnap Irene Adler (Charlotte Rampling). The telefilm proved popular with Holmes's followers.

A few months earlier, on June 16, 1976, NBC-TV presented the telefilm THE RETURN OF THE WORLD'S GREATEST DETECTIVE, starring Larry Hagman as Sherman Holmes, a modern-day policeman and follower of Sherlock Holmes. That year the British also starred Christopher Plummer as Holmes and Thorley Walters as Watson in "Silver Blaze" on the TV series "Classic Dark and Dangerous." Royal Dano also played a Sherlock Holmes–like character in the 1977 U.S. television special, "My Dear Uncle Sherlock" on "ABC Short Story Specials."

Christopher Plummer was quite good as Holmes on the big screen in 1979 when he played the part in MURDER BY DECREE, with James Mason as Dr. Watson. This British-Canadian co-production again had the sleuth trying to solve the Jack the Ripper murders, and it is no doubt the bloodiest of all Holmes features. The film is also overlong and a bit hard to follow, but it is a stylish affair and one worth watching.

In 1983 two of the best Sherlock Holmes features were issued, Sy Weintraub's productions of THE HOUND OF THE BASKERVILLES and THE SIGN OF FOUR, both starring Ian Richardson as Holmes. Richardson, who bears a resemblance to Basil Rathbone, was excellent in both films, with Donald Churchill as Watson in the HOUND and David Healy in THE SIGN OF FOUR. In fact, THE

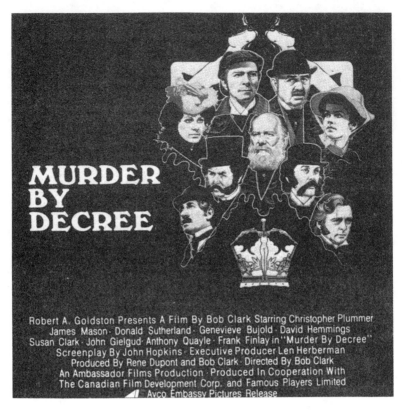

Robert A. Goldston Presents A Film By Bob Clark Starring Christopher Plummer
James Mason · Donald Sutherland · Genevieve Bujold · David Hemmings
Susan Clark · John Gielgud · Anthony Quayle · Frank Finlay in "Murder By Decree"
Screenplay By John Hopkins · Executive Producer Len Herberman
Produced By Rene Dupont and Bob Clark · Directed By Bob Clark
An Ambassador Films Production · Produced In Cooperation With
The Canadian Film Development Corp. and Famous Players Limited
Avco Embassy Pictures Release

Advertisement for MURDER BY DECREE (Avco/Embassy, 1979)

SIGN OF FOUR may well rank as one of the best Sherlock Holmes films of all time. Sadly, neither feature got much U.S. theatrical release, although both have been widely shown on cable TV.

Various stage presentations of William Gillette's play regained popularity in the U.S. and abroad in the 1970s. On November 15, 1981, Home Box Office telecast the mystery movie special SHERLOCK HOLMES, adapted from the Broadway production starring Frank Langella. The star repeated his role of Holmes with Richard Woods as Watson. Produced and directed by Peter Hunt, the film was set in London in 1891 and told of Holmes's attempts to retrieve valuable missives stolen from the home of Alice Faulkner (Laurie Kennedy). It was filmed at the Williamstown Theatre Festival. Four animated feature films for children, based on Doyle works, were made in Australia in 1984, with Peter O'Toole providing the voice of Holmes in SHERLOCK HOLMES AND THE BASKERVILLE CURSE, SHERLOCK HOLMES AND THE SIGN OF FOUR, SHERLOCK HOLMES AND A STUDY IN SCARLET, and SHERLOCK HOLMES AND THE VALLEY OF FEAR.

Peter Cushing returned to the role of Sherlock Holmes in the 1985 Tyburn release THE MASKS OF DEATH, with John Mills as Dr. Watson. Set in the early part of this century, the film had Scotland Yard persuading Holmes to come out of retirement to investigate a trio of London murders. The case eventually had him uncover a German plot to produce deadly gas to be released in London upon the outbreak of war between the two countries. Cushing was again excellent as the somewhat more aged Holmes, while Anne Baxter was Irene Adler, who aids her former lover in his investigation, and Ray Milland portrayed the Home Secretary. Peter Cushing also wrote the forewords to two books about Holmes, Peter Haining's *Sherlock Holmes Scrapbook* (1974), and *Holmes of the Movies: The Screen Career of Sherlock Holmes* (1976), by David Stuart Davies.

The exploits of Sherlock Holmes's younger years were detailed in YOUNG SHERLOCK HOLMES, a 1985 release which had student Sherlock Holmes (Nicholas Rowe) looking into a series of mysterious deaths, which include that of his mentor, a professor (Nigel Stock). He is helped by pal John Watson (Alan Cox), and while looking into the matter Holmes meets and falls in love with the late professor's lovely niece (Sophie Ward). At first Holmes thinks the professor was killed to get plans he had developed for a flying machine, but he comes to realize that satanists committed the crime in order to get the girl for a sacrifice. In the *New York Times*, Vincent Canby called it "one of the few really . . . entertaining American movies of 1985."

To celebrate the centennial of Sherlock Holmes's first case, *A Study in Scarlet* in 1887, the CBS-TV movie THE

RETURN OF SHERLOCK HOLMES was telecast January 10, 1987. Taking place in the present day, the film had the great-granddaughter of Dr. Watson, Jane Watson (Margaret Colin), finding Sherlock Holmes (Michael Pennington) in a state of suspended animation, in which her ancestor had placed him in 1901 in order to have time to find a cure for the bubonic plague from which he suffered. The young woman revives Holmes, who is cured by modern medicine and then asked by the U.S. government to look into a murder case. This involves him and Jane with crooked government agents, counterfeiters, a hijacker, and a mysterious woman (Connie Booth). The *Hollywood Reporter*'s Miles Beller commented, "RETURN takes some devilishly good twists, playing with the Holmes legend and infusing it with a fresh viewpoint."

In addition to films, Sherlock Holmes continued to be dramatized in such other mediums as radio and television. In 1954 the BBC of London broadcast the twelve-episode radio series "Sherlock Holmes" with John Gielgud as Holmes and Ralph Richardson as Watson. The last episode, "The Final Problem," guest starred Orson Welles as Moriarty. The series was syndicated on U.S. radio in the 1970s. In 1959 and running for a decade, BBC-Radio presented "Sherlock Holmes" starring Carleton Hobbs as Holmes and Norman Shelley as Dr. Watson. Nigel Stock portrayed Holmes in another BBC-Radio offering, a serialization of "The Hound of the Baskervilles" in 1969. In 1977 in the United States, "CBS Radio Mystery Theatre" began broadcasting a series of Sherlock Holmes adaptations hosted by E. G. Marshall. Written by Murray Bennett, these programs starred Kevin McCarthy as Holmes and Court Benson as Dr. Watson. It is interesting to note that in the broadcast of "A Study in Scarlet" the role of Inspector Lestrade was performed by Ian Martin, who had played Dr. Watson in the 1948–1949 radio season presentation of "The New Adventures of Sherlock Holmes" on Mutual with John Stanley as Holmes. In 1981 " CBS Radio Mystery Theatre" also broadcast a Halloween special of "The Hound of the Baskervilles."

Sherlock Holmes has continued to be popular on

recordings. In addition to the aforementioned Caedmon albums by Basil Rathbone, Holmes was also performed by Rathbone on "Sherlock Holmes Adventures" (Audio Book 611), and episodes of the radio series with Rathbone and Nigel Bruce have been issued on a variety of labels, including Biograph, Radiola, Varese International, Murray Hill, and Reichenbach Society. "The Adventure of the Innocent Murderess" was issued on Radio Greats (LP-107), starring Tom Conway as Holmes and Nigel Bruce as Watson. On September 25, 1938, Orson Welles portrayed Holmes in his adaptation of William Gillette's play on CBS radio's "Mercury Theatre of the Air," with Ray Collins as Watson; this broadcast has been issued on records as "The Immortal Sherlock Holmes" (Radiola 1143). Two episodes of the BBC-Radio show with John Gielgud and Ralph Richardson, "The Dying Detective/The Empty House," have been issued on Golden Age Records (LP-5030). Also from this series is a three-record set called "More Sherlock Holmes Adventures" on Murray Hill Records (LP-M51204). In 1970 Nigel Stock portrayed Holmes on four long-playing records issued in England on the Discourses label.

Perhaps Sherlock Holmes's greatest popularity in the 1980s has been derived from Jeremy Brett's work as the consulting detective in two series for Britain's Granada Television. In 1985 "The Adventures of Sherlock Holmes" was telecast co-starring David Burke as Dr. Watson. Thirteen one-hour segments, all adaptations of Arthur Conan Doyle stories, comprised the series. All were beautifully produced and highly entertaining, capturing the aura of England in the gaslight era. Jeremy Brett was particularly ingratiating as an emotionally insulated and distant Holmes, and his work as the detective has been especially popular with female viewers. In 1987 more Holmes segments appeared as "The Return of Sherlock Holmes," again with Brett as Holmes and Edward Hardwicke as Watson. All of these programs were originally telecast on the PBS-TV series "Mystery!" in the U.S., with some of them rerun on the USA Network and the Disney Channel.

Advertisement for THE RETURN OF SHERLOCK HOLMES (CBS-TV, 1987)

In the late summer of 1987 Frank Langella returned to the role of Sherlock Holmes in the Broadway production of "Sherlock's Last Case," by Charles Marowitz, with Donal Donnelly as Watson. *Daily Variety* said the production was "only sporadically entertaining." In 1988 ITC Entertainment filmed SHERLOCK AND ME in London. Like the 1987 play it is a spoof about a hard-drinking, unemployed actor (Michael Caine) retained by Dr. Watson (Ben Kingsley) to pretend he is Sherlock Holmes, since it is really the physician who is the master sleuth and who has used a nonexistent Holmes as a front. SHERLOCK AND ME was released in 1988 by Orion as WITHOUT A CLUE, to tepid box office returns.

In 1989 Ron Moody took the part in the London stage production "Sherlock Holmes—The Musical," with script and music by Leslie Bricusse.

For more than a century, Sherlock Holmes and his exploits have entertained millions around the world; no doubt the future holds more literary, film, stage, radio, television, and record outings for the Baker Street sleuth. Over the years, many have tried to explain the seemingly endless popularity of Holmes, but perhaps it was Sir Arthur Conan Doyle himself who summed it up best in "The Adventure of the Empty House" when he had Dr. Watson narrate, just as he and Holmes are embarking on another new exploit, "It was indeed like old times, when, at that hour, I found myself seated beside him in a hansom, my revolver in my pocket, and the thrill of adventure in my heart."

Filmography

1. SHERLOCK HOLMES BAFFLED. American Mutoscope & Biograph Company, 1900. 35 seconds.

2. ADVENTURES OF SHERLOCK HOLMES. Vitagraph, 1905. 8 minutes.
   D: J. Stuart Blackton. **SC:** Theodore Liebler.
   Cast: Maurice Costello (Sherlock Holmes).
   Alternate Title: HELD FOR RANSOM.

3. SHERLOCK HOLMES' ENEMY. Ambrosia Films [Italy], 1908. One reel.
   Alternate Title: RIVAL SHERLOCK HOLMES.

4. SHERLOCK HOLMES AND THE GREAT MURDER MYSTERY. Crescent Films, 1908. One reel.
   Based on the story "The Murders in the Rue Morgue" by Edgar Allan Poe.

5. SHERLOCK HOCHMES (Sherlock Holmes). Projectograph [Hungary], 1908. One reel.
   Cast: Bauman Karoly (Sherlock Holmes).

6. SHERLOCK HOLMES I LIVESFARE (Sherlock Holmes in Deathly Danger). Nordisk [Denmark], 1908. One reel.
   D-SC: Viggo Larsen.
   Cast: Viggo Larsen (Sherlock Holmes), Forrest Holger-Madsen (Raffles), Otto Dethlefsen (Professor Moriarty), Elith Pio (Little Billy), Aage Brandt, August Blom, Paul Gregaard, Gustav Lund.
   Also called SHERLOCK HOLMES RISKS HIS LIFE.

7. RAFFLES ESCAPES FROM PRISON. Nordisk, 1908. One reel.
   D-SC: Viggo Larsen.
   Cast: Viggo Larsen (Sherlock Holmes), Forrest Holger-Madsen (Raffles), Elith Pio (Little Billy).

8. SHERLOCK HOLMES I GASJELDEREN (Sherlock Holmes in the Gas Chamber). Nordisk, 1908. One reel.
   P-D: Viggo Larsen.
   Cast: Viggo Larsen (Sherlock Holmes), Forrest Holger-Madsen (Raffles), Elith Pio (Little Billy).

9. SANGERINDENS DIAMANTER (The Singer's Diamonds). Nordisk, 1909. One reel.
   P-D: Viggo Larsen.
   Cast: Viggo Larsen (Sherlock Holmes), Paul Gregaard (John Baxter), Aage Brandt (Singer), August Blom (Baxter's Uncle), Elith Pio (Little Billy).
   Also called THE THEFT OF THE DIAMONDS.

10. DROSKE NO. 519 (Cab No. 519). Nordisk, 1909. One reel.
    P-D: Viggo Larsen.
    Cast: Viggo Larsen (Sherlock Holmes), Elith Pio (Little Billy).

11. DEN GRAA DAME (The Grey Lady). Nordisk, 1909. One reel.
    P-D: Viggo Larsen. From *The Hound of the Baskervilles* by Arthur Conan Doyle.
    Cast: Viggo Larsen (Sherlock Holmes), Gustav Lund (Baron).

12. THE LATEST TRIUMPH OF SHERLOCK HOLMES. [France], 1909.

13. SHERLOCK HOLMES. Italia Films [Italy], 1909.

14. SHERLOCK HOLMES I BONDEFANGERKLOR (Sherlock Holmes in the Claws of the Confidence Men). Nordisk, 1910. One reel.
    Cast: Otto Lagoni (Sherlock Holmes), Elith Pio (Little Billy), Ellen Kornbech, Axel Boelsen.
    Also called THE CONFIDENCE TRICK and THE STOLEN WALLET.

15. SHERLOCK HOLMES CAPTURED. Nordisk, 1910. One reel.
    Cast: Otto Lagoni (Sherlock Holmes), Elith Pio (Little Billy), Ellen Kornbech, Axel Boelsen.
    Also called THE BOGUS GOVERNESS.

16. THE DIAMOND SWINDLER. Nordisk, 1910. One reel.
    Cast: Otto Lagoni (Sherlock Holmes), Elith Pio (Little Billy), Ellen Kornbech, Axel Boelsen.

17. ARSENE LUPIN VS. SHERLOCK HOLMES. Vitascope [Germany], 1910. One- and two-reel series.
    D: Viggo Larsen.
    Cast: Viggo Larsen (Sherlock Holmes, Paul Otto (Arsène Lupin).
    Series Titles: DER ALTE SEKRETAR (The Old Secretaire), DER BLAUE DIAMANT (The Blue Diamond), DIE FLASHEN REMBRANDTS (The Fake Rembrandts), DIE FLUCHT (Arsène Lupin's Escape), ARSENE LUPINS ENDE (The Finish of Arsène Lupin).

18. THE MILLION DOLLAR BOND. Nordisk, 1911. Two reels.
    Cast: Alwin Neuss (Sherlock Holmes).
    Also called SHERLOCK HOLMES' MASTERPIECE.

19. THE DISGUISED NURSE. Nordisk, 1911. Two reels.
    Cast: Alwin Neuss (Sherlock Holmes).

20. MEDLEM AF DEN SORTE HAND (The Member of the Black Hand). Nordisk, 1911. Two reels.
    Cast: Holger Rasmussen (Sherlock Holmes).
    Also called THE MURDER AT BAKER STREET and THE CONSPIRATORS.

21. HOTEL MYSTERIERNE (The Hotel Mystery). Nordisk, 1911. Two reels.
    Cast: Holger Rasmussen (Sherlock Holmes).
    Also called SHERLOCK HOLMES' LAST EXPLOIT.

22. SHERLOCK HOLMES CONTRA PROFESSOR MORYARTY (Sherlock Holmes vs. Professor Moriarty). Vitascope, 1911. Two reels.
    Cast: Viggo Larsen (Sherlock Holmes), Paul Otto (Professor Moriarty).

23. SHERLOCK HOLMES CHEATED BY RIGADIN. Eclair [France], 1911.

24. LES AVENTURES DE SHERLOCK HOLMES (The Adventures of Sherlock Holmes). Eclair, 1911.
    Cast: Henri Gouget (Sherlock Holmes).

25. SHERLOCK HOLMES. Franco-British Film Company, 1912. Two-reel series.
    Cast: Georges Treville (Sherlock Holmes), Mr. Moyse (Dr. Watson).
    Series Titles: THE SPECKLED BAND, THE SILVER BLAZE, THE MYSTERY OF BOSCOMBE VALE, THE COPPER BEECHES, THE STOLEN PAPERS, THE MUSGRAVE RITUAL, THE BERYL CORONET, THE REIGATE SQUIRES.

26. DIABOLICAL, MORE DIABOLICAL, AND THE MOST DIABOL-ICAL. Eclipse [France], 1912. Three reels.

27. SHERLOCK HOLMES SOLVES THE SIGN OF THE FOUR. Thanhouser, 1913. Two reels.
    Cast: Harry Benham (Sherlock Holmes).

28. GRIFFARD'S CLAW. Ambrosia, 1913.
    Also called IN THE GRIP OF THE EAGLE'S CLAW.

29. SHERLOCK HOLMES VS. THE BLACK HOOD. [German], 1913.

30. DER HUND VON BASKERVILLE (The Hound of the Basker-villes). Vitascope, 1914. Four reels.
    D: Rudolph Meinert. **SC:** Richard Oswald, from the novel by Arthur Conan Doyle. **SETS:** Hermann Warm.
    Cast: Alwin Neuss (Sherlock Holmes), Hanni Weiss (Laura Lyons), Erwin Fichtner (Lord Henry Baskerville), Friedrich Kuhne (Stapleton), Andreas Van Horne (Barrymore).

31. A STUDY IN SCARLET. G. B. Samuelson, 1914. 64 minutes.
    P: G. B. Samuelson. **D:** George Pearson. **SC:** Harry Engholm, from the novel by Arthur Conan Doyle.
    Cast: Fred Paul (Jefferson Hope), Agnes Glynne (Lucy Ferrier), Harry Paulo (John Ferrier), James Braginton (Sherlock Holmes), James Le Fre (Father), Winifred Pearson (Lucy as a Child).

32. A STUDY IN SCARLET. Universal, 1914. 20 minutes.
    D: Francis Ford.
    Cast: Francis Ford (Sherlock Holmes), Jack [John] Ford (Dr. Watson).

33. NIGHT OF TERROR. [Denmark], 1914.
    Cast: Emilie Sannom (Sherlock Holmes).

34. SHERLOCK HOLMES CONTRA DR. MOSS (Sherlock Holmes vs. Dr. Moss). Vitascope, 1914.
    Cast: Ferdinand Bonn (Sherlock Holmes), Friedrich Kuhne (Dr. Moss).

35. WHERE IS SHE? [Denmark], 1914.
    Cast: M. Gregers (Sherlock Holmes).

36. EIN SCHREI IN DER NACHT (A Scream in the Night). Decla [Germany], 1915. 30 minutes.
    Cast: Alwin Neuss (Sherlock Holmes), Edward Seefelu (Dr. Watson).

37. WILLIAM VOSS. Meinert Pictures [Germany], 1915.
    Cast: Alwin Neuss (Sherlock Holmes), Theodore Burgardt (William Voss).

38. DAS EINSAME HAUS (The Isolated House). Vitascope, 1915.
    D: Rudolph Meinert. **SC:** Richard Oswald.
    Cast: Alwin Neuss (Sherlock Holmes), Erwin Fichtner (Lord Henry Baskerville), Hanni Weiss (Lady Baskerville/Laura Lyons), Friedrich Kuhne (Stapleton), Andreas Van Horne (Barrymore).

39. WIE ENTSTAND DER HUND VON BASKERVILLE (How The Hound of the Baskervilles Returned). Vitascope, 1915.
    D-SC: Richard Oswald.
    Cast: Alwin Neuss (Sherlock Holmes), Erwin Fichtner (Lord Henry Baskerville), Hanni Weiss (Lady Baskerville), Friedrich Kuhne (Stapleton), Andreas Van Horne (Barrymore).

40. DAS UNHEIMLICHE ZIMMER (The Uncanny Room). Vitascope, 1915.
    D-SC: Richard Oswald.
    Cast: Alwin Neuss (Sherlock Holmes), Erwin Fichtner (Lord Henry Baskerville), Hanni Weiss (Lady Baskerville), Friedrich Kuhne (Stapleton), Andreas Van Horne (Barrymore).

41. DAS DUNKLE SCHLOSS. (The Dark Castle). Vitascope, 1915.
    D: Willy Zehn. **SC:** Robert Liebman.

Cast: Eugene Burge (Sherlock Holmes), Erwin Fichtner (Lord Henry Baskerville).

42. DR. MacDONALD'S SANITARIUM. Vitascope, 1915.
D: Willy Zehn. SC: Paul Rosenhaym.
Cast: Erich Kaisertitz (Sherlock Holmes).

43. THE HOUSE WITHOUT ANY WINDOWS. Vitascope, 1916.
D: Willy Zehn. SC: Paul Rosenhaym.
Cast: Erich Kaisertitz (Sherlock Holmes).

44. THE VALLEY OF FEAR. G. B. Samuelson, 1916. 6,500 feet.
P: G. B. Samuelson. D: Alexander Butler. SC: Harry Engholm, from the novel by Arthur Conan Doyle.
Cast: H. A. Saintsbury (Sherlock Holmes), Daisy Burrell (Ettie Shafter), Booth Conway (Professor Moriarty), Jack Macaulay (McGinty), Cecil Mannering (John McMurdo), Arthur M. Cullin (Dr. Watson), Lionel D'Aragon (Captain Marvin), Bernard Vaughan (Shafter), Jack Clair (Ted Baldwin).

45. SHERLOCK HOLMES. Essanay, 1916. 64 minutes.
D: Arthur Bethelt. SC: H. S. Sheldon, from the play by William Gillette.
Cast: William Gillette (Sherlock Holmes), Marjorie Kay (Alice Faulkner), Edward Fielding (Dr. Watson), Ernest Maupain (Professor Moriarty), William Pestance (Prince), Stewart Robbins (Benjamin Forman), Mario Marjeroni (James Larrabee), Grace Reals (Madge Larrabee), Fred Malatesta (McTague), Burford Hampden (Little Billy), Frank Hamilton (Leary), Hugh Thompson (Sir Edward Leighton), Ludwig Kreiss (Count Von Stalburg), Marion Skinner (Mrs. Faulkner), Miss Ball (Therese the Maid).

46. SHERLOCK HOLMES AND THE MIDNIGHT MEETING. Vitascope, 1916.
Cast: Alwin Neuss (Sherlock Holmes).

47. SHERLOCK HOLMES ON LEAVE. Vitascope, 1916.
Cast: Alwin Neuss (Sherlock Holmes).

48. SHERLOCK HOLMES. Kowo Film [Germany], 1917–1919. Two reels each.
D: Karl Heinz Rolf.
Cast: Hugo Flink (Sherlock Holmes).
Series Titles: DER ERDSTROMMOTOR (The Earthquake Motor), DIE KASSETTE (The Mysterious Casket), DER SCHLANGENRING (The Snake Ring), DIE INDISCHE SPINNE (The Indian Spider) [all issued in 1917].
D: Karl Heinz Rolf.

Cast: Ferdinand Bonn (Sherlock Holmes).
Series Titles: WAS DER SPIEGEL SAH (The Mirror of Death), DIE GIFTPLOMBE (The Poisoned Seal), DAS SCHICKSALDER RENATE YONGK (The Fate of Renate Yongk), DIE DOSE DES KARDINALS (The Cardinals' Snuffbox) [all issued in 1918].
D: Karl Heinz Rolf.
Cast: Kurt Brekendorff (Sherlock Holmes).
Series Title: DER MORD IM SPLENDID HOTEL (The Murder in the Hotel Splendid) [issued in 1919].

49. ROTTERDAM-AMSTERDAM. Meinert Films [Germany], 1918.
    Cast: Viggo Larsen (Sherlock Holmes).

50. A BLACK SHERLOCK HOLMES. Ebony Films, 1918.

51. THREE DAYS DEAD. Vitascope, 1919.
    Cast: Viggo Larsen (Sherlock Holmes).

52. THE ADVENTURES OF SHERLOCK HOLMES. Stoll, 1921. Two reels each.
    D: Maurice Elvey. **SC:** William J. Elliott.
    Series Titles:
    - THE DYING DETECTIVE.
        Cast: Eille Norwood (Sherlock Holmes), Hubert Willis (Dr. Watson), Cecil Humphreys (Culverton Smith), Madame d'Esterre (Mrs. Hudson).
    - THE DEVIL'S FOOT.
        Cast: Eille Norwood (Sherlock Holmes), Hubert Willis (Dr. Watson), Harvey Barban (Mortimer Tragennis), Hugh Buckler (Dr. Sterndale).
    - A CASE OF IDENTITY.
        Cast: Eille Norwood (Sherlock Holmes), Hubert Willis (Dr. Watson), Edna Flugrath (Mary Sutherland), Nelson Ramsey (Hosmer Angel).
    - YELLOW FACE.
        Cast: Eille Norwood (Sherlock Holmes), Hubert Willis (Dr. Watson), Clifford Heatherley (Grant Munro), Norman Whalley (Effie Munro).
    - THE RED-HEADED LEAGUE.
        Cast: Eille Norwood (Sherlock Holmes), Hubert Willis (Dr. Watson), Edward Arundell (Jabez Wilson), H. Townsend (Spalding).
    - THE RESIDENT PATIENT.
        Cast: Eille Norwood (Sherlock Holmes), Hubert Willis (Dr. Watson), C. Pitt-Chatham (Dr. Percy Trevelyan), Judd Green (Blessington), Wally Bosco (Moffatt).
    - A SCANDAL IN BOHEMIA.
        Cast: Eille Norwood (Sherlock Holmes), Hubert Willis (Dr.

Watson), Joan Beverley (Irene Adler), Alfred Drayton (King of Bohemia).
- THE MAN WITH THE TWISTED LIP.
    Cast: Eille Norwood (Sherlock Holmes), Hubert Willis (Dr. Watson), Robert Vallis (Neville St. Clair), Paulette del Baye (Mrs. St. Clair), Madame d'Esterre (Mrs. Hudson).
- THE BERYL CORONET.
    SC: Charles Barnett.
    Cast: Eille Norwood (Sherlock Holmes), Hubert Willis (Dr. Watson), Henry Vibart (Alexander Holder), Molly Adair (Mary), Lawrence Anderson (Arthur), Jack Selfridge (Sir George Burnwell), Madame d'Esterre (Mrs. Hudson).
- THE NOBLE BACHELOR.
    Cast: Eille Norwood (Sherlock Holmes), Hubert Willis (Dr. Watson), Arthur Bell (Inspector Lestrade), Cyril Percival (Simon), Temple Bell (Hetty Doran), Fred Earle (Moulton), Madame d'Esterre (Mrs. Hudson).
- THE COPPER BEECHES.
    Cast: Eille Norwood (Sherlock Holmes), Hubert Willis (Dr. Watson), Madge White (Violet Hunter/Ada), Lyell Johnson (Jephro Rucastle), Fred Raynham (Toller), Eve McCarthy (Mrs. Toller), Lottie Blackford (Mrs. Rucastle), Bobbie Harwood (Roger Wilson), William J. Elliott, Jr. (Japhat).
- THE EMPTY HOUSE.
    Cast: Eille Norwood (Sherlock Holmes), Hubert Willis (Dr. Watson), Austin Fairman (Ronald Adair), Cecil Kerr (Sir Charles Ridge), Arthur Bell (Inspector Lestrade), Madame d'Esterre (Mrs. Hudson).
- THE TIGER OF SAN PEDRO.
    Cast: Eille Norwood (Sherlock Holmes), Hubert Willis (Dr. Watson), Lewis Gilbert (Murillo), George Harrington (Scott Eccles), Arthur Walcott (Garcia), Arthur Bell (Inspector Lestrade), Madame d'Esterre (Mrs. Hudson).
- THE PRIORY SCHOOL.
    SC: Charles Barnett.
    Cast: Eille Norwood (Sherlock Holmes), Hubert Willis (Dr. Watson), Leslie English (Dr. Huxtable), C. H. Croker-King (Duke of Holderness), Irene Rooke (Duchess), Tom Ronald (Reuben Hayes), Patrick Kay (Lord Saltire), Cecil Kerr (Wilder), Madame d'Esterre (Mrs. Hudson).
- THE SOLITARY CYCLIST.
    Cast: Eillie Norwood (Sherlock Holmes), Hubert Willis (Dr. Watson), R. D. Sylvester (Carruthers), Violet Hewitt (Violet Ralph), Allan Jeayes (Woodley).

53. THE HOUND OF THE BASKERVILLES. Stoll, 1921. 5,500 feet.
    D: Maurice Elvey. **SC:** William J. Elliott & Dorothy Westlake, from the novel by Arthur Conan Doyle.

Cast: Eille Norwood (Sherlock Holmes), Hubert Willis (Dr. Watson), Rex McDougall (Sir Henry Baskerville), Catina Campbell (Beryl Stapleton), Lewis Gilbert (Stapleton), Robert English (Dr. Mortimer), Fred Raynham (Barrymore), Miss Walker (Mrs. Barrymore), Madame d'Esterre (Mrs. Hudson), Robert Vallis (Convict).

54. SHERLOCK HOLMES. Goldwyn Pictures, 1922. 109 minutes.
    P: E. J. Godsol. **D:** Albert Parker. **SC:** Marion Fairfax & Earle Brown, from the play by William Gillette.
    Cast: John Barrymore (Sherlock Holmes), Carol Dempster (Alice Faulkner), Gustav von Seyffertitz (Professor Moriarty), Roland Young (Dr. Watson), William Powell (Forman Wells), Hedda Hopper (Madge Larabee), Reginald Denny (Prince Alexis), David Torrence (Count von Stalberg), Anders Randolf (James Larabee), Louis Wolheim (Craigin), Percy Knight (Sid Jones), Peggy Bayfield (Rose Faulkner), Robert Schable (Alf Bassick), Jerry Devine (Little Billy), John Willard (Inspector Gregson).

55. THE FURTHER ADVENTURES OF SHERLOCK HOLMES. Stoll, 1922. Two reels each.
    D: George Ridgwell. **SC:** Robert L. Mannock & Geoffrey H. Malins.
    Series Titles:
    - CHARLES AUGUSTUS MILVERTON.
      Cast: Eille Norwood (Sherlock Holmes), Hubert Willis (Dr. Watson), Teddy Arundell (Inspector Hopkins), George Foley (Charles Augustus Milverton), Harry J. Worth (Butler), Tonie Edgar Bruce (Lady Eva Bracknell), Madame d'Esterre (Mrs. Hudson), Edith Bishop (Maid).
    - THE ABBEY GRANGE.
      Cast: Eille Norwood (Sherlock Holmes), Hubert Willis (Dr. Watson), Teddy Arundell (Inspector Hopkins), Madeleine Seymour (Lady Brackenstall), Lawford Davidson (Sir Eustace Brackenstall), Leslie Stiles (Captain Croker), Madge Tree (Theresa), Madame d'Esterre (Mrs. Hudson).
    - THE NORWOOD BUILDER.
      Cast: Eille Norwood (Sherlock Holmes), Hubert Willis (Dr. Watson), Teddy Arundell (Inspector Hopkins), Fred Wright (James Oldacre), Cyril Raymond (John McFarlane), Laura Walker (Miss McFarlane), Madame d'Esterre (Mrs. Hudson).
    - THE REIGATE SQUIRES.
      Cast: Eille Norwood (Sherlock Holmes), Hubert Willis (Dr. Watson), Teddy Arundell (Inspector Hopkins), Richard Atwood (Alec Cunningham), Edward O'Neill (Squire Cunningham), Arthur Lumley (Colonel Hayter), Madame d'Esterre (Mrs. Hudson).
    - THE NAVAL TREATY.
      Cast: Eille Norwood (Sherlock Holmes), Hubert Willis (Dr.

Watson), Jack Hobbs (Percy Phelps), Francis Duguid (Joseph Harrison), Nancy May (Miss Harrison).

- THE SECOND STAIN.
  Cast: Eille Norwood (Sherlock Holmes), Hubert Willis (Dr. Watson), Teddy Arundell (Inspector Hopkins), Cecil Ward (Lord Bellinger), Dorothy Fane (Miss Hope), Maria Minetti (Mrs. Lucas), Madame d'Esterre (Mrs. Hudson).
- THE RED CIRCLE.
  Cast: Eille Norwood (Sherlock Holmes), Hubert Willis (Dr. Watson), Teddy Arundell (Inspector Hopkins), Bertram Burleigh (Gennaro Lucca), Maresco Marescini (Gorgiano), Sybil Archdale (Amelia Lucca), Tom Beaumont (Leverton), Madame d'Esterre (Mrs. Hudson), Esmé Hubbard (Mrs. Warren).
- THE SIX NAPOLEONS.
  Cast: Eille Norwood (Sherlock Holmes), Hubert Willis (Dr. Watson), Teddy Arundell (Inspector Hopkins), George Bellamy (Beppo), Jack Raymond (Pietro Venucci), Alice Moffatt (Lucretia), Madame d'Esterre (Mrs. Hudson).
- THE BLACK PETER.
  Cast: Eille Norwood (Sherlock Holmes), Hubert Willis (Dr. Watson), Teddy Arundell (Inspector Hopkins), Fred Paul (Peter Carey), Hugh Buckler (Pat Cairns), Jack Jarman (John Neligan), Fred Rains (John Neligan, Sr.), Mrs. Willis (Mrs. Carey), Miss Willis (Miss Carey), Madame d'Esterre (Mrs. Hudson).
- THE BRUCE PARKINGTON PLANS.
  Cast: Eille Norwood (Sherlock Holmes), Hubert Willis (Dr. Watson), Teddy Arundell (Inspector Hopkins), Malcolm Tod (Cadogan West), Lewis Gilbert (Mycroft Holmes), Ronald Power (Colonel Valentine Walter), Edward Sorley (Hugh Oberstein), Leslie Brittain (Sidney Johnson).
- THE STOCKBROKER'S CLERK.
  Cast: Eille Norwood (Sherlock Holmes), Hubert Willis (Dr. Watson), Olaf Hytten (Hall Pycroft), Aubrey Fitzgerald (Pinner), George Ridgwell (Beddington).
- THE BOSCOMBE VALLEY MYSTERY.
  Cast: Eille Norwood (Sherlock Holmes), Hubert Willis (Dr. Watson), Hal Martin (Charles McCarthy), Roy Raymond (James McCarthy), Fred Raymond (John Turner), Thelma Murray (Miss Turner).
- THE MUSGRAVE RITUAL.
  Cast: Eille Norwood (Sherlock Holmes), Hubert Willis (Dr. Watson), Geoffrey Wilmer (Geoffrey Musgrave), Clifton Boyne (Brunton), Betty Chester (Rachel Howells).
- THE GOLDEN PINCE-NEZ.
  Cast: Eille Norwood (Sherlock Holmes), Hubert Willis (Dr. Watson), Teddy Arundell (Inspector Hopkins), Norma Whalley (Anna Coram), Cecil Morton York (Professor Coram).

- THE GREEK INTERPRETER.
    Cast: Eille Norwood (Sherlock Holmes), Hubert Willis (Dr. Watson), J. R. Tozer (Latimer), Robert Vallis (Wilson Kemp), Cecil Dane (Melas), Edith Saville (Sophy Katrides), H. Wheeler (Inspector Hopkins), Madame d'Esterre (Mrs. Hudson).

56. THE LAST ADVENTURES OF SHERLOCK HOLMES. Stoll, 1923. Two reels each.
    D: George Ridgwell. **SC:** Geoffrey H. Malins & P. L. Mannock.
    Series Titles:
- THE SILVER BLAZE.
    Cast: Eille Norwood (Sherlock Holmes), Hubert Willis (Dr. Watson), Knighton Small (Colonel Ross), Sam Marsh (Straker), Norma Whalley (Mrs. Straker), Sam Austin (Silas Brown), Bert Barclay (Groom), Tom Beaumont (Inspector Gregory).
- THE SPECKLED BAND.
    Cast: Eille Norwood (Sherlock Holmes), Hubert Willis (Dr. Watson), Lewis Gilbert (Dr. Grimsby Roylott), Cynthia Murtagh (Helen Stoner), Henry Wilson (Baboon), Madame d'Esterre (Mrs. Hudson).
- THE GLORIA SCOTT.
    Cast: Eille Norwood (Sherlock Holmes), Hubert Willis (Dr. Watson), Reginald Fox (Victor Trevor), Fred Raynham (James Trevor), Roy Raymond (Pendergast), Laurie Lewis (Hudson), Ernest Shannon (Evans).
- THE BLUE CARBUNCLE.
    Cast: Eille Norwood (Sherlock Holmes), Hubert Willis (Dr. Watson), Douglas Payne (Peterson), Gordon Hopkirk (Ryder), Sebastian Smith (Henry Barker), Mary Mackintosh (Mrs. Oakshoft), Archie Hunter (Breckinridge).
- THE ENGINEER'S THUMB.
    Cast: Eille Norwood (Sherlock Holmes), Hubert Willis (Dr. Watson), Bertram Burleigh (Hatherley), Ward McAllister (Ferguson), Mercy Hatton (Girl).
- HIS LAST BOW.
    Cast: Eille Norwood (Sherlock Holmes), Hubert Willis (Dr. Watson), Nelson Ramsey (Von Bork), Van Courtlan (Baron Herling), Kate Gurney (Martha), Watts Phillips (Officer).
- THE CARDBOARD BOX.
    Cast: Eille Norwood (Sherlock Holmes), Hubert Willis (Dr. Watson), Tom Beaumont (Inspector Lestrade), Hilda Anthony (Mary Browner), Johnny Butt (James Browner), Eric Lugg (Alec Fairborn), Maud Wulff (Miss Cushing).
- THE DISAPPEARANCE OF LADY FRANCES CARFAX.
    Cast: Eille Norwood (Sherlock Holmes), Hubert Willis (Dr. Watson), Tom Beaumont (Inspector Gregory), Evelyn Cecil

(Lady Frances Carfax), David Hawthorne (Philip Green), Cecil Morton York (Hily Peters), Madge Tree (Mrs. Peters).
- THE THREE STUDENTS.
  Cast: Eille Norwood (Sherlock Holmes), Hubert Willis (Dr. Watson), William Lugg (Soames), A. Harding Steerman (Bannister), L. Verne (Gilchrist).
- THE MISSING THREE-QUARTER.
  Cast: Eille Norwood (Sherlock Holmes), Hubert Willis (Dr. Watson), Hal Martin (Overton), Jack Raymond (Porter), Albert E. Rayner (Dr. Leslie Armstrong), Leigh Gabell (Staunton), Cliff Davies (Lord Mount James).
- THE MYSTERY OF THOR BRIDGE.
  Cast: Eille Norwood (Sherlock Holmes), Hubert Willis (Dr. Watson), A. B. Imeson (Mr. Gibson), Violet Graham (Miss Dunbar), Noel Grahame (Mrs. Gibson), Harry J. Worth (Inspector).
- THE STONE OF MAZARIN.
  Cast: Eille Norwood (Sherlock Holmes), Hubert Willis (Dr. Watson), Tom Beaumont (Inspector Gregory), Lionel D'Aragon (Count Sylvius), Laurie Leslie (Merton).
- THE MYSTERY OF THE DANCING MEN.
  Cast: Eille Norwood (Sherlock Holmes), Hubert Willis (Dr. Watson), Frank Goldsmith (Hilton Cubitt), Wally Bosco (Staney), Dezma du May (Mrs. Cubitt).
- THE CROOKED MAN.
  Cast: Eille Norwood (Sherlock Holmes), Hubert Willis (Dr. Watson), Jack Hobbs (Henry Wood), Gladys Jennings (Mrs. Barclay), Dora de Winton (Miss Morrison), Richard Lindsay (Major Murphy).
- THE FINAL PROBLEM.
  Cast: Eille Norwood (Sherlock Holmes), Hubert Willis (Dr. Watson), Percy Standing (Professor Moriarty), Tom Beaumont (Inspector Taylor).

57. THE SIGN OF FOUR. Stoll, 1923. 6,750 feet.
   D-SC: Maurice Elvey. From the novel by Arthur Conan Doyle.
   Cast: Eille Norwood (Sherlock Holmes), Isobel Elsom (Mary Morstan), Arthur Cullin (Dr. Watson), Fred Raynham (Prince Abdullah Khan), Norman Page (Jonathan Small), Humberston Wright (Dr. Sholto), Henry Wilson (Pygmy), Madame d'Esterre (Mrs. Hudson), Arthur Bell (Inspector Athelney Jones).

58. DER HUND VON BASKERVILLE (The Hound of the Baskervilles). Erda Film [Germany], 1929.
   D: Richard Oswald. **SC:** Herbert Jutke & Georg Klaren, from the novel by Arthur Conan Doyle. **PH:** Frederik Fulsang.
   Cast: Carlyle Blackwell (Sherlock Holmes), George Seroff (Dr. Watson), Alexander Murski (Sir Hugo Baskerville), Betty Bird

(Beryl Stapleton), Fritz Rasp (Stapleton), Alma Taylor (Mrs. Barrymore), Robert Garrison (Frankland), Erich Ponto, Valy Arnheim, Carla Bartheel, Jaro Furth.

59. THE RETURN OF SHERLOCK HOLMES. Paramount, 1929.
   P: David O. Selznick. **D:** Basil Dean. **SC:** Basil Dean & Garrett Ford. **PH:** William Steiner. **ED:** Helen Turner.
   Cast: Clive Brook (Sherlock Holmes), Betty Lawford (Mary Watson), H. Reeves-Smith (Dr. Watson), Charles Hay (Charles Longmore), Phillips Holmes (Roger Longmore), Donald Crisp (Colonel Sebastian Moran), Harry T. Morey (Professor Moriarty), Hubert Druce (Sergeant Gripper), Arthur Mack (Sparks).

60. PARAMOUNT ON PARADE. Paramount, 1930. 102 minutes.
   Segment: MURDER WILL OUT.
   EP: David O. Selznick. **D:** Frank Tuttle. **PH:** Harry Fishbeck & Victor Milner.
   Cast: Clive Brook (Sherlock Holmes), William Powell (Philo Vance), Warner Oland (Dr. Fu Manchu), Eugene Pallette (Sergeant Ernest Heath), H. Reeves-Smith (Dr. Watson), Jack Oakie (Victim).

61. THE SLEEPING CARDINAL. Twickenham, 1931 (released in U.S. by First Division). 84 minutes.
   P: Julius Hagen. **D:** Leslie S. Hiscott. **SC:** Cyril Twyford & H. Fowler Mear. **DIALOGUE:** Arthur Wontner. **PH:** Sydney Blythe. **ED-ASST DIR:** Jack Harris. **AD:** James Carter.
   Cast: Arthur Wontner (Sherlock Holmes), Norman McKinnel (Professor Moriarty), Leslie Perrins (Ronald Adair), Jane Welsh (Kathleen Adair), Ian Fleming (Dr. Watson), William Frazer (Thomas Fisher), Louis Goodrich (Colonel Sebastian Moran), Philip Hewland (Inspector Lestrade), Charles Paton (J. J. Godfrey), Minnie Rayner (Mrs. Hudson), Sidney King (Tony Rutherford), Gordon Begg (Marston), Harry Terry (Number 16).
   U.S. Title: SHERLOCK HOLMES' FATAL HOUR.

62. THE SPECKLED BAND. British & Dominions Studios, 1931 (released in the U.S. by First Division). 90 minutes.
   P: Herbert Wilcox. **D:** Jack Raymond. **SC:** W. P. Lipscomb. **PH:** Frederick A. Young. **ED:** P. M. Rogers.
   Cast: Lyn Harding (Dr. Grimesby Rylott), Raymond Massey (Sherlock Holmes), Athole Stewart (Dr. Watson), Angela Baddeley (Helen Stoner), Nancy Price (Mrs. Staunton), Marie Ault (Mrs. Hudson), Stanley Lathbury (Rodgers), Charles Paton (Builder), Joyce Moore (Violet).

63. THE HOUND OF THE BASKERVILLES. Gaumont British, 1931 (released in the U.S. by First Division). 75 minutes.

P: Michael Balcon. D: V. Gareth Gundrey. SC: Edgar Wallace & V. Gareth Gundrey, from the novel by Arthur Conan Doyle. PH: Bernard Knowles. ED: Ian Dalrymple.

Cast: Robert Rendel (Sherlock Holmes), John Stuart (Sir Henry Baskerville), Frederick Lloyd (Dr. Watson), Reginald Bach (Stapleton), Heather Angel (Beryl Stapleton), Wilfred Shine (Dr. Mortimer), Sam Livesey (Sir Hugo Baskerville), Henry Hallett (Barrymore), Sybil Jane (Mrs. Barrymore), Elizabeth Vaughn (Mrs. Laura Lyons), Leonard Hayes (Cartwright).

64. LELICEK VE SLUZBACH SHERLOCKA HOLMESE (Lelicek in the Service of Sherlock Holmes). Elektafilm [Czechoslovakia], 1932.
P: Jan Reiter. D: Karel Lamac. SC: Vaclav Wasserman & Hugo Vavrise. PH: Otto Heller & Jan Stallich.
Cast: Martin Fric (Sherlock Holmes), Vlasta Burinan (Frantisek Lelicek/Fernando XXIII), Lida Baarova (Queen Kralovna), Fred Bulin (Jeho Sluha James), Eva Jansenova (Conchita), Cenek Slegl (Count Marshal), Theodor Pistek (Prime Minister), Zvonimir Regez (Officer), Eman Fiala (Photographer).

65. THE MISSING REMBRANDT. Twickenham, 1932 (released in the U.S. by First Division). 83 minutes.
P: Julius Hagen. D: Leslie Hiscott. SC: H. Fowler Mear & Cyril Twyford, from the story "The Adventure of Charles Augustus Milverton" by Arthur Conan Doyle. PH: Sydney Blythe & Basil Emmott.
Cast: Arthur Wontner (Sherlock Holmes), Francis L. Sullivan (Baron von Guntermann), Ian Fleming (Dr. Watson), Miles Mander (Claude Holford), Jane Welsh (Lady Violet), Minnie Raynor (Mrs. Hudson), Dino Galvani (Carlo Ravelli), Philip Hewland (Inspector Lestrade), Herbert Lomas (Manning), Anthony Hollis (Marquis De Chaminade), Ben Welden (Agent), Takase (Chang Wu).

66. THE SIGN OF FOUR. Associated Talking Pictures, 1932 (released in the U.S. by World Wide). 75 minutes.
P: Basil Dean. D: Rowland V. Lee & Graham Cutts. SC: W. P. Lipscomb, from the novel by Arthur Conan Doyle. PH: Robert de Grasse & Robert G. Martin.
Cast: Arthur Wontner (Sherlock Holmes), Ian Fleming (Dr. Watson), Isla Bevan (Mary Morstan), Claire Greet (Mrs. Hudson), Miles Malleson (Thaddeus Sholto), Graham Soutten (Jonathan Small), Gilbert Davis (Athelney Jones), Edgar Norfolk (Captain Morstan), Herbert Lomas (Sholto), Roy Emerton (Bailey), Kynaston Reeves (Bartholomew), Mr. Burnhett (Tattoo Artist), Togo (Tonga).

67. SHERLOCK HOLMES. Fox, 1932. 68 minutes.
P: William Fox. D: William K. Howard. SC: Bertram Millhauser

& Bayard Veiller, from the play by William Gillette. **PH:** George Barnes. **ED:** Margaret Clancy. **AD:** John Hughes. **MUS:** George Lipschultz. **ASST DIR:** Philip Ford.

Cast: Clive Brook (Sherlock Holmes), Miriam Jordan (Alice Faulkner), Reginald Owen (Dr. Watson), Ernest Torrance (Professor Moriarty), Howard Leeds (Little Billy), Alan Mowbray (Inspector Gore-King), Herbert Mundin (Pub Operator), G. Montague Shaw (Judge), Arnold Lucy (Chaplain), Lucien Prival (Hans the Hun), Roy D'Arcy (Manuel Lopez), Stanley Fields (Tony Ardetti), Eddie Dillon (Ardetti's Henchman), Robert Graves, Jr. (Gaston Reux), Brandon Hurst (Erskine's Secretary), Claude King (Sir Albert Hastings), Ivan Simpson (Mr. Faulkner).

68. A STUDY IN SCARLET. World Wide/Fox, 1933. 70 minutes.

P: Burt Kelly, Samuel Bischoff & William Saal. **D:** Edwin L. Marin. **SC:** Robert Florey. **DIALOGUE:** Reginald Owen. **PH:** Arthur Edelson. **ED:** Rose Loewinger. **AD:** Ralph DeLacy. **RECORDER:** Hans Weeren. **MUS:** Val Burton.

Cast: Reginald Owen (Sherlock Holmes), Anna May Wong (Mrs. Pyke), June Clyde (Eileen Forrester), Warburton Gamble (Dr. Watson), J. M. Kerrigan (Jabez Wilson), Alan Dinehart (Thaddeus Merrydew), Alan Mowbray (Inspector Lestrade), Doris Lloyd (Mrs. Murphy), Billy Bevan (Will Swallow), Leila Bennett (Dolly), Cecil Reynolds (Baker), Tetsu Komai (Ah Yet), Halliwell Hobbes (Malcolm Dearing), Tempe Pigott (Mrs. Hudson), Wyndham Standing (Captain Pyke), Hobart Cavanaugh (Publican).

Also called THE SCARLET RING.

69. THE RADIO MURDER MYSTERY. Universal, 1933. 18 minutes.

P: Louis Sobol. **D:** Monte Brice. **SC:** H. D. Kusell.

Cast: Richard Gordon (Sherlock Holmes), Leigh Lovell (Dr. Watson).

70. THE TRIUMPH OF SHERLOCK HOLMES. Gaumont-British, 1935 (released in the U.S. by Olympia Macri Excelsior). 84 minutes.

P: Julius Hagen. **D:** Leslie S. Hiscott. **SC:** H. Fowler Mear, Cyril Twyford & Arthur Wontner, from the novel *The Valley of Fear* by Arthur Conan Doyle. **PH:** William Luff.

Cast: Arthur Wontner (Sherlock Holmes), Ian Fleming (Dr. Watson), Lyn Harding (Professor Moriarty), Jane Carr (Ettie Douglas), Leslie Perrins (John Douglas), Charles Mortimer (Inspector Lestrade), Minnie Raynor (Mrs. Hudson), Michael Shepley (Cecil Barker), Ben Welden (Ted Balding), Conway Dixon (Ames), Roy Emerson (Boss McGinty), Wilfred Caithness (Colonel Sebastian Moran), Edmund D'Alby (Captain Marvin), Ernest Lynds (Jacob Shafter).

71. DER HUND VON BASKERVILLE (The Hound of the Baskervilles). Ondra Film [Germany], 1937.
    P-D: Karl Lamac. **SC:** Carla von Stackelberg, from the novel by Arthur Conan Doyle. **PH:** Willy Winterstein. **MUS:** Paul Huhn.
    Cast: Bruno Guttner (Sherlock Holmes), Fritz Odemar (Dr. Watson), Peter Voss (Lord Henry Baskerville), Fritz Rasp (Barrymore), Friedrich Kayssler (Lord Charles Baskerville), Lilly Schonborn (Mrs. Barrymore), Erich Ponto (Stapleton), Alice Brandt (Beryl Stapleton), Ernest Rotmund (Dr. Mortimer), Paul Rehkipf (Convict), Gertrude Walle (Landlady), Hanna Waag (Lady Baskerville), Arthur Malkowski (Lord Hugo Baskerville), Laus Pohl, Horst Birr, Ernst A. Shaah, Ilka Thim, Kurt Lauermann.

72. SHERLOCK HOLMES UND DIE GRAUE DAME (Sherlock Holmes and the Gray Lady), Neue Film [Germany], 1937.
    P-D: Erich Engels. **SC:** Erich Engels & Hans Heuer.
    Cast: Herman Speelmans (Jimmy Ward/Sherlock Holmes), Ernst Karchow (Inspector Brown), Trude Marlen (Maria Iretzkaja), Eve Tinschmann (Frau Miller), Reinhold Bernt (Wilson), Elisabeth Wendt (Lola), Edwin Jurgensen (Baranoff), Teho Shall (Harry Morrel), Werner Finck (Ward's Servant), Werner Scharf (Jack Clark), Hans Halden (James Hewitt), Henry Lorenzen (Archibald Pepperkorn).

73. THE SILVER BLAZE. Twickenham, 1937 (released in the U.S. in 1941 by Monogram as MURDER AT THE BASKERVILLES). 71 minutes.
    P: Julius Hagen. **D:** Thomas Bentley. **SC:** H. Fowler Mear & Arthur Macrae, from the novel by Arthur Conan Doyle. **PH:** Sydney Blythe & William Luff.
    Cast: Arthur Wontner (Sherlock Holmes), Ian Fleming (Dr. Watson), Lyn Harding (Professor Moriarty), John Turnbull (Inspector Lestrade), Lawrence Grossmith (Sir Henry Baskerville), Robert Horton (Colonel Ross), Judy Gunn (Diana Baskerville), Martin Walker (John Straker), Eve Gray (Mrs. Straker), Arthur Macrae (Jack Trevor), Arthur Goulet (Colonel Sebastian Moran), Minnie Raynor (Mrs. Hudson), D. J. Williams (Silas Brown), Ralph Truman (Bert Prince), Gilbert Davis (Miles Stamford), Ronald Shiner (Stableboy).
    Also known as ADVENTURE AT THE BASKERVILLES.

74. DER MANN DER SHERLOCK HOLMES WAR (The Man Who Was Sherlock Holmes). UFA [Germany], 1937.
    D: Karl Hartl. **SC:** R. A. Stemmie & Karl Hartl. **PH:** Fritz Arno. **ED:** Gertrud Hinz. **AD:** Otto Hunte & Willy Schiller. **MUS:** Hans Sommer.
    Cast: Hans Albers (Sherlock Holmes), Heinz Ruhmann (Dr. Watson), Marieluise Claudius (Mary Berry), Hilde Weissner

(Madame Ganymar), Siegfried Schurenberg (Monsieur Lepin), Paul Bildt (Conan Doyle), Hansi Knoteck (Jane Berry), Franz W. Schroder-Schrom (Police Chief), Hans Junkermann (Exhibition Director), Eduard von Winterstein (Court Chairman), Edwin Jurgensen (Prosecutor), Hans Richter (Berliner), Ernest Waldow (Hotel Detective), Ernst Legal (Jean).

75. THE HOUND OF THE BASKERVILLES. 20th Century–Fox, 1939. 80 minutes.

P: Gene Markey. **D:** Sidney Lanfield. **SC:** Ernest Pascal, from the novel by Arthur Conan Doyle. **PH:** J. Peverell Marley. **ED:** Robert Simpson. **MUS:** Cyril Mockridge. **AD:** Richard Day & Hans Peters.

Cast: Richard Greene (Sir Henry Baskerville), Basil Rathbone (Sherlock Holmes), Wendy Barrie (Beryl Stapleton), Nigel Bruce (Dr. Watson), Lionel Atwill (Dr. Mortimer), John Carradine (Barryman), Barlowe Borland (Mr. Franklan), Beryl Mercer (Mrs. Mortimer), Morton Lowry (John Stapleton), Ralph Forbes (Sir Hugo Baskerville), Mary Gordon (Mrs. Hudson), Peter Willes (Roderick), Ian MacLaren (Sir Charles Baskerville), Nigel De Brulier (Convict), E. E. Clive (Cab Driver), Eily Malyon (Mrs. Barryman), John Burton (Bruce), Evan Thomas (Edwin), Ivan Simpson (Shepherd), Lionel Pape (Coroner), Dennis Green (Jon).

76. THE ADVENTURES OF SHERLOCK HOLMES. 20th Century–Fox, 1939. 85 minutes.

P: Gene Markey. **D:** Alfred L. Werker. **SC:** Edwin Blum & William Drake, from the play by William Gillette. **PH:** Leon Shamroy. **ED:** Robert Bishoff. **AD:** Richard Day & Hans Peters. **MUS:** Cyril Mockridge.

Cast: Basil Rathbone (Sherlock Holmes), Nigel Bruce (Dr. Watson), Ida Lupino (Ann Brandon), Alan Marshal (Jerrold Hunter), Terry Kilburn (Little Billy), George Zucco (Professor Moriarty), Henry Stephenson (Sir Ronald Ramsgate), E. E. Clive (Inspector Bristol), Arthur Hohl (Bassick), May Betty (Mrs. Jameson), Peter Willes (Lloyd Brandon), Mary Gordon (Mrs. Hudson), Holmes Herbert (Justice), George Regas (Mateo), Mary Forbes (Lady Conynham), Frank Dawson (Dawes), William Austin (Stranger), Ivan Simpson (Gates), Neil Fitzgerald (Court Clerk), Leonard Mudie (Barrows), Anthony Kemble-Cooper (Tony), Eric Wilton (Butler), Denis Green (Sergeant), Robert Noble (Foreman).

77. SHERLOCK HOLMES AND THE VOICE OF TERROR. Universal, 1942. 65 minutes.

AP: Howard Benedict. **D:** John Rawlins. **SC:** Lynn Riggs & Robert D. Andrews. **PH:** Woody Bredell. **ED:** Russell Schoengart. **MUS:** Charles Previn. **AD:** Jack Otterson.

Cast: Basil Rathbone (Sherlock Holmes), Nigel Bruce (Dr.

Watson), Evelyn Ankers (Kitty), Henry Daniell (Sir Alfred Lloyd), Reginald Denny (Sir Evan Barham), Thomas Gomez (Meade), Montagu Love (General Lawford), Olaf Hytten (Fabian Prentiss), Mary Gordon (Mrs. Hudson), Leyland Hodgson (Captain Ronald Shore), Hillary Brooke (Jill Grandis), Arthur Blake (Crosbie), Harry Stubbs (Taxi Driver).

78. SHERLOCK HOLMES AND THE SECRET WEAPON. Universal, 1942. 68 minutes.

AP: Howard Benedict. **D:** Roy William Neill. **SC:** Edward T. Lowe, W. Scott Darlin & Edmund Hartmann. **PH:** Lester White. **ED:** Otto Ludwig. **MUS:** Frank Skinner. **AD:** Jack Otterson.

Cast: Basil Rathbone (Sherlock Holmes), Nigel Bruce (Dr. Watson), Lionel Atwill (Professor Moriarty), Kaaren Verne (Charlotte Eberli), Dennis Hoey (Inspector Lestrade), William Post, Jr. (Dr. Tobel), Harry Woods (Kurt), George Burr MacAnnan (Gottfried), Paul Fix (Mueller), Holmes Herbert (Sir Reginald), Guy Kingsford (London Policeman), Leyland Hodgson, Leslie Denison, John Burton (Men), Mary Gordon (Mrs. Hudson), Henry Victor (Hoffner), Harold De Becker (Peg Leg), Gerard Cavin (Scotland Yard Man), Philip Van Zandt (Kurt), Harry Cording (Brady), Robert O. Davis (Brawn), Paul Bryar (Waiter), Vicki Campbell (Aviatrix), George Eldredge (Policeman).

79. SHERLOCK HOLMES IN WASHINGTON. Universal, 1943. 71 minutes.

AP: Howard Benedict. **D:** Roy William Neill. **SC:** Lynn Riggs & Bertram Millhauser. **PH:** Lester White. **ED:** Otto Ludwig. **MUS:** Charles Previn.

Cast: Basil Rathbone (Sherlock Holmes), Nigel Bruce (Dr. Watson), Marjorie Lord (Nancy Partridge), George Zucco (Richard Stanley/Heinrich Hinkle), Henry Daniell (William Raster), Thurston Hall (Senator Henry Babcock), John Archer (Lieutenant Peter Merriam), Gilbert Emery (Sir Henry Marchmont), Edmund MacDonald (Detective Lieutenant Grogan), Gavin Muir (Bart Lang), Don Terry (Howe), Bradley Page (Cady), Holmes Herbert (Mr. Ahrens), Ian Wolfe (Clerk).

80. SHERLOCK HOLMES FACES DEATH. Universal, 1943. 68 minutes.

P-D: Roy William Neill. **SC:** Bertram Millhauser, from the story "The Musgrave Ritual" by Arthur Conan Doyle. **PH:** Charles Van Enger. **ED:** Fred Feitchans. **MUS:** Hans J. Salter. **AD:** John Goodman & Harold MacArthur.

Cast: Basil Rathbone (Sherlock Holmes), Nigel Bruce (Dr. Watson), Hillary Brooke (Sally Musgrave), Dennis Hoey (Inspector Lestrade), Milburn Stone (Captain Vickery), Arthur Margretson (Dr. Sexton), Halliwell Hobbes (Brunton), Gavin Muir (Philip

Musgrave), Minna Phillips (Mrs. Howells), Vernon Downing (Lieutenant Clavering), Gerald Hamer (Major Langford), Olaf Hytten (Captain McIntosh), Frederick Worlock (Geoffrey Musgrave), Heather Wilde (Jenny), Norma Varden (Barmaid), Harold De Becker (Pub Proprietor), Peter Lawford (Sailor).

81. CRAZY HOUSE. Universal, 1943. 80 minutes.
   AP: Erle C. Kenton. **D:** Edward Cline. **SC:** Robert Lees & Frederick I. Rinaldo. **PH:** Charles Van Enger. **ED:** Arthur Hilton. **AD:** John Goodman & Harold MacArthur. **MUS:** Charles Previn.
   Cast: Ole Olsen (Himself), Chic Johnson (Himself), Cass Daley (Sadie), Patric Knowles (Eddie McLean), Martha O'Driscoll (Margie), Leighton Noble (Johnny), Percy Kilbride (Colonel Merriweather), Thomas Gomez (Wagstaff), Hans Conreid (Roco), Andrew Tombes (Gregory), Billy Gilbert (Stone), Chester Clute (Pud), Edgar Kennedy (Judge), Franklin Pangborn (Hotel Clerk), Shemp Howard (Mumbo), Fred Sanborn (Jumbo), Dorothy Jarnac (Specialty Dancer), Sol Haines, Buddy Lawler, Bob Lorraine, Jack Barnett (Lancers), Jim Rushing (Mr. 5X5), Pierre Watkin (Man), Ray Walker (Announcer), John Hamilton (Director), Jack Norton (Drunk), Paul McVey (Studio Executive), Emmett Vogan (Broker), Lane Chandler (Policeman), Earle Hodgins (Barker), Harry Powers (Waiter), Stanley Lawson (Skinny Man), Eddie Polo, George Gray, Francis Sayles (Stooges), Heinie Conklin (Keystone Kop), Dippy Diers (Specialty), Harold DeGarro (Stilt Walker), Charles Dorety (Swiss Bell Ringer), Tiny Ward (Dead End Character), Basil Rathbone (Sherlock Holmes), Nigel Bruce (Dr. Watson), Allan Jones, Johnny Mack Brown, the DeMarcos, Count Basie & Band, the Glenn Miller Singers, the Chandra Kaly Dancers, the Five Hertzogs, Ward & Van, the Layson Brothers, Edgar Barrier, Grace MacDonald, Alan Curtis, Marion Hutton, Ramsey Ames, Robert Paige, Lon Chaney, Evelyn Ankers, Gale Sondergaard, Leo Carrillo, Andy Devine, Turhan Bey, Louise Allbritton, the Delta Rhythm Boys (Themselves).

82. THE SPIDER WOMAN. Universal, 1944. 62 minutes.
   P-D: Roy William Neill. **SC:** Bertram Millhauser. **PH:** Charles Van Enger. **ED:** James Gibbon. **AD:** John Goodman & Martin Obzina. **MUS:** Hans J. Salter.
   Cast: Basil Rathbone (Sherlock Holmes), Nigel Bruce (Dr. Watson), Gale Sondergaard (Adrea Spedding), Dennis Hoey (Inspector Lestrade), Vernon Downing (Norman Locke), Alec Craig (Radlik), Arthur Hohl (Gilfower), Mary Gordon (Mrs. Hudson), Teddy Infuhr (Larry), Belle Mitchell (Fortune Teller), Stanley Logan (Colonel), Donald Stuart (Artie), John Roche (Croupier), John Burton (Announcer), Harry Cording (Fred Garvin), Marie de Becker (Charwoman), John Rogers (Clerk).

Also known as SHERLOCK HOLMES AND THE SPIDER WOMAN.

83. THE SCARLET CLAW. Universal, 1944. 74 minutes.
P-D: Roy William Neill. **SC:** Edmund L. Hartmann & Roy William Neill. **ST:** Paul Gangelin & Brenda Weisberg. **PH:** George Robinson. **ED:** Paul Landres. **AD:** John Goodman & Ralph DeLacy. **MUS:** Paul Sawtell. **SP EFF:** John P. Fulton.
Cast: Basil Rathbone (Sherlock Holmes), Nigel Bruce (Dr. Watson), Gerald Hamer (Potts/Tanner/Ramson), Paul Cavanagh (Lord Penrose), Key Harding (Marie Journet), Miles Mander (Judge Brisson), David Clyde (Sergeant Thompson), Ian Wolfe (Drake), Victoria Horne (Nora), Arthur Hohl (Emile Journet), George Kirby (Father Pierre), Frank O'Connor (Cab Driver), Harry Allen (Storekeeper), Gertrude Astor (Lady Penrose), William Desmond (Club Member).

84. THE PEARL OF DEATH. Universal, 1944. 69 minutes.
P-D: Roy William Neill. **SC:** Bertram Millhauser, from the story "The Adventure of the Six Napoleons" by Arthur Conan Doyle. **PH:** Virgil Miller. **ED:** Ray Snyder. **AD:** John Goodman & Martin Obzina. **MUS:** Paul Sawtell.
Cast: Basil Rathbone (Sherlock Holmes), Nigel Bruce (Dr. Watson), Evelyn Ankers (Naomi Drake), Miles Mander (Giles Conover), Ian Wolfe (Amos Hodder), Holmes Herbert (James Goodram), Dennis Hoey (Inspector Lestrade), Rondo Hatton (the Creeper), Mary Gordon (Mrs. Hudson), Richard Nugent (Bates), Charles Francis (Digby), Harry Cording (Man), Audrey Manners (Teacher), Harold De Becker (Boss), Leland Hodgson (Customs Officer).

85. THE HOUSE OF FEAR. Universal, 1945. 69 minutes.
P-D: Roy William Neill. **SC:** Roy Chanslor, from the story "The Adventure of the Five Orange Pips" by Arthur Conan Doyle. **PH:** Virgil Miller. **ED:** Saul A. Goodkind. **AD:** John Goodman & Eugene Lourie. **MUS:** Paul Sawtell.
Cast: Basil Rathbone (Sherlock Holmes), Nigel Bruce (Dr. Watson), Aubrey Mather (Bruce Alastair), Paul Cavanagh (Simon Merrivale), Dennis Hoey (Inspector Lestrade), Gavin Muir (Chaimers), Holmes Herbert (Alan Cosgrave), Harry Cording (John Simpson), David Clyde (Alex MacGregor), Sally Shepherd (Mrs. Monteith), Doris Lloyd (Bessie), Cyril Delevanti (Stanley Raeburn), Dick Alexander (Ralph King), Wilson Benge (Guy Davies), Fiorette Hillier (Alison MacGregor), Alec Craig (Angus), Leslie Denison (Sergeant Bleeker).

86. WOMAN IN GREEN. Universal, 1945. 68 minutes.
P-D: Roy William Neill. **SC:** Bertram Millhauser. **PH:** Virgil

Miller. **ED:** Edward Curtiss. **AD:** John Goodman & Martin Obzina. **MUS:** Mark Levant. **SP EFF:** John P. Fulton.

Cast: Basil Rathbone (Sherlock Holmes), Nigel Bruce (Dr. Watson), Henry Daniell (Professor Moriarty), Hillary Brooke (Lydia Marlowe), Matthew Boulton (Inspector Gregson), Tom Bryson (Williams), Paul Cavanagh (Sir George Fenwick), Eve Amber (Maude Fenwick), Frederick Worlock (Onslow), Mary Gordon (Mrs. Hudson), Sally Shepherd (Crandon), Percival Vivan (Dr. Simnell), Olaf Hytten (Norris), Harold De Becker (Shabby Man), Tommy Hughes (Newsman).

87. PURSUIT TO ALGIERS. Universal, 1945. 65 minutes.

    P-D: Roy William Neill. **SC:** Leonard Lee. **PH:** Paul Ivano. **ED:** Saul A. Goodkind. **AD:** John Goodman & Martin Obzina. **MUS:** Edgar Fairchild.

    Cast: Basil Rathbone (Sherlock Holmes), Nigel Bruce (Dr. Watson), Marjorie Riordan (Sheila Woodbury), Rosalind Ivan (Agatha Dunham), Martin Kosleck (Mirko), John Abbott (Jodri), Wee Willie Davis (Gubec), Morton Lowry (Sanford), Leslie Vincent (Nikolas), Gerald Hamer (Kingston), Frederick Worlock (Prime Minister), Rex Evans (Gregor), Tom Dillon (Restaurant Manager), Sven Hugo Borg (Johansson), Wilson Benge (Clergyman), Gregory Gaye (Ravez), Dorothy Kellogg (Woman).

88. TERROR BY NIGHT. Universal, 1946. 60 minutes.

    P-D: Roy William Neill. **SC:** Frank Gruber. **PH:** Maury Gertsman. **ED:** Saul A. Goodkind. **AD:** John Goodman. **MUS:** Mark Levant.

    Cast: Basil Rathbone (Sherlock Holmes), Nigel Bruce (Dr. Watson), Alan Mowbray (Major Duncan-Bleek/Colonel Sebastian Moran), Dennis Hoey (Inspector Lestrade), Renée Godfrey (Vivian Ledder), Billy Bevan (Porter), Mary Forbes (Lady Margaret), Geoffrey Steele (Ronald Carstairs), Boyd Davis (MacDonald), Janet Murdoch (Mrs. Shallcross), Skelton Knaggs (Sands), Frederick Worlock (Professor Kilbane), Leland Hodgson (Train Conductor), Gerald Hamer (Shallcross), Harry Cording (Mock), Charles Knight (Guard), Bobby Wissler (Young Mock).

89. DRESSED TO KILL. Universal, 1946. 72 minutes.

    P-D: Roy William Neill. **SC:** Leonard Lee & Frank Gruber. **PH:** Maury Gertsman. **ED:** Saul A. Goodkind. **AD:** Jack Otterson & Martin Obzina. **MUS:** Milton Rosen.

    Cast: Basil Rathbone (Sherlock Holmes), Nigel Bruce (Dr. Watson), Patricia Morison (Hilda Courtney), Edmond Breon (Julian Emery), Frederick Worlock (Colonel Cavanagh), Tom Dillon (Detective Sergeant Thompson), Harry Cording (Hamid), Carl Harbord (Inspector Hopkins), Mary Gordon (Mrs. Hudson), Ian Wolfe (Scotland Yard Commissioner), Patricia Cameron (Evelyn Clifford), Topsy Glyn (Child).

90. THE MAN WITH THE TWISTED LIP. Grand National, 1951. 35 minutes.

    P: Rudolph Carter. **D:** Richard M. Grey. From the story by Arthur Conan Doyle.

    Cast: John Longden (Sherlock Holmes), Campbell Singer (Dr. Watson), Beryl Baxter (Doreen), Hector Ross (Neville St. Clair), Walter Gotell (Luzato).

91. THE HOUND OF THE BASKERVILLES. Hammer Films/United Artists, 1959. 84 minutes. Color.

    P: Anthony Hinds. **EP:** Michael Carreras. **D:** Terence Fisher. **SC:** Peter Bryan, from the novel by Arthur Conan Doyle. **PH:** Jack Asher. **ED:** James Needs. **AD:** Bernard Robinson. **MUS:** James Bernard.

    Cast: Peter Cushing (Sherlock Holmes), André Morell (Dr. Watson), Christopher Lee (Sir Henry Baskerville), Marla Landi (Cecile Stapleton), Ewen Solon (Stapleton), David Oxley (Sir Hugo Baskerville), Miles Malleson (Bishop Frankland), Francis De Wolff (Dr. Mortimer), John Le Mesurier (Barrymore), Sam Kydd (Perkins), Judi Moyens (Servant Girl), David Birks (Servant), Michael Hawkins (Lord Chaphill), Ian Hewitson (Lord Kingsblood), Michael Mulcaster (Seldon), Helen Goss (Mrs. Barrymore), Elizabeth Dott (Mrs. Goodlippe).

92. SHERLOCK HOLMES UND DAS HALSBAND DES TODES (Sherlock Holmes and the Deadly Necklace). Constantin-Film/CCC/Omnia, 1962. 86 minutes.

    P: Arthur Brauner. **D:** Terence Fisher & Frank Witherstein. **SC:** Curt Siodmak, from the novel *The Valley of Fear* by Arthur Conan Doyle. **PH:** Richard Angst. **ED:** Ira Oberberg. **MUS:** Martin Slavin. **AD:** Paul Markwitz.

    Cast: Christopher Lee (Sherlock Holmes), Thorley Walters (Dr. Watson), Hans Sohnker (Professor Moriarty), Hans Nielsen (Inspector Cooper), Senta Berger (Ellen Blackburn), Ivan Desny (Paul King), Leon Askin (Charles), Wolfgang Lukschy (Peter Blackburn), Edith Schultze-Westrum (Mrs. Hudson), Bernard Larjarrie (French Police Inspector), Lindi Sini (Light Girl), Bruno W. Pantel (Auctioneer), Heinrich Gies (American), Roland Armontel (Doctor), Max Strassberg (Johnny), Danielle Argence (Librarian), Corrado Anicelli (Samuels), Franco Giacobini (Jenkins), Waldemar Frahm (Butler), Renate Huttner (Kellnerin), Kurt Hain (Postbeamter), Pierre Gualdi (Wirt).

    U.S. TV Title: SHERLOCK HOLMES AND THE DEADLY NECKLACE.

93. MR. MAGOO—MAN OF MYSTERY. UPA, 1964. 96 minutes, animated.

Cast: Jim Backus (Voice of Mr. Magoo), Paul Frees (Voice of Sherlock Holmes).

94. IBM PUPPET SHOWS. Eames, 1965. 9 minutes.
    D: Charles & Ray Eames.
    Episode Title: SHERLOCK HOLMES AND THE SINGULAR CASE OF THE PLURAL GREEN MUSTACHE.

95. A STUDY IN TERROR. Columbia, 1965. 94 minutes. Color.
    P: Henry E. Lester. **EP:** Herman Cohen. **AP:** Robert Sterne. **D:** James Hill. **SC:** Donald & Derek Ford. **PH:** Desmond Dickinson. **ED:** Henry Richardson. **AD:** Alex Vetchinsky. **MUS:** John Scott. **SP EFF:** Wally Veevers. **ASST DIR:** Barry Langley.
    Cast: John Neville (Sherlock Holmes), Donald Houston (Dr. Watson), Adrienne Corri (Angela), Anthony Quayle (Dr. Murray), John Fraser (Lord Carfax), Frank Finlay (Inspector Lestrade), Barbara Windsor (Annie Chapman), Peter Carsten (Max Steiner), Charles Regnier (Joseph Beck), Georgia Brown (Singer), Robert Morley (Mycroft Holmes), Barry Jones (Duke of Shires), Terry Downes (Chunky), Kay Walsh (Cathy Eldowes), Christine Maybach (Polly Nichols), Cecil Parker (Prime Minister), Dudley Foster (Home Secretary), John Cairney (Michael Osborne), Edina Romay (Mary Kelly), Avis Bunnage (Landlady), Barbara Leake (Mrs. Hudson), Patrick Newell (P.C. Benson), Liz Stride (Norma Foster), Judi Dench (Sally).
    Alternate Title: FOG.

96. THE PRIVATE LIFE OF SHERLOCK HOLMES. United Artists, 1970. 125 minutes. Color.
    P-D: Billy Wilder. **SC:** I. A. L. Diamond & Billy Wilder. **PH:** Christopher Challis. **ED:** Ernest Walter. **AD:** Tony Inglis. **MUS:** Miklos Rozsa. **SP EFF:** Wally Veevers & Cliff Richardson. **ASST DIR:** Tom Pevsner.
    Cast: Robert Stephens (Sherlock Holmes), Genevieve Page (Gabrielle Valladon), Colin Blakely (Dr. Watson), Tamara Toumanova (Petrova), Christopher Lee (Mycroft Holmes), Irene Handl (Mrs. Hudson), Clive Revill (Rogozhin), Catherine Lacey (Old Lady), Stanley Holloway (Head Gravedigger), Mollie Maureen (Queen Victoria), Peter Madden (Von Tirpitz), Robert Cawdron (Hotel Manager), Michael Elwyn (Cassidy), James Copeland (Guide), Alex McCrindle (Baggage Man), Kenneth Benda (Minister), Graham Armitage (Wiggins), Eric Francis (Other Gravedigger), John Garrie, Godfrey James (Carters), Ina de la Haye (Maid), Michael Balfour (Cabbie), Frank Thornton (Porter), George Benson (Inspector Lestrade), John Gatrell (Equerry), Philip Anthony (Lieutenant Commander), Philip Ross (McKellar), Annette Kerr

(Secretary), Martin Carroll, John Scott (Scientists), Daphne Riggs (Lady-in-Waiting).

97. TOUHA SHERLOCKA HOLMESE (The Longing of Sherlock Holmes). Czechoslovak Film, 1971.
    D: Stepan Skalsky. **SC:** Ilja Hurnik & Stepan Skalsky.
    Cast: Radovan Lukavsky (Sherlock Holmes), Vaclav Voska (Dr. Watson), Vlasta Fialova (Lady Abraham), Marie Rousulkova (Lady Oberon), Josef Patocka (Conan Doyle), Bohus Zahorsky (Maestro), Miroslav Machacek (Lord Biddleton), Eduard Kohout (Conductor), Vlastimil Brodsky (Mr. Wrubelski).

98. MR. SHERLOCK HOLMES IN LONDON. Sherlock Holmes Society of London, 1971. 43 minutes.
    Cast: Anthony D. Howlett (host).

99. THEY MIGHT BE GIANTS. Universal, 1971. 98 minutes. Color.
    P: Paul Newman & John Foreman. **D:** Anthony Harvey. **SC:** James Goldman, from his play. **PH:** Victor Kemper. **ED:** Barry Malkin. **MUS:** John Barry. **ASST DIR:** Louis A. Stroller.
    Cast: George C. Scott (Justin Playfair), Joanne Woodward (Dr. Mildred Watson), Lester Rawlins (Blevins Playfair), Rue McClanahan (Daisy), Jack Gilford (Wilbur Peabody), Ron Weyland (Dr. Strauss), Kitty Winn (Grace), Peter Fredericks (Grace's Boyfriend), Sudie Bond (Maud), Jenny Egan (Miss Finch), Al Lewis (Messenger), Michael McGuire (Telephone Guard), Eugene Roche (Policeman), Theresa Merritt (Peggy), Oliver Clark (Mr. Small), Jane Hoffman, Dorothy Greener (Telephone Operators), James Tolkan (Mr. Brown), Jacques Sandulescu (Brown's Driver), Candy Azzara (Teenager), Staats Cotsworth (Winthrop), Paul Benedict (Chestnut Vendor), Ralph Clanton (Store Manager), Ted Beniades (Cab Driver), John McCurry (Police Lieutenant), F. Murray Abraham (Usher), Tony Capodilupo (Chief).

100. THE HOUND OF THE BASKERVILLES. ABC-TV/Universal, 1972. 73 minutes. Color.
    P: Stanley Kallis. **D:** Barry Crane. **SC:** Robert E. Thompson, from the novel by Arthur Conan Doyle. **PH:** Harry Wolf. **ED:** Bill Mosher. **SP EFF:** Albert Whitlock.
    Cast: Stewart Granger (Sherlock Holmes), Bernard Fox (Dr. Watson), William Shatner (Stapleton), Jane Merrow (Beryl Stapleton), Anthony Zerbe (Dr. Mortimer), John Williams (Frankland), Sally Ann Howes (Laura Frankland), Ian Ireland (Sir Henry Baskerville), Brendan Dillon (Barrymore), Arlaine Anderson (Mrs. Barrymore), Billy Bowles (Cartwright), Alan Callou (Inspector Lestrade), Chuck Hicks (Seldon), Karen Kondon (Mrs. Mortimer), Arthur Malet (Higgins), Liam Dunn (Messenger), Elaine Church (Servant), Eric Brotherson (Porter), Barry Bernard (Manager),

Jenifer Shaw (Peasant Girl), Constance Cavendish (Eel Monger), Terence Pushman (Chestnut Vendor), Michael St. Clair (Constable).

101. MURDER IN NORTHUMBERLAND. West End Productions, 1974. Color.
   P-D: Paul Roach.
   Cast: Keith McConnell (Sherlock Holmes), Anthony Seerl (Dr. Watson).

102. THE ADVENTURES OF SHERLOCK HOLMES' SMARTER BROTHER. 20th Century–Fox, 1975. 91 minutes. Color.
   P: Richard A. Roth. **AP:** Charles Orme. **D-SC:** Gene Wilder. **PH:** Gerry Fisher. **ED:** James Clark. **AD:** Alan Tomkins. **MUS:** John Morris. **SP EFF:** Roy Whybrow. **ASST DIR:** David Tomblin.
   Cast: Gene Wilder (Sigi Holmes), Madeline Kahn (Jenny), Marty Feldman (Orville Sacker), Dom DeLuise (Gambetti), Leo McKern (Professor Moriarty), Douglas Wilmer (Sherlock Holmes), Thorley Walters (Dr. Watson), Roy Kennear (Assistant), John Le Mesurier (Lord Redcliff), George Silver (Bruner), Susan Field (Queen Victoria), Nicholas Smith (Hunkston), Tommy Godfrey (Fred), John Hollis (Colonel Von Stulberg), Aubrey Morris (Coach Driver), Joseph Behramannis (Russian), Wolfe Morris (Frenchman), Julian Orchard (Man in Tails), Kenneth Beade (Butler), Michael Crane (Renato), Tony Sympson (Opera Conductor).

103. THE AMERICAN ADVENTURES OF SURELICK HOLMES. Hand-in-Hand Productions, 1975.

104. THE RETURN OF THE WORLD'S GREATEST DETECTIVE. NBC-TV, 1976. 73 minutes. Color.
   P: Dean Hargrove & Roland Kibbee. **D:** Dean Hargrove. **SC:** Dean Hargrove and Roland Kibbee. **PH:** William Mendenhall. **ED:** John Kaufman, Jr. **MUS:** Dick DeBenedictis. **AD:** William L. Campbell.
   Cast: Larry Hagman (Sherman Holmes), Jenny O'Hara (Dr. Joan Watson), Nicholas Colasanto (Lieutenant Nick Tinker), Woodrow Parfrey (Himmel), Helen Verbit (Mrs. Hudson), Ivor Francis (Spiner), Charles Macauley (Judge Clement Harley), Ron Silver (Dr. Collins), Sid Haig (Vince Cooley), Booth Colman (Psychiatrist), Lieux Dressler (Mrs. Slater), Fuddle Bagley (Detective), Benny Rubin (Klinger), Robert Snively (Manager), Jude Farese (Caretaker), George Brenlin (Sergeant), Al Dunlap (Bailiff), Jefferson Kibbee (Delivery Man).

105. SHERLOCK HOLMES IN NEW YORK. NBC-TV/20th Century–Fox, 1976. 100 minutes. Color.
   P: John Cutts. **EP:** Nancy Malone. **D:** Boris Sagal. **SC:** Alvin

Sapinsley. **PH:** Michael Margulies. **ED:** Samuel E. Beetley **AD:** Lawrence G. Paull. **MUS:** Richard Rodney Bennett.

Cast: Roger Moore (Sherlock Holmes), Charlotte Rampling (Irene Adler), Patrick MacNee (Dr. Watson), John Huston (Professor Moriarty), Gig Young (Mortimer McGraw), David Huddleston (Inspector Lafferty), Signe Hasso (Frau Reichenbach), Leon Ames (Daniel Furman), John Abbott (Heller), Jackie Coogan (Hotel Haymarket Proprietor), Maria Grimm (Nicole Romaine), Marjorie Bennett (Mrs. Hudson), Geoffrey Moore (Scott Adler).

106. THE SEVEN PERCENT SOLUTION. Universal, 1976. 113 minutes. Color.

P-D: Herbert Ross. **EP:** Arlene Sellers & Alex Winitsky. **AP:** Stanley O'Toole. **SC:** Nicholas Meyer, from his novel. **PH:** Oswald Morris. **ED:** William Reynolds & Chris Barnes. **MUS:** John Addison. **AD:** Peter Lamont.

Cast: Nicol Williamson (Sherlock Holmes), Robert Duvall (Dr. Watson), Alan Arkin (Sigmund Freud), Vanessa Redgrave (Lola Deveraux), Joel Grey (Lowenstein), Samantha Eggar (Mary Watson), Laurence Olivier (Professor Moriarty), Jeremy Kemy (Baron von Leinsdorf), Georgia Brown (Mrs. Freud), Charles Gray (Mycroft Holmes), Regine (Madame), Anna Quayle (Freda), Jill Townsend (Mrs. Holmes), John Bird (Berger), Alison Leggatt (Mrs. Hudson), Frederick Jaeger (Marker), Erik Chitty (Butler), Jack May (Dr. Schultz), Gertan Klauber (The Pasha), Leon Greene (Squire Holmes), Michael Blagdon (Young Sherlock Holmes), Ashley House (Young Sigmund Freud), Sheila Shand (Nun), Erich Padalewsky (Station Master), John Hill (Train Engineer).

107. MURDER BY DEATH. Columbia, 1976. 94 minutes. Color.

P: Ray Stark. **AP:** Roger M. Rothstein. **D:** Robert Moore. **SC:** Neil Simon. **PH:** David M. Walsh. **ED:** Margaret Booth. **MUS:** Dave Grusin.

Cast: Eileen Brennan (Tess Skeffington), Truman Capote (Lionel Twain), James Coco (Milo Perrier), Peter Falk (Sam Diamond), Alec Guinness (Bensonmum), Elsa Lanchester (Jessica Marbles), David Niven (Dick Charleston), Peter Sellers (Sidney Wang), Maggie Smith (Dora Charleston), Nancy Walker (Yetta), Estelle Windwood (Miss Withers), James Cromwell (Marcel), Richard Narita (Willie Wang), Keith McConnell (Sherlock Holmes), Richard Peel (Dr. Watson).

108. THE HIDDEN MOTIVE. Kentucky Educational Television, 1976. 16 minutes. Color.

Cast: Leonard Nimoy (Sherlock Holmes), Burt Blackwell (Dr. Watson).

109. THE HOUND OF THE BASKERVILLES. Hemdale, 1978. 85 minutes. Color.
    P: John Goldstone. **EP:** Michael White & Andrew Braunsberg. **AP:** Tim Hampton. **D:** Paul Morrissey. **SC:** Peter Cook, Dudley Moore & Paul Morrissey, from the novel by Arthur Conan Doyle. **PH:** Dick Rush. **ED:** Richard Marden. **MUS:** Dudley Moore.
    Cast: Peter Cook (Sherlock Holmes), Dudley Moore (Dr. Watson/Mrs. Holmes/Spiggot), Denholm Elliott (Stapleton), Joan Greenwood (Beryl Stapleton), Terry-Thomas (Dr. Mortimer), Max Wall (Barrymore), Irene Handl (Mrs. Barrymore), Kenneth Williams (Sir Henry Baskerville), Hugh Griffith (Frankland), Dana Gillespie (Mary Frankland), Roy Kinnear (Ethel Seldon), Prunella Scales (Glynis), Penelope Keith (Receptionist), Spike Milligan (P.C.), Lucy Griffith (Iris), Jessie Matthews (Mrs. Tindale), Rita Webb (Masseuse), Geoffrey Moon (Perkins), Josephine Tewson (Nun), Anna Wing (Daphne), Henry Woolf (Shopkeeper), Pearl Hackney (Passenger).

110. MURDER BY DECREE. Avco/Embassy, 1979. 112 minutes. Color.
    P: René Dupont & Bob Clark. **EP:** Len Heberman & Robert Goldstone. **D:** Bob Clark. **SC:** John Hopkins, from the book *The Ripper File* by John Lloyd & Elwyn Jones. **PH:** Reginald Morris. **ED:** Stan Cole. **MUS:** Carl Zittrer.
    Cast: Christopher Plummer (Sherlock Holmes), James Mason (Dr. Watson), David Hemmings (Inspector Foxborough), Susan Clark (Mary Kelly), Anthony Quayle (Sir Charles Warren), John Gielgud (Prime Minister), Frank Finlay (Inspector Lestrade), Donald Sutherland (Robert Lees), Genevieve Bujold (Annie Crook), Chris Wiggins (Dr. Harding), Teddi Moore (Mrs. Lees), Peter Jonfield (William Slade), Roy Lansford (Sir Thomas Spivey), Catherine Kessler (Carrie), Ron Pember (Makins), June Brown (Annie Chapman), Terry Duggan (Dannie), Hilary Sista (Catherine Eddowes), Betty Woolfe (Mrs. Hudson), Iris Fry (Elizabeth Stride), Geoffrey Russell (Home Secretary), Victor Langley (Prince of Wales), Pamela Abbott (Princess Alexandra), Robin Marchall (Duke of Clarence), Danny Long (P. C.).

111. SHERLOCK HOLMES. Home Box Office, 1981. 100 minutes. Color.
    P-D: Peter H. Hunt. **AP:** Deborah A. Ross. From the play by William Gillette. **MUS:** Arthur B. Rubinstein. **STAGE DIRECTOR:** Gary Halvorson.
    Cast: Frank Langella (Sherlock Holmes), Richard Woods (Dr. Watson), George Morfogon (Professor Moriarty), Laurie Kennedy (Alice Faulkner), Susan Clark (Madge Larabee), Stephen Collins (James Larabee), Tom Akins (Craigin), William Duell (Parsons),

John Tillinger (Sir Edward), Dwight Schultz (Basil), Babette Tweed (Theresa).

112. THE SIGN OF FOUR. Mapleton Films, 1983. 100 minutes. Color.
    P: Otto Plaschkes. **EP:** Sy Weintraub. **D:** Desmond Davis. **SC:** Charles Pogue, from the novel by Arthur Conan Doyle. **PH:** Denis Lewiston. **ED:** Timothy Gee. **AD:** Eileen Diss. **MUS:** Harry Rabinowitz.
    Cast: Ian Richardson (Sherlock Holmes), David Healy (Dr. Watson), Thorley Walters (Major John Sholto), Cherie Lunghi (Mary Morstan), Terence Rigby (Inspector Layton), Joe Melia (Jonathan Small), Michael O'Hagan (Mordecai Smith), Clive Merrison (Bartholomew Sholto), Richard Heffren (Thaddeus Sholto), Darren Michael (Wiggins), Robert Russell (Williams), John Benefield (McMundro), John Pedrick (Tonga), Gordon Rollings (Mr. Sherman).

113. THE HOUND OF THE BASKERVILLES. Mapleton Films, 1983. 100 minutes. Color.
    P: Otto Plaschkes. **EP:** Sy Weintraub. **D:** Douglas Hickox. **SC:** Charles Pogue, from the novel by Arthur Conan Doyle. **PH:** Ronnie Taylor. **ED:** Malcolm Cooke. **MUS:** Michael J. Lewis.
    Cast: Ian Richardson (Sherlock Holmes), Donald Churchill (Dr. Watson), Martin Shaw (Sir Henry Baskerville), Nicholas Clay (Jack Stapleton), Denholm Elliott (Dr. Mortimer), Brian Blessed (Geoffrey Lyons), Ronald Lacey (Inspector Lestrade), Edward Judd (Barrymore), Glynis Barber (Beryl Stapleton), Eleanor Bron (Mrs. Barrymore), Connie Booth (Laura Lyons), Eric Richard (Cabbie), David Layton (Sir Charles Baskerville), Michael Burrell (Merchant).

114. SHERLOCK HOLMES AND THE BASKERVILLE CURSE. Pacific Arts, 1984. 70 minutes. Animated, color.
    D: Eddy Graham.
    Cast: Peter O'Toole (Voice of Sherlock Holmes).

115. SHERLOCK HOLMES AND THE SIGN OF FOUR. Pacific Arts, 1984. 48 minutes. Animated, color.
    D: Eddy Graham.
    Cast: Peter O'Toole (Voice of Sherlock Holmes).

116. SHERLOCK HOLMES AND A STUDY IN SCARLET. Pacific Arts, 1984. 49 minutes. Animated, color.
    D: Eddy Graham.
    Cast: Peter O'Toole (Voice of Sherlock Holmes).

117. SHERLOCK HOLMES AND THE VALLEY OF FEAR. Pacific Arts, 1984. 49 minutes. Animated, color.

D: Eddy Graham.
Cast: Peter O'Toole (Voice of Sherlock Holmes).

118. THE MASKS OF DEATH. Tyburn Entertainment, 1985. 82 minutes. Color.
   P: Norman Pridgen. **EP:** Kevin Francis. **D:** Roy Ward Baker. **SC:** N. J. Crisp. **ST:** John Elder. **PH:** Brendan J. Stafford. **ED:** Christopher Barnes. **MUS:** Philip Martell & Malcolm Williamson. **AD:** Geoffrey Tozer.
   Cast: Peter Cushing (Sherlock Holmes), John Mills (Dr. Watson), Anne Baxter (Irene Adler), Ray Milland (Home Secretary), Anton Diffring (Graf Udo von Felseck), Gordon Jackson (Alec MacDonald), Susan Penhaligon (Miss Derwent), Marcus Gilbert (Anton Von Felseck), Jenny Laird (Mrs. Hudson), Russell Hunter (Alfred Combs), James Cossine (Barnes), Eric Dodson (Lord Claremont), Georgia Coombs (Lady Claremont), James Head (Chauffeur), Dominic Murphy (Boot Boy).

119. YOUNG SHERLOCK HOLMES. Paramount, 1985. 110 minutes. Color.
   P: Mark Johnson. **D:** Barry Levinson. **SC:** Chris Columbus. **PH:** Stephen Goldblatt. **ED:** Stu Linder. **MUS:** Bruce Broughton. **DESIGN:** Norman Reynolds.
   Cast: Nicholas Rowe (Sherlock Holmes), Alan Cox (John Watson), Sophie Ward (Elizabeth), Anthony Higgins (Rathe), Susan Fleetwood (Mrs. Dribb), Freddie Jones (Cragwitch), Nigel Stock (Waxflatter), Roger Ashton Griffiths (Lestrade), Donald Eccles (Rev. Duncan Nesbitt), Patrick Newell (Bentley Bobster), Earl Rhodes (Dudley Babcock).

120. THE RETURN OF SHERLOCK HOLMES. CBS-TV, 1987. 100 minutes. Color.
   P: Nick Gillot. **D:** Kevin Connor. **SC:** Bob Shayne. **PH:** Tony Imi. **ED:** Bernard Gribble. **MUS:** Ken Thorne. **DESIGN:** Keith Wilson. **AD:** Simon Wakefield.
   Cast: Michael Pennington (Sherlock Holmes), Margaret Colin (Jane Watson), Barry Morse (Carter Morstan), Lila Kaye (Ms. Houston), Connie Booth (Violet), Nicholas Guest (Toby), Shane Rimmer (Stark), Paul Maxwell (Hopkins), Oliver Pierre (Hampton), Ray Jewers (Singer), Daniel Benzali (Ross), Sheila Brand (Kitty), Tony Steedman (Doctor), William Hootkins (Spelman).

121. SHERLOCK AND ME. ITC Entertainment Group, 1988.
   P: Marc Stirdivant. **D:** Thom Eberhardt. **SC:** Larry Strawther & Gary Murphy. **MUS:** Henry Mancini.
   Cast: Michael Caine (Reginald Kincaid/Sherlock Holmes), Ben Kingsley (Dr. Watson).

Chapter 14

THE WHISTLER

THE WHISTLER SERIES is different from most detective film groupings in that the title character is never seen as more than a fleeting shadow who whistles a brief, eerie refrain. Each of the eight features in Columbia's Whistler series had a different protagonist, and the Whistler himself stood for the fate which entwined a different individual in each plot line. The films were based on the popular CBS radio series "The Whistler," which was broadcast from 1942 to 1952, with Bill Forman (later Marvin Miller and Everett Clarke) in the title role.

When Columbia Pictures producer Rudolph C. Flothow began a series of films based on the radio program, popular leading man Richard Dix was hired to star in the features. Born in 1894, Dix (whose real name was Ernest Carlton Brimmer) had considerable stage experience before making his film debut in 1921 in NOT GUILTY. In the next few years he developed into a popular film star in such features as THE CHRISTIAN ('23), SOULS FOR SALE ('23), TO THE LAST MAN ('23), THE TEN COMMANDMENTS ('23), MANHATTAN ('24), THE LUCKY DEVIL ('25), THE QUARTERBACK ('26), SHANGHAI BOUND ('27), and REDSKIN ('29), before making a successful talkie debut in NOTHING BUT THE TRUTH ('29). Dix continued to be a popular leading man in sound films like SEVEN KEYS TO BALDPATE ('29), CIMARRON ('31), YOUNG DONOVAN'S KID ('31), PUBLIC DEFENDER ('31), THE LOST SQUADRON ('32), ROAR OF THE DRAGON ('32), THE CONQUERORS ('32), THE GREAT JASPER ('33), THE ARIZONIAN ('35), YELLOW DUST ('36), BLIND ALIBI

('38), MAN OF CONQUEST ('39), RENO ('39), CHERO-
KEE STRIP ('40), AMERICAN EMPIRE ('42), EYES OF
THE UNDERWORLD ('43), and THE GHOST SHIP ('43).
By the time he made the Whistler series, Dix was in poor
health, and he died following his seventh series entry,
THE THIRTEENTH HOUR ('47), in 1949.

For its initial entry in the new series, Columbia hired J.
Donald Wilson, who wrote the radio series, to do the story
for THE WHISTLER, which was issued in 1944 to generally
good reviews. The film was well written, and William
Castle's direction was tight and supplied the film with an
aura of suspense and horror. The plot has a businessman,
Earl Conrad (Richard Dix) despondent over the supposed
death of his wife. He hires an unknown man (J. Carrol
Naish) to kill him. When he finds out that his wife is
actually alive in a concentration camp, Conrad attempts to
cancel the murder contract, but his go-between (Don
Costello) is killed by the law, and Conrad must try to elude
the hit man, who eventually is killed. While the *New York
Times* complained the feature was a "weary, illogical
imitation of Alfred Hitchcock (plus an early Fritz Lang film)
. . . very dull," Don Miller more correctly opined in *B
Movies* (1973) that Eric Taylor's script "was suspenseful
and without waste motion, and Castle heightened the
tenseness with excellent economy of means while eliciting
exemplary performances from Dix and J. Carrol Naish as
the killer."

Later in 1944 William Castle directed the second series
outing, MARK OF THE WHISTLER, based on a Cornell
Woolrich original story. Dix was cast as bum Lee Nugent,
who comes across a newspaper story about an attempt to
locate the heir to an estate. He takes on the guise of the
man being sought and collects nearly $100,000 from a
dormant bank account, only to learn that he is being
sought by a hit man who is after the man whose identity he
has taken. Lee is aided by pretty newspaper reporter
Patricia Henley (Janis Carter) and street beggar Limpy
Smith (Paul Guifoyle) before he finally squares himself
with the law. The *New York Times* liked the follow-up better
than the initial film, saying the plot had "some fair to

middling interest." On the other hand, Kate Cameron in the *New York Daily News* called the film an "exciting picture" and the Whistler outings "a series of thrilling adventure films."

Lew Landers took over the direction for the third Whistler outing, THE POWER OF THE WHISTLER, issued in March 1945. Here Richard Dix played William Everest, a man who is hit by a car and suffers amnesia. Pretty Jean Lang (Janis Carter) and her sister Frances (Jeff Donnell) befriend the man and try to learn his identity from a few objects found in his pockets. Eventually they discover he is an escaped mental patient who is a homicidal maniac now threatening Jean, with whom he has fallen in love. The *New York Daily News* said director Landers "maintains considerable suspense" in the feature, while *Variety* dubbed it a "fair whodunit."

William Castle returned to the series for the fourth entry, VOICE OF THE WHISTLER, released for the 1945 Christmas holidays. The film's plot, however, was hardly a joyful one in its tale of a rich businessman, John Sinclair (Richard Dix), who finds out he has only six months to live. He asks his beautiful nurse, Joan Martin (Lynn Merrick), to marry him in return for inheriting his fortune. The young woman agrees in order to finance the career of her lover, medical intern Fred Graham (James Cardwell). Seven months pass and Sinclair and Joan have fallen in love, and his health is perfect. Jealous Fred Graham shows up at their luxury lighthouse home bent on killing Sinclair. Eventually he carries out his plan but Fred, too, dies, leaving Joan to live as a penitent recluse in the lighthouse. *Variety* complained, "Despite its eerie buildup, VOICE OF THE WHISTLER isn't as haunting as ballyhooed. A minor item."

THE MYSTERIOUS INTRUDER, released in March 1946, is considered by many to be the best film in the Whistler series. William Castle directed this, the fifth series affair and his last. Eric Taylor, who had done the screenplay for the initial film, THE WHISTLER, supplied the taut script. Richard Dix portrayed private eye Don Gale, who investigates a series of murders he discovers were insti-

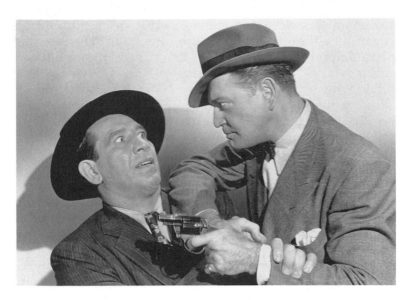

Mike Mazurki *(left)* and Richard Dix in MYSTERIOUS INTRUDER (Columbia, 1946)

gated for the control of two priceless Jenny Lind recordings. He finds that a Swedish millionaire is after the records and that he has hired monstrous killer Harry Pontos (Mike Mazurki) to carry out his dirty work. Motivated by his own desire to have the recordings, Gale soon finds himself at odds with Pontos as well as police Detective Taggart (Barton MacLane). In his article "Private Eyes" in *Focus on Film* (Autumn, 1975), Don Miller called the film "perhaps the best of the non-[Raymond] Chandler private eyes of the period," and said the film "possessed a haunting atmosphere all its own." *Variety* noted, "Direction of William Castle is nicely done. He keeps the action moving at a lively pace and the audience edged forward on their seats."

SECRET OF THE WHISTLER, the sixth series entry, was also issued in 1946. Veteran action director George Sherman led the project, which Jon Tuska in *The Detective in Hollywood* (1978) called "a letdown." He added, "None of the characters were sympathetic and there was no imagination in either the acting or the direction.'' The plot had artist Ralph Harrison (Richard Dix) married to sick but rich Edith (Mary Currier), who finds out he is having a love affair with beautiful model Kay Morrell (Leslie Brooks). When Edith accuses Ralph of infidelity and threatens to remove him from her will, the artist gives her poison which Edith does not take. She notes his actions in her diary. When Edith dies of a heart attack, Ralph thinks he is responsible; three months later he marries Kay. When a similar homicide appears in the newspaper, Ralph hunts for the diary. He learns that Kay has it and plans to turn him over to the law. Ralph strangles his new wife and is arrested, only to find out the police have cleared him in Edith's death.

Richard Dix's seventh and final Whistler film was THE THIRTEENTH HOUR, issued in 1947 and directed by

John Kellogg *(left)* and Richard Dix in THE THIRTEENTH HOUR (Columbia, 1947)

William Clemens, who had directed a trio of entries in the Falcon (see B/V) series. Dix portrayed trucking firm owner Steve Reynolds, who is engaged to diner operator Eileen Blair (Karen Morley), who has a young son Tommy (Mark Dennis). Policeman Don Parker (Regis Toomey) is also in love with Eileen. After having an accident while trying to avoid a reckless driver, Steve has his driver's license revoked by Parker. His competitor, Jerry Mason (Jim Bannon), tries to buy Steve out, but he refuses. Later a masked assailant tries to kill Steve, but it is Don who is murdered. Steve is blamed for the crime. He and Eileen, along with his mechanic Charlie (John Kellogg), try to prove his innocence. Steve learns the crime is linked to a diamond robbery and a hot car racket. *Film Daily* reviewed, "The plot has action requirements and is set off to good advantage in the directorial handling."

In 1948 Richard Dix suffered a severe heart attack and was unable to continue in the Whistler films, but Columbia made one more effort without Dix, the unsuccessful RETURN OF THE WHISTLER. The plot has a man (Michael Duane) meeting and falling in love with a beautiful French woman (Lenore Aubert). He plans to marry her, but she suddenly disappears. He hires a private investigator (Richard Lane) to find her, and it is discovered that she has been committed to an asylum by a man (James Cardwell) who claims that the woman, who is really a wealthy widow, is his wife. The man and the detective then try to prove the girl's identity and set her free from the confines of the institution, whose administrators are in the employ of the man who had her committed.

Overall, the Whistler films are an interesting and offbeat series of well-made programmers whose mystery and horrific content, plus solid direction, acting, and production values, made them a bit better than the average low-budget pictures of the period. With budgets in the $70,000 range per picture, the Whistler films were slick affairs highlighted by the work of Richard Dix in the first seven efforts. Although Dix's popularity had waned somewhat by the time he did the series, he still had a faithful following and this, coupled with the innate appeal of the films, made them box office winners for Columbia.

Filmography

1. THE WHISTLER. Columbia, 1944. 60 minutes.
   P: Rudolph C. Flothow. **D:** William Castle. **SC:** Eric Taylor. **ST:** J. Donald Wilson. **PH:** James S. Brown. **ED:** Jerome Thoms. **AD:** George Van Marter. **MUS:** Wilbur Hatch.
   Cast: Richard Dix (Earl Conrad), J. Carrol Naish (The Killer), Gloria Stuart (Alice Walker), Alan Dinehart (Gorman), Don Costello (Lefty Vigran), Joan Woodbury (Toni Vigran), Cy Kendall (Bartender), Trevor Bardette (Thief), Robert E. Keane (Charles McNear), Clancy Cooper (Briggs), George Lloyd (Bill Tomley), Byron Foulger (Flophouse Clerk), Charles Coleman (Jennings), Robert Homans (Dock Watchman).

2. MARK OF THE WHISTLER. Columbia, 1944. 61 minutes.
   P: Rudolph C. Flothow. **D:** William Castle. **SC:** George Bricker. **ST:** Cornell Woolrich. **PH:** George Meehan. **ED:** Reg Browne. **AD:** John Daut. **MUS:** Wilbur Hatch.
   Cast: Richard Dix (Lee Nugent), Janis Carter (Patricia Henley), Paul Guifoyle (Limpy Smith), Porter Hall (Joe Sorsby), John Calvert (Eddie Donnelly), Matt Willis (Perry Donnelly).

3. THE POWER OF THE WHISTLER. Columbia, 1945. 66 minutes.
   P: Leonard S. Picker. **D:** Lew Landers. **SC:** Aubrey Wisberg. **PH:** L. W. O'Connell. **ED:** Reg Browne. **AD:** John Daut. **MUS:** Wilbur Hatch.
   Cast: Richard Dix (William Everest), Janis Carter (Jean Lang), Jeff Donnell (Frances Lang), Tala Birell (Constantine Ivaneska), Loren Tindall (Charlie Kent), John Abbott (Kaspar Andropolos), Murray Alper (Joe Blaney), Cy Kendall (Druggist).

4. VOICE OF THE WHISTLER. Columbia, 1945. 60 minutes.
   P: Rudolph C. Flothow. **D:** William Castle. **SC:** Wilfred H. Petitt & William Castle. **ST:** Allan Rader. **PH:** George Meehan. **ED:** Dwight Caldwell. **MUS:** Mischa Bakaleinikoff.
   Cast: Richard Dix (John Sinclair), Lynn Merrick (Joan Martin), Rhys Williams (Ernie Sparrow), James Cardwell (Fred Graham), Tom Kennedy (Ferdinand), Donald Woods (Paul Kitridge), Egon Brecher (Dr. Rose), Gigi Perreau (Bobbie).

5. THE MYSTERIOUS INTRUDER. Columbia, 1946. 62 minutes.
   P: Rudolph C. Flothow. **D:** William Castle. **SC:** Eric Taylor. **PH:**

Philip Tannura. **ED:** Dwight Caldwell. **AD:** Hans Radon. **MUS:** Wilbur Hatch & Mischa Bakaleinikoff. **ASST DIR:** Carl Hiecke.

Cast: Richard Dix (Don Gale), Barton MacLane (Detective Taggart), Nina Vale (Joan Hill), Regis Toomey (James Summers), Mike Mazurki (Harry Pontos), Helen Mowry (Freda Hanson), Pamela Blake [Adele Pearce] (Elora Lund), Charles Lane (Detective Burns), Paul Burns (Edward Stillwell), Kathleen Howard (Rose Denning), Harlan Briggs (Brown).

Working Title: MURDER IS UNPREDICTABLE.

6. SECRET OF THE WHISTLER. Columbia, 1946. 62 minutes.

P: Rudolph C. Flothow. **D:** George Sherman. **SC:** Raymond L. Schrock. **ST:** Richard H. Landau. **PH:** Allen Siegler. **ED:** Dwight Caldwell. **AD:** Hans Radon. **MUS:** Wilbur Hatch & Mischa Bakaleinikoff. **ASST DIR:** Carter DeHaven, Jr. **SETS:** Robert Bradfield. **SOUND:** Howard Fogetti.

Cast: Richard Dix (Ralph Harrison), Leslie Brooks (Kay Morrell), Michael Duane (Jim Calhoun), Mary Currier (Edith Marie Harrison), Mona Barrie (Linda Vail), Ray Walker (Joe Conroy), Claire DuBrey (Laura), Charles Trowbridge (Dr. Winthrop), Arthur Space (Dr. Gunther), Jack Davis (Henry Loring), Barbara Woodell (Nurse).

7. THE THIRTEENTH HOUR. Columbia, 1947. 65 minutes.

P: Rudolph C. Flothow. **D:** William Clemens. **SC:** Edward Bock & Raymond L. Schrock. **ST:** Leslie Edgley. **PH:** Vincent Farrar. **ED:** Dwight Caldwell. **AD:** Hans Radon. **MUS:** Wilbur Hatch & Mischa Bakaleinikoff. **ASST DIR:** Carter DeHaven, Jr. **SETS:** Albert Rickard. **SOUND:** Howard Fogetti.

Cast: Richard Dix (Steve Reynolds), Karen Morley (Eileen Blair), John Kellogg (Charlie Cook), Jim Bannon (Jerry Mason), Regis Toomey (Patrolman Don Parker), Bernadene Hayes (Mable Sawyer), Mark Dennis (Tommy), Anthony Warde (Ranford), Ernie Adams (McCabe), Cliff Clark (Captain Linfield).

8. RETURN OF THE WHISTLER. Columbia, 1948. 61 minutes.

P: Rudolph C. Flothow. **D:** D. Ross Lederman. **SC:** Edward Bock & Maurice Tombragel. **ST:** Cornell Woolrich. **PH:** Philip Tannura. **ED:** Dwight Caldwell **AD:** George Brooks. **MUS:** Wilbur Hatch & Mischa Bakaleinikoff.

Cast: Michael Duane (Ted Nichols), Lenore Aubert (Alice Barclay), Richard Lane (Gayford Travers), James Cardwell (John), Anne Shoemaker (Mrs. Barclay), Sarah Padden (Mrs. Huls), Wilton Graff (Dr. Grantland), Olin Howlin (Jeff Anderson), Eddy Waller (Sam), Trevor Bardette (Arnold), Ann Doran (Sybil), Robert Emmett Keane (Hart), Edgar Dearing (Captain Griggs).

Chapter 15

OTHER MOVIE DETECTIVES

BILL AND SALLY REARDON

MELVYN DOUGLAS (1901–1981) had a long and distinguished acting career. He portrayed a number of screen sleuths, but he did only one detective film series—the two Bill and Sally Reardon features, THERE'S ALWAYS A WOMAN and THERE'S THAT WOMAN AGAIN. Douglas made his film debut in 1931 in the Gloria Swanson vehicle TONIGHT OR NEVER and was a leading man to most of the screen's top female stars. He also cut a niche in the detective genre appearing as a sleuth in such features as THE LONE WOLF RETURNS ('35) (see B/V), ARSENE LUPIN RETURNS ('38) (q.v.), FAST COMPANY ('38) (q.v.), and TELL NO TALES ('39). He won an Academy Award as best supporting actor for HUD ('63).

In a obvious attempt to create box office interest in a husband-and-wife sleuthing team, à la Nick and Nora Charles in the Thin Man (see B/V) features, Columbia Pictures purchased the screen rights to the characters of Bill and Sally Reardon from William Collison's magazine stories and cast Joan Blondell as Sally and Melvyn Douglas as her husband in THERE'S ALWAYS A WOMAN. Blondell had previously been very good as the amateur detective nurse in MISS PINKERTON ('32). In this outing she is the wife of a private eye who is down on his luck, and as a result takes back his old job with the district attorney. When a society woman (Mary Astor) is murdered, Sally decides to aid Bill in investigating the case, and her hair-brained schemes get him into a great deal of

From left: George Davis, Joan Blondell, Melvyn Douglas, and Marek Windheim in THERE'S ALWAYS A WOMAN (Columbia, 1938)

hot water with his boss until Sally, by accident, ends up solving the case. *Variety* noted, "All the elements of first-rate cinema entertainment are present." Highlights of the feature included a very funny sequence where Sally gets the third degree from the police, and the scene where Bill and Sally get tipsy. An interesting footnote to the film is that future screen siren Rita Hayworth was assigned an important supporting role, that of Sally's pal in the D.A.'s office, but most of her scenes were deleted upon the release of the picture. Apparently Hayworth was not available for the sequel, so her part was basically dropped. In 1939 Joan Blondell, Melvyn Douglas, and director Alexander Hall were reteamed for another comedy-mystery, THE AMAZING MR. WILLIAMS.

The second series outing, THERE'S THAT WOMAN AGAIN, was issued early in 1939 and although director Alexander Hall was back, as was star Melvyn Douglas,

Virginia Bruce replaced Joan Blondell as Sally Reardon. Here Sally tries to aid detective husband Bill in a case involving jewel thefts and two murders, the culprits being lovely Mrs. Nacelle (Margaret Lindsay) and her cohort Tony Croy (Stanley Ridges). In trying to solve the case herself, Sally not only endangers Bill's life and reputation but also ends up in a suspect's shower. Although the film moved at a fast clip and was a light, breezy mystery-comedy, it was not so popular as the initial feature, and no further adventures of Bill and Sally Reardon were forthcoming.

Filmography

1. THERE'S ALWAYS A WOMAN. Columbia, 1938. 82 minutes.
   D:Alexander Hall. SC: Joel Sayre, Philip Rapp, Gladys Lehman & (uncredited) Morrie Ryskind.
   Cast: Joan Blondell (Sally Reardon), Melvyn Douglas (Bill Reardon), Mary Astor, Frances Drake, Jerome Cowan, Thurston Hall, Robert Paige, Pierre Watkin, Walter Kingsford, Lester Matthews, Wade Boteler, Rita Hayworth, Arthur Loft, William H. Strauss, Marek Windheim, Bud Jamison, George Davis, Robert Emmet Keane, John Gallaudet, Eddie Fetherston, Josef De Stefani, Ted Oliver, Gene Morgan, Tom Dugan, Bud Geary, Billy Benedict, Lee Phelps, Eddie Dunn, George McKay.

2. THERE'S THAT WOMAN AGAIN. Columbia, 1939. 72 minutes.
   D: Alexander Hall. SC: Philip G. Epstein, James Edward Grant & Ken Englund.
   Cast: Melvyn Douglas (Bill Reardon), Virginia Bruce (Sally Reardon), Margaret Lindsay, Stanley Ridges, Gordon Oliver, Tom Dugan, Don Beddoe, Jonathan Hale, Pierre Watkin, Paul Harvey, Marc Lawrence, Charles Wilson, Donald [Don "Red"] Barry, Jack Hatfield, Harry Burns, Helen Lynd, Georgette Rhodes, Lilian Yarbo, Vivien Oakland, William Newell, Gladys Blake, Pat Flaherty, Dick Curtis, June Gittelson, Lucille Lund, John Dilson, Eric Mayne, Maurice Costello, Russell Heustis, Lola Jensen, Frank Hall Crayne, Charles McMurphy, Mantan Moreland, George Turner, Lee Shumway, Nell Craig, Lillian West, Allen Fox, Larry Wheat.

C. AUGUSTE DUPIN

EDGAR ALLAN POE created fiction's first detective in his 1841 short story, "The Murders in the Rue Morgue," in the person of the hermitlike eccentric C. Auguste Dupin. The next year Dupin's second case was "The Mystery of Marie Rôget," and in 1844 Poe wrote "The Purloined Letter," which many consider one of the finest detective stories ever written. Regarding Poe and his detective, Otto Penzler et al. wrote in *Detectionary* (1977), "Poe is the father of the detective story as well as the creator of the short story form as we know it today. His morbid, brooding personality was reflected in his tales of terror, and his brilliant mathematical mind is reflected in his Dupin tales of ratiocination (a word he invented)."

Due to its grisly title, "The Murders in the Rue Morgue" is probably the best known of the Dupin trilogy. It has been filmed at least five times. (SHERLOCK HOLMES AND THE GREAT MURDER MYSTERY [Crescent Films, 1908] was based on the Poe story, but in it Dupin was replaced by Sherlock Holmes.) The initial screen version came in 1914 when Sol A. Rosenberg produced and adapted THE MURDERS IN THE RUE MORGUE for the screen. Its tale of an ape being trained to carry out a series of murders may qualify this silent movie as the most accurate screen version of the Poe story but, unfortunately, the feature is lost to the ages.

The best-known version of THE MURDERS IN THE RUE MORGUE was made by Universal in 1932 with Bela Lugosi starring and Robert Florey adapting and directing the feature. Both craftsmen had been dismissed from the studio's production of FRANKENSTEIN ('31), and this feature was designed by Universal as a substitute for them. The result is a film which has little resemblance to the Poe story (detective Dupin becomes young medical student Pierre Dupin), and the thrust of the project became its horrific elements, which for its time were considerable. Briefly, the plot had sideshow performer and mad scientist Dr. Mirakle (Bela Lugosi) wanting to mate an ape with a woman and choosing beautiful Camille (Sydney Fox) for the experiment. The girl is loved by medical student Pierre Dupin (Leon [Ames] Waycoff), who eventually saves her from a fate certainly worse than death! Lugosi was quite good as the madman, and the production had a polished, eerie look about it. As Richard Bojarski noted in *The Films of Bela Lugosi* (1980), "Poe's nightmarish Paris was brought alive by Karl Freund's camera and Charles Hall's settings of narrow winding streets, eerie rooftop sequences and Mirakle's secret laboratory in the oldest part of the city." It should be noted that Arlene Francis made her film debut as a prostitute abducted by Mirakle in the early portion of the film, and it is claimed that Bette Davis tested for the part of Camille.

Exactly a century after the publication of "The Mystery of Marie Rôget," the story was brought to the screen by Universal in 1942. Poe had based his work on an actual case, in which the torso of a young woman had been found near Hoboken in the Hudson River. The writer set the case in Paris and the film did also, with the story taking place in 1889 with detective Dr. Paul Dupin (Patric Knowles), a chemist for the Paris police force, investigating the murders of two people whose corpses are found in the Seine. The case leads him to beautiful singer Marie Rôget (Maria Montez), who is plotting with Marcel Vignon (Edward Norris) to get rid of her younger sister Camille (Nell O'Day). THE MYSTERY OF MARIE ROGET was a pale progammer which used only the bare framework of the Poe story for its plot line. Rose London wrote in *Cinema of Mystery* (1975), "Yet though faithful to Poe, the film is unfaithful to the cinema, choosing a wearisome plot that not even the fires of Maria Montez as the victim can stoke up. She is at least allowed to play herself as a comedy star and to be resurrected—it was not her body in the Seine, after all."

In 1954 a third screen version of "The Murders in the Rue Morgue" was filmed, this time called PHANTOM OF THE RUE MORGUE and issued in 3-D. Here woman-hating Paris scientist Dr. Marais (Karl Malden) sends out his trained ape to murder young females, and the crimes are blamed on a professor, Paul Dupin (Steve Forrest), who must prove his innocence as well as save his lady love (Patricia Medina) from the simian. Here the detective is called Inspector Bonnard (Claude Dauphin), and the ape is played by Charles Gemora, who also did the role in the

Dolores Dorn in PHANTOM OF THE RUE MORGUE (Warner Bros.,
1954)

1932 version. The *New York Times* kidded, "At least the ape this time is as schizophrenic as his keeper, love-crazy over Patricia Medina and who can blame him?"

In 1971 American-International released its final Edgar Allan Poe film, the fourth screen version of THE MURDERS IN THE RUE MORGUE, filmed in Europe by British director Gordon Hessler with an international cast. The plot had almost nothing to do with the Poe story, and Dupin as the protagonist was eliminated. The story had Charron's (Jason Robards) acting troupe performing the Poe plot on stage with the actor's hated rival, Marot (Herbert Lom), allegedly returning from the dead to torment Charron's beautiful wife, Madeline (Christine Kaufmann), as well as to take on the guise of an ape to commit a series of murders. "A Sigh . . . A Gasp . . . A Scream! These are the sounds of . . . MURDERS IN THE RUE MORGUE" read the poster for the feature, which Phil Hardy in *The Encyclopedia of Horror Movies* (1986) called director Hessler's "finest achievement to date."

George C. Scott portrayed Detective Dupin in the fifth screen version of THE MURDERS IN THE RUE MORGUE, a 1986 CBS-TV movie filmed in Paris by director Jeannot Szwarc. This time, Dupin was investigating horrible double murders. *TV Guide* said this TV adaptation "compensates for its attenuated and murky teleplay by offering George C. Scott as sleuth C. Auguste Dupin."

Of the trio of C. Auguste Dupin stories, only the last, "The Purloined Letter," remains unfilmed. In the early 1960s, when American-International and producer-director Roger Corman were having success with a series of Edgar Allan Poe features, the property was mentioned for filming, but it never came to pass. It remains a shame that Dupin, fiction's first short story sleuth, has yet to be filmed properly.

Filmography

1. THE MURDERS IN THE RUE MORGUE. Rosenberg, 1914.
   SC: Sol. A. Rosenberg.

2. THE MURDERS IN THE RUE MORGUE. Universal, 1932. 65 minutes.
   D: Robert Florey. **SC:** Tom Reed, Dale Van Every & John Huston.
   Cast: Bela Lugosi, Sydney Fox, Leon [Ames] Waycott (Pierre Dupin), Bert Roach, Brandon Hurst, Noble Johnson, D'Arcy Corrigan, Betty Ross Clarke, Herman Bing, Arlene Francis, Charles Gemora, Joe Bonomo.

3. THE MYSTERY OF MARIE ROGET. Universal, 1942. 61 minutes.
   D: Phil Rosen. **SC:** Michael Jacoby.
   Cast: Patric Knowles (Dr. Paul Dupin), Maria Montez, Maria Ouspenskaya, Lloyd Corrigan, John Litel, Nell O'Day, Edward Norris, Frank Reicher, Clyde Fillmore, Norma Drury, John Maxwell, Bill Ruhl, Paul Bryar, Paul Burns, Charles Middleton, Reed Hadley, Paul Dubov, Joe Bernard, Frank O'Connor, Ray Bailey, Charles Wagenheim, Lester Dorr, Alphonse Martel, Francis Sayles, Jimmie Lucas, Beatrice Roberts, Caroline Cooke.
   Reissued by Realart as PHANTOM OF PARIS.

4. PHANTOM OF THE RUE MORGUE. Warner Bros, 1954. 84 minutes. Color.
   D: Roy Del Ruth. **SC:** Harold Medford & James R. Webb.
   Cast: Karl Malden, Claude Dauphin, Patricia Medina, Steve Forrest (Paul Dupin), Allyn McLerie, Anthony Caruso, Veola Vonn, Dolores Dorn, Merv Griffin, Paul Richards, Rolfe Sedan, Erin O'Brien-Moore, The Flying Zacchinis, Charles Gemora, Frank Lackteen, Henry Kulky.

5. THE MURDERS IN THE RUE MORGUE. American-International, 1971. 87 minutes. Color.
   D: Gordon Hessler. **SC:** Christopher Wicking & Henry Selsar.
   Cast: Jason Robards, Herbert Lom, Christine Kaufmann, Lilli Palmer, Michael Dunn, Adolfo Celi, Maria Perschy, Peter Arne, Dean Selmeir, Marshall Jones, Jose Calvo, Werner Umberg, Luis Rivera, Rosalind Elliot, Virginia Stach, Ruth Platt, Maria Martin, Xan Das Bolas, Sally Longley, Pamela McInnes, Rafael Hernandez.

DUNCAN MacLAIN

DETECTIVE DUNCAN MACLAIN, as created by Baynard H. Kendrick, was a different kind of sleuth in that he was totally blind. According to the books about his adventures, MacLain was blinded while serving as an intelligence officer in World War I. Returning home, he developed his other senses and opened a New York City detective agency, assisted by two guide dogs. Between 1937 and 1961 a baker's dozen books about MacLain's adventures were published, and the sightless sleuth was also featured in a trio of films.

The initial Duncan MacLain novel was *The Last Express*, published by Doubleday in 1937 in its Crime Club series. Universal Pictures began a series of "Crime Club" films from books in the Doubleday series, and in 1938 THE LAST EXPRESS was filmed under Otis Garrett's direction. For the only time in his film career, however, Duncan MacLain was fully sighted, but other than that the film was a fairly faithful adaptation of the Kendrick novel, highlighted by fine photography by Stanley Cortez. The plot finds Gotham detective Duncan MacLain (Kent Taylor) and his partner Spud Savage (Don Brodie) on the trail of documents stolen from City Hall under orders from a special prosecutor (Edward Raquello) who is murdered. Two other murders also take place as MacLain investigates the case and romances pretty Amy Arden (Dorothea Kent). *Variety* said the script "is fairly intriguing despite meandering route taken. This murder mystery vehicle seems to be an instance where the audience wonders why the mystifying elements were not more clearly developed."

Duncan MacLain was correctly portrayed on film in two well-made Metro-Goldwyn-Mayer programmers by popular character actor Edward Arnold, who had a lengthy career as a cinema sleuth. Arnold (1890-1956) appeared as a detective in such features as THE SECRET OF THE BLUE ROOM ('33), THE PRESIDENT VANISHES ('34), REMEMBER LAST NIGHT? ('35), CRIME AND PUNISHMENT ('35), and MEET NERO WOLFE ('36) (see B/V), and among his other films were RASPUTIN AND THE EMPRESS ('32), JENNIE GERHARDT ('33), MADAME SPY ('34), SADIE McKEE ('34), CARDINAL RICHELIEU ('35), THE GLASS KEY ('35), DIAMOND JIM ('35), SUTTER'S GOLD ('36), COME AND GET IT ('36), THE TOAST OF NEW YORK ('37), IDIOT'S DELIGHT ('39), MR. SMITH GOES

TO WASHINGTON ('39), LILLIAN RUSSELL ('40), ALL THAT MONEY CAN BUY ('41), JOHNNY EAGER ('42), KISMET ('44), MAIN STREET AFTER DARK ('45), WEEKEND AT THE WALDORF ('45), THE HUCKSTERS ('47), COMMAND DECISION ('49), ANNIE GET YOUR GUN ('50), BELLES ON THEIR TOES ('52), and THE AMBASSADOR'S DAUGHTER ('56).

EYES IN THE NIGHT was the first of the two Duncan MacLain films Edward Arnold starred in, and it was issued in the fall of 1942 and was based on the 1942 novel *Odor of Violets*. Duncan MacLain is hired by a wealthy woman (Ann Harding) to investigate a man (John Emery) who wants to marry her stepdaughter (Donna Reed). When an invention belonging to the woman's husband (Reginald Denny) is stolen, the detective uncovers the fact that a spy ring is behind the theft. Foreign agents capture MacLain, but he is rescued by his dog Friday. *Variety* commented, "Except for the opening phases, yarn moves at a fast clip, with plenty of suspenseful, though stereotyped, sequences, making it a strong bet for secondary bookings." In *B Movies* (1973), Don Miller wrote the feature "held interest from beginning to the end, which was action-paced in a way not customarily provided by the rather staid MGM scripting department."

It was three years before another Duncan MacLain feature appeared, as THE HIDDEN EYE was issued in the summer of 1945. From an original script by George Harmon Coxe and Harry Ruskin, the film was designed, like EYES IN THE NIGHT, as a dual-biller, although it was slickly produced. A trio of murders are committed, and at the scene blind detective Duncan MacLain (Edward Arnold) notices the odor of an Oriental perfume. A young man (Paul Langton) is the chief suspect in the crimes, but MacLain believes he is innocent and eventually has a showdown with the real murderer. Despite his handicap, the sleuth is able to beat the culprit in a fistfight. As in the first feature, the detective relies heavily on his guide dog Friday for support. The *New York Times* termed the film a "unique melodrama" but added, "The only trouble with

From left: Paul Langton, Frances Rafferty, William "Bill" Phillips, and Edward Arnold in THE HIDDEN EYE (M-G-M, 1945)

this whodunit is . . . that it is not very interesting. Most of the time the characters just stand around talking and what they have to say is not very enlightening."

Although Duncan MacLain was not featured in any further films, the character was portrayed on television in the 1950s by Robert Middleton in an anthology segment, and MacLain was the basis for the character of Mike Longstreet, a blind New Orleans insurance company investigator played by James Franciscus in the series "Longstreet" (ABC-TV, 1971/1972).

Filmography

1. THE LAST EXPRESS. Universal, 1938. 63 minutes.
     D: Otis Garrett. **SC:** Edmund L. Hartman, from the novel by Baynard Kendrick.

Cast: Kent Taylor (Duncan MacLain), Dorothea Kent, Don Brodie, Greta Grandstedt, Paul Hurst, Samuel Lee, Albert Shaw, Edward Raquello, Robert Emmett Keane, Charles Trowbridge, Addison Richards, J. Farrell MacDonald.

2. EYES IN THE NIGHT. Metro-Goldwyn-Mayer, 1942. 80 minutes.
   D: Fred Zinnemann. SC: Guy Trosper & Howard Emmett Rogers, from the novel *Odor of Violets* by Baynard Kendrick.
   Cast: Edward Arnold (Duncan MacLain), Ann Harding, Donna Reed, Katherine Emery, Horace [Stephen] McNally, Allen Jenkins, Stanley Ridges, Reginald Denny, John Emery, Rosemary De Camp, Erik Rolf, Barry Nelson, Reginald Sheffield, Steven Geray, Mantan Moreland, Friday.

3. THE HIDDEN EYE. Metro-Goldwyn-Mayer, 1945. 70 minutes.
   D: Richard Whorf. SC: George Harmon Coxe & Harry Ruskin. ST: George Harmon Coxe.
   Cast: Edward Arnold (Duncan MacLain), Frances Rafferty, Ray Collins, Paul Langton, William "Bill" Phillips, Thomas Jackson, Morris Ankrum, Robert Lewis, Francis Pierlot, Sondra Rodgers, Theodore Newton, Jack Lambert, Ray Largay, Leigh Whipper, Byron Foulger, Lee Phelps, Eddie Acuff, Bob Pepper, Russell Hicks, Friday.

FATHER BROWN

UNLIKE MOST DETECTIVES who wanted to bring the unjust to justice, G. K. Chesterton's Father Brown was interested in saving souls. Beginning in 1911, Chesterton wrote several volumes of short stories about the adventures of the dull-appearing but quick-witted clergyman. His initial volume, *Innocence of Father Brown*, included the story "Blue Cross" about the priest's most notable adversary, Flambeau, and this story has served as the basis for both feature films made about Father Brown.

In 1935 Paramount issued FATHER BROWN, DETECTIVE, directed by Edward Sedgwick. Here suave thief Flambeau (Paul Lukas) plans to steal a diamond cross which is in the trust of Father Brown (Walter Connolly). To carry out his plan, Flambeau romances lovely Evelyn Fisher (Gertrude Michael) as he also plans to rob her wealthy father (Halliwell Hobbes) and then use the girl to

From left: Gertrude Michael, Walter Connolly, and Paul Lukas in FATHER BROWN, DETECTIVE (Paramount, 1935)

help him steal the cross. Flambeau is able to carry out his theft of the holy object, and by being found in Evelyn's bedroom he assures himself of her silence. Father Brown knows that Flambeau took the cross, and he tells the police chief (Robert Loraine) that he wants the thief to see the error of his ways. The policeman scoffs at Father Brown's attempt to redeem Flambeau, who manages to escape a police dragnet. Due to the priest's words, he sees the error of his ways and returns the cross and plans to begin life anew with Evelyn. *Variety* thought the film "clean and wholesome."

The same plot was in evidence for the second film about the Chesterton character, the 1954 British production of FATHER BROWN, which Columbia released in the U.S. in 1955 as THE DETECTIVE. This time out Father Brown (Alec Guinness) is assigned to guard a valuable cross during its trip to Rome for use at a holy congress. Using various disguises, Flambeau (Peter Finch) manages to take the cross. In order to get it back, Father Brown tries to bait Flambeau with a priceless chess set in the possession of Lady Warren (Joan Greenwood), and again Flambeau is successful in his theft. This time, however, Father Brown stays on his trail and at a Burgundy château he shows the thief how he has gone wrong in life. The man repents and returns the items he has stolen. Alec Guinness was particularly good in the title role of this appealing, wry picture.

Besides the two films about the detective-priest, Karl Swenson had the title role in the 1945 radio program "The Adventures of Father Brown"; Kenneth More played the character in the 1974 ATV series "Father Brown" on British television; and Bernard Cornwell starred in the 1986/1987 PBS-TV series also titled "Father Brown."

Filmography

1. FATHER BROWN, DETECTIVE. Paramount, 1935. 66 minutes.
     D: Edward Sedgwick. **SC:** Harry Meyers & C. Gardner Sullivan.
     Cast: Walter Connolly (Father Brown), Paul Lukas, Gertrude Michael, Halliwell Hobbes, Una O'Connor, Robert Loraine, Peter Hobbes, E. E. Clive, Bunny Beatty, Robert Adair, Gwenllian Gill, King Baggott, Eldred Tilbury.

2. FATHER BROWN. Columbia, 1954. 91 minutes.
     D: Robert Hamer. **SC:** Thelma Schnee & Robert Hamer.
     Cast: Alec Guinness (Father Brown), Joan Greenwood, Peter Finch, Cecil Parker, Bernard Lee, Sidney James, Gerard Oury, Ernest Thesiger, Ernest Clark, Everley Gregg, Austin Trevor, Marne Maitland, Eugene Deckers, Jim Gerald, Noel Howlett, John Salew, Matisconia de Macon Singers & Dancers.
     U.S. Title: THE DETECTIVE.

FLASH CASEY

JACK "FLASHGUN" CASEY was a crime photographer who worked for various Boston newspapers. He was the fictional creation of George Harmon Coxe, and unlike most sleuths his career in books did not begin until after his film career was over. Two feature films about Casey's exploits were made in the 1930s, and both were based on Coxe short stories about the tough crime-fighting photographer. Casey, however, is probably better known for his radio and TV adventures than for his brief movie career.

Flash Casey made his screen debut in 1936 in the Metro-Goldwyn-Mayer film WOMEN ARE TROUBLE, based on an original screen story by George Harmon Coxe. Here Casey (Stuart Erwin) teams with reporter Ruth (Florence Rice) in combating crooks out to get an illegal cut of the city's booze business. City editor Blaine (Paul Kelly), who is having alimony troubles with ex-wife Frances (Margaret Irving), urges them on, and they get help from police Inspector Matson (Cy Kendall). The feature was a mixture of comedy and action, and *Variety* opined, "It's

From left: Stuart Erwin, Florence Rice, and Paul Kelly in WOMEN ARE TROUBLE (M-G-M, 1936)

strictly a program picture, short on running time, so-so in marquee weight, and riveted against a framework that milks laughs and hypos suspense."

George Harmon Coxe's short story "Return Engagement" was the basis for Flash Casey's second and final screen appearance in Grand National's 1937 release, HERE'S FLASH CASEY. The story had Casey (Eric Linden) winning a photography prize while in college, getting his first newspaper job, and becoming involved with murder, kidnapping, and blackmail while falling in love with society editor Kay Lansing (Boots Mallory). Grand National had hoped to produce a series of Flash Casey features, but the reception given to HERE'S FLASH CASEY was tepid at best, and future projects for the crime photographer were dropped.

The radio adventures of Flash Casey began in the 1930s, but the character's best-known airwaves outing was in the CBS series "Casey, Crime Photographer," starring Staats Cotsworth as Casey. The series ran from 1946 to 1954 and was also called "Casey, Press Photographer" and "Flash Gun Casey." In 1942 George Harmon Coxe produced his first Flash Casey novel, *Silent Are the Dead,* and two more followed during the decade: *Murder for Two* (1943) and *Flash Casey, Detective* (1946), made up of four novelettes. During that decade Casey was also the subject of an experimental television series in New York City.

Casey came to national television in the spring of 1951 in the half-hour CBS-TV series, "Crime Photographer," also called "Casey, Crime Photographer." Richard Carlyle portrayed Casey, and Jan Minor was reporter Ann Williams, a part she also played on the CBS radio series about Casey. The series had Casey working as an investigator for the *New York Morning Express.* After several episodes, Richard Carlyle was replaced by Darren McGavin, who played Casey until the series ended in June 1952.

In the 1960s Flash Casey returned to the literary world when George Harmon Coxe turned out another trio of books about the detective. Published by Knopf, who did the first two Casey books in the 1940s, they were *Error of*

Judgment (1961), *The Man Who Died Too Soon* (1962), and *Deadly Image* (1964).

Filmography

1. WOMEN ARE TROUBLE. Metro-Goldwyn-Mayer, 1936. 60 minutes.
   D: Errol Taggart. **SC:** Michael Fessler.
   Cast: Stuart Erwin (Casey), Florence Rice, Paul Kelly, Margaret Irving, Cy Kendall, John Harrington, Harold Huber, Raymond Hatton, Kitty McHugh.

2. HERE'S FLASH CASEY. Grand National, 1937. 57 minutes.
   D: Lynn Shores. **SC:** John Krafft, from the story "Return Engagement" by George Harmon Coxe.
   Cast: Eric Linden (Casey), Boots Mallory, Cully Richards, Holmes Herbert, Joseph Crehan, Howard Lang, Victor Adams, Harry Harvey, Suzanne Kaaren, Matty Kemp, Dorothy Vaughn, Maynard Holmes.

FRANK CANNON

FRANK CANNON, like Theo Kojak (q.v.), is a product of television, and the movies about the character have all been done for the small screen. Cannon, however, has his roots in radio and film, as he is quite similar to the character of Brad Runyon, the Fat Man, who was played on radio and in the 1952 feature film THE FAT MAN by J. Scott Smart. Runyon was a private eye created by Dashiell Hammett as the antithesis of his corpulent villain Caspar Gutman in *The Maltese Falcon*. Frank Cannon was a former policeman who became a very high-paid private investigator. William Conrad proved perfect for the part, and at the age of fifty-one, the role made Conrad a star after years of being a character actor in films, radio, and television.

Born in 1920, William Conrad came to films in 1946 in THE KILLERS and appeared in such features as BODY AND SOUL ('47), SORRY, WRONG NUMBER ('48), THE RACKET ('51), FIVE AGAINST THE HOUSE ('55), THE RIDE BACK ('57), -30- ('59), in which he was impressive as

a newspaper editor, and TV's BROTHERHOOD OF THE
BELL ('70). On radio he was the voice of Matt Dillon on
"Gunsmoke" (CBS, 1949-1961). He directed such films as
TWO ON A GUILLOTINE ('65), MY BLOOD RUNS COLD
('65), BRAINSTORM ('65), and ASSIGNMENT TO KILL
('68), and produced a number of films, such as THE RIDE
BACK ('57), CHUBASCO ('68), and THE LEARNING
TREE ('69). Conrad also guest-starred on many television
programs and directed for the small screen such TV movies
as THE SKIN GAME ('70).

The television feature film CANNON was telecast by
CBS-TV on March 26, 1971, as the pilot for the "Cannon"
series which debuted that fall and ran until 1977. The
telefilm had private eye Frank Cannon hired by Diana
Langston (Vera Miles), his old girlfriend, to investigate the
murder of her husband. Diana has been charged with the
killing, and Cannon arrives in her small Western home-
town to find the area controlled by hoodlums, with the law
unable to keep them under control. Cannon is warned off
the case, but he persists and eventually brings in the real
killer. *Movies on TV* (1978) commented, "Playing for
realism, producer Quinn Martin often uses hand-held
cameras while filming near Las Cruces, New Mexico. . . .
When the plot complications tend to wear the viewer
down, Martin shores it up with fine location work,
Conrad's imposing presence, and a supporting cast featur-
ing Vera Miles, Barry Sullivan, J. D. Cannon, Keenan
Wynn, and Earl Holliman." Judith Crist in *TV Guide* noted
the Conrad film was "routine for him—and us." *TV Movies
and Video Guide* (1988) felt the film's "too many subplots
make for confusion after halfway mark," but called it
"above average."

The third season of the "Cannon" TV series kicked off
with a two-hour episode called "He Who Digs a Grave" on
September 12, 1973, and the segment has since been issued
to TV as a feature film called CANNON: HE WHO DIGS A
GRAVE. Filmed on location in Grass Valley, California, the
film has Frank Cannon (William Conrad) arriving in a small
cattle town to defend an old wartime pal (David Janssen)
who has been accused of two murders. The real killer tries

William Conrad in CANNON: HE WHO DIGS A GRAVE (CBS-TV, 1973)

to shoot Cannon, as well as catch him in a cattle stampede and a fire, but the private eye eventually clears his friend's name by bringing in the murderer.

The "Cannon" TV series left the air in 1977 for continued popularity in syndication. On November 1, 1980, the character returned to network television in the CBS-TV film THE RETURN OF FRANK CANNON. Now private eye Cannon (William Conrad) is retired and running a seafood restaurant, but when the daughter (Allison Argo) of an old army buddy asks him to look into her father's mysterious death, he takes the case. Although the man was supposed to have committed suicide, Cannon, who once loved the man's wife (Diana Muldaur), discovers that it was murder and that the CIA and a mysterious doctor (Arthur Hill) are involved in the case. The *New York Times* called the telefilm "a pleasant and undemanding way to pass a couple of hours."

Although THE RETURN OF FRANK CANNON was William Conrad's last work in the role to date, the actor has kept up small screen investigating by starring in the title role of the Nero Wolfe (NBC-TV, 1981) series and as a district attorney on "Jake and the Fatman" (CBS-TV, from 1987).

Filmography

1. CANNON. CBS-TV, 1971. 104 minutes. Color.
   D: George McGowan. **SC:** Edward Home.
   Cast: William Conrad (Frank Cannon), Vera Miles, Barry Sullivan, Keenan Wynn, Earl Holliman, Lynda Day, J. D. Cannon, Murray Hamilton, John Fiedler, Lawrence Pressman, Ross Hagen.
   Working Title: STARR.

2. CANNON: HE WHO DIGS A GRAVE. CBS-TV, 1973. 106 minutes. Color.
   D: Richard Donner.
   Cast: William Conrad (Frank Cannon), David Janssen, Anne Baxter, Barry Sullivan, Lee Purcell, Martine Bartlett, Royal Dano, Tim O'Connor, Virginia Gregg, Murray Hamilton, R. G. Armstrong, Dennis Rucker.

3. THE RETURN OF FRANK CANNON. CBS-TV, 1980. 100 minutes. Color.

    D: Corey Allen. **SC:** James D. Buchanan & Ronald Austin.

    Cast: William Conrad (Frank Cannon), Allison Argo, Burr DeBenning, Taylor Lacher, Diana Muldaur, Ed Nelson, Joanna Pettet, William Smithers, Arthur Hill, Rafael Campos, James Hong, Hank Brandt, Hector Elias, Rene Enriquez, Gary Grubbs, Evelyn Guerrero, John Steadman, James Gavin.

HANK HYER

RUDOLPH KAGEY, using the pseudonym Kurt Steel, wrote a series of entertaining mystery novels in the 1930s about private eye Hank Hyer and his newspaperman pal Sim Perkins. Paramount acquired the rights to the 1936 novel *Murder Goes to College,* apparently intent on doing a series of Hank Hyer films. Two were produced—one good and one poor—and nothing more resulted. This is a pity since the initial film, MURDER GOES TO COLLEGE, was well done, and the casting of Lynne Overman as Hank Hyer and Roscoe Karns as Sim Perkins proved to be a delight, making it a shame that more Steel novels were not filmed.

    Lynne Overman (1887–1943) was a very popular character actor known for his droll comedic abilities in such features as RUMBA ('35), THE JUNGLE PRINCESS ('36), THREE MARRIED MEN ('36), WILD MONEY ('37), HOTEL HAYWIRE ('37), TYPHOON ('40), ROXIE HART ('42), and DIXIE ('43). Overman and Roscoe Karns had teamed previously for THREE MARRIED MEN before making their two Hank Hyer films. Roscoe Karns (1893–1970) came to films toward the end of the silent period and became a popular character actor in the sound era in films like THE FRONT PAGE ('30), NIGHT AFTER NIGHT ('32), IT HAPPENED ONE NIGHT ('34), CLARENCE ('37), THEY DRIVE BY NIGHT ('40), WILL TOMORROW EVER COME? ('47), and ONIONHEAD ('58). On television he had the title role in "Rocky King, Inside Detective" (DuMont, 1950–1954) and co-starred in "Hennesey" (CBS-TV, 1959–1962).

From left: Harvey Stephens, Barlow Borland, Roscoe Karns, Lynne Overman, Purnell Pratt, and Charles Wilson in MURDER GOES TO COLLEGE (Paramount, 1937)

MURDER GOES TO COLLEGE, issued in March 1937, had private detective Hank Hyer (Lynne Overman) and newspaperman friend Sim Perkins (Roscoe Karns) investigating the murder of a college professor, much to the chagrin of local police Inspector Simpson (Charles Wilson) who is in charge of the case. Their snooping gets Hank and Sim in trouble with racketeer Strike Belno (Larry "Buster" Crabbe) as well as the various suspects, including the dead man's young wife (Astrid Allwyn), a former nightclub singer hooked up with the gangster. Hyer, putting the pieces of the puzzle together, is eventually able to solve the homicide. *Variety* said the film was "moulded along smart comedy lines smacking of the 'Thin Man' school of sleuth drama . . . Dialog crackles with humor and up-to-date wit." In *B Movies*, (1973), Don Miller commented, "It was neat, with Overman's dry wit aiding greatly."

The novel *Murder Goes to College* was also credited as the source for the second Hank Hyer feature, PARTNERS IN CRIME, released in the fall of 1937, but the film had nothing to do with the Kurt Steel novel on which it was allegedly based. Instead, the feature has Hank Hyer (Lynne Overman) and Sim Perkins (Roscoe Karns) working to rid their city of its corrupt mayor (Russell Hicks) by supporting a reform candidate who is forced to withdraw from the race when pretty Odette Le Vin (Muriel Hutchison) claims he is her father. Hank finds out that the girl is actually in the pay of the mayor, and he leads a movement to draft Sim for the job, and along the way he investigates a murder. Sim wins the race, but the murder turns out to be bogus. When it is discovered that Perkins is not an American citizen, both he and Hank are booted out of town! The *New York Daily News* complained, "The Bureau of Standards may have a case in the canned nonsense in PARTNERS IN CRIME. The humor specified by recipe is sadly deficient." The same year that Roscoe Karns appeared in the two Hank Hyer films, he also played Sergeant Ernest Heath in the Philo Vance film, A NIGHT OF MYSTERY (see B/V) for Paramount.

Filmography

1. MURDER GOES TO COLLEGE. Paramount, 1937. 77 minutes.
    D: Charles Riesner. **SC:** Brian Marlow, Robert Wyler & Eddie Welch, from the novel by Kurt Steel.
    Cast: Roscoe Karns (Sim Perkins), Lynne Overman (Hank Hyer), Marsha Hunt, Astrid Allwyn, Harvey Stephens, Larry "Buster" Crabbe, Earl Foxe, Anthony Nace, John Indrisano, Barlow Borland, Purnell Pratt, Charles Wilson, James Blaine, Robert Perry, James H. Carson, Edward Emerson, Nick Lukats.

2. PARTNERS IN CRIME. Paramount, 1937. 66 minutes.
    D: Ralph Murphy. **SC:** Garnett Weston, from the novel *Murder Goes to College* by Kurt Steel.
    Cast: Lynne Overman (Hank Hyer), Roscoe Karns (Sim Perkins), Muriel Hutchison, Anthony Quinn, Inez Courtney, Lucien Littlefield, Charles Halton, Charles Wilson, June Brewster, Esther Howard, Nora Cecil, Russell Hicks, Don Brodie, Archie Twitchell, Arthur Hoyt, Oscar "Dutch" Hendrian, Ruth Warren.

INSPECTOR HORNLEIGH

GORDON HARKER AND Alastair Sim headlined a trio of well-paced detective thrillers in the Inspector Hornleigh series which 20th Century–Fox produced in England. The films were based on the popular "Inspector Hornleigh" BBC-Radio series by Hans Wolfgang Priwin.

For the initial film, INSPECTOR HORNLEIGH, a 1939 release, 20th Century–Fox sent director Eugene Forde to England to lead the project. Forde directed a number of fine mystery films for the studio, including CHARLIE CHAN IN LONDON ('34), THE GREAT HOTEL MURDER ('35), CHARLIE CHAN AT MONTE CARLO ('37), CHARLIE CHAN ON BROADWAY ('37), CHARLIE CHAN'S MURDER CRUISE ('40), MICHAEL SHAYNE, PRIVATE DETECTIVE ('40), SLEEPERS WEST ('41), DRESSED TO KILL ('41), and THE CRIMSON KEY ('47), and two entries in Columbia's Crime Doctor series, THE CRIME DOCTOR'S STRANGEST CASE and SHADOWS IN THE NIGHT (both '44). Forde's deft touch with mystery films was evident in INSPECTOR HORNLEIGH, which was adapted to the screen by Edgar Wallace's son, Bryan Edgar Wallace. The plot revolved around wealthy foreigner, Kavanos (Steven Geray), who has caused several murders and is out to steal the Chancellor of the Exchequer's budget plans. Scotland Yard Inspector Hornleigh (Gordon Harker) and his bumbling assistant, Detective Sergeant Bingham (Alastair Sim), are assigned to the case, which leads them to an inn where the proprietors (Hugh Williams and Miki Hood) are involved with the scheme. *Variety* said the feature contained "above-average thrill values."

Later in 1939 the second series entry, INSPECTOR HORNLEIGH ON HOLIDAY, was issued. Here Hornleigh (Gordon Harker) and Bingham (Alastair Sim) have gone on a two-week holiday at the seaside. As their vacation ends, they become involved in the investigation of the death of a man who burned to death when his car went over a cliff. The local authorities think it is an accident, but Hornleigh feels the man was murdered. He

Gordon Harker *(left)* and Alastair Sim in INSPECTOR HORNLEIGH ON HOLIDAY (20th Century–Fox, 1940)

and Bingham uncover an insurance fraud scheme in which a local gang substitutes victims for their members who have taken out large insurance policies and then collect the money. Hornleigh and Bingham are able to round up the gang. "This is an absorbing melodorama having an original plot unfolded with much comedy, filmed with a wealth of detail and a cast that makes for first-rate screen entertainment" (*Variety*).

The third film in the series, INSPECTOR HORNLEIGH GOES TO IT, was released in Britain early in 1941 but it was not shown in the U.S. until that summer, when it was called MAIL TRAIN, perhaps in an attempt to connect it with another popular British spy thriller, NIGHT TRAIN TO MUNICH ('40). Scotland Yard Inspector Hornleigh (Gordon Harker) is demoted from covering a spy case to looking into the theft of military supplies. By accident he and associate Bingham (Alastair Sim) find the spy gang, and when a dentist who is a member of the fifth columnists is killed, Hornleigh and Bingham trail the gang to a school and then to a mail train, with the inspector working as a mail sorter as he and Bingham trap the spies. "Very British and good fun" is how David Quinlan summed up the thriller in *British Sound Films: The Studio Years, 1928–1959* (1984).

Gordon Harker (1885–1967) was ideally cast as the methodic Inspector Hornleigh; the cockney impersonator made his stage debut in 1903 and came to the movies in 1927. Among his many films were THE WRECKER ('28), ELSTREE CALLING ('30), THE SQUEAKER ('30), THE RINGER ('31), THE FRIGHTENED LADY ('32), ROME EXPRESS ('32), THE AMATEUR GENTLEMAN ('36), THE FROG ('37), RETURN OF THE FROG, ('38), CHANNEL INCIDENT ('40), WARN THAT MAN ('43), HER FAVORITE HUSBAND ('50), SMALL HOTEL ('57), and his last film, LEFT, RIGHT AND CENTER ('59). Equally well cast as the dense, but well-meaning Scottish associate Bingham, Alastair Sim (1900–1976) was considered the Dean of British Comedians. A stage star by 1930, Sim came to films in 1935 with THE RIVERSIDE MURDER, and his screen appearances included TROUBLED WATERS ('36), THE

SQUEAKER ('37), THE TERROR ('38), LAW AND DISOR-
DER ('40), COTTAGE TO LET ('41), WATERLOO ROAD
('44), GREEN FOR DANGER ('46), HUE AND CRY ('46),
STAGE FRIGHT ('50), LAUGHTER IN PARADISE ('51), A
CHRISTMAS CAROL (SCROOGE) ('51), INNOCENTS IN
PARIS ('53), AN INSPECTOR CALLS ('54), THE BELLES OF
ST. TRINIAN'S ('54), BLUE MURDER AT ST. TRINIAN'S
('57), LEFT, RIGHT AND CENTER ('59), SCHOOL FOR
SCOUNDRELS ('60), COLD COMFORT FARM ('72), and
ROYAL FLASH ('75).

Filmography

1. INSPECTOR HORNLEIGH. 20th Century–Fox, 1939. 87 minutes.
    D: Eugene Forde. **SC:** Bryan Edgar Wallace, Gerald Elliott &
    Richard Llewellyn.
    Cast: Gordon Harker (Inspector Hornleigh), Alastair Sim (Ser-
    geant Bingham), Miki Hood, Hugh Williams, Steven Geray, Wally
    Patch, Edward Underdown, Gibb McLaughlin, Ronald Adam, Eliot
    Makeham.

2. INSPECTOR HORNLEIGH ON HOLIDAY. 20th Century–Fox, 1939.
    87 minutes.
    D: Walter Forde. **SC:** Frank Launder & Sidney Gilliat.
    Cast: Gordon Harker (Inspector Hornleigh), Alastair Sim (Ser-
    geant Bingham), Linden Travers, Wally Patch, Edward Chapman,
    Philip Leaver, Kynaston Reeves, John Turnbull, Wyndham Goldie,
    Cyril Conway, Eileen Bell.

3. INSPECTOR HORNLEIGH GOES TO IT. 20th Century–Fox, 1941.
    87 minutes
    D: Walter Forde. **SC:** Frank Launder, Val Guest & J.O.C. Orton.
    Cast: Gordon Harker (Inspector Hornleigh), Alastair Sim (Ser-
    geant Bingham), Phyllis Calvert, Edward Chapman, Raymond
    Huntley, Charles Oliver, Percy Walsh, David Horne, Peter Gaw-
    thorne, Wally Patch, Betty Jardine, O. B. Clarence, John Salew, Cyril
    Cusack, Bill Shine, Sylvia Cecil, Edward Underdown, E. Turner,
    Marie Makine, Richard Cooper.
    U.S. Title: MAIL TRAIN.

JACK PACKARD AND DOC LONG

JACK PACKARD AND Doc Long, along with Reggie York, were

the three detective heroes of Carleton E. Morse's long-running radio adventure program, "I Love a Mystery" (NBC, later Mutual, 1939–1951). The radio series usually had the three sleuths battling evil in the Orient, and Jim Bannon portrayed Jack Packard, Barton Yarborough was Doc Long, and Michael Raffetto played Reggie York. Yarborough and Raffetto also played the parts in a 1948 ABC radio summer spin-off series called "I Love Adventure," and in 1954 CBS made an unsuccessful attempt to revive "I Love a Mystery" on radio. In 1945 Columbia Pictures acquired the rights to the Morse series and brought Jim Bannon and Barton Yarborough to Hollywood to make three films in its "I Love a Mystery" series. The Reggie York character was not included in the trio of films.

I LOVE A MYSTERY, issued by Columbia early in 1945, was produced by Wallace MacDonald, a former actor and

From left: Barton Yarborough, Jim Bannon, and George Macready in I LOVE A MYSTERY (Columbia, 1945)

scripter, who also produced the other two series entries. The story had wealthy Jefferson Monk (George Macready) being offered $10,000 for his head by a mysterious Oriental society which needs it to bring back its founder. The man's beautiful young wife Ellen (Nina Foch) asks detectives Jack Packard (Jim Bannon) and Doc Long (Barton Yarborough) to investigate, and eventually they prove that the wife is behind the offer in an effort to scare her husband to death and to inherit his large estate. *Variety* termed the film "a fairly suspenseful low-budget chiller."

The next "I Love a Mystery" outing was THE DEVIL'S MASK, released in 1946. Here Jack Packard (Jim Bannon) and Doc Long (Barton Yarborough) are hired by Eve Mitchell (Mona Barrie), who thinks her stepdaughter Janet (Anita Louise) plans to harm her because the girl blames Eve for the disappearance of her father, explorer Quentin Mitchell (Frank Mayo), who was reported missing in the Jivaro country of South America. Another private eye, Rex Kennedy (Michael Duane), is hired by Janet, and through him she meets a friend of her father, taxidermist Leon Hartman (Paul E. Burns). When Jack and Doc learn that a shrunken head in a local museum is actually that of the missing explorer, they are able to deduce that Hartman is the culprit. He nearly kills them and Janet before he dies after being clawed by his trained leopard, Diablo.

The year 1946 also saw the last film in the Columbia trilogy, THE UNKNOWN. Its plot found young heiress Nina Arnold (Jeff Donnell) returning to the Southern mansion where she was born to see her mother (Karen Morley). She finds the estate inhabited by relatives she did not know existed. Nina hires Jack Packard (Jim Bannon) and Doc Long (Barton Yarborough) to investigate, and they uncover insanity and a plot to get the young woman's fortunes. In order to breathe some life into the proceedings, the script had such horror film trappings as a supposedly haunted house, grave robbers, secret panels and passages, and a cloaked phantom. Despite being atmospheric, THE UNKNOWN was a tepid effort.

Jim Bannon began working in radio in the late 1930s and

came to Hollywood with the "I Love a Mystery" Columbia series. He starred in features like THE MISSING JUROR ('44), SOUL OF A MONSTER ('44), and THE GAY SENORITA ('46), before taking the title role in Eagle-Lion's Red Ryder series in 1949. After that he turned to character roles and remained active in films and television into the 1970s, when he wrote his autobiography, *The Son Who Rose in the West*. Once married to actress Bea Benadaret, he was the father of actor Jack Bannon. Jim Bannon died in 1984. Barton Yarborough (1900–1951) also appeared in several Hollywood productions, like GHOST OF FRANKEN-STEIN ('42) and CAPTAIN TUGBOAT ANNIE ('45), although he was primarily regarded as a radio actor. Yarborough created the role of Sergeant Ben Romero on NBC radio's "Dragnet" series in 1949, and he played the part when the series came to TV with a special preview on "Chesterfield Sound Off Time" late in 1951. A few days later, Yarborough died of a heart attack; he was eventually replaced by Ben Alexander.

I LOVE A MYSTERY became a TV movie in 1967 as a pilot for a proposed small-screen revival of the Carleton E. Morse series. Unfortunately the telefilm was so poor that it was not shown until February 27, 1973, when it was telecast by NBC-TV. The six-year delay negated any chance the project had for becoming a series. Leslie Stevens wrote and directed the telefilm, which had private investigators Jack Packard (Les Crane), Doc Long (David Hartman), and Reggie York (Hagan Beggs) being engaged by an insurance company to locate a man who has disappeared before claiming large policy proceeds. The sleuths trace the missing man to a remote island castle where he is the prisoner of mad scientist Randolph Cheyne (Ida Lupino), who captures the trio, planning to mate them with her three gorgeous daughters (Karen Jensen, Deanna Lund, and Melodie Johnson). Donald F. Glut and Jim Harmon wrote in *The Great Television Heroes* (1975) that the TV movie "ridiculed the whole concept of mystery and adventure stories, and told the audience—correctly—that they were fools for watching this piece of trash."

Filmography

1. I LOVE A MYSTERY. Columbia, 1945. 69 minutes.
   D: Henry Levin. **SC:** Charles O'Neal.
   Cast: Jim Bannon (Jack Packard), Nina Foch, George Macready, Barton Yarborough (Doc Long), Carole Matthews, Lester Matthews, Gregory Gay, Leo Mostovoy, Frank O'Connor, Isabel Withers, Joseph Crehan, Kay Dowd, Ernie Adams.

2. THE DEVIL'S MASK. Columbia, 1946. 66 minutes.
   D: Henry Levin. **SC:** Charles O'Neal & Dwight Babcock.
   Cast: Anita Louise, Jim Bannon (Jack Packard), Michael Duane, Mona Barrie, Barton Yarborough (Doc Long), Ludwig Donath, Paul E. Burns, Frank Wilcox, Thomas Jackson, Richard Hale, John Elliott, Edward Earle, Frank Mayo.

3. THE UNKNOWN. Columbia, 1946. 70 minutes.
   D: Henry Levin. **SC:** Charles O'Neal & Dwight Babcock.
   Cast: Jim Bannon (Jack Packard), Karen Morley, Jeff Donnell, Robert Wilcox, Barton Yarborough (Doc Long), James Bell, Wilton Graff, Robert Scott, Boyd Davis, Helen Freeman, J. Louis Johnson.

4. I LOVE A MYSTERY. NBC-TV, 1973. 100 minutes. Color.
   D-SC: Leslie Stevens.
   Cast: Ida Lupino, Les Crane (Jack Packard), David Hartman (Doc Long), Hagan Beggs (Reggie York), Jack Weston, Don Knotts, Terry-Thomas, Melodie Johnson, Karen Jensen, Deanna Lund, André Philippe, Francine York, Peter Mamakos, Lewis Charles.

JOE DANCER

FOLLOWING HIS SUCCESS as a police detective on "Baretta" (ABC-TV, 1975–1978), Robert Blake attempted to return to the small screen as private eye Joe Dancer. He starred in three telefilm pilots, all produced in 1981, about the character, but the project failed to sell as a series. Joe Dancer was a tough Hollywood private eye whose cases led him through the film world's upper crust as well as the underworld. He was assisted by Charley, a wheelchair-ridden associate, and in all three Joe Dancer telefilms the part was enacted by Sondra Blake, the wife of the star, who also served as the films' executive producer.

Robert Blake and Veronica Cartwright in JOE DANCER (NBC-TV, 1981)

Born in 1933, Robert Blake is a veteran of the film industry, having appeared in the "Our Gang" comedies from 1939 to 1944 under his real name of Mickey Gubitosi. Changing his name to Bobby Blake, he appeared as Little Beaver in Republic's Red Ryder series with William Elliott and Allan Lane. He also was in feature films like THE BIG NOISE ('44), THE HORN BLOWS AT MIDNIGHT ('45), and THE TREASURE OF SIERRA MADRE ('48). He left acting for a decade and then returned to television and films billed as Robert Blake and appearing on the big screen in such films as PORK CHOP HILL ('59), THE PURPLE GANG ('60), THE GREATEST STORY EVER TOLD ('65), IN COLD BLOOD ('67), TELL THEM WILLIE BOY IS HERE ('69), ELECTRA GLIDE IN BLUE ('73), and the TV movie BLOOD FEUD ('83), in which he portrayed Jimmy Hoffa. In 1985 he played a ghetto priest in the TV film HELL TOWN, which became a short-running series.

THE BIG BLACK PILL, telecast on NBC-TV on January 29, 1981, was the first Joe Dancer adventure. In this TV movie, Hollywood detective Joe Dancer finds himself accused of murder. In order to clear himself, he investigates the case and finds that Beverly Hills politicans and wealthy families are involved in a web of corruption. At one point the crooks try to kill him and a nun (Veronica Cartwright) who get in their way. *TV Movies and Video Guide* (1988) termed the telefilm "average." Two months after the initial Joe Dancer film, NBC-TV telecast THE MONKEY MISSION on March 23, 1981. The plot had Joe Dancer hired by a client to obtain a valuable vase which was stolen from the client's family during World War II. The vase is now in a museum, and in order to steal it, Dancer enlists the aid of electronics whiz Stump Harris (Keenan Wynn) and animal trainer Jimmy Papadopolous (John Fiedler) and his trained chimp Gregor. The film tried to play down Dancer's hard-boiled image in favor of comedy, but *Movies on TV* (1981) commented, "A better yarn is needed—not another animal act!" Since the Joe Dancer series did not sell, the third Dancer telefilm, MURDER ONE, DANCER ZERO, was not shown until June 5, 1983, when it was broadcast by NBC-TV. Here Joe

Dancer is hired to investigate a Hollywood scandal and ends up being accused of manslaughter as a smokescreen to keep him off the case, which could ruin a star's career and bring about the downfall of a major studio. Like its two predecessors, the telefilm was only an average effort—the major reason the Joe Dancer project never got past the pilot stage. Unlike most proposed series, however, it did produce three pilots.

Filmography

1. THE BIG BLACK PILL. NBC-TV, 1981. 100 minutes. Color.
   D: Reza S. Badiyi. **SC:** Michael Butler.
   Cast: Robert Blake (Joe Dancer), JoBeth Williams, James Gammon, Neva Patterson, Veronica Cartwright, Carol Wayne, Edward Winter, Philip R. Allen, Sondra Blake, Eileen Heckart, Wilford Brimley, Kevin Major Howard, Kenneth Tigar, Bubba Smith, Robert Phillips, Stanton Coffin, Deborah LeVine, Marie Todd.

2. THE MONKEY MISSION. NBC-TV, 1981. 100 minutes. Color.
   D: Burt Brinckerhoff. **SC:** Robert Crais.
   Cast: Robert Blake (Joe Dancer), John Fiedler, Keenan Wynn, Clive Revill, Sondra Blake, Pepe Serna, Mitchell Ryan, Andy Wood, Logan Ramsey, Alan Napier, Elizabeth Haliday, Laura Jacoby, Jennifer Gordon, Norman Rice, Domonic Bando, Willy the Monkey.

3. MURDER ONE, DANCER ZERO. NBC-TV, 1983. 100 minutes. Color.
   D: Reza S. Badiyi. **SC:** Ed Waters.
   Cast: Robert Blake (Joe Dancer), Kenneth McMillan, Jane Daly, William Prince, Sondra Blake, Joel Bailey, Royal Dano, Sydney Lassick, Robin Dearden, Sam Anderson, Deborah Geffner, Gino Conforti, Kelly Lange, Heather Mathey, Harry Caesar, Joseph DiReda, Kelly Grant, C. Jay, Glenn Robards, Reed Rondell, Larry Williams.
   Working Titles: JOE DANCER III and LIGHTS, CAMERA . . . MURDER.

JOEL AND GARDA SLOANE

Since it had it had considerable box office success with the Thin Man series (see B/V) about husband and wife sleuths Nick and Nora Charles, Metro-Goldwyn-Mayer hoped to have a partner series in the exploits of spouses Joel and Garda Sloane, whose adventures were penned by Marco Page in his 1938 book *Fast Company*. The studio purchased the property and cast Melvyn Douglas and Florence Rice in the lead roles. Douglas had just starred in the first of his two Bill and Sally Reardon (q.v.) films, THERE'S ALWAYS A WOMAN, which was issued four months after FAST COMPANY, in the spring of 1938. In both films, Thurston Hall was cast as the district attorney.

FAST COMPANY, which is called THE RARE BOOK MURDERS on TV, tells of Joel Sloane (Melvyn Douglas) and his wife Garda (Florence Rice), rare book collectors, with Joel doing detective work for insurance companies in settling claims on the loss of such volumes. When rare book dealer Otto Brockler (George Zucco) is bumped off, the main suspect is former employee Ned Morgan (Shep-

Melvyn Douglas and Florence Rice in FAST COMPANY (M-G-M, 1938)

pard Strudwick) who is in love with the dead man's daughter (Mary Howard). Joel and Garda, however, come up with a trio of other suspects, and the two eventually bring the case to a close by naming the killer. The *New York Post* dubbed the feature a "thoroughly entertaining comedy-drama," while *Variety* noted, "It is in the groove of the better supporting features . . . Production is smartly mounted and technically excellent."

Marco Page had co-scripted his novel for FAST COMPANY, and it had been produced by Frederick Stephani. For the follow-up film, Stephani again produced and the book *Fast Company* was again the basis for the feature FAST AND LOOSE, issued early in 1939. This time Robert Montgomery played Joel Sloane while Rosalind Russell, in her first major film role, was cast as Garda. Here Joel is assigned to look into the disappearance of some rare tomes from the collection of rich Nicholas Torent (Ralph Morgan). As a result, a trio of murders take place as Joel and Garda try to get to the bottom of the case, which is centered around the theft of an original Shakespeare manuscript worth a half-million dollars. *Variety* complained somewhat, "Interest is generated more in the antics and adventures of Montgomery than in the whodunits at hand, but that seems to be the intent of the picture from the start."

Frederick Stephani produced the third and final feature in the series, FAST AND FURIOUS, released in the fall of 1939. This time the film was based on an original screenplay and not Marco Page's book, and musical film director Busby Berkeley was assigned to direct. Again new leads were cast, Franchot Tone as Joel and Ann Sothern as Garda. The budget for this outing was obviously lower than for the two previous entries, and director Berkeley seemed most at home with staging the film's beauty contest sequences rather than its comedy-mystery elements. The plot had Joel and Garda at the beach for a vacation. There they meet their friend, news hawk Ted Bentley (Allyn Joslyn), and he and Joel are asked to judge a local beauty contest, much to Garda's chagrin. When a murder occurs, Ted is blamed, and Joel and Garda try to prove his innocence. They are almost done in by the real killer before naming the culprit, who was involved in fixing the beauty pageant. *Variety* thought it to be "pleasantly entertaining throughout" with a "tasty blend of comedy and mystery suspense."

The three films M-G-M produced about Joel and Garda Sloane are enjoyable mystery-comedies, but the failure of the studio to sustain the same lead players in each film prevented audiences from becoming more than peripherally involved with the protagonists and their cases. Well produced, written, and paced, the trio of features had the stuff for a sustained series, but without stars identified with the two leads such a series was impossible for any length of time.

Filmography

1. FAST COMPANY. Metro-Goldwyn-Mayer, 1938. 75 minutes.
   D: Edward Buzzell. **SC:** Marco Page & Harold Tarshis, from the novel by Page.
   Cast: Melvyn Douglas (Joel Sloane), Florence Rice (Garda Sloane), Claire Dodd, Sheppard Strudwick, Louis Calhern, Nat Pendleton, Douglass Dumbrille, Mary Howard, George Zucco, Minor Watson, Donald Douglas, Dwight Frye, Thurston Hall, Horace MacMahon, Roger Converse, Natalie Garson, Henry Sylvester, Edward Hearn, James B. Carson, Ronnie Rondell, Jack Foss, Barbara Bedford.
   TV Title: THE RARE BOOK MURDERS.

2. FAST AND LOOSE. Metro-Goldwyn-Mayer, 1939. 78 minutes.
   D: Edwin L. Marin. **SC:** Harry Kurnitz, from the novel *Fast Company* by Marco Page.
   Cast: Robert Montgomery (Joel Sloane), Rosalind Russell (Garda Sloane), Reginald Owen, Ralph Morgan, Alan Dinehart, Joan Marsh, Etienne Girardot, Jo Ann Sayers, Anthony Allan, Tom Collins, Sidney Blackmer, Donald Douglas, Ian Wolfe, Mary Forbes, Leonard Carey.

3. FAST AND FURIOUS. Metro-Goldwyn-Mayer, 1939. 70 minutes.
   D: Busby Berkeley. **SC:** Harry Kurnitz.
   Cast: Franchot Tone (Joel Sloane), Ann Sothern (Garda Sloane), Ruth Hussey, Lee Bowman, Allyn Joslyn, John Miljan, Mary Beth Hughes, Bernard Nedell, Cliff Clark, James Burke, Frank Orth, Margaret Roach, Gladys Blake, Granville Bates.

KITTY O'DAY

MONOGRAM PRODUCER Lindsley Parsons joined forces with veteran director William Beaudine and actor-writer Tim Ryan to begin a series of films based on the exploits of sleuth Kitty O'Day who had been created in an original story by Victor Hammond. By the mid-1940s the popularity of female detectives had ebbed following the 1930s' series about such sleuths as Hildegarde Withers, Torchy Blane, Nancy Drew (see B/V), and Nurse Sarah Keate (q.v.). Gail Patrick had played a lady peeper in MURDER AT THE VANITIES ('34), Jane Wyman had done the same in PRIVATE DETECTIVE ('39); in the 1940s at Republic, Stephanie Bachelor had the title role in THE UNDERCOVER WOMAN ('46), while Adele Mara was a sleuth in EXPOSED ('47). Aside from these one-shots, Kitty O'Day was the only female detective with a sustained series, and she lasted for only three entries. In the last she suffered the same ignominy as Lew Archer (q.v.) did two decades later, when her name was changed.

DETECTIVE KITTY O'DAY opened the series in the spring of 1944, and its plot has lovers Kitty O'Day (Jean Parker) and Johnny Jones (Peter Cookson) in the employ of businessman Wentworth (Edward Earle), not realizing he is a fence for stolen bonds and securities. When Wentworth is found murdered, police Detective Miles (Tim Ryan) suspects Kitty and Johnny of the crime, along with Wentworth's lawyer (Herbert Heyes), a man (Douglas Fowley) who was friendly with Wentworth's wife (Veda Ann Borg) and his butler (Olaf Hytten). Kitty and Johnny decide to play sleuth in order to clear themselves and stumble onto two more murders before unmasking the killer who then threatens the couple. With Jean Parker's name to carry the film at the marquee, DETECTIVE KITTY O'DAY proved to be popular.

George Callahan, who scripted a number of the Monogram Charlie Chan (see B/V) features, joined forces with Tim Ryan and Victor Hammond to write the screenplay for ADVENTURES OF KITTY O'DAY with Lindsley Parsons

Advertisement for ADVENTURES OF KITTY O'DAY (Monogram, 1944)

again producing and William Beaudine back as the director. The dual-biller was released late in 1944, and it had
Kitty O'Day (Jean Parker) working as a hotel telephone
operator. She and boyfriend Johnny Jones (Peter Cookson)
become involved in a trio of murders, with the local police
inspector (Tim Ryan) trying to solve the homicides without
Kitty's nosy sleuthing. Eventually, though, she and
Johnny learn that the crimes are tied to the theft of precious
jewels. "Story and dialog hold promise for the writers
involved, and some of the comedy material clicks in a
moderate way," wrote *Variety*.

When the third series entry, FASHION MODEL, came
out in March 1945, several changes took place. William
Strohbach took over as producer, and Kitty O'Day became
Peggy Rooney, and her lover Johnny Jones was now called
Jimmy O'Brien. Marjorie Weaver took over the feminine
lead while the leading man was Robert Lowery, who later

was married to the series' former star, Jean Parker. This "good light comedy" (*Variety*) found model Peggy Rooney trying to clear her boyfriend, stock boy Jimmy O'Brien, who is accused of committing two murders at the swank store where they both work. Police Inspector O'Hara (Tim Ryan) believes Jimmy is guilty after a third murder takes place. Peggy eventually saves him and points out the real killer—but not before she nearly is done in herself. Following FASHION MODEL, no more comedy-mystery collaborations about female sleuths came from the Monogram team of director William Beaudine and scripters Tim Ryan (who played the police detective in all three entries) and Victor Hammond.

Filmography

1. DETECTIVE KITTY O'DAY. Monogram, 1944. 63 minutes.
   D: William Beaudine. **SC:** Tim Ryan & Victor Hammond.
   Cast: Jean Parker (Kitty O'Day), Peter Cookson, Tim Ryan, Veda Ann Borg, Douglas Fowley, Edward Gargan, Edward Earle, Herbert Heyes, Pat Gleason, Olaf Hytten.

2. ADVENTURES OF KITTY O'DAY. Monogram, 1944. 63 minutes.
   D: William Beaudine. **SC:** Tim Ryan, George Callahan & Victor Hammond.
   Cast: Jean Parker (Kitty O'Day), Peter Cookson, Tim Ryan, Ralph Sanford, William Ruhl, Lorna Gray [Adrian Booth], Jan Wiley, Shelton Brooks, William Forrest, Hugh Prosser, Dick Elliott, Byron Fougler.

3. FASHION MODEL. Monogram, 1945. 59 minutes.
   D: William Beaudine. **SC:** Tim Ryan & Victor Hammond.
   Cast: Marjorie Weaver (Peggy Rooney), Robert Lowery, Tim Ryan, Lorna Gray [Adrian Booth], Dorothy Christy, Dewey Robinson, Sally Yarnell, Jack Norton, Harry Depp, Nell Craig, Edward Keane, John Valentine, Cedric Stevens.
   Working Title: THE MODEL MURDERS.

KOJAK

THEO KOJAK PROVED to be one of television's most popular police detectives as Telly Savalas played the part on

Telly Savalas as Kojak.

CBS-TV's "Kojak" from 1973 to 1978. The character has also been featured in four telefilms, one of which was issued abroad theatrically. Bald, sardonic, and lollipop-addicted, Kojak was a detective who used brains, brawn, and an ingratiating personality to solve his cases. The character was played to perfection by Telly Savalas.

Born in 1924, Telly Savalas worked on television before coming to films in 1959 in THE YOUNG SAVAGES. Among his other features are BIRDMAN OF ALCATRAZ ('62), CAPE FEAR ('63), BATTLE OF THE BULGE ('65), THE SCALPHUNTERS ('68), CROOKS AND CORONETS ('69), THE LAND RAIDERS ('69), MacKENNA'S GOLD ('69), A TOWN CALLED HELL ('71), PANCHO VILLA ('71), HORROR EXPRESS ('72), INSIDE OUT ('75), and MY PALIKARI ('82).

"Kojak" first came to the small screen on March 8, 1973, in the CBS-TV/Universal telefilm THE MARCUS-NELSON MURDERS, based on Selwyn Rabb's book *Justice in the Back Room*. The film has some historical importance in that it was based on the 1963 Manhattan Wylie-Hoffert murders which eventually resulted in the Supreme Court's 1966 Miranda decision mandating that all suspects be informed of their right to legal counsel. This "taut" (Judith Crist, *TV Guide*) drama had New York City police detective Theo Kojak (Telly Savalas) investigating the murders of two teenage girls and believing a young black man was innocent of the crimes, even though he confessed to them after being arrested on another charge. Kojak finds himself hindered by fellow law enforcement officials who seem only to want a fast conviction in the matter. Director Joseph Sargent and scripter Abby Mann, who was also the film's executive producer, won Emmy Awards for the telefilm, and Telly Savalas was also nominated for the award as best actor. As a result of the pilot, the television series debuted that fall on CBS-TV and ran for five seasons. Besides Telly Savalas in the title role (making famous the question "Who loves ya, baby?"), "Kojak" featured Dan Frazer as his partner, Frank McNeil, Kevin Dobson as Lieutenant Bobby Crocker, and the star's brother George

Savalas (billed as Demosthenes for the first two seasons) as Detective Stavros.

The second season of "Kojak" opened with the two-hour episode, THE CHINATOWN MURDERS, which was later shown on TV as a feature film and as such was issued theatrically abroad. In this outing Kojak (Telly Savalas) finds himself in the middle of a feud between two Mafia families which almost becomes an all-out street war when one of them is kidnapped, but it turns out the culprits are three Chinese-Americans who aim to get a cut of the families' profits. The detective then must free the captive in order to avert a bloody gang war. The film was made partially on location in New York City's Chinatown.

On February 16, 1985, CBS-TV telecast KOJAK: THE BELARUS FILE, which advertising called "The case that brought Kojak back." Taken from John Loftus's novel *The Belarus Secret*, the telefilm had Kojak (Telly Savalas) investigating the murders of a trio of Russian immigrants who came to this country after World War II. The State Department refuses to aid Kojak in his investigation although an official (Suzanne Pleshette) of the department is sympathetic to his cause. The case gets complicated when an old friend (Max von Sydow) goes into hiding and the investigation turns up possible Nazi spies and connections back to the days when the friend was in a concentration camp. In *TV Guide* Judith Crist noted, "Everyone is in good form . . . and the New York locations as vivid as ever." She added, "And the case itself, reaching back to the Nazi occupation of a part of the Soviet Union, is grimly significant."

Kojak returned to the airwaves on February 21, 1987, in the CBS-TV film KOJAK: THE PRICE OF JUSTICE, which was shown on the "CBS Saturday Movie." Here Kojak (Telly Savalas), now a police inspector, is assigned to investigate a case where a society woman (Kate Nelligan) is accused of murdering her two young sons. He finds the that woman has a questionable past, that a Mafia don (Jeffrey DeMunn) is involved in the case, that a tabloid writer (Jack Thompson) is also digging into the matter, and that Kojak's superiors want the case solved quietly before the upcoming city elections. Miles Beller wrote in the *Hollywood Reporter*, "Telly tells it like it is, a New York police officer just looking to cut back on crime, just looking to do his job." He noted the telefilm had "a fast-paced script."

Filmography

1. THE MARCUS-NELSON MURDERS. CBS-TV/Universal, 1973. 148 minutes. Color.

   D: Joseph Sargent. **SC:** Abby Mann, from the novel *Justice in the Back Room* by Selwyn Rabb.

   Cast: Telly Savalas (Theo Kojak), Marjoe Gortner, Jose Ferrer, Ned Beatty, Allen Garfield, Chita Rivera, Lloyd Gough, Gene Woodbury, William Watson, Val Bisoglio, Lorraine Gary, Roger Robinson, Harriet Karr, Antonia Rey, Bruce Kirby, Robert Walden, Lynn Hamilton, Tol Avery, Bill Zuckert, Lawrence Pressman, John Sylvester White, Carolyn Nelson, Paul Jenkins, Helen Page Camp, Ellen Moss, George Savalas, Alan Manson, Fred Holliday, Henry Brown, Jr., Joshua Shelley, Patricia O'Connel, Alex Colon, Ben ˙ꞮIammer, Elizabeth Berger, Lora Kaye, Steven Gravers.

   ˙Ɪɔ **called** KOJAK AND THE MARCUS-NELSON MURDERS.

2. THE CHINATOWN MURDERS. CBS-TV/Universal, 1974. 100 minutes. Color.

   D: Jeannot Szwarc.

   Cast: Telly Savalas (Theo Kojak), Dan Frazer, Kevin Dobson, Michael Constantine, Sheree North, Tige Andrews, Leonardo Cimino, Demosthenes [George Savalas], Robert Ito, Shirlee Kong, Patrick Adiarte, Val Bisoglio.

3. KOJAK: THE BELARUS FILE. CBS-TV/Universal, 1985. 100 minutes. Color.

   D: Robert Markowitz. **SC:** Albert Ruben, from the novel *The Belarus Secret* by John Loftus.

   Cast: Telly Savalas (Theo Kojak), Suzanne Pleshette, Max von Sydow, Besty Aidem, Alan Rosenberg, Herbert Berghof, Charles Brown, David Leary, George Savalas, Dan Frazer, Clarence Felder, Adam Klugman, Harry Davis, Vince Conti, Mark Russell.

4. KOJAK: THE PRICE OF JUSTICE. CBS-TV/Universal, 1987. 100 minutes. Color.

   D: Alan Metzger. **SC:** Albert Ruben, from the novel *The Investigation* by Dorothy Uhnak.

Cast: Telly Savalas (Theo Kojak), Kate Nelligan, Pat Hingle, Jack Thompson, Brian Murray, John Bedford-Lloyd, Jeffrey DeMunn, Tony Di Benedetto, Ron Frazier, Stephen Joyce, Earl Hindman, James Rebhorn, Martin Shaker, Joseph Carberry, Fausto Bara, Novella Nelson, Kenneth Ryan, Candace Savalas, Lee Wallace, Norman Matlock, Miriam Cruz, Margaret Thompson, Stanley Tucci, Angela Pietropinto, Nicholas Savalas, Alvin A. Carmines, E. Eric Donlan, Naya G. Tolischus, Nick Georgiade.

LEW ARCHER (HARPER)

LEW ARCHER IS THE Ross Macdonald–created Los Angeles detective whom many view as the modern counterpart of Sam Spade and Philip Marlowe. A former policeman and military intelligence agent, Archer was once married, but his wife did not like his profession. Well educated, Lew Archer is a modern-day knight fighting corruption in the smog-filled environs of a city he does not like but remains in because of the need for his services. Since 1949 Ross Macdonald has penned a score of books about Archer's various adventures.

While Lew Archer has had steady success in literature, his screen career has been erratic to say the least. In the two feature films about him, both based on Macdonald novels, Archer's name was changed to Lew Harper, allegedly because star Paul Newman felt more at ease playing a character whose surname began with *H!* Only in the TV movie THE UNDERGROUND MAN ('74) with Peter Graves did Lew Archer carry his correct name in a film. This also occurred in the brief-running 1975 TV series "Archer," with Brian Keith in the title role.

Ross Macdonald's first Lew Archer book was 1949's *Moving Target,* and it was the basis for HARPER in 1966 starring Paul Newman. In need of money to handle his divorce from his wife Susan (Janet Leigh), private investigator Lew Harper (Paul Newman) takes a case for an old pal, lawyer Albert Graves (Arthur Hill). He agrees to find a missing millionaire named Sampson. He learns that the man has an unhappy, crippled wife, Elaine (Lauren

Bacall), and two grown children, Miranda (Pamela Tiffin) and pilot Alan Taggert (Robert Wagner). The case leads him to fat, has-been movie star Fay Estabrook (Shelley Winters), doper-singer Betty Fraley (Julie Harris), and religious cult leader Claude (Strother Martin). As the case continues, Harper finds himself in a morass of murder, blackmail, smuggling, and lust before bringing the affair to a close. Called THE MOVING TARGET in England, the film grossed a hefty $6 million in the U.S. and was a fairly faithful adaptation of the Macdonald novel, except for the changing of Lew Archer's name to Harper.

On May 6, 1974, NBC-TV telecast the two-hour made-for-television movie, THE UNDERGROUND MAN, based on Ross Macdonald's 1971 novel. Here Lew Archer appeared under his own name. Peter Graves was well cast in this production about the Los Angeles private eye trying to find out who kidnapped his ex-girlfriend's son and uncovering several old murder cases, including that of a man who has been investigating his father's murder. *Movies on TV* (1981) opined, "Ross Macdonald's best-seller is adapted with care and attention by producer Howard Koch. Graves makes a fairly convincing Lew Archer—Macdonald's laconic, compassionate sleuth—and there's a fine class supporting cast." On the other hand, Alvin H. Marrill felt, in *Movies Made for Television* (1984), that Graves was "completely miscast as private eye Lew Archer." The telefilm was the pilot for the "Archer" TV series, but when it debuted on NBC-TV in January 1975, Brian Keith played Lew Archer. The one-hour melodrama was not a success and ran for only three months before being cancelled.

Paul Newman returned to the role of Lew Harper in the 1975 Warner Bros. theatrical release, THE DROWNING POOL, from Ross Macdonald's 1950 novel of the same title, which refers to a hydrotherapy room in a mental institution, the setting of the last portion of the feature which moved the detective from his Los Angeles environs to the Louisiana bayous. Harper's ex-love, Iris Devereaux (Joanne Woodward), asks for his help. He comes to Louisiana where she tells him that her wealthy husband (Richard Derr) is blackmailing her, supposedly over a love

Paul Newman in THE DROWNING POOL (Warner Bros., 1975)

affair which did not take place. Iris's mother-in-law, Olivia Devereaux (Coral Browne), is murdered, and her chauffeur (Andy Robinson) is the suspect. With the help of his sister (Helen Kallianoites), Harper proves his innocence, but as a result he becomes involved with a land and oil baron (Murray Hamilton) after Olivia's oil-rich tidal lands, a corrupt cop (Tony Franciosa), who was once Iris's lover, and his associate (Richard Jaeckel), plus a bevy of other sordid characters. The feature was pale indeed when compared to HARPER, and *Variety* said, "It all adds up to zero." Since the failure of THE DROWNING POOL, no further Lew Archer adventures have been filmed, although the private eye continues to remain very popular in print.

Filmography

1. HARPER. Warner Bros. 1966. 121 minutes. Color.
   D: Jack Smight. **SC:** William Goldman, from the novel *The Moving Target* by Ross Macdonald.
   Cast: Paul Newman (Lew Harper), Lauren Bacall, Julie Harris, Arthur Hill, Janet Leigh, Pamela Tiffin, Shelley Winters, Robert Wagner, Robert Webber, Harold Gould, Strother Martin, Roy Jensen, Martin West, Jacqueline De Wit, Eugene Iglesias, Richard Carlyle.
   British title: THE MOVING TARGET.

2. THE UNDERGROUND MAN. NBC-TV/Paramount, 1974. 100 minutes. Color.
   D: Paul Wendkos. **SC:** Douglas Heyes, from the novel by Ross Macdonald.
   Cast: Peter Graves (Lew Archer), Sharon Farrell, Celeste Holm, Jim Hutton, Kay Lenz, Biff McGuire, Vera Miles, Jo Ann Pflug, Judith Anderson, Jack Klugman, Arch Johnson, Bill McKinney, Lee Paul, Ian John Tanza, Judson Morgan, Bill Stout, Maxine Stuart, Jay Varela, Brick Hines, Sheila Dabney, Carlena Gower, Bonita Ralen, Lawrence Montaigne.

3. THE DROWNING POOL. Warner Bros., 1975. 108 minutes. Color.
   D: Stuart Rosenberg. **SC:** Tracy Keenan Wynn, Lorenzo Semple, Jr., & Walter Hill, from the novel by Ross Macdonald.
   Cast: Paul Newman (Lew Harper), Joanne Woodward, Tony Franciosa, Murray Hamilton, Gail Strickland, Melanie Griffith, Linda

Haynes, Richard Jaeckel, Paul Koslo, Joe Canutt, Andy Robinson, Coral Browne, Richard Derr, Helen Kallianoites, Leigh French, Peter Dassinger.

LORD PETER WIMSEY

THE CREATION OF PROLIFIC writer Dorothy L. Sayers, Lord Peter Wimsey first appeared in the 1923 novel *Whose Body?* and he continued in a dozen more novels by the author through "Talboys," published after the author's death. Typically British upper class, Wimsey appeared to be something of a snob, criminology was a hobby for him, and he proved quite adept at deductions. In most of his adventures he is aided by manservant Bunter, his ex-sergeant during World War I service. He clears writer Harriet Vane of a murder charge, and they are married. Lord Peter Wimsey's short stories and novels have continued to be reprinted, and after a brief 1930s film career, the character was successfully revived on British TV in the 1970s and 1980s, with the episodes being shown stateside on PBS-TV.

Peter Haddon portrayed Lord Peter Wimsey in the 1935 Associated British production of THE SILENT PASSENGER. This complicated thriller had Wimsey coming to the aid of a man (John Loder) whose wife (Mary Newland) was the victim of a murdered blackmailer (Leslie Perrins). The crime was actually committed by railroad detective Camberley (Donald Wolfit), who killed the blackmailer and placed his body in the trunk belonging to the accused. Eventually Wimsey puzzles out the case and brings in the real murderer. Although not issued theatrically in the United States, the film does appear on television.

In 1936 Dorothy L. Sayers and Muriel St. Claire Byrne wrote the play *Busman's Honeymoon*, which appeared in London with Denis Arundell as Lord Peter Wimsey. The next year Sayers novelized the work under the same title; in 1940 it was filmed in Britain by Metro-Goldwyn-Mayer as BUSMAN'S HONEYMOON, and it was issued in the U.S. by the same studio as HAUNTED HONEYMOON.

England's entry into World War II caused production troubles for the feature, as director Arthur Woods was an RAF pilot and could work on the film only when given official permission. The Germans threatened to bomb the studio where the picture was being made, and leading lady Maureen O'Sullivan returned to the U.S. and was replaced by Constance Cummings. The plot had Lord Peter Wimsey (Robert Montgomery) and his bride, mystery author Harriet Vane (Constance Cummings), going to a remote cottage on the moors for their honeymoon only to discover a corpse there. Suspects abound, and the couple find Scotland Yard Inspector Kirk (Leslie Banks) no help in the matter. They solve the case themselves in order to get on with their honeymoon. Bosley Crowther in the *New York Times* opined, "Imagine Englishmen trifling with such stuff as a musty mystery while Norway was being invaded and the Low Countries overrun."

While nothing more has been seen of Lord Wimsey cinematically, the character was successfully revived in 1970 by BBC-TV, with Ian Carmichael as a very good Wimsey in a serialized version of some of the Sayers works. Through 1975 Carmichael starred in "Murder Must Advertise," "Unpleasantness at the Bellona Club," "Clouds of Witness," "The Nine Tailors," and "Five Red Herrings." Beginning in the fall of 1974, these episodes were shown in the U.S. on the PBS-TV series "Masterpiece Theatre." In the mid-1980s British television filmed more Lord Peter Wimsey adventures with Edward Petherbridge in the title role and Harriet Walter as Harriet Vane. PBS-TV's "Mystery!" telecast "Strong Poison," "Have His Carcase," and "Gaudy Night" in the United States.

Filmography

1. THE SILENT PASSENGER. Associated British, 1935. 75 minutes.
   D: Reginald Denham. **SC:** Basil Mason, from a story by Dorothy L. Sayers.
   Cast: Peter Haddon (Lord Peter Wimsey), Mary Newland, John Loder, Donald Wolfit, Leslie Perrins, Austin Trevor, Aubrey Mather, Robb Wilton, Ralph Truman, Percy Rhodes, Frederick Burtwell, Gordon McLeod, George de Warfaz, Vincent Holman, Ann Codring-

Ian Carmichael in MURDER MUST ADVERTISE (BBC-TV, 1971)

ton, Dorice Fordred, Annie Esmond.

2. BUSMAN'S HONEYMOON. Metro-Goldwyn-Mayer, 1940. 83 minutes.

   D: Arthur Woods. **SC:** Monckton Hoffe, Angus Macphail & Harold Goldman, from the novel by Dorothy L. Sayers and the play by Dorothy L. Sayers & Muriel St. Claire Byrne.

   Cast: Robert Montgomery (Lord Peter Wimsey), Constance Cummings (Harriet Vane), Leslie Banks, Seymour Hicks, Robert Newton, Googie Withers, Frank Pettingell, Joan Kemp-Welch, Aubrey Mallalieu, James Carney, Roy Emerton, Louise Hampton, Eliot Makeham, Reginald Purdell.

   U.S. Title: HAUNTED HONEYMOON.

PHILIP TRENT

"THE FINEST DETECTIVE story of modern times" is how G. K. Chesterton, the author of the Father Brown (q.v.)

stories, termed Edmund Clerihew Bentley's 1912 novel
Trent's Last Case, which was called *The Woman in Black* in
the United States. The Bentley novel was dedicated to
Chesterton, a longtime friend who illustrated three volumes of nonsense verses composed by Bentley. Bentley
also wrote two other books, *Trent's Own Case* (1936) and
Trent Intervenes (1938), about the adventures of Philip
Trent, an artist who accidentally becomes interested in a
murder case, and as a result of his findings solves the case
and goes to work for a London newspaper.

Three movies have been adapted from *Trent's Last Case*,
but none of them has successfully captured the flavor of
the Bentley work; the definitive movie study of Philip
Trent's adventures has yet to be filmed. The initial film
version came from Great Britain in 1920 by Broadwest
Films. A millionaire commits suicide but frames his
secretary for the "murder," and Philip Trent (Gregory
Scott) tries to puzzle out the affair and save the accused
man.

In March of 1929, Fox Film Corporation issued TRENT'S
LAST CASE starring Raymond Griffith as Philip Trent, but
the popular actor had a voice defect which made him
sound hoarse, and the primitive sound equipment did not
help matters. Wealthy Sigsbee Manderson (Donald Crisp)
is supposedly murdered. Police Inspector Murch (Edgar
Kennedy) interrogates the suspects who include the dead
man's wife Evelyn (Marceline Day), his secretary Jack
Marlowe (Lawrence Gray), who is in love with Evelyn, his
uncle (Raymond Hatton), and two servants (Anita Garvin
and Nicholas Soussanin). Family friend Philip Trent is
present during the investigation, and while Murch suspects Marlowe of the crime, Trent proves that Manderson
killed himself in such a way as to make Marlowe look
guilty, since he was jealous because his wife and secretary
were lovers. Howard Hawks directed this stilted film
which was supervised by Bertram Millhauser, who later
scripted several of the Universal Sherlock Holmes (q.v.)
features. At the time of its release, *Photoplay* thought the
film "very good." Despite being made at the beginning of
the sound era, the feature was done with only sound

effects and a music score, while a totally silent version was issued in England.

The best-known film version of the E. C. Bentley novel is the 1952 British Lion production of TRENT'S LAST CASE, directed by Herbert Wilcox. The plot line stays close to the previous two versions in its tale of a corrupt international financier, Sigsbee Manderson (Orson Welles) being found dead on his country estate and the inquest jury returning a verdict of suicide. London newspaper reporter Philip Trent (Michael Wilding), however, feels that the man was murdered and investigates the case along with Scotland Yard Inspector Murch (Sam Kydd). Trent learns that the dead man's wife, Margaret (Margaret Lockwood), was having an affair with his secretary, John Marlowe (John McCallum), and that his uncle, Burton Cupples (Miles Malleson), also had a motive for the murder. Trent is then able to retrace the events which led up to Manderson's demise. *Variety* reported, "While the suspense is adroitly

Michael Wilding *(center)* in TRENT'S LAST CASE (British Lion, 1952)

kept going and the climax has all the elements of surprise, the film suffers from an excess of wordage. All the characters talk too much, and do very little. There is hardly any action."

Filmography

1. TRENT'S LAST CASE. Broadwest Films, 1920. 5,500 feet.
    D: Richard Garrick. **SC:** P. L. Mannock, from the novel by E. C. Bentley.
    Cast: Gregory Scott (Philip Trent), Pauline Peters, Clive Brook, George Foley, Cameron Carr, P. E. Hubbard, Richard Norton.

2. TRENT'S LAST CASE. Fox, 1929. Six reels.
    D: Howard Hawks. **SC:** Scott Darling & Malcolm S. Boylan, from the novel by E. C. Bentley.
    Cast: Raymond Griffith (Philip Trent), Marceline Day, Donald Crisp, Lawrence Gray, Raymond Hatton, Edgar Kennedy, Anita Garvin, Nicholas Soussanin.

3. TRENT'S LAST CASE. British Lion, 1952. 90 minutes.
    D: Herbert Wilcox. **SC:** Pamela Bower, from the novel by E. C. Bentley.
    Cast: Michael Wilding (Philip Trent), Margaret Lockwood, Orson Welles, John McCallum, Miles Malleson, Hugh McDermott, Sam Kydd, Jack McNaughton, Henry Edwards, Kenneth Williams, Eileen Joyce.

THE ROVING REPORTERS

PRODUCER SOL M. WURTZEL had several successful detective series at 20th Century–Fox, including Charlie Chan and Mr. Moto (see B/V), and he initiated another such grouping with the Roving Reporters, about New York City ace reporter Barney Callahan and his photographer pal Snapper Doolan. Although only a trio of movies were made in the series, they were action filled, well made, and entertaining, with top-notch direction by H. Bruce Humberstone, who handled several of the Chan features for Wurtzel, for the first two, and by former screen idol Ricardo Cortez in the finale.

Michael Whalen and Chick Chandler starred in all three outings in the roles of Barney Callahan and Snapper Doolan. Born Joseph Kenneth Shovlin in 1907, Michael Whalen was a staple leading man at 20th Century–Fox in the 1930s in the studio's B-unit in such outings as COUNTRY DOCTOR ('36) and SPEED TO BURN ('38). He continued to do lead roles well into the 1940s in films like SIGN OF THE WOLF ('41) before going into supporting roles in the late 1940s and 1950s. He died in 1974. Chick Chandler had one of the most diverse careers in films, often as a sidekick or in supporting roles in big features and as the star of lower-budget outings. Born in 1905 he appeared in scores of features such as MELODY CRUISE ('33), SWANEE RIVER ('40), I WAKE UP SCREAMING (HOT SPOT) ('41), SAILORS ON LEAVE ('41), SEVEN DOORS TO DEATH ('44), THE LOST CONTINENT ('47), BATTLE CRY ('55), and IT'S A MAD, MAD, MAD, MAD WORLD ('63).

Late in the summer of 1938, the first entry in the Roving Reporters series, TIME OUT FOR MURDER, was released. The movie was first titled MERIDIAN 7-1212, New York City's telephone number for the correct time, but it was given a more general title for mass release. The plot has rich socialite Peggy Norton (Ruth Hussey) murdered, and the police captain (Cliff Clark) handling the investigation arrests a bank messenger (Robert Kellard) for the crime. Newsman Barney Callahan (Michael Whalen), along with photographer Snapper Doolan (Chick Chandler), believes that the accused is innocent, and the duo investigate the case themselves. The trail leads them to gangster Dutch Moran (Douglas Fowley) and banker Philip Gregory (Lester Matthews). As Barney works on the case, he also plays a cat-and-mouse game with bill collector Margie Ross (Gloria Stuart). In *B-Movies* (1973), Don Miller noted that Michael Whalen and Chick Chandler "teamed well . . . with Humberstone's direction pacing the action succinctly."

TIME OUT FOR MURDER proved so popular that director H. Bruce Humberstone quickly turned out a follow-up, WHILE NEW YORK SLEEPS, which 20th

From left: Michael Whalen, William Demarest, Harold Huber, Joan Woodbury, and Marc Lawrence in WHILE NEW YORK SLEEPS (20th Century–Fox, 1938)

Century–Fox got into theaters for the Christmas holiday season in 1938. The plot, which was padded by a nicely interpolated nightclub sequence, finds Callahan (Michael Whalen) and pal Snapper Doolan (Chick Chandler) investigating a suicide which the reporter feels is really a murder. The case takes them to a cabaret where Barney fails for singer Judy King (Jean Rogers) who works for mobster Joe Marco (Harold Huber), whom the investigators feel is involved in the homicide, which Barney proves was part of a bond swindle. *Variety* called the picture "a fast moving newspaper-murder mystery yarn" and gave co-star Chick Chandler praise: "Chandler, as the irrepressible flashlight hound, enlivens the proceedings with wisecracks and good-natured raillery that's infectious."

In the spring of 1939, INSIDE STORY, the final Roving Reporters programmer was issued, and the direction was taken over by former silent film idol Ricardo Cortez, making his directorial debut in good fashion. The film also gave Jean Rogers her second lead in the series, following her supporting role in the initial outing, TIME OUT FOR MURDER. When a gangland massacre occurs in a cabaret, reporter Barney Callahan (Michael Whalen) and photographer Snapper Doolan (Chick Chandler) arrive on the scene and come to the aid of hostess June White (Jean Rogers), who witnessed the killings and is marked for murder by the gangsters. While the main suspect is mobster Gus Brawley (Douglas Fowley), Barney outsmarts the police chief (Cliff Clark) and uncovers the real culprits while romancing beautiful June. While Cortez's direction was smooth and pleasing, the plot line was mundane. *Variety* said the feature "has little to distinguish it from a host of similar clip-joint yarns."

Although INSIDE STORY was not up to its two predecessors, it was not a poor film, and certainly the Roving Reporter series could have continued, but producer Wurtzel dropped it in favor of an even briefer grouping called the Camera Daredevils. SHARPSHOOTERS ('38) and CHASING DANGER ('39), the latter directed by Ricardo Cortez, were globe-trotting adventure dual-billers centered around the activities of newsreel cameramen.

Filmography

1. TIME OUT FOR MURDER. 20th Century–Fox, 1938. 73 minutes.
   D: H. Bruce Humberstone. **SC:** Jerry Cady.
   Cast: Michael Whalen (Barney Callahan), Gloria Stuart, Chick Chandler (Snapper Doolan), Douglas Fowley, Robert Kellard, Jean Rogers, Jane Darwell, June Gale, Ruth Hussey, Cliff Clark, Peter Lynn, Lester Matthews, Edward Marr.
   Original Title: MERIDIAN 7-1212.

2. WHILE NEW YORK SLEEPS. 20th Century–Fox, 1938, 61 minutes.
   D: H. Bruce Humberstone. **SC:** Frances Hyland & Albert Ray.
   Cast: Michael Whalen (Barney Callahan), Jean Rogers, Chick Chandler (Snapper Doolan), Harold Huber, Joan Woodbury, Robert Kellard, Marc Lawrence, Sidney Blackmer, William Demarest.

3. INSIDE STORY. 20th Century–Fox, 1939. 61 minutes.
   D: Ricardo Cortez. **SC:** Jerry Cady.
   Cast: Michael Whalen (Barney Callahan), Jean Rogers, Chick Chandler (Snapper Doolan), Douglas Fowley, John King, Jane Darwell, June Gale, Spencer Charters, Theodore Von Eltz, Cliff Clark, Charles D. Brown, Charles Lane, Jan Duggan, Louise Carter, Bert Roach.

RUSS ASHTON

IN 1947 SCREEN GUILD issued two short feature films about a Los Angeles private eye named Russ Ashton, a screen original conceived by Maury Nunes and Carl K. Hittleman, each of whom produced one of the films. Tom Neal essayed the role of the gumshoe in both films, while Allen Jenkins was his thickheaded pal, Pamela Blake portrayed Ashton's loving but somewhat screwy secretary, and Virginia Sale was Jenkins's easily flattered waitress girl-friend. Both films were directed by veteran Lambert Hillyer, whose career began in 1917 and continued into the early 1950s on television.

THE HAT BOX MYSTERY was released in August 1947, and it was followed the next month by THE CASE OF THE BABY SITTER. The initial film opened with the actors introducing themselves in character, giving THE HAT BOX MYSTERY a film noir mystique which continued in its plot of a mysterious man (Leonard Penn) coming to Russ Ashton's (Tom Neal) detective agency wanting the sleuth to take incriminating pictures of his two-timing wife for a divorce case. Ashton is out of town, so his secretary-girlfriend Susan (Pamela Blake) decides to carry out the assignment, since the agency is very low on funds. She takes the camera the client gives her to take the pictures, but when she attempts to take the photos the camera turns out to be rigged with a hidden gun and the woman is killed. Susan is arrested for murder, and Ashton returns to try to save her with the aid of his none-too-bright associate Harvard (Allen Jenkins). Russ eventually gets Susan off

Zon Murray, Ed Keane, Tom Neal, and Leonard Penn in THE HAT BOX MYSTERY (Screen Guild, 1947)

the hook by proving that it was the client who fired the fatal shot from a hiding place across the street from where Susan allegedly committed the crime. *Variety* wrote, "Streamlined 44 minutes, contains the usual excitement quota of mystery fare."

While THE HAT BOX MYSTERY got the Screen Guild series off to a good start, the second featurette, THE CASE OF THE BABY SITTER, was so poor that it brought the grouping to a halt. "Pic has been crudely assembled with deficient lighting, inferior camera work, and bare settings framing a weak screenplay," complained *Variety*. Detective Russ Ashton (Tom Neal) and assistant Harvard (Allen Jenkins) are hired by a young couple (George Meeker and Rebel Randall) supposedly to guard their baby after a kidnap threat, but in reality the sleuths are guarding jewels stolen by the man and woman. Trouble develops when a rival gang tries to steal the stones and kidnap Ashton's secretary-lover Susan (Pamela Blake) and almost kill her before Russ comes to her rescue. The reaction to the film was so feeble that no further Russ Ashton featurettes followed, thus causing Screen Guild to curtail the series of short feature films it had began in 1946 with two Russell Hayden north-woods Mountie adventures, 'NEATH CANADIAN SKIES and NORTH OF THE BORDER, which were followed in 1947 by two more Hayden efforts, WHERE THE NORTH BEGINS and TRAIL OF THE MOUNTIES.

The most interesting aspect of the Russ Ashton featurettes is the casting of movie tough guy Tom Neal as the gumshoe. Born in 1914, the actor worked on Broadway before coming to films in the late 1930s. He appeared in such features as OUT WEST WITH THE HARDYS ('38), ANOTHER THIN MAN ('39), THE COURAGEOUS DR. CHRISTIAN ('40), SKY MURDER ('40), FLYING TIGERS ('42), CHINA GIRL ('43), BEHIND THE RISING SUN ('43), FIRST YANK INTO TOKYO ('45), CLUB HAVANA ('45), and the film noir no-budget classic DETOUR ('45), as well as the serials JUNGLE GIRL ('41) and the title role in BRUCE GENTRY, DAREDEVIL OF THE SKIES ('49). In 1951 Neal made headlines when he battered actor Franchot Tone over the affections of actress Barbara Payton. Although he and Payton were teamed for THE GREAT JESSE JAMES RAID ('53), the confrontation ended his screen career, and Neal turned to landscape work. In 1965 Neal was sent to prison for the involuntary manslaughter of his wife, Gail, who had been shot in their Palm Springs home. Neal spent six years in prison, was released in 1971, and died from heart failure the next year.

Filmography

1. THE HAT BOX MYSTERY. Screen Guild, 1947. 44 minutes.
   D: Lambert Hillyer. **SC:** Don Martin & Carl K. Hittleman.
   Cast: Tom Neal (Russ Ashton), Pamela Blake, Allen Jenkins, Virginia Sale, Ed Keane, Leonard Penn, William Ruhl, Zon Murray, Olga Andre.

2. THE CASE OF THE BABY SITTER. Screen Guild, 1947. 41 minutes.
   D: Lambert Hillyer. **SC:** Carl K. Hittleman & Ande Lamb.
   Cast: Tom Neal (Russ Ashton), Pamela Blake, Allen Jenkins,

Virginia Sale, George Meeker, Rebel Randall, Keith Richards, Lona Andre, Crane Whitley.

SHAFT

WITH THE PROLIFERATION of tough, streetwise detectives in the late 1960s and early 1970s, it was only a matter of time before such a figure would emerge from the black community. This occurred in 1970 when Ernest Tidyman created the character of John Shaft in the novel *Shaft*. In the next five years Tidyman wrote a half-dozen more John Shaft adventures, and the character appeared in a trio of motion pictures as well as a TV series. The character of John Shaft is a handsome, tough, ruthless, and lusty detective who lives by his wits in Gotham and its environs.

In 1971 director Gordon Parks brought SHAFT to the screen with location shooting in Harlem. Richard Roundtree portrayed John Shaft. The story had the gumshoe out to find the abducted daughter of a black gangster, being helped on the case by his friend, police Lieutenant John Anderozzi (Charles Cioffi). It turns out that the mob is behind the kidnapping. When Shaft gets too close, the gangsters kill Anderozzi, and the detective wreaks a brutal revenge for his friend's murder. Made on a $1.5 million budget, SHAFT grossed almost $8 million and earned Isaac Hayes an Academy Award for best original film score.

The success of SHAFT, which was based on Tidyman's initial novel about the shamus, brought about a sequel, SHAFT'S BIG SCORE, taken from Tidyman's Shaft novel of the same title. The book came out in 1972, and that year saw the release of the second series film, which director Gordon Parks made for $2 million. A quarter of a million dollars is stolen by a renegade gangster who wants it to be used for a Harlem child welfare group. Both the man's cohorts and the Mafia in Queens want the loot. Shaft (Richard Roundtree) is out to retrieve the money and get it to the people for whom it was intended. Like SHAFT, this sequel was heavily laced with violence and sex, and it grossed $4 million.

In 1973, Metro-Goldwyn-Mayer issued its third and final Shaft opus, SHAFT IN AFRICA, which director John Guillermin filmed on location in Ethiopia, Spain, and New York City. The plot has African diplomats hiring detective John Shaft (Richard Roundtree) to put a stop to an international slave ring run by African slave trader Amafi (Frank Finlay). The adventure takes Shaft to the Dark Continent, where he opposes the slaver, in addition to bedding various women, including the daughter (Vonetta McGee) of one of his employers and Amafi's mistress (Debebe Esthetu). Budgeted at $2 million, the film grossed only $1.5 at the box office, and no further Shaft movies were made.

Neda Arneric and Richard Roundtree in SHAFT IN AFRICA (M-G-M, 1973)

On October 9, 1973, Richard Roundtree premiered in the television series "Shaft" on CBS-TV. The small-screen effort continued the adventures of the black detective, but his activities were toned down for television. "Shaft" shared a time period, and alternated with, James Stewart's series "Hawkins" and "The New CBS Tuesday Night Movies" for one season before its final telecast on August 20, 1974. In the "Shaft" episodes, Ed Barth co-starred as police Lieutenant Al Rossi, Shaft's cop pal.

Richard Roundtree obtained cinema stardom in the role of tough John Shaft. Born in 1937, the actor has appeared in such films as EMBASSY ('72), CHARLEY ONE EYE ('72), EARTHQUAKE ('74), and MAN FRIDAY ('75). Ernest Tidyman, who wrote the Shaft novels, was a scriptwriter and television producer whose writings also included his Academy Award–winning script for THE FRENCH CONNECTION ('74), HIGH PLAINS DRIFTER ('74), and REPORT TO THE COMMISSIONER ('75), which he co-wrote with Abby Mann, the creator of "Kojak" (q.v.).

While Shaft may have opened the door for other black detectives—such as James McEachin in "Tenafly" (NBC-TV, 1973–1974) and Fred Williamson as Jesse Crowder in two 1976 Atlas releases, NO WAY BACK and DEATH JOURNEY—the series actually lacked innovation. Richard Meyers noted in *For One Week Only* (1983), "SHAFT was little more than a dark Sam Spade. In the television series based on the trilogy of SHAFT movies . . . he was nothing more than MANNIX with black skin."

Filmography

1. SHAFT. Metro-Goldwyn-Mayer, 1971. 100 minutes. Color.
   D: Gordon Parks. **SC:** John D. F. Black & Ernest Tidyman, from Tidyman's novel.
   Cast: Richard Roundtree (John Shaft), Moses Gunn, Charles Cioffi, Christopher St. John, Gwenn Mitchell, Lawrence Pressman, Victor Arnold, Sherri Brewer, Rex Robbins, Camille Yarbrough, Margaret Warncke, Joseph Leon, Arnold Johnson, Dominic Barto, George Strus, Edmund Hashim, Drew Bundini Brown, Tommy Lane, Al Kirk, Shimen Ruskin, Antonio Fargas.

2. SHAFT'S BIG SCORE. Metro-Goldwyn-Mayer, 1972. 104 minutes. Color.
   D: Gordon Parks. **SC:** Ernest Tidyman, from his novel.
   Cast: Richard Roundtree (John Shaft), Moses Gunn, Drew Bundini Brown, Joseph Mascolo, Kathy Imrie, Wally Taylor, Julius W. Harris, Rosalind Miles, Joe Santos, Angelo Nazzo, Don Blakely, Melvin Green, Jr., Thomas Anderson, Evelyn Davis, Richard Pittman, Robert Kya-Hill.

3. SHAFT IN AFRICA. Metro-Goldwyn-Mayer, 1973. 112 minutes. Color.
   D: John Guillermin. **SC:** Stirling Silliphant.
   Cast: Richard Roundtree (John Shaft), Frank Finlay, Vonetta McGee, Neda Arneric, Debebe Esthetu, Spiros Focas, Jacques Herlin, Jho Jhenkins, Willie Jonah, Adolfo Lastretti, Marne Maitland, Frank MacRae.

THATCHER COLT

IN THE 1930s FULTON OURSLER, under the pseudonym of Anthony Abbott, wrote several books about the exploits of New York City Police Commissioner Thatcher Colt, who solved murder cases by the methodic use of police procedures. The fictional Thatcher Colt was a dapper, handsome man who was highly intelligent and a romantic. The books about him proved to be popular mystery fare during the Depression. In 1932 Columbia Pictures ideally cast Adolphe Menjou as Colt in two top-notch programmers, but the studio failed to follow up on these two successful movies.

Since he was noted as one of the screen's best-dressed men, Adolphe Menjou fitted the role of Thatcher Colt and handled it to perfection. After stage work Menjou, who was born in 1890, began working in films around 1919 and continued to appear in movies until 1960. Among his many films are A WOMAN OF PARIS ('23), THE KISS ('29), THE FRONT PAGE ('30), MOROCCO ('31), MORNING GLORY ('32), A FAREWELL TO ARMS ('32), LITTLE MISS MARKER ('34), STAGE DOOR ('37), A BILL OF DIVORCEMENT ('40), FATHER TAKES A WIFE ('41), ROXIE HART ('42), HI DIDDLE DIDDLE ('43), THE

HUCKSTERS ('47), STATE OF THE UNION ('48), ACROSS THE WIDE MISSOURI ('51), PATHS OF GLORY ('58), and his last, POLLYANNA ('60). Vehemently anti-Communist, Menjou had difficulty finding work in Hollywood in later years due to his political beliefs. He died in 1963.

In 1932 Columbia Pictures released THE NIGHT CLUB LADY, taken from the 1931 novel *About the Murder of the Night Club Lady*. When she is threatened with death, hateful nightclub singer Lola Carewe (Mayo Methot) goes to Gotham Police Commissioner Thatcher Colt (Adolphe Menjou) for protection. That night in his presence, along with his associate Tony (Skeets Gallagher) and other policemen, she dies. Believing the woman has been murdered, Colt investigates her past and finds she has been blackmailing several different men, all of them with motives for killing her. Colt is then able to deduce how Lola was murdered and bring in her killer. The *New York Times* noted, "Irving Cummings' direction is excellent. The picture moves rapidly and interestingly."

The second Thatcher Colt feature was THE CIRCUS QUEEN MURDER, based on *About the Murder of the Circus Queen*, published in 1932. Released in the spring of 1933, the feature found Thatcher Colt (Adolphe Menjou) on holiday in a small town and attending a circus. During one of the acts high-wire artist Josie La Tour (Greta Nissen) falls. Although it is believed that the young woman died from the fall, Colt proves that she was killed by a poison arrow. He investigates the killing and finds that Josie's estranged husband (Dwight Frye), whom she thought was dead, was planning to kill her lover, aerialist Sebastian (Donald Cook). Regarding Menjou's work as Colt, *Variety* opined, "Adolphe Menjou . . . proves one of the screen's best bets for detective roles. He does the job so realistically that the audience's mind is distracted from the usual bromidic strains." Despite the good reviews and audience acceptance of the two Thatcher Colt features, Columbia dropped the series.

An NBC radio series titled "Thatcher Colt," with Hanley Stafford in the title role, ran from 1936 to 1938.

Donald Cook *(crouching)*, Greta Nissen, George Rosener *(left)*, and Adolphe Menjou in THE CIRCUS QUEEN MURDER (Columbia, 1933)

Nearly a decade after Columbia ended its Thatcher Colt series, the detective returned to the screen in THE PANTHER'S CLAW, which was based on a short story by Anthony Abbott. Made by Producers Releasing Corporation, the feature got better reviews than were normally given a PRC production. "This is a tight, fast-moving murder mystery . . . exceedingly well acted and carries a punch in dialog and situations . . . Direction is brisk and camerawork excellent," wrote *Variety*. Opera star Nina Politza (Gerta Rozan) is murdered and opera company wigmaker Everett Digberry (Byron Foulger) is the suspect. Thatcher Colt (Sidney Blackmer) investigates the case and learns that Digberry wrote extortion letters to all the opera cast members in order to shield his attempt to lend money to the murdered diva. Colt, however, proves the man is innocent and points out the actual murderer.

With only a trio of feature films to his credit, Thatcher Colt proved to be an interesting cinematic detective who was showcased in carefully made and entertaining programmers. Like the Anthony Abbott literary efforts about him, Thatcher Colt may well be a prime candidate for cinematic revival.

Filmography

1. THE NIGHT CLUB LADY. Columbia, 1932. 70 minutes.
   D: Irving Cummings. **SC:** Robert Riskin, from the novel *About the Murder of the Night Club Lady* by Anthony Abbott.
   Cast: Adolphe Menjou (Thatcher Colt), Mayo Methot, Skeets Gallagher, Albert Conti, Blanche Frederici, Nat Pendleton, Ruthelma Stevens, Gerald Fielding, Greta Grandstedt, Ed Brady, Lee Phelps, George Humbart, Niles Welch, William von Bricken, Teru Shimada.

2. THE CIRCUS QUEEN MURDER. Columbia, 1933. 65 minutes.
   D: Roy William Neill. **SC:** Jo Swerling, from the novel *About the Murder of the Circus Queen* by Anthony Abbott.
   Cast: Adolphe Menjou (Thatcher Colt,) Greta Nissen, Ruthelma Stevens, Dwight Frye, Donald Cook, Harry Holman, George Rosener.

3. THE PANTHER'S CLAW. Producers Releasing Corporation, 1942. 72 minutes.
   D: William Beaudine. **SC:** Martin Mooney.
   Cast: Sidney Blackmer (Thatcher Colt), Byron Foulger, Rick Vallin, Herbert Rawlinson, Gerta Rozan, Lynn Starr, Barry Bernard, John Ince, Martin Ashe, Joaquin Edwards, Walter James.

TONY ROME

WITH THE POPULARITY of hard-hitting detectives like Mike Hammer (q.v.) and Lew Archer (q.v.), who was brought to the screen successfully as HARPER (q.v.) in 1966, it was only natural that Miami-based tough gumshoe Tony Rome would come to films, and he was well portrayed by Frank

Sinatra in two big-budget efforts. Marvin H. Albert used the pseudonym of Anthony Rome in writing his novels about Tony Rome, who lived on a houseboat and walked many a mean street fighting corruption and romancing beautiful women.

Anthony Rome's Tony Rome adventure, *Miami Mayhem* (1960), was the source for the first feature, TONY ROME, which 20th Century–Fox issued in the autumn of 1967. *Variety* felt that Frank Sinatra was "excellent as [the] private eye" and added that the picture was a "fast-moving suspenser relying heavily on burly comedy. Top notch production values." The adventure found Tony Rome (Frank Sinatra) doing a favor for his former partner (Robert J. Wilkie) and becoming embroiled in the family of rich construction magnate Kosterman (Simon Oakland), whose wife Rita (Gena Rowlands) wants him to look into the activities of her stepdaughter Dina (Sue Lyon), recently married to an older doctor (Jeffrey Lynn). Tony's girl-friend, Anne Archer (Jill St. John), tells him Diana's mother's (Jeanne Cooper) jewelry collection has been replaced by phonies and that the girl has been paying her money. Kosterman is murdered, and police Lieutenant Santini (Richard Conte) suspects that Rome is hiding information about the case. He also learns that Rita's ex-husband (Buzz Henry) is involved in the matter. Eventually Rome solves the complicated case but loses Anne, who goes back to her former husband. Don Miller wrote in "Private Eyes" in *Focus on Film* (Autumn 1975), "TONY ROME benefitted from Miami locations, occasional risible lines and Sinatra's impudent bravado. That the story never became quite clear was beside the point. Most of it was fun, barring some graphic scenes of mayhem, and the frequent inside jokes . . . helped make it a pleasant time-killer."

Following TONY ROME, Frank Sinatra portrayed a tough police investigator in THE DETECTIVE, which 20th Century–Fox released in the spring of 1968. In late fall of that year came the second Tony Rome adventure for the studio, LADY IN CEMENT. Like the initial effort, the film was produced by Aaron Rosenberg and directed by

Gordon Douglas, but this time out author Marvin H. Albert co-scripted his 1960 Anthony Rome novel of the same title. Again set in Miami, the feature had Tony Rome (Frank Sinatra) diving for sunken treasure, his hobby, and finding the body of a naked young woman whose feet are encased in cement. When it was proved that she was murdered, gangster Gronsky (Dan Blocker) hires Tony to find out if she is his missing girlfriend, a go-go dancer named Sandra. Sandra's roommate Maria (Lainie Kazan) sends Tony to socialite Kit Forrest (Raquel Welch) who knew the woman, but she is a drunk and does not remember her. Al Mungar (Martin Gabel), a one-time Mafia kingpin, tells Rome to leave Kit alone. The detective proves Sandra was the murdered woman, but Maria, too, is killed and an attempt is made on Gronsky's life. After finding out that Kit and Sandra both loved Mungar's son Paul (Steve Peck) and had fought over him, Tony is accused of killing Danny Yale (Frank Raiter), the proprietor of a club for homosexuals. When Lieutenant Santini (Richard Conte) tries to arrest him, Tony escapes. Trying to solve the case and clear himself, Rome learns that many of the people involved took part in a huge robbery. Eventually he is able to track down the killer, and at the finale finds romance with Kit. *Variety* thought the feature was a "dull potboiler," while the *New York Times* felt "Frank Sinatra has some fairly crude material, this time carelessly handled . . . Sinatra, himself, is all right, no more." LADY IN CEMENT failed to generate much notice at the box office, and no further adventures of Tony Rome were produced.

Filmography

1. TONY ROME. 20th Century–Fox, 1967. 110 minutes. Color.
   D: Gordon Douglas. **SC:** Richard Breen, from the novel *Miami Mayhem* by Anthony Rome.
   Cast: Frank Sinatra (Tony Rome), Richard Conte, Jill St. John, Sue Lyon, Gena Rowlands, Simon Oakland, Jeffrey Lynn, Lloyd Bochner, Robert J. Wilkie, Virginia Vincent, Buzz Henry, Joan Shawlee, Richard Krisher, Lloyd Gough, Babe Hart, Templeton Fox, Rocky

Graziano, Elisabeth Fraser, Shecky Greene, Jeanne Cooper, Harry Davis, Stan Ross, Deanna Lund, Michael Romanoff, Tiffany Bolling.

2. LADY IN CEMENT. 20th Century–Fox, 1968. 93 minutes. Color.
   D: Gordon Douglas. **SC:** Marvin H. Albert [Anthony Rome] & Jack Guss, from the novel by Anthony Rome.
   Cast: Frank Sinatra (Tony Rome), Richard Conte, Raquel Welch, Martin Gabel, Lainie Kazan, Dan Blocker, Pat Henry, Steve Peck, Virginia Wood, Richard Deacon, Frank Raiter, Peter Hock, Alex Stevens, Christine Todd, Mac Robbins, Tommy Uhlar, Ray Baumel, Pauly Dash, Andy Jarrell, Joe E. Lewis.

TRAVIS McGEE

JOHN D. MACDONALD'S fictional detective Travis McGee has been the subject of a score of books. His exploits have been centered around his Florida-based stolen-property recovery business. Each of the books about McGee has a color in its title, and the detective himself lives on a boat called the *Busted Flush,* is helped by pal Meyer as he tries to be honest with everyone but finds few who reciprocate. To date, two films have been made about Travis McGee, one for theaters and one for TV.

Taken from MacDonald's 1966 novel, DARKER THAN AMBER was issued by National General Pictures in 1970 in an apparent attempt to cash in on the box office popularity of such 1960s screen operatives as Lew Harper (Archer) (q.v.) and Tony Rome (q.v.). The complicated plot has private detective Travis McGee (Rod Taylor) and his buddy Meyer (Theodore Bikel) fishing in the Florida Keys when they see a young woman about to be murdered. An iron boot has been placed on her leg, and she is pushed off a bridge. McGee and Meyer are able to rescue the girl (Suzy Kendall) but learn only that her name is Vangie Bellemer. One of the assailants (William Smith) kills McGee's friend Burk (James Booth) while trying to find the girl, who has gone ashore in Fort Lauderdale when McGee's boat docks there. She is later killed in her apartment, and McGee identifies her body at the morgue. Investigating Vangie's past, McGee is abducted by one of her killers (Robert

Lobby card for DARKER THAN AMBER (National General Pictures, 1970)

Phillips), who takes him to a deserted beach, but in a fight the man is killed. McGee learns from Noreen Walker (Janet MacLachlan) that she and Vangie were prostitutes who worked for Del (Ahna Capri) and that they were employed to get wealthy men on cruises so Del's henchmen, the two men who murdered Vangie, could rob and murder the victims. Noreen agrees to aid McGee in avenging Vangie's murder. They find Del in Nassau, and they hire a look-alike for Vangie, ballerina Merrimay Lane (Suzy Kendall), to help them. The trio then carry out the revenge against Del and the remaining henchman.

An interesting aspect of DARKER THAN AMBER came at the finale when McGee rejected the sexual advances of the ballerina. Although Jane Russell provided a slick cameo performance as a hooker called the Alabama Tiger, overall the feature was not successful. Somehow its rough tale of drug smuggling, prostitution, and unrequited love did not find much appeal with theater goers, although Rod Taylor was properly stalwart as hero Travis McGee.

In 1983 a second attempt was made at filming a MacDonald book, this time *The Empty Copper Sea* (1978) became the TV movie TRAVIS McGEE, which also served as the pilot for a series which did not sell. Here McGee (Sam Elliott) comes to the aid of a pal, Van Harder (Richard Farnsworth), a charter boat operator who has been accused of causing the drowning of one his passengers when he got drunk and wrecked his boat. Since the victim was not found, McGee feels something is awry. He comes to believe that Van Harder was drugged, and he and associate Meyer (Gene Evans) investigate the case and uncover a number of suspects, including the supposedly dead man's business partner (Geoffrey Lewis). The locale of the movie was changed from Florida to California, and the script allowed the detective to find romance with one of the suspects, played by Katharine Ross. Although *TV Guide's* Judith Crist was "delighted that this is a pilot" and that Sam Elliott "is just fine" as McGee, the TV movie failed to sell as a weekly series.

Filmography

1. DARKER THAN AMBER. National General Pictures, 1970. 97 minutes. Color.

   D: Robert Clouse. **SC:** Ed Waters, from the novel by John D. MacDonald.

   Cast: Rod Taylor (Travis McGee), Suzy Kendall, Theodore Bikel (Meyer), Jane Russell, James Booth, Janet MacLachlan, William Smith, Ahna Capri, Robert Phillips, Chris Robinson, Jack Nagle, Sherry Faber, James H. Frysinger, Oswaldo Calvo, Jeff Gillen, Michael De Beausset, Judy Wallace, Harry Wood, Marcy Knight, Warren Bauer, Wayne Bauer, Don Schoff.

2. TRAVIS McGEE. ABC-TV, 1983. 100 minutes. Color.

   D: Andrew V. McLaglen. **SC:** Stirling Silliphant, from the novel *The Empty Copper Sea* by John D. MacDonald.

   Cast: Sam Elliott (Travis McGee), Gene Evans (Meyer), Richard Farnsworth, Katharine Ross, Vera Miles, Geoffrey Lewis, Barry

Corbin, Amy Madigan, Marshall Teague, Maggie Wellman, Walter
Olkewicz, Jack Murdock, Greta Blackburn, Owen Orr, Pilar Del Rey.

WALLY BENTON

RED SKELTON HAS BEEN one of the most sucessful and
beloved of all comedians, with success in vaudeville, radio,
movies, television, and personal appearances. Skelton
came to films in 1938 in HAVING A WONDERFUL TIME,
but it was not until three years later that he acquired his
first feature starring role in WHISTLING IN THE DARK at
Metro-Goldwyn-Mayer, playing radio sleuth Wally Benton, also known as the Fox. The film was so successful that
Skelton repeated the part in two follow-ups, WHISTLING
IN DIXIE in 1942 and WHISTLING IN BROOKLYN in
1943. In each of the features Wally Benton was radio
detective the Fox who broadcast for WHN radio and was
sponsored by "The Tonic for the Chronic," Grape-O Mix.
Each of the adventures had Wally getting involved in a
mystery, aided by fiancée Carol (Ann Rutherford) and a
dopy pal, played by Rags Ragland. In *The Great Movie
Comedians* (1978), Leonard Maltin wrote, "In retrospect,
the WHISTLING films are among Skelton's best screen
endeavors, not only because they showcase him so well,
but because they are such unpretentious and spirited
outings."

WHISTLING IN THE DARK had actually been filmed by
M-G-M in 1933 with Ernest Truex as a radio announcer
who pines to be a whodunit author; today that feature
plays on TV as SCARED. The plot was used for Red
Skelton's first M-G-M starrer, and it had Wally Benton and
girlfriend Carol Lambert (Ann Rutherford), along with her
friend Fran Post (Virginia Grey), being abducted by crook
Joseph Jones (Conrad Veidt) who orders Wally to come up
with the perfect murder so that Jones can do in a man who
is in his way in obtaining a fortune. Eventually Wally and
the women escape. Using a radio receiver attached to a

From left: Conrad Veidt, Ann Rutherford, Red Skelton, Virginia Grey, and Rags Ragland in WHISTLING IN THE DARK (M-G-M, 1941)

telephone, Wally is able to thwart Jones's plan during his radio broadcast.

The success of WHISTLING IN THE DARK led to the release of WHISTLING IN DIXIE, issued in the fall of 1942. It was directed by S. Sylvan Simon, who directed all three of the Wally Benton features. The plot has Wally's girlfriend Carol Lambert (Ann Rutherford) ushering him to Georgia to solve a supposed murder involving a relative of one of Carol's sorority sisters (Diana Lewis). Once there the two uncover a plot by a corrupt local lawman (George Bancroft) and a drunken judge (Guy Kibbee) to keep hidden Confederate gold. "Plenty of fun is poked at the melodramatics of soap operas, with the curse taken off by having the crazy airshow script angles actually work out for the salvation of Skelton and his friends," wrote *Variety*.

WHISTLING IN BROOKLYN, the final Wally Benton outing, was issued in the fall of 1943, and the *New York Times* called it a "broadly slapstick excursion." This time out a murderer sends a letter to the police saying that it is really Wally Benton, the Fox, who has been perpetrating the city's plague of killings. By a series of accidents, it appears that Wally really is the culprit. The police get on his trail as does the real murderer, who feels that the radio sleuth is too close to solving the case. Aided by fiancée Carol Lambert (Ann Rutherford), Wally ends up at Ebbets Field pitching in a baseball game against the Brooklyn Dodgers, and the chase then leads him to an abandoned ship where in a showdown he is able to unmask the real murderer.

Filmography

1. WHISTLING IN THE DARK. Metro-Goldwyn-Mayer, 1941. 76 minutes.
    D: S. Sylvan Simon. **SC:** Robert MacGunigle, Harry Clark & Albert Mannheimer.
    Cast: Red Skelton (Wally Benton), Ann Rutherford, Conrad Veidt, Virginia Grey, Rags Ragland, Henry O'Neill, Eve Arden, Paul Stanton, Don Douglas, Don Costello, William Tannen, Reed Hadley, Mariska Aldrich, Lloyd Corrigan, George Carleton, Will Lee, Ruth Robinson.

2. WHISTLING IN DIXIE. Metro-Goldwyn-Mayer, 1942. 74 minutes.
    D: S. Sylvan Simon. **SC:** Nat Perrin.
    Cast: Red Skelton (Wally Benton), Ann Rutherford, George Bancroft, Guy Kibbee, Diana Lewis, Peter Whitney, Rags Ragland, Celia Travers, Lucien Littlefield, Louis Mason, Mark Daniels, Pierre Watkin, Emmett Vogan, Hobart Cavanaugh.

3. WHISTLING IN BROOKLYN. Metro-Goldwyn-Mayer, 1943. 87 minutes.
    D: S. Sylvan Simon. **SC:** Nat Perrin & Wilkie Mahoney.
    Cast: Red Skelton (Wally Benton), Ann Rutherford, Jean Rogers, Rags Ragland, Ray Collins, Henry O'Neill, Arthur Space, William Frawley, Sam Levene, Robert Emmett O'Connor, Steven Geray, Howard Freeman, Tom Dillon, the Brooklyn Dodgers.

BIBLIOGRAPHY

THE FOLLOWING IS A listing of the novels about the fictional detectives covered in the text. Translated titles are used for books published abroad.

ARSENE LUPIN

Author: Maurice Leblanc (1864–1941)
  Arsène Lupin (1907)
  Arsène Lupin vs. Herlock Sholmes (1908)
  The Hollow Needle (1909)
  813 (1910)
  The Crystal Stopper (1912)
  Teeth of the Tiger (1914)
  The Memoirs of Arsène Lupin (1925)

C. AUGUSTE DUPIN

Author: Edgar Allan Poe (1809–1849)
  "The Murders in the Rue Morgue" (1841)
  "The Mystery of Marie Rôget" (1842)
  "The Purloined Letter" (1844)

DUNCAN MacLAIN

Author: Baynard H. Kendrick (1894–1977)
  The Last Express (1937)

The Whistling Hangman (1937)
The Odor of Violets (1941)
Blind Man's Bluff (1943)
Death Knell (1945)
Out of Control (1945)
Make Mine MacLain (1947)
You Diet Today (1952)
Blind Allies (1954)
Reservations or Death (1957)
Clear and Present Danger (1958)
The Aluminum Turtle (1960) (in Britain: *The Spear Gun Murders*)
Frankincense and Murder (1961)

FATHER BROWN

Author: G. K. Chesterton (1874–1936)
The Innocence of Father Brown (1911)
The Wisdom of Father Brown (1914)
The Incredulity of Father Brown (1926)
The Secret of Father Brown (1927)
The Scandal of Father Brown (1935)
The Father Brown Omnibus (1951)

FLASH CASEY

Author: George Harmon Coxe (1901–   )
Silent Are the Dead (1942)
Murder for Two (1943)
Flash Casey, Detective (1946)
Error of Judgment (1961)
The Man Who Died Too Soon (1962)
Deadly Image (1964)

FRANK CANNON

Author: Richard Gallagher
  Murder by Gemini (1971)
Author: Paul Denver
  The Falling Blonde
  It's Lonely on the Sidewalk

HANK HYER

Author: Kurt Steel [Rudolph Kagey]
  Murder of a Dead Man (1935)
  Murder Goes to College (1936)
  Murder for What? (1936)
  Murder in G-Sharp (1937)

HERCULE POIROT

Author: Agatha Christie (1891–1976)
  The Mysterious Affair at Styles (1920)
  Murder on the Links (1923)
  Poirot Investigates (1925)
  The Murder of Roger Ackroyd (1926)
  The Big Four (1927)
  The Mystery of the Blue Train (1928)
  Peril at End House (1932)
  Thirteen at Dinner (1933) (in Britain: *Lord Edgware Dies*)
  Murder in the Calais Coach (1934) (in Britain: *Murder on the Orient Express)*
  Murder in Three Acts (1934) (in Britain: *Three-Act Tragedy)*
  Death in the Air (1935) (in Britain: *Death in the Clouds)*
  The A.B.C. Murders (1936)
  Murder in Mesopotamia (1936)
  Cards on the Table (1937)
  Poirot Loses a Client (1937) (in Britain: *Dumb Witness)*

Dead Man's Mirror (1937) (in Britain: *Death in the Mews)*
Death on the Nile (1938)
Appointment with Death (1938)
Murder for Christmas (1938) (in Britain: *Hercule Poirot's Christmas)*
The Regatta Mystery (1939)
Sad Cypress (1940)
The Patriotic Murders (1941) (in Britain: *One, Two, Buckle My Shoe)*
Evil under the Sun (1941)
Murder in Retrospect (1942) (in Britain: *Five Little Pigs)*
The Hollow (1946)
The Labors of Hercules (1947)
There Is a Tide (1948) (in Britain: *Taken at the Flood)*
Witness for the Prosecution and Other Stories (1948)
Three Blind Mice and Other Stories (1950)
The Under Dog and Other Stories (1951)
Mrs. McGinty's Dead (1952)
Funerals Are Fatal (1953) (in Britain: *After the Funeral)*
Hickory, Dickory, Death (1955) (in Britain: *Hickory, Dickory, Dock)*
Dead Man's Folly (1956)
Cat among Pigeons (1960)
The Adventure of the Christmas Pudding and Other Stories (1960)
Double Sin and Other Stories (1961)
The Clocks (1964)
Third Girl (1967)
Hallowe'en Party (1969)
Elephants Can Remember (1972)
Curtain (1975)

INSPECTOR MAIGRET

Author: Georges Simenon (1903–1989)
   The Crime of Inspector Maigret (1932)
   The Death of Monsieur Gallet (1932)
   The Crossroad Murders (1933)

The Strange Case of Peter the Lett (1933)
The Shadow in the Courtyard and the Crime at Lock 14 (1934)
The Patience of Inspector Maigret (1940)
Maigret Abroad (1940)
Maigret Travels South (1940)
Maigret to the Rescue (1941)
Maigret Keeps a Rendezvous (1941)
Maigret Sits It Out (1941)
Maigret and M. Labbe (1942)
No Vacation for Maigret (1953)
Maigret and the Strangled Stripper (1954)
Maigret and the Killers (1954)
Maigret in New York's Underworld (1955)
Inspector Maigret and the Dead Girl (1955)
Inspector Maigret and the Burglar's Wife (1956)
The Methods of Maigret (1957)
None of Maigret's Business (1958)
Madame Maigret's Own Case (1959)
The Short Cases of Inspector Maigret (1959)
Versus Inspector Maigret (1960)
Maigret Rents a Room (1961)
Maigret's Dead Man (1964)
Five Times Maigret (1964)
Maigret Cinq (1965)
Maigret's Pickpocket (1968)
Maigret and the Headless Corpse (1968)
Maigret and the Calame Report (1969)
Maigret in Vichy (1969)
Maigret Hesitates (1970)
Maigret's Boyhood Friend (1970)
Maigret and the Killer (1971)
Maigret and the Wine Merchant (1971)
Maigret Sets a Trap (1972)
Maigret and the Madwoman (1972)
Maigret and the Informer (1973)
A Maigret Trio (1973)
Maigret Loses His Temper (1974)
Maigret and the Millionaires (1974)
Maigret and the Bum (1974)
Maigret and the Loner (1975)

Maigret and the Man on the Bench (1975)
Maigret and the Apparition (1976)
Maigret and the Black Sheep (1976)
Maigret and the Spinster (1977)

JOEL and GARDA SLOANE

Author: Marco Page [Harry Kurnitz] (1908–1968)
  Fast Company (1938)

KOJAK

Author: Abby Mann (1927–   )
  Kojak (1974)

Author: Victor B. Miller
  Siege (1974)
  Requiem for a Cop (1974)
  The Girl in the River (1975)
  Therapy in Dynamite (1975)
  Death Is Not a Passing Grade (1975)
  A Very Deadly Game (1975)
  The Take-Over (1975)
  Gun Business (1975)
  The Trade-Off (1975)
  Marked for Murder (1975)

LEW ARCHER

Author: Ross Macdonald [Kenneth Millar] (1915–1983)
  The Moving Target (1949)
  The Drowning Pool (1950)
  The Way Some People Die (1951)

The Ivory Grin (1952)
Find a Victim (1954)
The Name Is Archer (1955)
The Barbarous Coast (1956)
The Doomsters (1958)
The Galton Case (1959)
The Wycherly Woman (1961)
The Zebra-Striped Hearse (1962)
The Chill (1964)
The Far Side of the Dollar (1965)
Black Money (1966)
The Instant Enemy (1968)
The Goodbye Look (1969)
The Underground Man (1971)
Sleeping Beauty (1973)
The Blue Hammer (1976)
Lew Archer, Private Investigator (1977)

LORD PETER WIMSEY

Author: Dorothy L. Sayers (1893–1957)
Whose Body? (1923)
Clouds of Witness (1927)
The Dawson Pedigree (1928) (in Britain: *Unnatural Death)*
The Unpleasantness at the Bellona Club (1928)
Lord Peter Views the Body (1929)
Strong Poison (1930)
Suspicious Characters (1931) (in Britain: *The Five Red Herrings)*
Have His Carcase (1932)
Murder Must Advertise (1933)
Hangman's Holiday (1933)
The Nine Tailors (1934)
Gaudy Night (1936)
Busman's Honeymoon (1937)
In the Teeth of the Evidence (1940)
Lord Peter Omnibus (1964)
Lord Peter (1972)

MIKE HAMMER

Author: Mickey Spillane (1918–   )
  I, the Jury (1947)
  Vengeance Is Mine! (1950)
  My Gun Is Quick (1950)
  The Big Kill (1951)
  One Lonely Night (1951)
  Kiss Me, Deadly (1952)
  The Girl Hunters (1962)
  The Snake (1964)
  The Twisted Thing (1966)
  The Body Lovers (1967)
  Survival . . . Zero! (1970)
  The Killing Man (1989)

MISS JANE MARPLE

Author: Agatha Christie (1891–1976)
  Murder at the Vicarage (1930)
  The Tuesday Club Murders (1933) (in Britain: *The Thirteen Problems)*
  The Regatta Mystery and Other Stories (1939)
  The Body in the Library (1942)
  The Moving Finger (1942)
  Three Blind Mice and Other Stories (1950)
  A Murder Is Announced (1950)
  Murder with Mirrors (1952) (in Britain: *They Do It with Mirrors)*
  A Pocket Full of Rye (1954)
  What Mrs. McGillicuddy Saw! (1957) (in Britain: *4:50 from Paddington)*
  The Adventure of the Christmas Pudding and Other Stories (1960)
  Double Sin and Other Stories (1961)
  The Mirror Crack'd (1963) (in Britain: *The Mirror Crack'd from Side to Side)*
  A Caribbean Mystery (1965)

At Bertram's Hotel (1966)
Nemesis (1971)
Sleeping Murder (1976)

NURSE SARAH KEATE

Author: Mignon G. Eberhart (1899–   )
The Patient in Room 18 (1929)
While the Patient Slept (1930)
Mystery of Hunting's End (1930)
From This Dark Stairway (1931)
Murder by an Aristocrat (1932)
Wolf in Man's Clothing (1942)
Man Missing (1954)

PERRY MASON

Author: Erle Stanley Gardner (1889–1970)
The Case of the Velvet Claws (1933)
The Case of the Sulky Girl (1933)
The Case of the Lucky Legs (1934)
The Case of the Howling Dog (1934)
The Case of the Curious Bride (1934)
The Case of the Counterfeit Eye (1935)
The Case of the Caretaker's Cat (1935)
The Case of the Sleepwalker's Niece (1936)
The Case of the Stuttering Bishop (1936)
The Case of the Dangerous Dowager (1937)
The Case of the Lame Canary (1937)
The Case of the Substitute Face (1938)
The Case of the Shoplifter's Shoe (1938)
The Case of the Perjured Parrot (1939)
The Case of the Rolling Bones (1939)
The Case of the Baited Hook (1940)
The Case of the Silent Partner (1940)
The Case of the Haunted Husband (1941)

The Case of the Empty Tin (1941)
The Case of the Drowning Duck (1942)
The Case of the Careless Kitten (1942)
The Case of the Buried Clock (1943)
The Case of the Drowsy Mosquito (1943)
The Case of the Crooked Candle (1944)
The Case of the Black-Eyed Blonde (1944)
The Case of the Golddigger's Purse (1945)
The Case of the Half-Wakened Wife (1945)
The Case of the Borrowed Brunette (1946)
The Case of the Fan-Dancer's Horse (1947)
The Case of the Lazy Lover (1947)
The Case of the Lonely Heiress (1948)
The Case of the Vagabond Virgin (1948)
The Case of the Dubious Bridegroom (1949)
The Case of the Cautious Coquette (1949)
The Case of the Negligent Nymph (1950)
The Case of the One-Eyed Witness (1950)
The Case of the Fiery Fingers (1951)
The Case of the Angry Mourner (1951)
The Case of the Moth-Eaten Mink (1952)
The Case of the Grinning Gorilla (1952)
The Case of the Hesitant Hostess (1953)
The Case of the Green-Eyed Sister (1953)
The Case of the Fugitive Nurse (1954)
The Case of the Runaway Corpse (1954)
The Case of the Restless Redhead (1954)
The Case of the Glamorous Ghost (1955)
The Case of the Sunbather's Diary (1955)
The Case of the Nervous Accomplice (1955)
The Case of the Terrified Typist (1956)
The Case of the Demure Defendant (1956)
The Case of the Gilded Lily (1956)
The Case of the Lucky Loser (1957)
The Case of the Screaming Woman (1957)
The Case of the Daring Decoy (1957)
The Case of the Long-Legged Model (1958)
The Case of the Footloose Doll (1958)
The Case of the Calendar Girl (1958)
The Case of the Deadly Toy (1959)

The Case of the Mythical Monkeys (1959)
The Case of the Singing Skirt (1959)
The Case of the Waylaid Wolf (1959)
The Case of the Duplicate Daughter (1960)
The Case of the Shapely Shadow (1960)
The Case of the Spurious Spinster (1961)
The Case of the Bigamous Spouse (1961)
The Case of the Reluctant Model (1962)
The Case of the Blonde Bonanza (1962)
The Case of the Ice-Cold Hands (1962)
The Case of the Mischievous Doll (1963)
The Case of the Step-Daughter's Secret (1963)
The Case of the Amorous Aunt (1963)
The Case of the Daring Divorcée (1964)
The Case of the Phantom Fortune (1964)
The Case of the Horrified Heirs (1964)
The Case of the Troubled Trustee (1965)
The Case of the Beautiful Beggar (1965)
The Case of the Worried Waitress (1966)
The Case of the Queenly Contestant (1967)
The Case of the Careless Cupid (1968)
The Case of the Fabulous Fake (1969)
The Case of the Crimson Kiss (1970)
The Case of the Crying Swallow (1971)
The Case of the Irate Witness (1972)
The Case of the Fenced-In Woman (1972)
The Case of the Postponed Murder (1973)

PHILIP MARLOWE

Author: Raymond Chandler (1888–1959)
  The Big Sleep (1939)
  Farewell, My Lovely (1940)
  The High Window (1942)
  Lady in the Lake (1943)
  The Little Sister (1949)
  The Long Goodbye (1953)
  Playback (1958)

PHILIP TRENT

Author: E. C. Bentley (1875–1956)
Trent's Last Case (1913) (in U.S.: *The Woman in Black)*
Trent's Own Case (1936)
Trent Intervenes (1938)
Trent's Case Book (1953)

RAFFLES

Author: E. W. Hornung (1866–1921)
The Amateur Cracksman (1899)
Raffles: Further Adventures of the Amateur Cracksman (1901)
The Shadow of the Rope (1902)
Thief in the Night (1905)
Mr. Justice Raffles (1909)

Author: Barry Perowne
The Return of Raffles (1933)
Raffles in Pursuit (1934)
Raffles under Sentence (1934)
She Married Raffles (1936)
Raffles vs. Sexton Blake (1937)
They Hang Them in Gibraltar (1939)
Raffles and the Key Man (1940)
Raffles Revisited: New Adventures of a Famous Gentleman Crook (1974)

SHAFT

Author: Ernest Tidyman (1928–1984)
Shaft (1970)
Shaft's Big Score (1972)
Shaft among the Jews (1972)
Shaft Has a Ball (1973)
Shaft's Carnival of Killers (1974)

Goodbye Mr. Shaft (1974)
The Last Shaft (1975)

THE SHADOW

Author: Maxwell Grant [Walter B. Gibson] (1897–1985)
  The Shadow and the Living Dead (1940)
  The Shadow and the Master of Evil (1941)
  The Shadow and the Ghost Makers (1942)
  The Weird Adventures of the Shadow (1966)
  The Mask of Mephisto and Murder by Magic (1975)
  The Crime Oracle and the Teeth of the Dragon (1975)

Author: Maxwell Grant [Dennis Lynds] (1924–   )
  The Return of the Shadow (1963)
  The Shadow Strikes (1964)
  Cry Shadow (1965)
  The Shadow's Revenge (1965)
  Shadow Beware (1965)
  Shadow—Go Mad! (1966)
  Mark of the Shadow (1966)
  The Night of the Shadow (1966)
  The Shadow: Destination Moon (1967)

Author: Maxwell Grant
  The Living Shadow (1974)
  The Mobsmen on the Spot (1974)
  The Shadow (1975)
  Hands in the Dark (1975)
  Double Seven (1975)
  The Crime Cult (1975)
  The Shadow: The Red Menace (1975)
  The Romanoff Jewels (1975)
  The Silent Seven (1975)
  Shadowed Millions (1976)
  Kinds of Crime (1976)
  Green Eyes (1977)
  The Creeping Death (1977)
  Fingers of Death (1977)

Murder Trail (1977)
Gray Fist (1977)
Zemba (1977)
The Death Giver (1978)
The Silent Death (1978)
The Wealth Seekers (1978)
The Shadow and the Golden Master (1984)

SHERLOCK HOLMES

Author: Arthur Conan Doyle (1859–1930)
  A Study in Scarlet (1888)
  The Sign of Four (1890)
  The Adventures of Sherlock Holmes (1892)
  The Memoirs of Sherlock Holmes (1894)
  The Hound of the Baskervilles (1902)
  The Return of Sherlock Holmes (1905)
  The Valley of Fear (1915)
  His Last Bow (1917)
  The Case Book of Sherlock Holmes (1927)
  The Complete Sherlock Holmes (1953)

Author: D. R. Bensen
  Sherlock Holmes in New York (1976)

Author: Adrian Conan Doyle & John Dickson Carr
  The Exploits of Sherlock Holmes (1976)

Author: Loren D. Estelman
  Sherlock Holmes vs. Dracula; or, The Adventure of the Sanguinary Count (1979)

Author: Robert Lee Hull
  Exit Sherlock Holmes (1977)

Author: Lee A. Mathias
  Sherlock Holmes and Harry Houdini in the Adventure of the Pandora Plague (1984)

Author: Manley W. Wellman & Wade Wellman
Sherlock Holmes' War of the Worlds (1975)

Author: Nicholas Meyer (1946–   )
The Seven Percent Solution (1974)
The West End Horror (1976)

Author: Ellery Queen [Frederic Dannay (1905–1982) & Manfred Lee (1905–1971)]
A Study in Terror (1966) (in Britain: *Sherlock Holmes vs. Jack the Ripper)*

Author: Michael Shepherd
Sherlock Holmes and the Case of Doctor Freud (1985)

Author: Vincent Starrett
The Private Life of Sherlock Holmes (1975)

Author: Frank Thomas (1922–   )
Sherlock Holmes and the Treasure Train (1979)
Sherlock Holmes and the Golden Bird (1979)
Sherlock Holmes and the Sacred Sword (1980)

Author: Michael Hardwick (1924–   )
Prisoner of the Devil (1979)
The Revenge of the Hound (1987)

THATCHER COLT

Author: Anthony Abbott [Charles Fulton Oursler] (1893–1952)
About the Murder of the Night Club Lady (1931)
About the Murder of the Clergyman's Mistress (1931) (in Britain: *The Crime of the Century)*
About the Murder of Geraldine Foster (1931)
About the Disappearance of Agatha King (1932)
About the Murder of the Circus Queen (1935)
About the Murder of a Startled Lady (1937)
About the Man Afraid of Women (1937)

TONY ROME

Author: Anthony Rome [Marvin H. Albert] (1924–   )
  Miami Mayhem (1960)
  Lady in Cement (1960)
  My Kind of Game (1963)

TRAVIS McGEE

Author: John D. MacDonald (1916–1986)
  Deep Blue Good-By (1964)
  Nightmare in Pink (1964)
  Purple Place for Dying (1964)
  The Quick Red Fox (1964)
  Bright Orange for the Shroud (1965)
  Deadly Shade of Gold (1965)
  Darker than Amber (1966)
  One Fearful Yellow Eye (1966)
  Girl in the Plain Brown Wrapper (1968)
  Pale Gray for Guilt (1968)
  Dress Her in Indigo (1969)
  Long Lavender Look (1970)
  Tan and Sandy Silence (1972)
  The Scarlet Ruse (1973)
  The Turquoise Lament (1973)
  Dreadful Lemon Sky (1975)
  The Empty Copper Sea (1978)
  The Brass Cupcake (1979)

ADDITIONS AND CORRECTIONS
TO THE BASE VOLUME

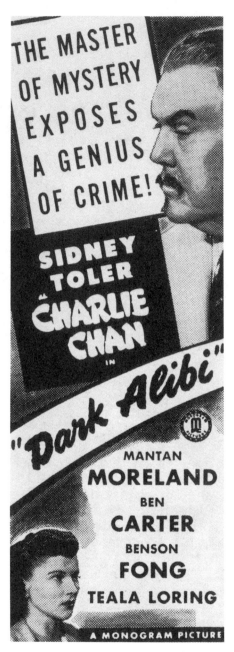

Advertisement for DARK ALIBI (Monogram, 1946) (B/V, p. 58)

Poirot (q.v., vol. II) six times in films and on TV, was a terrible Chan, and some Chinese-Americans protested his being cast in the role. The *Boston Globe* called the film "unrestrained, unfunny, unmysterious, catastrophic collage." *Variety* reported, "on the whole, the film consists of wholly unbelievable characters trapped in a dubious, convoluted mystery over a series of murders too cute for their own good."

THE HOUSE WITHOUT A KEY. Photography: Edward Snyder.

68 *Addenda:* 4A. ERAN TRECE. Fox, 1932. Director: David Howard. Screenplay: Barry Connors & Philip Klein, from the novel *Charlie Chan Carries On* by Earl Derr Biggers. CAST: Manuel Arbo (Charlie Chan), Juan Torena, Ana Maria Custodio, Raul Roulien, Blanca de Castejon, Martin Garralaga, Antonio Vidal, Joe Nieto, Rafael Calvo, Miguel Ligero, Amelia Sante, Luana Alcaniz, Carmen Rodriguez. Spanish-language version of the 1931 Fox feature CHARLIE CHAN CARRIES ON.

69 THE BLACK CAMEL. Producer-Director: Hamilton MacFadden. Photography: *add* Joseph August. *Add to cast:* Victor Varconi (Robert Fyfe).

CHARLIE CHAN'S CHANCE. *Delete:* Producer: Joseph August. Photography: Joseph August.

CHARLIE CHAN'S COURAGE. Producer: John Stone.

70 CHARLIE CHAN IN LONDON. Settings: Duncan Cramer.

CHARLIE CHAN IN PARIS. Producer: John Stone, *not* Sol M. Wurtzel. Settings: Duncan Cramer & Albert Hogsett.

71 CHARLIE CHAN IN EGYPT. *Add to cast:* Jameson Thomas (Dr. Antone Racine), Frank Reicher (Dr. Japor).

CHARLIE CHAN IN SHANGHAI. Photography: Barney McGill, *not* Rudolph Mate. Editor: Nick De Maggio. Art Directors: Duncan Cramer & Lewis Creber. Music Director: Samuel Kaylin.

72 CHARLIE CHAN AT THE CIRCUS. Art Director: Duncan Cramer. Music Director: Samuel Kaylin.

73 CHARLIE CHAN ON BROADWAY. Photography: Harry Jackson.

74 CHARLIE CHAN AT MONTE CARLO. Art Director: Bernard Herzburn. Assistant Director: Saul Wurtzel. CHARLIE CHAN IN RENO. Art Directors: Richard Day & David Hall. Sets: Thomas Little. Music Director: Samuel Kaylin. *Add to cast:* Fred Kelsey (Police Desk Clerk).

76 CHARLIE CHAN'S MURDER CRUISE. Based on the novel *Charlie Chan Carries On* by Earl Derr Biggers. Art directors: Richard Day & Chester Gore. Music Director: Samuel Kaylin.

77 MURDER OVER NEW YORK. Art Directors: Richard Day & Lewis Creber. Music Director: Emil Newman. CHARLIE CHAN IN RIO. Based on the novel *The Black Camel* by Earl Derr Biggers. Sets: Thomas Little.

79 BLACK MAGIC. Alternate title: CHARLIE CHAN IN BLACK MAGIC.

80 THE SHANGHAI COBRA. *Add to cast:* George Chandler (Joe), Cyril Delevanti (Larkin). THE RED DRAGON. Working title: CHARLIE CHAN IN MEXICO. DARK ALIBI. Working titles: CHARLIE CHAN IN ALCATRAZ and FATAL FINGERPRINTS.

81 SHADOWS OVER CHINATOWN. Working title: THE MANDARIN SECRET. THE TRAP. British title: MURDER AT MALIBU BEACH.

82 DOCKS OF NEW ORLEANS. Assistant Director: Theodore Loos.

83 THE GOLDEN EYE. Art Director: Dave Milton. Recording: Franklin Hansen.

84 THE FEATHERED SERPENT. Editor: Ace Herman. Music: Edward J. Kay. Special Effects: Ray Mercer. Recording: Tom Lambert. Technical Director: Dave Milton. Assistant Director: William Callahan. Production Manager: Allen K. Wood. CAST: Erville Alderson (Professor Scott), Charles Stevens (Manuel).

84   THE SKY DRAGON. Production Manager: Allen K. Wood. Music: Edward J. Kay. Special Effects: Ray Mercer. Recording: Tom Lambert.
Addenda: THE RETURN OF CHARLIE CHAN. Universal/ABC-TV, 1979. Color. 97 minutes. Producer: Jack Laird. Executive Producer: John J. Cole. Director: Daryl Duke. Script: Gene Kearney. Story: Gene Kearney & Simon Last. Photography: Richard C. Glouner. Editor: Frank Morris. Music: Robert Prince. Art Director: Frank Arrigo. CAST: Ross Martin (Charlie Chan), Richard Haydn (Andrew Kidder), Louise Sorel (Ariane Hadrachi), Joseph Hindy (Paul Hadrachi), Kathleen Widdoes (Irene Hadrachi), Don Gordon (Lambert), Peter Donat (Noel Adamson), Leslie Nielsen (Alexander Hadrachi), Rocky Gunn (Peter Chan), Virginia Ann Lee (Doreen Chan), Oh Soon-Teck (Stephen Chan), Ernest Harada (Oliver Chan), Pat Gage (Sylvia Gromach), Ted Greenlagh (Dr. Howard Jamison), Graham Campbell (Inspector McKenzie), Neil Dainard (Richard Lovell), John Guiliani (Giancarlo Tui), Otto Lowy (Anton Gromach), Pearl Hong (Jan Chan), Adele Yoshioda (Mai-Ling Chan). Working and British title: CHARLIE CHAN: HAPPINESS IS A WARM CLUE.
Addenda: CHARLIE CHAN AND THE CURSE OF THE DRAGON QUEEN. American Cinema, 1981. Color. 97 minutes. Producer: Jerry Sherlock. Executive Producers: Michael Leone & Alan Belkin. Director: Clive Donner. Screenplay: Stan Burns & David Axelrod. Story: Jerry Sherlock. Photography: Paul Lohmann. Editors: Walt Hanneman & Phil Tucker. Music: Patrick Williams. Assistant Directors: Richard Luke Rothschild, Rafael Elortegui & Pamela Eilerson. Production Design: Joel Schiller. Costumes: Jocelyn Richards. CAST: Peter Ustinov (Charlie Chan), Angie Dickinson (Dragon Queen), Lee Grant (Mrs. Lupowitz), Brian Keith (Chief of Police), Roddy McDowall (Gillespie), Rachel Roberts (Mrs. Dangers), Richard Hatch (Lee Chan, Jr.), Michelle Pfeiffer (Cordelia Farrington III), Paul Ryan (Masten), Johnny Seeka

(Stefan), Bennett Ohta (Chief of Police in Hawaii), David Hirokane (Lee Chan), Karlene Crockett (Brenda Lupowitz), Michael Fairman (Bernard Lupowitz), James Ray (Haynes), Momo Yashima (Dr. Yu Sing), Alison Hong (Maysie Ling).

90 *Photograph:* Frances Morris, *not* Sarah Padden.

91 CRIME DOCTOR. Screenplay: Graham Baker and Louis Lantz.

94 CRIME DOCTOR'S GAMBLE. Screenplay: Edward Bock.

CRIME DOCTOR'S DIARY. Editor: Jerome Thoms.

100 DELUGE was an RKO release, *not* Universal.

106 *Addenda:* Warren Beatty produced, directed, and played the title role in the 1990 Buena Vista release DICK TRACY. Co-stars were Sean Young as Tess Truehart and Madonna as nightclub singer Breathless Mahoney, along with George C. Scott, Al Pacino, Glenne Headley, William Hickey, and Michael J. Pollard. Bo Goldman's script was filmed mainly in primary colors to get the look of Chester Gould's comic strip.

116 ELLERY QUEEN, MASTER DETECTIVE was based on the story "John Braun's Body," *not* the novel *The Door Between.*

125 ELLERY QUEEN. Photography: Howard Schwartz.

141 THE FALCON AND THE CO-EDS. *Add to cast:* Olin Howlin (Driver), Ian Wolfe (Undertaker Marley), Dorothy Christy (Mrs. Harris).

143 THE FALCON IN SAN FRANCISCO. Editor: Ernie Leadlay.

144 APPOINTMENT WITH MURDER. Photography: Walter Strenge.

148 The nuptials for Miss Withers and Oscar Piper were cancelled in the unfilmed second book *Murder on Wheels* (1932).

152 MRS. O'MALLEY AND MR. MALONE was based on the story "Once upon a Train," *not* a book.

154 THE PENGUIN POOL MURDER. Cast: William Le Maire (MacDonald).

Tom Conway and Amelita Ward in THE FALCON AND THE CO-EDS
(RKO Radio, 1943) (B/V, p. 133)

MURDER ON THE BLACKBOARD. *Add to cast:* Jed Prouty (Dr. Levine), Tom Herbert (McTeague).
MURDER ON A HONEYMOON. Photography: Nicholas Musuraca.

155   FORTY NAUGHTY GIRLS. *Add to cast:* Bob McKenzie (Max).

157   It is Louis Joseph Vance, *not* Joseph Louis Vance, throughout the book.

170   Lewis Shayon, *not* Louis Shean.

175   CHEATERS AT PLAY. Photography: Ernest Palmer.

178   SECRETS OF THE LONE WOLF. Photography: Philip Tannura.
COUNTER-ESPIONAGE. Photography: Philip Tannura.

183   *Dividend on Death* was published in 1938.

185   Quinny Hite.

186   BLUE, WHITE AND PERFECT was based on the 1934 story "Diamonds of Death."

191   MICHAEL SHAYNE, PRIVATE DETECTIVE. Photography: George Schneiderman. Editor: Alfred De Gaetano.

193   LARCENY IN HER HEART. Cast: Douglas Fowley (Doc Patterson), Paul Bryar (Tim), Gordon Richards (Stallings). *Add to cast:* Gene Roth (Orderly). Issued to television in a 30-minute version called STAND-IN FOR MURDER by Official Films.

197   THANK YOU, MR. MOTO was issued in the summer of 1937.

199   THE MYSTERIOUS MR. MOTO was *not* based on the novel *Mr. Moto's Last Warning,* nor was the film of that title.

202   THINK FAST, MR. MOTO. Art Director: Lewis Creber.

203   MR. MOTO'S GAMBLE. *Add to cast:* Pierre Watkin, [*not* Addison Richards] (District Attorney), Fred Kelsey (Mahoney), Syd Saylor (Hotel Clerk), Paul Fix (Gangster), Edwin Stanley (Doctor), Olin Howland (Sheriff Tuttle), Irving Bacon (Sheriff), Edward Earle (Medical Examiner), Dick Elliott (Kansas City Bettor), George Chandler (Spectator), David Newell, Frank

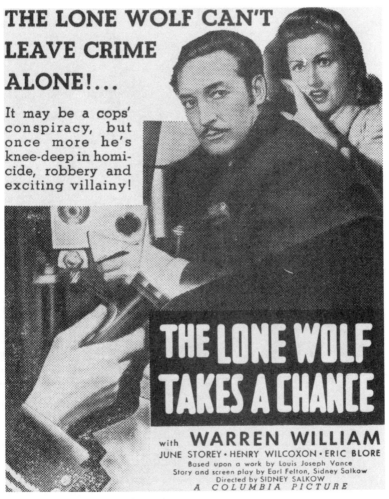

Advertisement for THE LONE WOLF TAKES A CHANCE (Columbia, 1941) (B/V, p. 168)

Lloyd Nolan and Elizabeth Patterson in MICHAEL SHAYNE, DETEC-
TIVE (20th Century–Fox, 1940) (B/V, p. 184)

McGlynn, Jr. (Detectives), Landers Stevens (Doctor), Frank Fanning (Turnkey), Dick Dickinson (Knock-down Timer), Bob Perry, George Blake (Referees), Lester Dorr, Allen Fox, Franklin Parker, Dick French (Reporters), George Magrill, Bob Ryan, Harry Strang, Stanley Blystone, Dick Rush, Adrian Morris, Max Wagner, Lee Shumway (Policemen).
THE MYSTERIOUS MR. MOTO. *Not based on a novel.* Photography: Virgil Miller. Art Directors: Bernard Herzbrun & Lewis Creber.

204 MR. MOTO'S LAST WARNING. Photography: Virgil Miller.

208 *Photograph:* Hooper Atchley (on floor), *not* Lucien Prival.

213 DOOMED TO DIE. *Add to cast:* William Desmond (Doctor), Angelo Rossitto (Newsboy).

221 *Photograph:* Frank Reicher, *not* Leslie Fenton.

224 *Photograph:* George Anderson, *not* Harvey Stephens.

235 *Meet the Tiger* was Leslie Charteris's first "Saint" novel.

236 Louis Hayward was born in South Africa, *not* South America.

244 One hundred ten segments of "The Saint" TV series were produced, and all of them were aired in the U.S. by NBC-TV.

246 *Addenda:* A half-dozen Simon Templar, "The Saint" television movies were produced in 1989 by DLT Entertainment as a part of the syndicated "Mystery Wheel of Adventure" package, which was rounded out with four "Dick Francis" adventures. Simon Dutton portrayed the Saint in all six telefilms: BRAZILIAN CONNECTION and SOFTWARE MURDERS, filmed in Great Britain; BLUE DULAC and BIG BANG, lensed in France; and the West German–made REAL ESTATE CAPER and WRONG NUMBER. All six films had budgets of between $3 million and $4 million.
THE SAINT STRIKES BACK. CAST: James Burke (Sergeant). *Add to cast:* Willie Best (Alganon), Gerald Hamer (Butler).

247 THE SAINT IN LONDON. *Add to cast:* John Abbott (The Count).

249 LE SAINT MENE LA DANCE. U.S. TV Title: DANCE OF DEATH.

250 *Addenda:* THE SAINT AND THE BRAVE GOOSE. ITC, 1980. Color. Producer: Robert S. Baker. Director: Cyril Frankel. Screenplay: John Kruse. CAST: Ian Ogilvy (Simon Templar), Gayle Hunnicutt. Telefilm taken from episodes of the 1977 syndicated TV series "The Return of the Saint."
Addenda: Andrew Clarke starred as Simon Templar in the television pilot film "The Saint" telecast June 12, 1987, on CBS-TV. The one-hour crime drama had the Saint coming to the aid of a ballerina (Liliana Kimorowska) who is threatened by a doll with broken legs.

259 SATAN MET A LADY. Editor: Warren Low. Art Director: Max Parker.

263 THE THIN MAN had a budget of $230,000, *not* $2 million.

265 Paul Fix played the hoodlum, while Teddy Hart was a crooked lawyer.

269 William Powell was nominated for an Academy Award for LIFE WITH FATHER, but did not win.

272 ANOTHER THIN MAN. CAST: Sheldon Leonard (Phil Church).

281 SMART BLONDE & FLY-AWAY BABY. Screenplay: Kenneth Gamet.

285 THE WESTLAND CASE. A woman is murdered, and Bill Crane is hired by her husband, who is accused of the crime.

303 *Addenda:* 1. BRELAN D'AS (Full House). Pathé Consortium, 1952. 118 minutes. Director: Henri Verneuil. Screenplay: Jacques Campanez. Photography: André German. Editor: Georges Rongier. CAST: Michel Simon (Inspector Maigret), Raymond Rouleau (Wens), Van Dreelan (Lemmy Caution), Arlette Merry (Florence), Natalie Nattier, Christian Fourcade (Christian). A three-part French film with stories from the works of Georges Simenon, Peter

Cheney, and S. A. Steeman. Cheyney's Lemmy Caution story "I Am an Easy Guy" was adapted for the film with Dutch actor Van Dreelan as Lemmy Caution.

Addenda: 9. TANGO DURCH DEUTSCHLAND (Tango through Germany). Mommartz/ZDP, 1980. 90 minutes. Color. CAST: Eddie Constantine (Lemmy Caution), Maya Farber-Jansen.

311 *Addenda:* In 1977 ABC-TV/Paramount made a pilot telefilm, NERO WOLFE, based on Rex Stout's novel *The Doorbell Rang.* Nero Wolfe (Thayer David) is hired by a wealthy woman (Anne Baxter) to find out why she and her family are being tailed by the FBI. Tom Mason played Archie Goodwin. The star, Thayer David, died shortly after the film was made, and it was not shown until late in 1979. The movie got good reviews, and in 1981 the "Nero Wolfe" TV series had a brief run on NBC-TV with William Conrad in the title role, with Lee Horsley as Archie Goodwin. The series was a good one but did not last long because it was placed in a time period which did not permit it to build its ratings quickly.

Addenda: NERO WOLFE. ABC-TV/Paramount, 1979. 97 minutes. Color. Producer: Everett Chambers. Executive Producer: Emmet G. Lavery, Jr. Director: Frank Gilroy. Script: Frank Gilroy, from the novel *The Doorbell Rang* by Rex Stout. Photography: Ric Waite. Editor: Harry Keller. Music: Leonard Rosenman. Art Director: John Beckman. CAST: Thayer David (Nero Wolfe), Tom Mason (Archie Goodwin), Anne Baxter (Rachel Bruner), Brooke Adams (Sarah Cacos), Biff McGuire (Inspector Cramer), Sarah Cunningham (Mrs. Althaus), John Randolph (Lou Cohen), David Hurst (Fritz Brenner), Allen Case (Fredericks), John Hoyt, Frank Campanella, John O'Leary, David Lewis.

316 PHANTOM RAIDERS & SKY MURDER. Screenplay: William R. Lipman.

317 CAST: Sorrell Booke, *not* Brooke.

Addenda: The character of Nick Carter returned to the screen in the Czech feature ADELA JESTE NEVECH-

ERLA, issued in the U.S. in 1978 by Dimension as DINNER FOR ADELE. The film was also called NICK CARTER IN PRAGUE and ADELE HASN'T HAD HER SUPPER YET. Set in Prague in 1900, it had Nick Carter (Michal Docolomansky) on the trail of a killer that turns out to be a large carnivorous plant. *Addenda:* ADELA JESTE NEVECHERLA. Dimension/CFP/Barrandov, 1978. Color. 100 minutes. Director: Oldrich Lipsky. Screenplay: Jiri Brdecka. Photography: Jaroslav Kucera. Music: Lubos Fiser. Special Effects: Jan Svankmaier. CAST: Michal Docolomansky (Nick Carter), Rudolf Hrusinksy, Milos Kopecky, Nada Konvalinkova, Ladislav Pesek.
U.S. Titles: DINNER FOR ADELE, NICK CARTER IN PRAGUE, and ADELE HASN'T HAD HER SUPPER YET.

319   CHARLIE CHAN
Author: Unknown
    Charlie Chan (1937)
    Charlie Chan: Villainy on the High Seas (1938)
    Inspector Charlie Chan of the Honolulu Police (1939)
    Charlie Chan Solves a New Mystery (1940)

Author: Michael Avallone
    Charlie Chan and the Curse of the Dragon Queen (1981)
CRAIG KENNEDY
    Dream Doctor (1914)
    The War Terror (1915)
    Gold of the Gods (1916)
    The Social Gangster (1916)
    The Ear in the Wall (1916)
    The Adventuress (1917)
    The Soul Scar (1919)
    Atavar (1924)
    Fourteen Points (1925)
    Pandora (1926)
    Kidnap Club (1932)
    Stars Scream Murder (1936)
DICK TRACY
Author: Chester Gould (1900–1985)

The Adventures of Dick Tracy (1932)
Dick Tracy from Colorado to Nova Scotia (1933)
Dick Tracy and Dick Tracy, Jr. (1933)
Dick Tracy Solves the Penfield Mystery (1934)
Dick Tracy and the Stolen Bonds (1934)
Dick Tracy and the Boris Arson Gang (1935)
Dick Tracy and the Racketeer Gang (1935)
Dick Tracy in Chains of Crime (1936)
Dick Tracy and Federal Agents (1936)
Dick Tracy and the Spider Gang (1937)
Dick Tracy and the Hotel Murders (1937)
Dick Tracy and the Maroon Gang (1938)
Dick Tracy and the Man with No Face (1938)
Dick Tracy, the Super Detective (1939)
Dick Tracy vs. Crooks in Disguise (1939)
Dick Tracy and the Blackmailers (1939)
Dick Tracy and the Phantom Ship (1940)
Dick Tracy and His G-Men (1941)
Dick Tracy and the Frozen Bullet Murders (1941)
Dick Tracy, Special F.B.I. Operative (1943)
Dick Tracy, Ace Detective (1943)
Dick Tracy Meets the Night Crawler (1943)
Dick Tracy and the Wreath Kidnapping Case (1946)
Dick Tracy and Yogee Yamma (1946)
Dick Tracy and the Woo-Woo Sisters (1947)
Dick Tracy and the Mad Killer (1947)
The Celebrated Cases of Dick Tracy: 1931-1951 (1981)
Dick Tracy: America's Most Famous Detective (1987)

Author: Helen Berke
Dick Tracy and the Bicycle Gang (1948)
Dick Tracy and the Tiger Lily Gang (1949)

Author: Paul S. Newman
Dick Tracy Encounters Facey (1967)

ELLERY QUEEN
Ellery Queen in the Adventure of the Last Man Club (1940)
Ellery Queen and the Adventure of the Murdered Millionaire (1942)

Ellery Queen's Aces of Mystery (1975)

321 HILDEGARDE WITHERS
Murder on Wheels (1932) should precede *Murder on the Blackboard* (1932)
The Puzzle of the Red Stallion (1935) (in Britain: *The Puzzle of the Briar Pipe* [1936])
The Puzzle of the Blue Banderilla (1937)
The Puzzle of the Happy Hooligan (1941)
The Puzzle of the Hildegarde Withers (1947)
The Green Ace (1950)
The Monkey Murder (1950)
Cold Poison (1954) (in Britain: *Exit Laughing)*

322 THE LONE WOLF
The Lone Wolf (1914) should be listed first

323 MICHAEL SHAYNE
Dividend on Death (1938)
A Taste for Cognac (1944)
Marked for Murder (1945)
Dangerous Dames (1955)
Never Kill a Client (1962)

325 NANCY DREW
Author: Carolyn Keene (Harriet S. Adams) (1908–1983)
The Secret of the Old Clock (1930) should be listed first followed by *Hidden Staircase* (1930), *Bungalow Mystery* (1930), and *Mystery at Lilac Inn* (1930)
Nancy's Mysterious Letter (1932)
Sign of the Twisted Candles (1933)
Password to Larkspur Lane (1933)
Clue of the Broken Locket (1934)
Mystery of the Ivory Charm (1936)
Mystery at the Moss-Covered Mansion (1941)
Secret in the Old Attic (1944)
Mystery of the Tolling Bell (1946)
Clue in the Old Album (1947)
Mystery at the Ski Jump (1952)
The Witch Tree Symbol (1955)
The Hidden Window Mystery (1956)
The Secret of Mirror Bay (1972)

The Sky Phantom (1976)
Nancy Drew Mystery Activity Book No. 1 (1977)
Nancy Drew Mystery Activity Book No. 2 (1977)
Nancy Drew and the Secret of the Twin Puppets (1977)
Mystery of Crocodile Island (1978)
The Mountain Peak Mystery (1978)
The Thirteenth Pearl (1979)
The Flying Saucer Mystery (1979)
Triple Hoax (1979)
The Secret in Old Lace (1980)
The Greek Symbol Mystery (1981)
The Swami's Ring (1981)
The Kachina Doll Mystery (1981)
The Twin Dilemma (1981)
The Captive Witness (1981)
Mystery of the Winged Lion (1982)
Race against Time (1982)
The Sinister Omen (1982)
The Elusive Heiress (1982)
Clue in the Ancient Disguise (1982)
The Broken Anchor (1982)
The Silver Cobweb (1983)
The Haunted Carousel (1983)
Nancy Drew Ghost Stories No. 1 (1983)
Nancy Drew Ghost Stories No. 2 (1983)
Enemy Match (1984)
The Mysterious Image (1984)
The Emerald-Eyed Cat Mystery (1984)
The Bluebeard Room (1985)
The Ghost in the Gondola (1985)
The Case of the Disappearing Diamonds (1987)
Never Say Die (1987)
Stay Tuned for Danger (1987)
This Side of Evil (1987)
Trial by Fire (1987)
Two Points to Murder (1987)
White Water Terror (1987)
Wings of Fear (1987)
Heart of Danger (1987)

Buried Secrets (1987)
Deadly Doubles (1987)
Deadly Intent (1987)
The Double Horror of Fenley Place (1987)
False Moves (1987)
Fatal Ransom (1987)
Circle of Evil (1987)
Sisters in Crime (1988)
The Mardi Gras Mystery (1988)
The Phantom of Venice (1988)
Secrets Can Kill (1988)
Murder on Ice (1988)
Smile and Say Murder (1988)
Hit and Run Holiday (1988)
Very Deadly Yours (1988)
Recipe For Murder (1988)
Fatal Attraction (1988)
Sinister Paradise (1988)
Till Death Do Us Part (1988)
Rich and Dangerous (1989)
Playing with Fire (1989)
Most Likely to Die (1989)
The Black Widow (1989)
Pure Poison (1989)
Death by Design (1989)
Trouble in Tahiti (1989)
High Marks for Malice (1989)
Danger in Disguise (1989)
Vanishing Act (1989)
Bad Medicine (1989)

Nancy Drew and the Hardy Boys
Authors: Carolyn Keene and Franklin W. Dixon
The Secret of the Knight's Sword (1984)
Danger on Ice (1984)
The Feathered Serpent (1984)
Secret Cargo (1984)
Nancy Drew and the Hardy Boys, Super Sleuths (1984)

Nancy Drew and the Hardy Boys, Super Sleuths No. 2 (1984)

Nancy Drew and the Hardy Boys Campfire Stories (1984)

The Alaskan Mystery (1985)

The Missing Money Mystery (1985)

Jungle of Evil (1985)

Ticket to Intrigue (1985)

Double Crossing (1988)

A Crime for Christmas (1988)

Shock Waves (1989)

328 PHILO VANCE

The Gracie Allen Murder Case (1938) was retitled *The Smell of Murder* (1950)

THE SAINT

The Million Pound Day was a reissue title for *The Holy Terror* (1932)

The Saint and the Fiction Makers (1968)

The Saint Abroad (1969)

The Saint's Choice (1969)

The Saint in Pursuit (1970)

The Saint and the People Importers (1972)

Send for the Saint (1977)

The Saint and the Templar Treasure (1979)

INDEX

Page numbers in italics refer to photographs.